The Real Estate Investment Handbook

THE FRANK J. FABOZZI SERIES

The Real Estate Investment Handbook

G. TIMOTHY HAIGHT
DANIEL SINGER

WILEY
John Wiley & Sons, Inc.

For general information on our other products and services, or technical support, please contact our Customer Care Department within the United States at 800-762-2974, outside the United States at 317-572-3993, or fax 317-572-4002.

Wiley also publishes its books in a variety of electronic formats. Some content that appears in print may not be available in electronic books.

For more information about Wiley, visit our web site at www.wiley.com.

ISBN: 0-471-64922-8

Printed in the United States of America

10 9 8 7 6 5 4 3 2 1

G. Timothy Haight
This book is dedicated to my loving wife Ann, who has supported me both in my professional and personal development.

Daniel Singer
This book is dedicated to my fellow investors, partners, and colleagues for their help, support, encouragement, and friendship over the years.

Contents

The Real Estate Investment Handbook is designed to be a tool for current and aspiring commercial real estate investors in developing and evaluating commercial real estate properties. In general, the commercial real estate market has been very "hot" since 2000 and gives every indication of remaining so throughout at least the middle of the decade. As a result of Federal government tax and monetary policies, commercial real investment provides excellent risk-return opportunities that enable many individuals to build a secure foundation for their wealth. In addition, most high income individuals are overinvested in the stock market. The portfolio of these individuals would benefit from diversification into commercial real estate. Unlike equity securities, commercial real estate often generates a substantial and predictable cash flow over time. The compounding effect of this cash flow can significantly enhance the performance of most investment portfolios.

Investing in commercial real estate is not for those whose mindset is to "get rich quick." Investing in commercial real estate involves a deliberate trade-off between up-front investment costs and a stream of cash returns over a five-to-ten-year time horizon. This cash flow is normally augmented by a favorable tax treatment that can yield substantial benefits to the high income investor. The fact that such benefits are received over time lends a compounding effect to real estate returns that may lack the "flash" of a quick kill in the stock market, but more than compensates for this by a predictable income stream.

The market for commercial real estate is differentiated by both size and type. Investing in a condo, second residence, or even a small office building is well within the reach of middle income investors. Opportunities also exist for much larger investments. The point is that commercial real estate provides opportunities for both the small and large investor.

Different types of real estate investment also abound, ranging from single-family rental properties to industrial parks. These investments vary by the function they serve, the required skill and experience of the potential investor, and the characteristics of their cash flow. A given investor might not have the proclivity and experience to invest in a self-

storage or athletic facility, but would definitely have the attributes necessary to invest in a motel or restaurant location. The great thing about
commercial real estate is that whatever the capabilities of the investor,
there is a commercial property out there that is right for them.

Throughout this book the authors have attempted to present this
human side of commercial real estate investing. Successful real estate
investing is not just about the net operating profits after taxes, net
income, or the cash flow of an investment, it is about the fit between the
investor and the investment.

It is the authors hope that the vignettes and analytical tools presented in the *Real Estate Investment Handbook* will prepare every
investor for success as a commercial real estate investor.

About the Authors

G. Timothy Haight received his DBA from George Washington University. He is the author of several books and more than 80 articles dealing with a wide range of business topics. Dr. Haight is the Chairman of the Board of Commonwealth Business Bank (Los Angeles), and is dean of the College of Business and Economics at California State University, Los Angeles. Dr. Haight resides in Orange County, California.

Daniel Singer holds a Ph.D. in Economics from the University of Colorado and has published numerous books and articles in professional journals. Dr. Singer has extensive experience in real estate investing, having owned a substantial portfolio of residential properties for over 30 years and has developed, owned, and operated four franchise restaurants in the Midwest. Dr. Singer currently resides in Baltimore, Maryland, where he is a Professor of Finance at Towson University and consults extensively with local real estate developers.

CHAPTER 1

A Portfolio Approach to Investing in Commercial Real Estate

Investing in real estate is not the path to easy riches, but it does provide a path to wealth creation that is surprisingly available to middle and upper income Americans. This path is both available and largely unused. Successful real estate investing is hard work, but it rewards those who are willing to do the work. Many elderly have had a comfortable retirement because of successful real estate investments, many students have gone to college funded by successful real estate investments, and many boats and vacation homes have been financed by real estate investments. Such accomplishments cannot be taken for granted. Successful real estate investors must have the skill, knowledge, and energy to find appropriate properties, evaluate them as investments, arrange for financing, and either manage these properties or find a buyer for them.

Not surprisingly, many individuals are already into real estate ownership—about two-thirds of Americans own their own home. Even though individuals are primarily motivated to own a home because they need a place to live or like the amenities it offers, homeownership has been a financial boon to many middle-class Americans. Homes constitute the largest and most profitable asset the majority of Americans own. To a considerable extent, the economic benefits of home ownership have been incidental to the home's function as a residence.

This book is about commercial real estate investment. Commercial real estate investment implies investing in real estate for a specific economic end—to make a profit. It does not matter if the property under consideration is a single-family home, a duplex, a condo, an office building or an ice rink. Purchasing such a property to make a profit makes it a commercial activity.

The fact of the matter is that, when many people think about investing today, they think about putting their money into a savings account, buying a CD (certificate of deposit, not the type that plays music), buying some stock, or buying mutual fund shares. That is unfortunate because there is an overlooked world of opportunity in commercial real estate. Most people who could or should be investing in commercial real estate fail to do so because they lack the knowledge of how to do it, feel they do not have the money to do so, or they feel it is strictly an area for professionals. While an individual may lack the knowledge of how to be a successful real estate investor, that can be rectified. The other assertions are not true. You do not need "big bucks" to play in this game and the opportunities are there for all. The only limits are the ones you place on yourself!

There are many individuals who feel they have managed their portfolios well because they have matched or beat the "market" (the stock market as measured by the Dow Jones Industrial Index or S&P 500). The fallacy in that thinking was revealed when the markets plunged in 2000. Others have experienced first hand the many pitfalls encountered in "playing the market." Solely relying on a strategy of investing in equities as "the" vehicle for wealth creation is a defective strategy because owning different stocks does not mean an individual is diversified. Most stocks are tightly linked to the performance of the overall market. "A falling tide lowers all boats." Such investors would have been much better off had they diversified some of their wealth into real estate.

This book is about how to do that. Different sectors of the market are described (not all, but enough to give an investor a flavor of what commercial real estate investing is all about), and illustrations of investing opportunities are offered to prepare readers to evaluate their own opportunities. Working through the material and illustrations in this book will give investors the knowledge that they need to be successful wealth creators.

THE HISTORICAL PERFORMANCE OF REAL ESTATE VERSUS STOCKS

The stock market has an excellent public relations team. The drumbeat in the business sections of newspapers, business magazines, and business radio and television shows focuses on stock market performance and the performance of individual stocks. This is because attention to the stock market feeds a $500 billion market composed of stockbrokers, stock brokerages, investment banks, mutual funds, stock market researchers, stock market analysts, stock market writers, and personal financial consultants. This is what they do. They talk and write about stocks and the stock market. The average investor is exposed to a constant litany of advice and commentary. All this attention creates the impression that stocks are the best way to invest. Even textbooks in personal finance, when they address this issue, present a chart that shows the relative performance over time of a savings account, T-bills, federal long-term bonds, corporate long-term bonds, and the stock market as measured by some broad-based stock index such as the Standard and Poor's 500 or the Dow Jones Industrial Index. The stock market always shows the highest returns that it should because it is the riskiest of all the investment alternatives shown. But where is commercial real estate?

It can be argued that such presentation overstate stock market performance for a number of theoretical and statistical reasons.[1] These reasons include a lack of randomness in the observation, the biases introduced by the selection of arbitrary time periods and the high degree of covariance among individual stocks. While data on the investment performance of specific types of commercial real estate is lacking, considerable work has been done on the performance of publicly listed *Real Estate Investment Trusts* (REITs) relative to home ownership, large stocks, small stocks, international stocks, bonds, and T-bills.[2] The basic findings of this research is that the portfolios of investing homeowners would have benefited from the inclusion of REITs in their portfolios both in terms of higher return and lower volatility (risk.) While there would not necessarily be a correlation between the stock performance of these REITs and a specific commercial real estate investment, such findings are suggestive of the fact that many stock market investors could benefit from diversifying into commercial real estate. In addition, because REITs are freely traded on the major exchanges, they provide the investor with liquidity, a commodity not readily available in other types of real estate ownership.

NOW IS THE TIME

The first decade of the 21st century will prove itself a great time to invest in commercial real estate. Interest rates are at historic lows. Cap-

---

[1] See http://economymodels.com/stocktime.asp

[2] Jack Goodman, "Homeownership and Investment in Real Estate Stocks," *National Association of Real Estate Investment Trusts*, January 2003; J. K. Brueckner, "Consumption and Investment Motives and the Portfolio Choices of Homeowners," *Journal of Real Estate Finance and Economics*, 15:2, 1997; M. Flavin and T. Yamashita, "Owner-Occupied Housing and the Composition of the Household Portfolio," *American Economic Review*, March 2002.

ital is readily available. Inflation is low. The real estate market appears poised for substantial growth. The Jobs and Growth Tax Relief Reconciliation Act of 2003 has created a number of substantial tax advantages for commercial real estate investors. All these factors point to the fact that this is the time to buy. This is a situation that will continue through the end of the decade.

Understanding the commercial real estate market today should begin with an understanding of its historical context. In the late 1980s, a real estate boom was moving toward its peak. Interest rates and inflation were climbing. Real estate was widely seen as a way to "beat inflation." The stock market was in the doldrums. When lenders became overextended and the monetary authorities contracted credit, the market collapsed. This was not a good time to buy. Sophisticated investors were selling, while neophyte investors were buying. By the early 1990s, the real estate market in almost all areas had collapsed. Many commercial real estate developers were bankrupted. A lot of office buildings, hotels, motels, houses, and apartment buildings were sold for pennies on the dollar. Real estate investors were completely discouraged. It was a great time to buy, but it required nerves of steel. Bottoms are hard to see when you are there, just as tops are hard to see just before you go over.

Today's real estate market appears to have moved out of that dismal environment in the mid-1990s and to be on its way to prosperous times. What the future will bring is hard to predict. In the beginning of 2004, interest rates hover near historical lows, stubbornly refusing to rise. Inflation, as measured by the CPI is also low. Capital gains taxes, dividend taxes, and a variety of stimulative tax measures have created greater opportunities for real estate investors. Conditions have been created that favor real estate investing. Certainly, there are no guarantees in this area. Real estate markets have exhibited great volatility in the past and will undoubtedly do so in the future. However, buying real estate now appears to give the wise investor, who has "bought right," the opportunity to gain a foothold for compounding future earnings that constitute the surest form of wealth creation. Buying right requires understanding the basic conditions for success in a particular real estate sector and having the capability of evaluating the financial dynamics of a particular investment opportunity.

The Importance of Location

Real estate properties are differentiated from most other financial or real assets by their uniqueness. No two hotels are exactly alike, no two pieces of undeveloped land are alike, no two office buildings are alike, no two shopping centers are alike, and so on. Commercial real estate is not a commodity. Each property is different because it is in a different physical location. This makes location one of the most important attributes of any piece of commercial real estate.

The first thing to understand about location is that location is not an absolute. There is no such thing as a generically "good" location (or a generically "bad" location.) The desirability of a particular site is relevant only in terms of its intended purpose. A property that is good for a residential dwelling is not necessarily good for an apartment, an office building, a factory, and the like. Assessing the value of a property always requires the strategic perspective: What is the purpose intended for this property?

Only in that context are the actual physical attributes of that site relevant. Physical attributes of a site would include the current use of the property, its location with respect to traffic patterns, relevant zoning laws, the contour of the land, the attributes and uses of adjacent or neighboring parcels of land (an otherwise desirable piece of land for a single-family residence might be made undesirable if the adjacent property were a mobile home park or a rendering plant), the effective marketing area or impact zone of the property and trends in adjacent, neighbor, local, or regional land use.

Another factor to consider in the valuation of commercial real estate is the impact of subjective perception. Certainly, a piece of property has an objective reality. However, that objective reality may not be as important as the subjective lens through which that property is viewed. An objective reality might describe 50 acres of rugged land surrounding a dismal swamp located 20 miles from the nearest urban area. A subjective perspective might be to consider land as a nature preserve, featuring select executive home sites surrounding ecologically important wetlands, that provide protection for a living environmental laboratory. The objective reality might be a rundown hotel adjacent to a metropolitan central business district whose desirability is threatened by crime in the neighborhood. The subjective perspective might be that the (refurbished) hotel could become a badly needed retirement community for area residents that is distinguished by its access to urban amenities and its significant architectural and historic significance. An investment in such a property could be thought of as a beacon of successful urban renewal that could revitalize the neighborhood.

It is all in the perspective. A lot of highly successful commercial real estate development occurs because someone is able to think "outside the box."

The Importance of Diversification

A key to successful investing, in general, is diversification. Specifically, diversification has that wonderful property of lowering risk without necessarily lowering gain (and often raising gain). We argue in this book that most investors should be diversified into real estate. We now wish to argue for diversification within the real estate sector for the same reasons.

In the middle of 1984, the market for office space in the Baltimore–Washington metropolitan area had been moribund for two years, with vacancy rates averaging around 14%. Manekin LLC, a private developer and broker of office buildings was not doing well as a result. Rather than downsize its staff, the organization looked at the residential market that had been red hot the last three years and decided to get into this real estate sector. Richard Alter, Manekin LLC President was quoted as saying, "Going forward, depending on market conditions, we expect to see 40% residential, 50% office, and 10% retail."

Moreover, in this area (as in most metropolitan areas), land for developments of any size was becoming increasingly difficult to find. In addition, local planning and zoning boards were becoming increasingly demanding. It turns out that the trend among these regulators is towards mixed-use development. This makes diversification a natural fit for a company like Manekin.

MIE Properties, a real estate development company that is also in the Baltimore–Washington metropolitan area, held about 2 million square feet of office space and 2 million square feet of retail space in 2004 and was in the same boat as Manekin. So, they began developing an 800-unit residential property that had a much brighter profit outlook. "We look at a piece of land and say, 'What would maximize the value?'" said Ed St. John, MIE Properties President. "We're not stuck with what we do. We do it all."

"If one end of the market takes a hit, you have something else to fall back on. It never hurts to be diversified," says J. William Miller Senior V.P. at the commercial real estate firm NAI KLNB.

The Dynamics of Wealth Creation and Preservation

Creating and preserving wealth starts with saving. Sad to say, there is no shortcut here. Those individuals who maxed out their credit cards in 2000 and 2001 to invest in the stock market paid an awful price for trying to go the easy way. Creating wealth is the classic example of the tortoise and the hare. To become wealthy, it is not necessary to make a one-time "killing." A much better approach to creating wealth is to use the power of compound interest.

One dollar invested for 20 years at 4% is equal to $2.19 (double your money), at 6% your money triples to $3.20, at 10% it increases to $6.72, and at 14% your initial investment will grow to a fabulous $13.74. No need to make a killing. All that is needed is patience and a sound investment strategy.

Commercial real estate opportunities offer rates of return that will have big payoffs through the power of compound interest. The trick to remember here is that higher returns go hand-in-hand with higher risk. When you receive an offer to have more return with less risk, watch your wallet and run for cover. Still, opportunities with superior returns relative to the risk abound in today's commercial real estate market and this situation is likely to continue for some time.

Risk and Danger Are Not the Same

Danger is something to be avoided at all costs. A sign that says "Danger—Unexploded Ordinance" means keep away. Rational individuals do not trespass. Risk is different. Risk needs to be embraced by investors because without risk there is little, if any, return. All forms of investment are risky. Avoiding risk is not the issue. Getting compensated adequately for bearing risk is the issue. All commercial real estate opportunities have risk, just as all other investments have risk. However, as commercial real estate is underused as an investment vehicle, the returns relative to the risk tend to be larger than those available in more traditional investment vehicles. If Prudential Insurance has an AA-credit rating and its 10-year bonds pay 9%, what is wrong with doing a build-to-suit lease for one of their regional offices that looks to earn a return of 22%? In both cases the obligation is secured by the general credit of the corporation. Which is preferable to the knowledgeable investor?

For investors the risk they are exposed to is not simply the sum of the riskiness of all their individual investments. Rather, it is the risk inherent in their entire portfolio. The risk of individual investments is not the same thing as the risk in the portfolio. This is because the risks of the different investments in your portfolio are more or less correlated with the risks of other investments in your portfolio. The effect of diversification among different types of investments is generally to reduce the risk of the overall portfolio without necessarily reducing return. This happens because the individual risk on one element in the portfolio may be largely independent of the risk of another element in your portfolio, so the risk of the portfolio itself declines. A property and casualty company's portfolio of homes they insure for fire hazard may illustrate this concept. If the probability of one home burning down is 0.001 (one in a thousand) and the probability of another home burning down is also 0.001, then the probability of them both burning down is 0.000001 (one in a million.) So adding elements to the portfolio whose risks are independent lowers the risk of the portfolio itself, even though the elements are equally risky.

An important implication of this concept is that investors should not evaluate the risk and return on an individual investment in terms of the riskiness of that particular investment alone. Instead, the risk should be judged by the impact of that investment on the riskiness of the overall portfolio itself. This means that it is possible to add a relatively risky investment to a portfolio and have the total riskiness of the portfolio go down. This reflects the way in which the riskiness of that investment is correlated with the riskiness of the existing investments in the portfolio.

Sometimes what is true for the individual is not true for the whole. Logicians call this phenomenon the "Fallacy of Composition." If it is true that one person at a football game can see better by standing up, it is not true that everyone can see better if they all stand up. It turns out that what is not true for an individual investment—more return with less risk—may be true for your portfolio, that is, it is possible to have more return with less risk because of diversification.

There are a lot of highly technical and mathematical ways to measure risk. All of them suffer from a variety of imperfections. Indeed, they are so mind numbing in their complexity, that the best approach to evaluating risk for the individual investor is common sense.

The common sense approach to risk is that while diversification is generally good, it needs to be evaluated within a set of priorities focusing on the life style context of the individual and his or her family. A young family needs to invest in a home and life insurance before they think about stocks. A retired police sergeant and his dependent wife living on his pension have no need to diversify by investing in a risky stock market option. A 45-year-old professional, with a family income of $145,000 a year, a house with substantial equity, and $200,000 in mutual funds as his sole financial asset, should be thinking about getting commercial real estate. Diversification in this case makes sense if the goal is wealth creation.

The whole point of this book is that an upper middle-class individual who today has a good job, is educated, owns a home, has paid off his or her credit card debt, and typically owns a fair amount of individual stocks or mutual funds, can probably stand to diversify into commercial real estate. Such diversification, if done correctly, can increase the individual's overall (portfolio) performance and decrease its risk. However, commercial real estate is not an area to take lightly. Each type of commercial property tends to have unique attributes with which the individual investor should be familiar. Given this knowledge then, a financial analysis of a specific project must be undertaken to figure out exactly what the risk return parameters of the property are. Then, the time comes for the investor to step up to the plate or not, as he or she deems appropriate.

SPECIFIC ADVANTAGES TO INVESTING IN REAL ESTATE

Financial Leverage

"Give me where to stand, and I will move the earth." said Archimedes, referring to the notion that with a long enough lever he could move the earth itself. The power of leverage is that great. This is as true in finance as it is in physics. Leverage is simply the extent to which debt is used to finance real estate. For example, let us assume that an individual purchases a house for $100,000. If Federal Housing Administration (FHA) financing is available, the owner may put down as little as 5% of the purchase price and borrow the rest ($5,000 equity and a $95,000 mortgage). Now, let us assume that the house rises in value to $110,000. This results in a gain of 10% on the house. By employing leverage, the owner of the house experiences a gain of 200%. This is due to his $5,000 equity investment growing to $15,000. Leverage makes the investor's money work harder.

Leverage is not unique to real estate. Stockbrokers typically offer "margin" financing on stocks bought through their brokerage. However, more leverage is generally available for real estate investment. This is because that while the commercial real estate market certainly has its ups and downs, it has nothing like the volatility of the stock market. Lenders feel more secure about their ability to recover their obligations when the value of those obligations is secured by a mortgage to real property whose value stays relatively constant.

Successful real estate investors optimize (not maximize!) their leverage. The general rule is "Borrow to buy, sell for cash." More leverage can make a good investment a great investment. Wise real estate investors generally look for those properties that provide the most financing. That is why single-family residences make such attractive investments. The government, in its desire to encourage home ownership, has created a set of institutions and policies to encourage individuals to purchase homes even with almost nothing down. While such programs are often targeted for the poorest and most disadvantaged in our society, there is a lot of carryover that can benefit almost anyone. Even outside residential properties, an eager seller can be interested in "taking back some paper" to minimize the investor's up-front cash requirements.

To optimize leverage, many investors have a specific strategy that they use in identifying investment opportunities. This involves acquisition strategies that minimize the cash necessary to get into a project and divestiture strategies that look to all cash exits. Such strategies would include minimizing the down payment, borrowing the down payment, extending the life of the loan, and borrowing interest only with a balloon payment for the principal.

The reason investors want to optimize leverage, rather than maximize it, is that increased leverage brings about increased risk. In this case the additional risk comes from the fixed obligations to pay interest (and perhaps principal.) Real estate investing always involves juxtaposing an uncertain cash flow coming in against a certain cash flow that must be paid out. Where this cash flow coming in is used to fund the cash flow going out (as is usually the case), this raises the possibility that the funds that were supposed to come in do not. This then puts the highly leveraged investor in a hard place. Money can fail to come in because the lessee is unable to pay, an argument with the lessee goes to court (the legal process is unbelievably slow and typically works to the disadvantage of the creditor), or the lessee, for some other reason, does not want to pay. Compelling such a person to pay is typically a long and arduous process, and while this process goes on, no money is coming in. Thus, how much leverage to use is ultimately a decision the investor makes based upon his or her preferred trade-off between risk and return.

Operating Leverage

Operating leverage is a characteristic commonly found in real estate properties due to its large proportion of fixed cost to total costs. This characteristic can be described in terms of the relationship between sales volume and profitability of a piece of property. Commercial real estate generally has a large degree of operating leverage due to its fixed costs. When fixed costs are large relative to variable costs, then small increases in sales will generate large increases in profits. The other side of the coin is that large fixed costs require a substantial volume of sales to break even.

The presence of such operating leverage means that when the revenues are large, the project is wildly successful, but if the revenue is not there, disaster looms. The point about operating leverage is that very small differences in sales can make for very large differences in profits. This makes predicting the failure or success of a real estate project more difficult.

Operating leverage is a form of business risk. Even where the real estate investor intends to take a very passive role in a development as a lessor, he or she is still effectively a partner with the lessee. Where the lessee is successful, the course of the lease will run successfully and both parties will be happy. Where the lessee is unsuccessful, the course of the lease will be troubled and both parties will be unhappy.

Inflation Resistance

Real estate values tend to rise with inflation. In fact, much real estate often rises faster than inflation because it is in relative limited supply compared to other consumer goods and services. Because real estate supply tends to be inelastic (insensitive to prices), as demand increases prices will rise faster in this sector.

Of course, a word of caution is necessary. Not all real estate rises in lockstep with inflation. There are variations in the price of real estate between regions, within regions, within states, within cities, and even within neighborhoods. Much depends on location and the demand for property at that location. Great care must be exercised in the selection of specific commercial real estate opportunities.

Tax Advantages

Real estate ownership is encouraged by the tax system. Two important advantages come into play here. The first is interest costs. The second has to do with the concept of depreciation. Both of these factors combine to make real estate investing very attractive.

Interest costs can be fully tax deductible for your personal residence (up to a limit) or for any commercial real estate investment. This means the cost of funds is reduced by your marginal tax rate. As a home owner, if you finance a house at 8% and you are in the 40% tax bracket, your real cost of financing the house will be 8% × (1 − 0.4) = 4.8%.

The second important tax advantage to owning real estate is the ability to depreciate any property (the buildings, not the land) being rented. Depreciation is a legitimate (noncash) deduction used to offset revenue that would otherwise be subject to taxes. This means you can show a loss on your real estate investment, use that loss to reduce your personal income, and thus lower your taxes. Anything to do with taxes tends to be a bit tricky and depreciation is no exception. Real estate rental is considered a passive activity and losses from a passive activity can only be used to offset passive income (not wages and salaries). However, if an individual actively participates in managing the rental property (as evidenced by selecting tenants, collecting rents, visiting the property, and doing maintenance—all of which are tax deductible in themselves), then the individual may deduct up to $25,000 from earned income, provided he or she does not have adjusted gross income in excess of $100,000 when the amount of loss that can be deducted is phased down to where adjusted gross income reaches $150,000 and no loss at all may be applied to earned income. There are a number of other constraints here having to do with marital status, and the like. There is also something called an *Alternative Minimum Tax* (ATM) to consider. An investor needs to consult with a tax professional to see how he or she may be impacted by the tax code. If an investor can write off $25,000 of paper losses due to depreciation and is in the 40% tax bracket, then he or she will receive a tax saving—a bottom line—of $10,000 in real dollars.

Investing in Real Estate Is Like Owning Your Own Business

Many individuals want to gain more "control" over their lives. The regimen of working for someone else, taking orders, and being subject to an array of arbitrary rules may feel stultifying. It is not uncommon for such individuals to want to "start their own business" to gain more control over their lives. For many people, this may not be a practical alternative. However, there may be another path to financial independence. Commercial real estate is an activity you control entirely. You find the opportunities, arrange the financing, bring all the elements together, and create something where there was nothing before. An individual can enter this business starting small and staying small, with the real estate investing being a profitable hobby. As an alternative, an investor can start small and over time, with a few good moves, grow his or her business into a high-paying full-time job.

Debt in an Inflationary World Is Good

Commercial real estate investors are debtors. They borrow money now to pay it back later. In an inflationary environment this confers a tremendous advantage to the buyer. In theory, interest rates adjust for the level of inflation by adding an inflation premium to the real rate of interest. In the real world, this adjustment process appears slow and uncertain. There have been a number of times within the past two decades where the rate of inflation exceeded the nominal rate of interest. Monetary history suggests a pattern in the world of modern finance where debtors have benefited from borrowing more valuable dollars and paying back with less valuable dollars.

The value of a dollar (or any unit of currency) is ultimately determined by what it will buy. What it will buy is determined by the price level of goods and services that, in turn, is determined by the demand for and supply of those goods and services. While government statistics show little inflation in the first few years of the decade, these indices do not necessarily reflect the buying pattern of real estate investors. It may be argued that broad-based indices (such as the Consumer Price Index), which rely on fixed market baskets of goods and services really understate the true level of inflation relevant to business decision makers.

There are a number of possible causes of inflation. One of the most common causes of inflation can result from the money supply increasing as a result of increasing government debt. Government debt increases because politicians basically find that, when they vote for benefits for people, they get congratulated for doing a good job by those people affected. When they vote for more taxes, they generally get voted out of office. Therefore, politicians tend to spend more without generating the needed tax revenues. The only way that can be done is to create more debt. What is the future for inflation in the United States? The effects of inflation are so powerful and pervasive that economists see inflation as a primary factor in redistributing wealth in our society. The real question is which side of this transfer will you be on?

Compounding Cash Flows

A hallmark of commercial real estate investment is that such investments yield compounding cash flows. Taking advantage of this requires a fairly long-term horizon, but that gets back to the tortoise and hare metaphor. An individual can go to Las Vegas, put down $10,000 on black at a casino roulette table, and double his or her money—or lose it all! The odds are against winning and there is a high degree of risk, but at least the issue is decided quickly. Or an individual can put $10,000 down on a well-located duplex apartment that will earn 21% annually over the next 15 years with very little risk. It takes a long time, but the $10,000 turns into $174,494! This is the miracle of compound interest. In finance, the tortoise not only finishes the race, the tortoise wins the race too! Rabbits show a burst of speed that looks good for a short time, but they rarely finish the race and almost never win the race. Compounding cash flows are the surest way to wealth creation.

Starting Small

This book is predominantly written for individuals who have already accumulated significant net worth. It is possible that such individuals have overly concentrated their wealth in traditional stocks and bonds and can benefit from diversification into commercial real estate.

What of individuals just beginning the process of wealth accumulation? Individuals whose chief problem is a lack of net worth and, perhaps, even a lack of good credit, are not necessarily left out in the cold. It turns out that real estate offers a great opportunity for such individuals. Social policy in the United States encourages home ownership. This has resulted in financial and banking policies that make acquiring a home relatively easy. This happens because houses can be bought for very little cash up front (many FHA mortgages require as little as 3% equity) and interest payments are subsidized by making them deductible against earned income. Even a person with very little income can enjoy the benefits of financial leverage.

Owning a home financed with a conventional 30-year mortgage have monthly payments that combine the interest owed and equity. The payment on equity is like forced savings. When a house is first purchased, the equity payment is very small but grows larger and larger over time—even though the monthly payment is fixed. That equity is actually building wealth. In addition, if the house is well located, it should appreciate over time rather than depreciate. Not only does your wealth increase as the value of the house increases, this gain is likely to be tax-free. Under certain circumstances, capital gains on the sale of a personal residence under $250,000 for an individual (and $500,000 for a couple) are completely free of tax. Even the smallest home owner gets (1) easy access to capital, (2) a subsidized interest rate, (3) forced savings, and (4) wealth appreciation as the house grows in value.

The really good news is that much of these benefits can apply to the purchase of a second (vacation) home. This is a great path to becoming a successful real estate investor. A second home in the mountains, on the coast, or even on a boat (with eating and toilet facilities) can give you a tax deduction for 2004. Mortgage interest on a second home may be deductible if the mortgage does not exceed the fair market value of the home and the mortgages on both your primary residence and the second home do not exceed $1 million. Points paid on the mortgage to acquire the second home may also be deductible if you itemize, but they must be amortized over the life of the loan rather than deducted completely for the year of purchase (as in the case of a personal residence.)

A caveat: Tax law is so complicated and subject to so many special circumstances that one cannot rely on the above generalities. *A tax professional should be consulted prior to making a real estate investment to make certain how the tax laws apply to your particular situation.*

SPECIFIC DISADVANTAGES RELATING TO REAL ESTATE

Lack of Liquidity

Liquidity in finance refers to the ability of an asset to be exchanged for cash without loss of value. Publicly traded stocks have good liquidity. (That is the purpose of having "stock markets.") Commercial real estate investments typically do not. If you have invested in a small office building and the time has come to liquidate that investment, it cannot be done overnight, or, at least, it cannot be done overnight without great loss of value.

Of course, much will depend on prevailing supply and demand conditions. It is possible that an investor will decide to liquidate in a period of high demand and short supply. In that case, a sale may be arranged in a few weeks. If the decision is made to liquidate, when market conditions are adverse, then arranging a sale may take months or years.

Difficulties in Determining Property Value

This issue is closely related to liquidity. If real estate is inherently illiquid, that means it takes time to realize the property's value. But what is its value anyway? This is certainly an area that it is easy to disagree on.

When investors are selling a commercial property, they are really selling a stream of income. Valuing this stream of income requires two factors to be considered. First, one must quantify the stream of income itself, and secondly, one must determine the risk associated with that stream of income.

When investors refer to the stream of income, what exactly are they talking about? It is possible that this refers to *net income*. Net income is a residual, resulting from taking all legitimate tax-deductible expenses from revenue and then subtracting the required tax from that sum. This may or may not be a good measure of the property's value. One reason for this is that the calculation of net income results from including, as tax deductible expenses, both business costs and financing costs. While the business costs are likely to remain the same if ownership changes, the financing costs may not. This is because the new owner may use a different capital structure (mix of debt and equity) than the current owner. Thus, net income not only reflects the operating characteristics of the property, but the financial characteristics as well.

As a consequence, some analysts prefer to use *earnings before interest and taxes* (EBIT) as a measure of income. This allows a focus on the purely business aspect of the property. The calculation of EBIT is closely related to that of *net operating profits after taxes* (NOPAT). NOPAT is basically EBIT after taxes. The nature of the tax code is so arbitrary that taxes paid may, or may not, have something to do with firm performance. Using EBIT is preferable in measuring income in situations where the tax is going to be determined by considerations other than those pertaining to the property. NOPAT is preferable if the tax liability is systematically related to firm performance.

Another problem with net income is that depreciation expense, one of the legally permitted deductions from revenue, is not a "cash" expense. Indeed, it is not paid to anyone but merely serves as a device to shelter income from taxes. The property owner retains this portion of revenues. As such, the sum of net income and depreciation is typically referred to cash flow. Cash flow is probably the most commonly used measure of income after net income. Cash flow should probably be used more commonly than net income as a measure of income because it makes greater economic sense. The reason that net income is more commonly used as a measure of income than cash flow is because real estate value is most commonly expressed in terms of income multiples. For example, it is very common to say, "That type of business will sell for five times earnings." Thus, net income is the traditional measure of earnings in the real estate business.

Yet another measure of income is possible. Real estate properties frequently require regular maintenance to preserve their value. Painting, patching, repairing, clearing drains, replacing worn elevator parts, and so on. The nature of these expenditures is that they may be deferred. While this may lead to a long-term deterioration of the property, such deference will have the effect of reducing the tax-deductible expenses and thus result in a larger net income figure. Consequently, some analysts prefer to take cash flow and deduct necessary maintenance expenses from it. This is a great concept, but in practice it is very hard to identify necessary maintenance expenditures. When this is done, however, such a measure of income is called *free cash flow.*

An additional issue with respect to income is its level. We generally know a lot about income in the present, but less about income in the future. When it is said that the value of the property depends on the income it can generate the reference is to income now and in the future. In many situations, future income can reasonably be expected to grow. In some circumstances, decline is possible. The future level of income can be a very important element in determining income.

The second element (after determining income) in determining value is determining the risk associated with that value. This risk has to do with the fact that the income anticipated might not occur, or its value may in some sense be diminished. The use of a discount factor is commonly used to adjust the cash flows to take this into account. Thus, discounting that income to its present value explicitly quantifies the risk associated with income.

If a property is generating an income stream of $10,000 per year, and that condition is expected to persist for the foreseeable future and a discount factor of 20% is considered appropriate to the risk level of that income, then the value of that property may be determined by the following equation (where n is any number of periods of time):

$$\text{Value} = \$10{,}000_1/(1 + 0.2)^1 + \$10{,}000_2/(1 + 0.2)^2 + \ldots$$

$$+\$10{,}000_n/(1 + 0.2)^n \tag{1.1}$$

$$\text{Value} = \$10{,}000/0.2 = (5)\$10{,}000 = \$50{,}000 \tag{1.2}$$

Equation (1.1) says that the value of the property is the present value of its income (however measured) discounted at a rate of 20%. (Stated in real estate lingo "its value is equal to five times earnings.") This is the general rule for determining the value of every kind of commercial real estate property. That is, ultimately its future earnings and its corresponding risks determine real estate's value. In this case the income level is determined to be $10,000 and those earnings in the future are discounted at an annual rate of 20%. The exponential in this series allows for the compounding effect to take place.

Where disagreements over value take place (and divergent opinions are common in this area), those disagreements center either on the quantity of earnings or the riskiness of those earnings. That is, whether this property is really generating $10,000 in income, or whether there is another way to look at it. Where the buyers and sellers forecast of future earning differ, each will arrive at different valuations. Furthermore, perhaps the seller is basing his analysis on cash flow, while the buyer thinks the net income figure would be more appropriate.

The future is always hard to predict. One way to deal with the risk of the unknown is to increase the discount rate to reflect that risk. A seller might be offering the property for the $50,000, as shown in equation (1.2), because he or she has confidence in the future ability of the property to generate that $10,000 year after year. Potential buyers may not share that confidence. For example, potential buyers may know less about the property and thus, may have less confidence in the property's ability to generate income in the future. Thus, prospective buyers might want to discount that $10,000 at a higher rate, say 40%, to compensate for that uncertainty. Therefore, these buyers will offer to buy the property at 2.5 (1/0.4) times earnings. When market conditions deteriorate, buyers become increasingly fearful of what the future might bring. They respond by seeing the real estate as deserving of higher discount rates. That is why prices fall on the downside of the market.

Another variation of equation (1.1) commonly encountered is where future income is likely to grow. (In equation (1.1), future income was projected to be constant.). This situation is expressed in equation (1.3).

$$\text{Value} = \$10{,}000_1(1 + g)/(1 + 0.2)^1 + \$10{,}000_2(1 + g)^2/(1 + 0.2)^2 + \ldots$$

$$+\$10{,}000_n(1 + g)n/(1 + 0.2)^n, \text{ and where } g = 10\% \qquad (1.3)$$

$$\text{Value} = \$10{,}000/(0.2 - 0.1) = (10)\$10{,}000 = \$100{,}000 \qquad (1.4)$$

Again, equation (1.4) is just a simpler way of expressing equation (1.3), which says that the property is now worth $100,000 (10 times earnings) because this income stream is expected to grow at 10% annually. Here again the assumptions underlying the valuation may cause differing views as to the property's value. If it is easy to disagree on the income measure to be used and what the appropriate discount rate is determined to be, then it is really easy to disagree on what the future rate of growth will be.

Equation (1.4) is the most commonly used framework to determine value. That is, the value of a commercial real estate property depends on how much income it will generate, the appropriate rate at which that income should be discounted, and how much that future is likely to grow in the future.

Overextended Borrowing

Leverage is a good thing, but too much leverage can be a bad thing. Leverage increases the potential return on a project, while at the same time increasing the risk associated with that project. This is why it is better to optimize leverage than maximize it. Too much borrowing jeopardizes the success of a real estate investment as surely as too little leverage. It is a matter of balance to be decided by the investor's taste and preference for the trade-off between risk and return.

Management Expertise Required

Where ownership of the property is direct, the commercial real estate investor is going to need to be involved with searching for the project, evaluating the project, financing the project, and (if acquired) managing the project. Even where the commercial real estate investment involves a sale–lease-back arrangement and there is no property to search for, and the evaluation is cut and dry, the project will still not manage itself. There are always ongoing issues to be dealt with between the lessor and lessee. Commercial real estate investment is not a passive activity. It requires active, focused, intense participation or things are likely to go terribly wrong. Commercial real estate investment is not for the detached.

SUMMARY

Many investors have an excessive concentration of equities in their investment portfolios. Whether such equities are directly held, the result of employer offered stock options or held indirectly through mutual funds, such investors can achieve significant reductions in risk without loss of potential return through investment in real estate. Indeed, the astute investor can often both increase return and reduce risk through real estate investment. This "magic" is accomplished through diversification and the power of compounding returns. The tried-and-true approach to building wealth over time comes from a portfolio of one-third equities and long-term debt, one-third real estate, and one-third liquid assets. Diversification minimizes risk and wealth grows by compounding earnings. This is a bedrock foundation for wealth building that will withstand the storms of adversity that are sure to come. Portfolio structures composed of trendy stocks are built on sand and inevitably collapse.

Real estate provides a mosaic of opportunities and risks. No one sector is inherently better than another. Office buildings may be hot in California, but dead in New York. Residential housing can be going great guns in Arizona, but suffering from oversupply in Tennessee. The good news for investors is that the market is so complex and dynamic, there are always good investment opportunities to be found somewhere. Of course, not all real estate investments are appropriate for all investors. Investors will vary by their degree of expertise, their willingness to commit time and energy to an investment, their ability to use the tax advantages inherent in real estate, their need for liquidity, their access to capital, and their taste for risk. Still somewhere within this mosaic, the patient real estate investor will find the opportunity that is right for him or her.

Table 1.1 presents a synopsis of the strengths and weaknesses of the different types of commercial real estate investment. Potential real estate investors should use this chart to find that combination of traits that are most appealing and then go to the relevant chapter to learn more about the area should use this chart.

All strengths and weaknesses are rated on a scale of low to high. It should be noted that these are general rankings. Local market conditions, or unique circumstances characterizing a particular project, could alter this rating in that instance. These rating should only be used as a general guide. More detailed information is contained in the referenced chapters.

Most forms of real estate investing permit or encourage a high degree of financial leverage. Greater financial leverage means an increased ability to fund a project with debt. The ability to use financial leverage in real estate investing is an advantage because financial leverage will give the investor a greater return per unit of equity capital. For example, a single-[family residence is bought for $100,000 with $5,000 equity and a mortgage of $95,000 and the property appreciates 10% to $110,000 in one year. Then the investor's gain is not 10% but 200%, that is, the $5,000 of equity has now become $15,000 of equity. Of course, financial leverage can also be a disadvantage because it implies an increased interest expense. Interest expenses are fixed and increase break-even points as a result.

Operating leverage occurs when a rise in sales or revenues brings about a more than proportionate increase in profits. Almost all real estate properties have high-operating leverage because the bulk of real estate expenses are fixed. This property of real estate simultaneously makes real estate such an attractive proposition in terms of potential return and increases the risk of failure if those fixed costs cannot be covered by receipts.

TABLE 1.1 Advantage and Disadvantage Comparisons by Types of Commercial Real Estate

Type of Property	Chapter	Financial Leverage	Operational Leverage	Inflation Resistance	Tax Advantage	Own Business	Compounding Properties	Lack of Liquidity	Valuation Difficulty	Management Expertise
Single-family	6	High	Medium	High	High	High	High	Medium	Medium	Medium
Apartments	7	High	High	High	High	High	High	Medium	Medium	High
Condos	8	High	High	Medium	High	High	Medium	Medium	Medium	Medium
Time shares	9	Medium	Medium	Medium	Low	Medium	Low	High	High	Low
Undeveloped land	10	Medium	High	Medium	Very low	Medium	High	High	High	Low
Self-storage	11	High	High	High	Medium	High	Medium	High	Medium	Medium
Restaurants	12	High	High	Medium	High	High	Medium	High	High	High
Shopping centers	13	Medium	Medium	Medium	Medium	Medium	Medium	High	Medium	High
Athletic facilities	14	Medium	Medium	Medium	High	High	Medium	High	Medium	High
Office buildings	15	High	High	High	High	Medium	High	High	Medium	Medium
Industrial	16	High	Medium	Medium	Medium	Medium	High	High	Low	Low
Parking lots	17	High	High	High	Medium	High	High	High	High	Medium
Hotels & Motels	18	High	Medium	High	High	High	Medium	Medium	Medium	High

Real estate properties are capable of functioning as an inflation hedge. That is, when prices in general go up, the rents or fees derived from owning real estate will also rise. This attribute of real estate combines with the use of leverage in real estate. Where the debt carries a fixed interest rate, the effect of inflation is to lower the value of the debt repayments. Under this scenario, creditors lose and debtors win.

Real estate property may generate tax savings that augment the real value of the property. In general, tax advantages arise from the use of depreciation and the fact that interest expense is tax deductible. Many real estate investments are not profitable until the tax advantages are considered.

Investing in real estate is not necessarily a passive business. Even if there are no operational demands on the investor, managing a portfolio of properties requires many administrative tasks that can amount to a full-time job. In addition, the investors may also elect to take on certain operational responsibilities with respect to the property owned. An office building owner may wish to take charge of the maintenance function, for example, or a shopping center owner may wish to find tenants on his or her own. Some investors may well consider the opportunity to support themselves by running their portfolio as their own business as a good thing. The framework used above treats the ownership attributes of a type of property as a good thing.

One of the most important components of the wealth building process is the ability to compound earnings. As a general rule, real estate properties are very good for facilitating this process because of the opportunities naturally provided to reinvest in a property already owned or a similar property.

In all real estate markets, there are times of excess demand. Converting the value of a property into cash by selling it is not a problem. Sadly, all real estate sectors sooner or later experience conditions of excess supply. Under these conditions, it can be very hard to access the value of a property through a cash sale. Frequently, the property becomes impossible to sell without significant reductions in price, or without some form of seller financing. Lack of liquidity constitutes a serious risk to all real estate investors.

Because real estate properties tend to be unique as a result of location or the characteristics of the improvements located on that property, determining the value of that property may be difficult. Of course, "comps"—comparisons—can always be found, but frequently those comps are not really comparable for one reason or another. Valuation difficulty can create a liquidity problem.

Management expertise is often required with any type of real estate investment. The owner-investor must always make a host of decisions

TABLE 1.2   Suitability Index for Investors by Type of Investment

Type of Property	Chapter	Suitability for an Investor Based on Experience
Single-family	Chapter 6	Little experience
Apartments	Chapter 7	Some experience
Condos	Chapter 8	Little experience
Time shares	Chapter 9	Little experience
Undeveloped land	Chapter 10	Little experience
Self-storage	Chapter 11	Little experience
Restaurants	Chapter 12	Some experience
Shopping centers	Chapter 13	Lots of experience
Athletic facilities	Chapter 14	Some experience
Office buildings	Chapter 15	Lots of experience
Industrial	Chapter 16	Lots of experience
Parking lots	Chapter 17	Some experience
Hotels & Motels	Chapter 18	Lots of experience

from determining the value of a property to financing the property and to taking care of an array of details associated with ownership (e.g., liability insurance.) Of course, this expertise will be less for some types of properties and more for others.

The manner in which these advantages and disadvantages impact the different property types are discussed in the referenced chapters. However, these advantages and disadvantages may be summed up in the "Suitability Index" shown in Table 1.2.

Success in real estate investing is a function of the experience (knowledge and expertise) of the investor. The first-time investor should not go for an industrial or office building property unless very special circumstances are present. Success in this area comes best to the novice who starts small and simple and acquires the necessary experience for success over time.

CHAPTER 2

Interpreting Financial Statements for Successful Real Estate Investing

Investing, in whatever form, deals with uncertainty. This is true for stocks, bonds, and, most importantly, commercial real estate. Uncertainty about the future translates into risk. Financial statements are tools of tremendous power that can be used to reduce that uncertainty. Financial statements may not lead the investor to the answer. However, they will lead to a better understanding of these risks.

Income statements are often not what they seem. "The devil is in the details" is never truer than when it comes to determining what financial statements mean. Income statements attempt to show how a business performs over specified period of time. Most commonly, income statements are presented on a year, a quarter, or monthly basis. If the purpose of the income statement is to provide insight into a firm's performance, an immediate problem arises over what "performance" means. Performance is often discussed in generalities like "profit," "earnings," or "the bottom line." There is nothing wrong with using such terms per se. The problem is they tend to mean different things to different people. Using such terms without defining them leads to misunderstandings and misunderstandings lead to mistakes.

It would be a nicer world if income statements presented the results of performance in a simple, unambiguous form. Unfortunately, that is not the case because reality intrudes. The underlying business is often not simple and unambiguous. Rather, the underlying business is complex, multidimensional, and engaged in all sorts of behavior relative to its performance that are not reflected on the income statement. Therefore, the best way to understand an income statement is to approach it from a different perspective. In our analysis of commercial real estate investments, we will generally approach evaluating an investment's performance by examining the income statement's NOPAT, net income, and cash flow. Each of these measures sheds light on a property's underlying value.

There are two basic kinds of income statements. They bear some similarity, but are, in fact, quite different. They are most powerful when used in combination. One type of income statement depicts past performance. Thus, a property's revenues, expenses, profits and losses are reported for a specific time period. As investors, we are generally more interested in the future than the past. Thus, the true worth of these historic financial reports is that they may give us some hints into the future. The statements can help us in constructing the second type of income statement, which is called a pro forma income statement. A standard income statement of the first type for a commercial real estate property (in this case, a parking lot) might appear as in Table 2.1.

The first thing to understand about this simple statement is that it does not show cash flows. This income statement for Express Parking Corporation does not mean that we actually received $250,000 cash for our services. For example, while the statement suggests that there was a

TABLE 2.1   Express Parking Corporation, Income Statement, January 1–December 31, 2003

Revenues	$250,000
Cost of service	50,000
Gross profit	200,000
Overhead	25,000
Depreciation	100,000
EBIT[a]	125,000
Interest	30,000
EBT[b]	95,000
Taxes	38000
Net income	57,000
Depreciation	100,000
Cash flow	157,000

[a] Earnings before interest and taxes
[b] Earnings before taxes
Tax rate (tx) = Taxes/EBT = $38,000/95000 = 40%
NOPAT = EBIT(1 − tx) = 125,000(1 − 0.4) = $75,000

$30,000 outflow for interest, it may not necessarily be the case. This is because income statements are constructed on an accrual basis. This basically means that we can apportion revenues and expenses to a particular period of time, even if we did not receive cash or spend cash, as long as we do this in accordance with *generally acceptable accounting principles* (GAAP). This is not necessarily a bad thing; it may even be a good thing, making the income statement more reflective of the firm's actual performance.

For example, suppose of that $250,000 revenue, $50,000 was from a corporate account whose employees regularly used our parking lot during this period of time, but they have not yet paid for it (the check is in the mail). It makes sense to apportion this revenue to this period, even though we have not yet been paid because this is when we sold the service. Since we did not get the money, the books balance by increasing "accounts receivable" on the balance sheet. So the $250,000 reflects performance if the accounts receivable can actually be collected, but will not reflect performance if those accounts receivable have to be written off as bad debt. It is impossible to say which is the best way to deal with this, because the future event (paying or not paying) has not yet occurred. (Remember income statements are historical.)

Similarly with respect to the $30,000 interest charge, it is shown as an expense; but perhaps we have not paid it yet. Perhaps the loan was an interest-only loan, where the actual interest is to be paid after the first of the year. Perhaps in the overhead, we have $5,000 of legal fees that we are nominally obligated to pay, but we were dissatisfied with the lawyer's service, have not paid him yet, and intend to renegotiate the fee.

From these examples, we can see that income statements do not necessarily represent a version of a firm's performance that is carved in stone. That is not to say the income statement is written in the sand either. Income statements should be seen as malleable, suggesting reality rather than depicting it.

Given the numbers in Table 2.1 as reasonably depicting reality, there is still some concern over how to interpret these numbers.

One perspective is to focus on EBIT. EBIT is very important because it shows the ability of the business to pay its debts. Recall, that the primary reason for real estate investing in the first place is the opportunity to use leverage. Using financial leverage means employing debt. The use of financial leverage means that interest and principal must be paid at some point in time. EBIT is the measure of the firm's ability to support these debt service requirements. As such, it is a prime factor in determining the basic desirability of the investment.

This brings us to a consideration of NOPAT. As can be seen from Table 2.1, NOPAT is basically EBIT adjusted for taxes. Taxes represent real payments to the government and should be taken account of as an expense, just as any other payment for resources that a business uses. Thus, NOPAT represents the funds available to pay for both the debt and equity capital used by the organization. As such, NOPAT allows the investor to look at the tradeoffs he or she will have (as the supplier of equity capital) between paying for debt (leverage) and paying himself. EBIT's perspective is the ability to pay for debt. NOPAT's perspective is the ability to pay for both debt and equity.

This brings us to net income, which is the number most traditionally associated with profit or the "bottom line." It is true that this is the most widely used measure of firm performance. However, it is not true that this is necessarily the best measure of firm performance. It is a measure of firm performance. Net income results from the definitions used by the tax code to describe revenues minus expenses and that amount, less taxes. Its most powerful perspective is that this is what is left after all is said and done to reward the investor. If this is a Subchapter S corporation, then net income is what is available to pay the owners in the form of dividends.

However, strictly speaking, that common interpretation is not true. Depreciation as an expense is not paid out. Depreciation is retained by the organization. This means the funds represented by depreciation are still in the firm to pay the owners. For this reason, it is common to add depreciation back to net income to get cash flow. From that perspective, cash flow is a superior way to evaluate the performance of a business. Cash flow is really what you get back from investing in a business. Tax laws and accounting principles define net income, but the cash investors get back from their investments tells the tale of success or failure!

Because of the importance of debt financing in commercial real estate investing, there has historically been a tendency to evaluate all commercial real estate projects in terms of their *debt capacity ratio* (DCR). This is defined as the ratio of EBIT divided by the interest owed for that period (NOPAT/interest.) In accounting textbooks, this ratio is often called the *times interest-earned ratio* (TIE.) In some circles, the decision to invest or not invest is largely dependent on achieving a satisfactory DCR (usually of 2).

This approach reflects the fact that financial leverage is a sword that cuts both ways. When conditions are favorable, financial leverage makes you look even better. However, when conditions are unfavorable, financial leverage raises the terrifying specter of bankruptcy. Long-term commercial investors, who have experienced both the ups and downs of the market, are rightly aware of the importance of a healthy DCR. Nevertheless, the DCR should not be the "go, no go" criteria for real estate projects.

The decision to invest in commercial real estate always involves a tradeoff between risk and return. The return on a project is found by focusing on cash flow and the resultant NPVs and IRRs a project generates. The risk of a project may be approached by considering both the break-even attributes of that project and its DCR ratio.

PRO FORMA INCOME STATEMENTS

Income statements, as a matter of historical record, sometimes do change. As more data become available, firms frequently revisit their income statement to "restate" them. Occasionally, such restatements are large, but for the most part they are relatively minor. After all, such income statements are grounded in a finite reality.

Pro forma income statements are absolutely necessary to the investor in commercial real estate. They are an indispensable "tool of the trade." The reason for this necessity is that conventional income statements are always looking backward. To be sure, "He who fails to understand history is condemned to repeat it," but this means the primary reason for looking backward is to look forward. Looking forward is what it is all about from the investor's perspective. Success or failure will come from future events, not past ones. Pro forma income statements are valuable because they are not grounded in the past reality.

Pro forma refers to the fact that these are anticipated numbers, expected numbers, possible numbers, or (in the worst case) imaginary numbers wholly without relevance to the real world. Pro forma income statements are a blank canvas on which any forecaster can paint what they would like.

Properly constructed, pro forma income statements are powerful vehicles for organizing one's thoughts about the future. Thus, they lead to a better understanding of that future. Pro forma income statements have two claims to legitimacy. The first is that they are an extension of historical income statements. That is not to say pro forma income statements should be mere extrapolations of the past. Rather the relationships embedded in the numbers of an income statement in the past existed for some reason. Those relationships may or may not be expected to hold in the future. This can be discovered through the examination of evidence pertaining to those relationships and the use of logic. This analysis can then be used to formulate a set of assumptions that will drive the pro forma numbers. The validity of any pro forma income statement thus depends on its relationship to historical income statements and the quality of the assumptions embedded in those numbers.

A pro forma income statement is presented in Table 2.2 for the Express Parking Corporation as above.

TABLE 2.2 Express Parking Corporation, Pro Forma Income Statement

	2003	2004	2005	2006	2007	Percentage Increase 2003–2007
Revenues	$250,000	$267,500	$286,225	$306,261	$327,699	31%
Cost of service	50,000	51,500	53,045	54,636.35	56,275.4405	13%
Gross profit	200,000	216,000	233,180	251,624	271,424	36%
Overhead	25,000	24,750	24,502.5	24,257.475	24,014.90025	–4%
Depreciation	100,000	100,000	100,000	100,000	100,000	0%
EBIT1	125,000	142,750	161,723	182,003	203,684	63%
Interest	30,000	33,000	36,300	39,930	43,923	46%
EBT2	95,000	109,750	125,423	142,073	159,761	68%
Taxes	38,000	43,900	50,169	56,829.31	63,904.4409	68%
Net income	57,000	65,850	75,254	85,244	95,857	68%
Depreciation	100,000	100,000	100,000	100,000	100,000	0%
Cash flow	157,000	165,850	175,254	185,244	195,857	25%
NOPAT	75,000	85,650	97,034	109,202	122,210	63%

The first thing one could ask about the anticipated sales growth at Express Parking is why is it growing at 7% a year for a total of 31% over the 4-year period? Why doesn't it grow at 5% or 10% instead? Seven percent could be a reasonable expectation of future revenues at Express Parking or not. What assumption does this reflect? Is this an extension of a historical trend? Are there some outside forces (like a new nearby office building) or inside forces (like an anticipated rise in parking fares) driving this estimate. Why are costs only going up 3% a year for a total of 13%? What does this say about the relationship between fixed and variable cost? Why is overhead expected to fall slightly? Does management have specific plans to implement some changes in this area? Why is depreciation held constant? Isn't new capital equipment going to be added during this period? Won't existing capital equipment continue to depreciate?

All these trends may be perfectly valid and reasonable, but they should be supported by evidence and justified by logic. The assumptions embedded in these trends drive EBIT, NOPAT, net income, and Cash Flow. Different assumptions would yield different conclusions. While no one can predict the future, pro forma income statements will shed additional light on the factors that will influence an investment's future success or failure.

Investors serious about commercial real estate will see a lot of pro formas. Generally, the sellers who have a vested interest in making the development look good prepare these pro formas. Investors need to be skeptical about such income statements. They may be perfectly reasonable guides to future performance or they may be treacherously deceptive about what the future is likely to hold. Thus, it is incumbent upon the investor to carefully evaluate the pro forma statements' underlying assumptions and substitute his or her own assumptions where it is merited.

Commercial real estate investors are both consumers and producers of pro forma income statements. They are consumers when they are being sold an idea. After they have accepted an idea, then the investor becomes a producer by preparing a pro forma statement as part of an application to borrow funds. Lenders are generally very good at distinguishing between pro formas that are within the realm of possibility and those that are made out of whole cloth. To maintain their credibility with a lender, an investor should be careful about providing supporting documentation for these pro forma statements. Unrealistic projections will not only diminish the value of the property in the eyes of the lender, but the investor's knowledge and integrity as well.

EVALUATING INVESTMENTS

The framework adopted in this text for evaluating commercial real estate investments is an extension of the cash flow concept. Whatever name is put on cash flows coming in or going out, it is the difference between these two over time that will prove the investment worthwhile or not.

The approach that should be used to evaluate an investment is to isolate and identify all real cash flows provided by the investor and to compare them with all real cash flows accruing to the investor. The framework for this analysis should be time sensitive, as money now is always more valuable than money in the future. The framework for actually comparing the different cash flows is called *Net Present Value* (NPV.) Net present value discounts all future cash flows to the present and thus makes them comparable so that the absolute benefit of the investment is identified in terms of its present value. A companion concept is that of the *Internal Rate of Return* (IRR.) The IRR identifies that rate of return that would equate the value of the cash flows going out with the value of the cash flows coming in. As such, it is appropriate to think of the IRR as the percentage return on an investment over that period of time. The mechanics of calculating the IRR means that where the cash flows are irregular, or alternate between the positive and negative over time, it is not possible to compute a value for the IRR. IRR values will be shown where it is possible to calculate them.

The general framework for evaluating investments using this cash flow methodology is depicted in Table 2.3. Table 2.3 collects all cash flows in and out (capital contributions and mortgage equity payments out and net income, depreciation, and cash gain on sale of land in.) These cash flows are then brought to their net present value by discounting all of the cash flows at 12% back to the present. In this case, it can be seen that the value of the NPV is $461,804, and this yields the investor a return of 24% annually over the contemplated 10-year time horizon.

The investor can then use this tool to assess whether or not this return is appropriate for the perceived risk.

Assessing Risk

A problem with income statements is that they address only the issue of return. Investors, on the other hand, are always interested in the relationship between return and risk on any given project. Risk does not appear on the income statement. Risk must be inferred from the income statement.

There are two basic ways to infer risk from income statements. One approach involves the calculation and interpretation of financial ratios. The second involves performing a break-even analysis.

TABLE 2.3 Express Parking Corporation

| | | | Cash Flow Statement | | |
Year	Net Income	Depreciation	Mortgage Equity Payments	Capital Contributions	Cash Gain on Sale of Land	Net Cash Flows[a]
0				$750,000		-$750,000
1	$65,850	$100,000	$39,678			$165,850
2	75,254	100,000	37,694			175,254
3	85,244	100,000	35,809			185,244
4	95,857	100,000	34,019			195,857
5	99,691	105,000	32,318			204,691
6	103,679	102,900	30,702			206,579
7	107,826	100,842	29,167			208,668
8	112,139	98,825	27,709			210,964
9	116,624	96,849	26,323			213,473
10	121,289	94,912	25,007		$546,980	763,181

[a] Net income + Depreciation – Mortgage equity payments – Capital contribution + Cash gain on sale of land.
NPV at 12% = $461,804
IRR = 24%

Ratio Analysis

Ratio analysis involves the comparison of certain components of the financial statements with other components of the financial statements. There are literally hundreds of financial ratios that can be calculated to shed light on a firm's performance and risk. These are generally grouped into four major categories: profitability, liquidity, efficiency, and leverage. There is nothing wrong with this type of approach if you are an accountant. For a real estate investor who wants a quick assessment on the underlying risk of a particular project, that's another matter.

A much more efficient and direct approach for the individual investor, for whom time is at a premium and studying financial statements not a delight, is to (1) focus on the liquidity of a project and (2) apply the DuPont equations. This approach will yield a great deal of insight for relatively little effort.

Liquidity Ratios

Liquidity tells us about the cash situation for a project. Current assets are all those items that we expect to turn into cash within one year. Current liabilities are all those items that we intend to pay out during the same year. As a general rule, the ratio of current assets to current liabilities, commonly referred to as the *current ratio*, should be 2.0 or higher to indicate a healthy situation, although this ratio may vary from industry to industry. In this case, Express Parking looks healthy. As we look at the

TABLE 2.4   Express Parking Corporation

Balance Sheet			
Cash	$5,000	Accounts payable	$25,000
Accounts receivable	50,000	Notes due	20,000
Inventory	125,000	Accrued expenses	10,000
Current assets	$180,000	Current liabilities	55,000
Fixed plant & Equipment	1,000,000	Long-term debt	200,000
less depreciation	320,000	Total liabilities	255,000
Net fixed plant & Equipment	680,000	Owners equity	605,000
		Total liabilities and	
Total Assets	860,000	Owners equity	860,000

Liquidity ratios:
Current ratio = Current assets/Current liabilities = 3.27
Quick ratio = (Current assets − Inventories)/Current liabilities = 1.00

balance sheet however, we notice the relatively large inventory item ($125,000.) What if these inventories cannot be sold for some reason or another? That is why we look at a second liquidity ratio, commonly called the *quick ratio*. It adjusts for inventories, because these are so hard to value and may or may not be very liquid. Express Parking has a quick ratio of 1. As a general rule, healthy situations may have a quick ratio of 1 or higher, although again this can vary from industry to industry.

Liquidity ratios tell one about the health of a firm or project, just as your temperature tells your physician about your health. Express Parking has a current ratio of 3.27—a sign of health. You have a temperature of 98.6°—you are healthy. A current ratio of 0.7 indicates big problems below the surface, just as if you had a temperature of 102° tells the physician that all is not right with you.

DuPont Ratios

DuPont ratios tell us about how well the firm is meeting its customers' needs and how efficient it is. Upon these two basic attributes of a firm, performance rests. In Table 2.5, we see that advance parking profit to sales ratio is increasing. Whether 17% is a good ratio depends upon the industry. For example, 17% would be great for a supermarket where the industry averages 2% and terrible for a jeweler where the ratio averages 50%. This rising trend suggests that their service is being well received in the marketplace.

The sales-to-asset ratio tell us about efficiency. In 2003, every $1 of assets produced $1.30 worth of sales. We see a period where efficiency fell off here and then increased again. Whether or not this represents a desirable level of efficiency will depend on the industry. (GM has an efficiency ratio of 0.53; Wal-Mart has an efficiency ratio of 2.58.)

Together market performance and efficiency tell us Express Parking's *return on investment* (ROI). This is a measure of business performance that abstracts from leverage considerations. As a result of Express Parking's

TABLE 2.5   Express Parking Corporation DuPont Ratios

DuPont Ratios	2003	2004	2005	2006	2007
Profit to sales	0.14	0.15	0.16	0.17	0.17
Sales-to-Total assets	1.3	1.2	1.0	1.2	1.4
Return on investment	18.20%	18.00%	16.00%	20.40%	23.80%
Total assets to owners' equity	1.8	1.7	1.7	1.8	1.8
Return on equity	32.76%	30.60%	27.20%	36.72%	42.84%

market performance and efficiency, we can see ROI trending up. Our conclusion: This is a healthy company. However, this does not tell us about the total performance of the firm, which includes business performance plus the effect of leverage.

Financial leverage is measured here as the ratio of total assets to owners' equity. It tells us how many dollars of assets are supported by a single dollar of equity. The higher this ratio, the greater the financial leverage. At Express Parking we can see this ratio has been fairly constant.

Return on equity (ROE) is our most global measure of business performance. It takes into account both business performance (as measured by ROI) and financial leverage. The result at Express Parking is a very healthy ROE.

If these results showed problems or downward trends, they would be suggestive to the investor of the measure of risk in the project. The DuPont analysis allows us to determine the source of the risk. Is its source the efficiency of the operation or its profitability? It is always up to the investor, in the end, to judge the risk. The liquidity and DuPont numbers can be important inputs into that process.

BREAK-EVEN ANALYSIS

Break-even analysis is a simple, yet powerful, tool to assess project risk. This concept is used extensively throughout this book for the purpose of assessing project risk. Break-even analysis has to do with the relationship between fixed and variable costs in a project. While this certainly allows us to find the minimal level of sales necessary to "break even," it also has a lot to say about potential profitability.

The break-even point for a project is where total revenues are equal to total costs.

$$\text{Total revenues} = \text{Total costs} \qquad (2.1)$$

Total costs are seen to be a function of fixed costs and variable costs. Variable costs are so called because they are a function of total revenue. Usually, the relationship between variable costs and total revenue is depicted as a constant. This assumption tends to be more valid for the short run. Fixed costs are so-called because they do not necessarily change as total revenue changes. They may well vary considerably over time.

$$\text{TC} = \text{FC} + \text{VC} \qquad (2.2)$$

where $\text{VC} = b\text{TR}$ and b is some constant percent.

Therefore the *break-even point* (BEP) is

$$TR + TC; TR = FC + VC; TR = FC + bTR; \text{ so } BEP = FC/(1 - b) \qquad (2.3)$$

In the case of Express Parking above (Table 2.1), variable cost will be the cost of service/sales or 20%. Fixed costs will be equal to overhead, depreciation and interest or $155,000.

Therefore the BEP at Express is $155,000/(1 − 0.2) = $193,750.

With revenues at Express Parking well above that level (Table 2.1) and projected to continue to be above that level (Table 2.2), there seems little danger of Express Parking failing. Further, we know about Express Parking that for every $1 they increase their revenue, they generate $.80 which goes either towards defraying their fixed costs or to increased profits. This relationship is referred to as *operating leverage*.

Most commercial real estate investments have high operating leverage because they have high fixed costs. Projects with high fixed costs are revenue dependent. Accurate sales forecasts are critical in commercial real estate investing. The difference between a little bit less of revenues and a little bit more of revenues is often the difference between a disastrous loss and a handsome gain.

SUMMARY

Financial statements are inherently difficult to use for assessing the potential for success or failure of a project. One problem involves their construction in an accrual format. Another problem is that convention and tax law, rather than market value, generally drive the definitions of cost and revenue under GAAP. A third problem is that most real estate projects are forced to analyze pro forma data, which is all about assumptions, that may or may not be accurate.

The framework used as an indicator of success or failure is to use a cash flow statement (as constructed above in Table 2.3) that adds a measure of market reality to estimating the potential return from a real estate project. Risk is then assessed using break-even analysis to generate an understanding of the variance in outcome associated with unfavorable events. All projects are then examined in terms of both their potential return and potential risk.

CHAPTER 3

Depreciation

Tax policy has three goals: (1) to raise revenue, (2) to achieve the social end of greater income equality, and (3) to foster desirable economic policies all of which are sought in a highly politicized context. This has resulted in a tax system characterized by what many feel is undue complexity. Tax policy has become a political tool, influenced by the politics of the executive and legislative branches of government.

This can be seen clearly in the case of depreciation (now officially referred to as "cost recovery"). If the government wants to stimulate growth in business, it will shorten the defined life of an asset class or increase the speed with which it is depreciated, so businesses can attain a higher write-off. This tends to stimulate business investment spending by making capital investment more profitable. If the agenda of the day is "closing loopholes" and "taxing the rich," the taxing authorities will lengthen the life of an asset class or retard the speed at which the asset can be depreciated. This will have the effect of making capital investment less attractive. Unfortunately, these actions tend to be implemented in nontransparent ways, making it very difficult to see what has actually been accomplished by changes in tax legislation.

The Jobs and Growth Tax Relief Reconciliation Act of 2003, signed into law by President Bush on May 28, 2003, is a good example of the use of tax law as an instrument of economic policy. This legislation was broad reaching and reduced the tax liability of most individuals and businesses. The specifics of these changes are discussed below. The significance of this situation is that further tax law changes are likely as policy and politics change. It should be noted, however, that the changes due to the passage of the Jobs and Growth Act were particularly beneficial to potential investors in commercial real estate. For the present, that has contributed to create a very favorable environment for real estate investment.

37

THE BASICS OF DEPRECIATION[1]

The idea behind a tax on income is to tax the difference between revenues and expenses that can and should be charged against that revenue. When expenses are made on labor and goods or services that will be quickly consumed in the production process, this is a relatively straightforward matter. A problem arises when a business purchases an item that will last more than a year. Such an expense is called a *capital expense*. The point here is that the capital item will give up its value over a period of years, hence it should be "expensed" over a period of years. Allowing the entire expense of the capital item to be charged in the year of purchase or acquisition would give the firm an "unfair" tax break, by inordinately reducing its tax liability in that year. Thus, the tax legislation purpose is to match revenue with the capital acquired to generate it. Depreciation has come to be the term describing that portion of the capital item that is expensed in a particular year.

However, the investor may elect in some circumstances to expense (write-off immediately) rather than depreciate (spread out the expense) certain capital items. A business may elect to fully expense certain qualifying property in the year that it is placed in service. This is referred to as a *Section 179* (of the Internal Revenue Code) *deduction*. Qualifying property includes tangible personal property such as machinery and equipment, property attached to a building (e.g., signs), gasoline storage tanks, and livestock. Land improvements (buildings, parking areas, fences, etc.) are specifically excluded from a Section 179 deduction. Also qualifying for a Section 179 deduction would be single-purpose agricultural or horticultural structures and petroleum storage facilities.

A business frequently has the choice of electing to take the Section 179 deduction or not. The reason for this may be that the business does not generate sufficient income to take advantage of the deduction at the time, or, perhaps, the election of this option prevents the business from using other exemptions and deductions.

For capital items that will be depreciated, there are two different depreciation systems: the *General Depreciation System* (GDS) and the *Alternative Depreciative System* (ADS.) The difference between the two systems is largely that ADS specifies a longer recovery period than GDS. The GDS is most commonly used, but the ADS may be required or elected in a number of situations.

ADS is required for:

---

[1] Depreciation is fully explained in "How to Depreciate Property," *IRS Publication 946*, 2002, a 107-page opus of everything you wanted to know about depreciation.

■ Listed property used 50% or less for business. Listed property includes any automobile or transportation vehicle, any property used for entertainment or recreation, any computers and peripherals (unless used in a place of business), and cellular telephones.
■ Property used outside the United States.
■ Tax-exempt property.
■ Tax-exempt financed property.
■ Property used in farming under certain circumstances.
■ Imports covered by an Executive Order of the President of the United States.

When it comes down to the practical matter of how much of a capital item should be expensed in a given year, there are two variables to be considered: (1) the economic life of the asset, and (2) the rate at which the capital item should be expensed.

The length of life of a particular type of capital used continues to be a matter of continuing dispute between the IRS and various businesses until the Tax Reform Act of 1986, which established life-specific classes for different types of capital equipment called *ACRS* (Accelerated Cost Recovery System, pronounced "acres"). These life classes were subsequently revised into nine separate property classes with recovery periods of 3, 5, 7, 10, 15, 20, 25, 27.5 (residential rental property), and 39 years (nonresidential real property) under what has become known as the *Modified Accelerated Cost Recovery System* (MACRS, pronounced "makers.") For example, automobiles fall in the 5-year class, office furniture falls in the 7-year class, and building improvements fall in the 15-year class.

Depreciation rates may be straight line, double-declining balance, or 1.5-declining balance. Double-declining balance generally applies to 3-, 5-, 7-, and 10-year property. One-hundred-and-fifty-percent declining balance generally applies to 15- and 20-year property, and all 27.5- and 39-year property must be straight-line depreciated. As a general rule, the sooner the asset can be depreciated, the greater the tax advantage to the depreciating party.

Straight-line depreciation means that each year's depreciation is equal to every other year. So, a property in the 27.5-year category will depreciate 1/27.5 years each year of its life. In contrast, a 150%-declining balance takes the straight-line depreciation for the first year and multiplies it by 1.5. That is that year's depreciation rate and it is applied to the basis of the capital item. Then, in the second year, the first year's depreciation is subtracted from the original basis and that amount is multiplied by the same depreciation rate to determine the depreciation in that year. The process is then repeated over the remainder of the items life. A double-declining asset goes through exactly the same process except that the multiplier is 2.0 rather than 1.5. The process is further modified by the fact that if at any point, the accelerated depreciation is less than what has been generated by straight-line depreciation, straight-line depreciation is used. Fortunately the relevant year-by-year depreciation percentages are presented in Form 946.

This whole process is made even more complicated by the use of partial year conventions. This is to prevent a business from purchasing a capital item in late December and gaining the same depreciation charge, as if it were purchased in the beginning of January of that same year. Hence, the depreciation formulas are adjusted to provide for which quarter in the tax year the property was acquired.

One of the implications of this is that if a 5-year asset class capital item is acquired midyear, so it only captures a portion of its depreciation the first year, it will need to be depreciated in the sixth year, in order to capture that last half year of life. So a capital asset with a 5-year life will be depreciated over six years. A similar adjustment is made for all asset life classes. Fortunately, the relevant percentages are also presented in Form 946.

It must be remembered that depreciation is a noncash expense. The capital item was purchased initially, and there was a cash outflow at that time, but none since. As this noncash expense is subtracted from revenues, its effect is to lower the tax liability. The advantage to depreciation comes from a reduction in taxes. If, in a given year, an investment project has $100,000 of pretax earnings and its tax rate is 40%, then it will pay $40,000 in taxes and have $60,000 in net income. If, as an added cost, there is $20,000 of depreciation charged against revenue, EBT will be $80,000, the tax paid will be $32,000, and net income will be $48,000. Where is the gain? There is no gain if net income is the criteria of "profit." However, the depreciation was not paid to anyone, so the investor still has it. The investor's cash flow is thus $68,000 ($48,000 net income and $20,000 depreciation). So, net income goes down from $60,000 to $48,000, but the cash flow rises from $60,000 to $68,000 leaving the investor better off by $8,000. Furthermore, the value of depreciation increases as the tax rate increases.

The effect of the length of time required to depreciate an asset can be seen in Table 3.1. This Table compares three capital items each with a basis (depreciable cost) of $100,000. One capital item is in the 5-year class and depreciates on a double declining basis. Another capital item is in a 15-year life class and depreciates at 150%. While the third item is in the 39-year class and its depreciation is straight lined. All assets are subject to the half-year convention. (The assumption being that the assets were purchased midyear and only get 50% of the first year's

TABLE 3.1 Tax Savings of Different Asset Life Classes[a]

	5-Year			15-year			39-year		
Year	Basis	Asset Depreciation	Tax Saving	Basis	Asset Depreciation	Tax Savings	Basis	Asset Depreciation	Tax Savings
1	$100,000	$20,000	$8,000	$100,000	$5,000	$2,000	$100,000	$1,282.05	$513
2	80,000	32,000	12,800	95,000	$9,025	3,610	98,718	$2,531.23	1,012
3	48,000	19,200	7,680	85,975	$7,351	2,940	96,187	$2,466.33	987
4	28,800	11,520	4,608	78,624	$6,054	2,422	93,720	$2,403.09	961
5	17,280	11,520	4,608	72,570	$5,029	2,012	91,317	$2,341.47	937
6	5,760	5,760	2,304	67,541	$4,208	1,683	88,976	$2,281.43	913
NPV of tax savings at 12%:		$29,524			$10,290			$3,572	

[a] Assuming a 40% tax bracket, using the half-year convention.

41

depreciation.) The assumed holding period for each asset is six years, and at that time the asset is presumed sold for its depreciated value if any. Thus, the value of the tax savings can be compared between the three investments.

Comparing the tax savings on this basis reveals the clear advantage of shorter depreciation periods. Since the tax savings occur over time, an adjustment must be made to convert tax savings in the different years back to their "present value." This is done using a NPV calculation that discounts all cash flows (at 12%) back to the original year. Thus, the 5-year asset captures a tax saving worth $29,524, compared to the $10,290 of the 15-year asset and the $3,572 of the 39-year asset. Clearly, the length of time allocated to depreciation makes a big difference.

RECENT TAX LAW CHANGES

As described above, the cost of property is depreciated over its recovery period, a period assigned by the IRS. For example, equipment is generally depreciated over five years or seven years, automobiles are depreciated over five years, and rental real estate is depreciated over 27.5 years. However, the Jobs and Growth Tax Relief Reconciliation Act of 2003 have temporarily suspended these rules for many types of capital expenditures.

There are two provisions that allow you to deduct more depreciation than you can under the usual rules: the Section 179 Deduction and the Special Depreciation Allowance. The Section 179 Deduction (now called *Code Section 179*) allows taxpayers to expense—that is, write off in one year—up to $100,000 (up from $24,000) of the cost of eligible business property through 2005. This deduction applies no matter when during the year the equipment is purchased.

The deduction can be used only for property purchased. For example, the deduction cannot be used for a property acquired in trade, except to the extent you paid cash. Also, this deduction can be used only if the property is used more than 50% for business.

The deduction is reduced if more than $400,000 of eligible property is purchased for this year (up from $200,000 in previous years.) Also, off-the-shelf software purchased for business may be deducted as well. The deduction cannot exceed your business taxable income figured without regard to this deduction. In other words, this election cannot be used to generate a loss. Business taxable income includes self-employment income and wages and salaries. If you are married and file a joint return, you can take into account your spouse's business income. Real property is not eligible for this deduction.

There is another restriction as well. If the property is sold before the end of its recovery period, you have to include in income the excess of the Section 179 deductions, which you claimed over the depreciation, that you would have claimed for the time you owned it.

Whether or not the Section 179 deduction should be elected instead of using the normal depreciation procedure will depend on a number of factors: (1) Your current tax bracket compared to your future tax bracket (higher expected future tax rates would argue against the use of Section 179); (2) your ability to use (as a tax offset) the current tax savings; and (3) how long you expect to keep the property for which you claim the deduction.

In addition, this Jobs and Growth Act creates a *special depreciation allowance*. In addition to the Section 179 deduction, a special depreciation allowance of 50% of the basis of the eligible property may be claimed. (This is an increase from the previous requirement of 30%.) If you also claim the Section 179 deductions for the property, the special allowance is figured using the basis reduced by the Section 179 deductions.

Eligible property for the special deduction includes most depreciable property with a recovery period of 20 years or less and computer software that is depreciated over three years. This property must have been purchased between May 6, 2003, and December 31, 2004, and placed in service (i.e., used in the business) before 2005. You must be the first person to use the property. Business use of the property must be more than 50 percent (as in the case of the Section 179 deduction).

The limit on the depreciation for vehicles bought in 2002 with a gross weight of less than 6,000 pounds is $10,710 ($7,650 bonus depreciation plus the $3,060 "regular" auto depreciation) multiplied by the business-use percentage.

Unlike the Section 179 deductions, there is no business-taxable income limit. Therefore, you can claim this deduction even if your business shows a loss. There is also no dollar limit. The special allowance must be claimed for all property in a particular class (see the caution note below), whereas the Section 179 deductions are claimed on a property-by-property basis.

Table 3.2 permits a comparison of the alternative cost recovery mechanisms (Section 179, *Special Bonus*, and regular double declining balance) for a $50,000 purchase of office furniture that falls into the 7-year life class. Using the Section 179 deduction yields a tax saving of $17,857. Using the Special Bonus provision yields a tax saving of $15,738, while the normal tax saving generated would be $13,619. This suggests that there is a clear advantage to using Section 179 (assuming it is able to be

TABLE 3.2 Comparison of Alternative Cost Recovery Mechanisms[a]

Year	Basis	Section 179 Election Depreciation	Tax Saving	Basis[b]	Special Depreciation	Tax Savings	Basis	Normal Depreciation	Tax Savings
1	$50,000	$50,000	$20,000	$25,000	$28,573	$11,429	$50,000	$7,145.00	$2,858
2		0	0	21,428	6,123	2,449	42,855	12,245	4,898
3		0	0	15,305	4,373	1,749	30,610	8,745	3,498
4		0	0	10,933	3,123	1,249	21,865	6,245	2,498
5		0	0	7,810	2,233	893	15,620	4,465	1,786
6		0	0	5,578	2,230	892	11,155	4,460	1,784
7		0	0	3,348	2,233	893	6,695	4,465	1,786
8		0	0	1,115	1,115	446	2,230	2,230	892
NPV of tax saving at 12%:			$17,857			$15,738			$13,619

[a] Assuming a 40% tax bracket, using the half-year convention.
[b] Basis after 50% exclusion for bonus depreciation.

used by the presence of enough income for an offset). However, it can be seen that the Special Bonus provides a significant tax saving in its own right. Because this would be applicable to all real property, it serves as a powerful incentive to commercial real estate investors to take advantage of this provision.

SUMMARY

Depreciation represents a tax shield for revenues. Recent tax policy changes have shifted the amount of depreciation that can be charged to the life of the capital asset to a shorter time period and "front-loaded" the amount that can be depreciated in a given year. Both of these changes make real estate investment more attractive. The competitive nature of the real estate investment process can put pressure on profit margins. The tax advantages derived from depreciation can make the difference between a mediocre outcome and a great outcome for the real estate investor.

CHAPTER 4

Business Organizational Forms

Statutes relevant to real estate transactions vary significantly from state to state. Therefore, the following discussion is intended only to familiarize the reader with the general way in which the law applies to real estate transactions and business organizations. Investors find knowledgeable attorneys experienced in real estate transactions invaluable to their success. Such attorneys should always be consulted before, during, and after any contemplated real estate investment. Not to do so is "penny wise and pound foolish."

Real estate investors will often make use of real estate brokers in buying or selling commercial real estate. Indeed, there are brokers who specialize in commercial real estate, or various types of commercial real estate, and can often be of great service in providing relevant information about that real estate. As a buyer, the real estate investor should be aware that the real estate agent is an agent for the seller. As a seller, the investor will need to sign a listing agreement with the brokerage that details the rights and responsibilities of all parties to the listing as well obligating the investor to pay the broker a commission if the broker finds a willing and qualified buyer.

Once a buyer and seller of commercial real estate come to terms, their agreement must be expressed in a written contract called a "purchase and sale agreement." This contract will identify the parties to the contract, describe the property, and specify the purchase price and deposit. After the purchase and sale contract is signed, the buyer must make sure the deed to the property is "marketable" and free and clear of liens and encumbrances. It is also appropriate for the buyer to have the property thoroughly inspected.

Following this process, there will be a "closing," in which the buyer receives a deed to the property and the seller receives his money. The deed to the property can take a number of forms. The most common

47

form is "fee simple absolute" (fee simple), which is the most complete interest you can have in a piece of real estate. A deed may take the form of a "defeasible fee" in which circumstance ownership is conditional upon some act or behavior. For example, where the deed states that this land may not be used for manufacturing purposes. If the land is so used, it will revert to its original owners. Deeds may also contain "easements," "profits," or "covenants." An easement gives someone the right to go into and use your property for some purpose. For example, a property bordering a lake may give others the right to use your property to gain access to the lake. A profit gives someone else the right to take some resource from the land such as timber, or coal. Covenants are agreements to do something (mow the lawn once a week) or not do something (convert the facade of a building to another style).

Deeds themselves take specific forms. There is a *general warranty deed*, in which the seller promises that they own the property and have an unfettered right to sell it. This means that if there is a challenge to the deed, the seller will have to defend the right of ownership. A *grant deed* warrants that the seller has not conveyed the property to anyone else and that the property is free of encumbrances. In this deed, the seller does not have to defend the buyer if there is a challenge to the title. A *bargain and sale deed* makes no express warranties, but there is an implied warranty that the seller is conveying an unfettered marketable title. A *quit-claim deed* releases the seller's interest in the property, if the seller has any interest at all. It is a good deed if there are no other claimants to the property.

It is important for the investor to understand the difference between leases for residential property and business leases. In a business lease, the landlord gives the key to the property to the tenant and the tenant is on his or her own, unless there is an explicit stipulation to the contrary in the lease. In a residential lease, the landlord retains considerable responsibility. The landlord will often be held responsible for making all but the most minor repairs, maintaining the property in livable condition, injuries to tenants and their guests that occur in any "common" area such as halls, walkways, or recreational areas, and for allowing the tenant "quiet enjoyment," which means the landlord must give sufficient notice before entering the property. Most states today have laws that curtail the landlord's right to evict tenants for failure to pay the rent of major lease violations. It is not unusual to take two or three months to evict a tenant for failure to pay rent. This highlights the importance of maintaining good landlord-tenant relations.

BUSINESS ORGANIZATIONAL FORM

The choice of which business form to adopt, as a vehicle to invest in commercial real estate, is critical to the success of the real estate investor. Different business forms have different tax implications, different implications for investor liability, different implications for control, and different implications for cost. There is no one "best" business form. The business form adopted should be the one that best meets the individual investor's needs. The investor's needs have to do with the investor's goals, personal situation, and the particular type of investment being considered. In this context the investor must weigh the tradeoffs between tax advantages, liability, control, and cost.

Perhaps the most important issue impacting the business form chosen is the potential liability for the investor by the business organization or agents of the business organization. The legal principle is *qui facet per alium, facet per se*. That is, "who acts through another, acts himself."

All business forms are governed by the concept of *agency*. Agency is a legal relationship in which one person (real—or artificial, i.e., a corporation, limited liability company, etc.) represents another and is authorized to act on his or her behalf. Agency law is quite broad and covers the whole body of rules that society recognizes and enforces in regards to situations where one person acts for another. Without agency law, business could not act. Each individual would only be able to represent himself.

The form that the business takes affects the liability of the owners. To what extent is the business and the investor the same? To the extent they are the same, the investor will be responsible for torts of any agents of the business. (A tort is damage, injury or a wrongful act done willfully, negligently, and not involving breach of contract. If the issue is a breach of contract, then the issue is dealt with in a civil suit.)

Agents of a business include employees and those to whom the business has given a power of attorney. Independent contractors are not considered agents. Principals in a business are generally responsible for the acts of their employees. (Exactly who is a principal will be defined by the form the business takes.) Agency can be created by contract, by conduct that implies agency or by "estoppel" (apparent authority). This means an employee of the business may bind the principal contractually, whether the employee has the actual authority to do so, as long as the employee has the apparent authority to do so. Further, even though the owner has committed no act of negligence, the principle can be held negligent if that employee is acting within the scope of their employment.

Agents are expected by law to exhibit a high degree of fidelity to the principal. This would include obeying instructions, acting with skill, protecting confidential information, and the duty to avoid a conflict of interest. The principal, in turn, has a duty to compensate the agent and inform him or her of any risks associated with the agency. When an agent acting within the scope of their employment commits a tort, both the employee, and the principal can be held liable for the tort. This is known as the doctrine of joint and several liability.

The legal framework for business organizations is created at the state level. Although the forms are similar across state lines, the keyword here is similar. A form that would provide a desired advantage in one state may well not do so in another. There is no barrier choosing to create a business form in a state offering the most advantages. The laws of the state in which it is formed, not the state in which it operates, govern the liability and internal affairs of a business entity. While forming the business in your home state may offer simplicity and cost savings, states such as Delaware and Nevada may, in most cases, offer superior liability and other offsetting advantages.

The following discussion deals with the attributes of these business forms in general. The specific needs of an investor should always be discussed with an experienced attorney to determine the relevance of the laws in that state to the investor's need.

The relative attributes of different organizational forms are presented in Table 4.1

Sole Proprietorship

This is the easiest, most convenient, and least expensive form of business organization. Unfortunately, for the real estate investor interested in increasing and preserving wealth, it is not very good.

This form of business only has one owner. No formal requirements to create or operate this form. The owner has unlimited, personal liability for all of the business's debts. The owner personally hires all employees, and thus the owner has unlimited, personal liability for the acts of employees. A sole proprietorship is not a separate taxpaying entity. Income is reported on the owner's personal tax return and does not require the filing of a separate tax return. For these reasons, this form of business should usually be avoided.

General Partnership (also Called "Partnership")

This business form must have two or more owners. No formal requirements are necessary to create and/or operate this form. Some states provide for the filing of "Articles of Partnership," so that the arrangement is a matter of public record. All owners have unlimited, personal liability for all of the businesses debts. All owners personally hire all employees,

TABLE 4.1 Attributes of Business Forms

Organizational Form	Tax Implications	Liability	Control	Cost
Sole proprietorship	No distinction between business and owner.	Complete owner liability for business.	Complete control of business.	No cost; created by mere declaration or behavior.
General partnership	Business income prorated to partners.	Complete liability for business.	Control diluted by other partners.	Minimal; state filing optional.
Limited partnership	Business income prorated to partners.	General partner has unlimited liability; limited partners have limited liability.	Control is vested in general partner; limited partners may not participate in management.	Minimal; most states require registration and annual filing.
Limited liability partnership	Business income prorated to partners.	All partners have full or partial limited liability; may be restricted to professional partnerships.	Control is embedded in partnership agreement and bylaws.	Modest; most states require certificate registration and annual filing.
Registered limited liability partnership	Business income prorated to partners.	All partners have full or partial limited liability; may be restricted to professional partnerships.	Control is embedded in partnership agreement and bylaws.	Modest; where this form exists, registration and filing are required.
Limited liability limited partnerships	Business income prorated to partners.	Both general and limited partners have limited liability.	Control is embedded in partnership agreement and bylaws.	Modest; more formal registration and filing requirements.
Close corporations	Business income taxed at the corporate level; distributions to owners taxed as dividends.	All owners have limited liability; number of possible owners is limited.	Control is embedded in the director(s) of the corporation who are elected by the shareholders according to the articles of incorporation and bylaws.	Less expensive; nominal registration, filing, and reporting requirements.
Limited liability company	Business income prorated to partners.	All owners have limited liability; the LLC exists independently of its owners.	Control is embedded in the owners by the charter and bylaws.	More expensive; formal registration, filing, and reporting requirements.

51

TABLE 4.1 (Continued)

Organizational Form	Tax Implications	Liability	Control	Cost
Professional limited liability company	Business income prorated to partners.	All owners have limited liability; the PLLC exists independently of its owners.	Control is embedded in the charter and bylaws.	More expensive; formal registration, filing, and reporting requirements.
C corporations	Business income taxed at the corporate level; distributions to owners taxed as dividends.	All owners have limited liability.	Control is embedded in the director(s) of the corporation who are elected by the shareholders according to the articles of incorporation and bylaws.	Expensive; the most formal registration, filing, and reporting requirements.
Subchapter S corporations	Business income not taxed at corporate level, but prorated to shareholders.	All owners have limited liability.	Control is embedded in the director(s) of the corporation who are elected by the shareholders according to the articles of incorporation and bylaws.	Less expensive; nominal registration, filing, and reporting requirements.
Professional corporations	Business income taxed at the corporate level; distributions to owners taxed as dividends.	Owners have partial limited liability; restricted to recognized professional groups.	Control is embedded in the director(s) of the corporation who are elected by the shareholders according to the articles of incorporation and bylaws.	More or less expensive, varying by state; the formality of reporting and filing requirements also varies by state.
Professional associations	Business income taxed at the corporate level; distributions to owners taxed as dividends.	Owners have partial limited liability; restricted to recognized professional groups.	Control is embedded in the director(s) of the corporation who are elected by the shareholders according to the articles of incorporation and bylaws.	More or less expensive, varying by state; the formality of reporting and filing requirements also varies by state.
Service corporations	Business income taxed at the corporate level; distributions to owners taxed as dividends.	Owners have partial limited liability; restricted to recognized professional groups.	Control is embedded in the director(s) of the corporation who are elected by the shareholders according to the articles of incorporation and bylaws.	More or less expensive, varying by state; the formality of reporting and filing requirements also varies by state.

and thus all of the owners have unlimited, personal liability for the acts of employees. In addition, each owner has unlimited, personal liability for the acts of all of the other owners. Partnerships are a separate tax-paying entity: Income is prorated to the owners' personal tax returns and the business files only an information return with the IRS. Partnerships are a relatively simple business form to create and operate. Exposure to liability is so great in this form that it should not be used. Thus, this form is in a tie for the worst form of business with sole proprietorship.

Limited Partnership (LP)

This business form must have two or more owners. Limited partnerships are formally created under state law. One or more owners of the LP must be a general partner who has unlimited, personal liability in all of the same ways as a partner in a in a general partnership. At least one owner must be a limited partner (frequently all of the other owners will be limited partners) who has limited liability. Owners who are limited partners are prohibited from participating in the management of the business. Limited partnerships are frequently used to build tax shelters and for estate planning purposes. Income to the partnership is passed through to the owners' personal tax returns and the business files only an information return with the IRS.

Limited Liability Partnership (LLP)

The LLP requires two or more owners as a limited partnership. This business form is formally created under state law as is an LP; but all of the owners have limited liability for the business's debts. In many states, however, this "limited liability" is less than that afforded to the owners of an LLC or a corporation. In some states, notably California and New York, the LLP may only be used in "professional" practices. Income is passed through to the owners' personal tax returns and the business files only an information return with the IRS.

Limited Liability Limited Partnership (LLLP)

In some states, the LP can register as an LLLP that has the effect of giving the general partner limited liability. Therefore all of the owners of the LLLP have limited liability for the business's debts. LLLPs are usually more costly to start and maintain than an LP because they are subject to more formal statutory rules regarding officers and record keeping. Income is passed through to the owners' personal tax returns and the business files only an information return with the IRS.

Registered Limited Liability Partnership (RLLP)

Some states provide for the creation of *"registered"* limited liability *partnerships* (RLLP). This occurs where the LLP is really a general partnership that has "registered" in the LLP form to achieve some version of limited liability for all of the owners of the business.

Limited Liability Company (LLC)

This is a recently developed business form. The LLC may have one or more owners. This business form is created by state statute where all of the owners have limited liability for the business's debts. A LLC is usually less costly than a corporation to create and maintain, because it has more relaxed, less burdensome rules governing operation compared to a corporation. The LLC is not a separate taxpaying entity: Income is reported on the owner's personal tax returns and does not require the filing of a separate tax return when there is only one owner.

In many states, the business interests of the owners of an LLC are protected from the claims of the owners' personal creditors. This advantage is not enjoyed in the corporation or the *limited liability partnership* (LLP). This advantage may be significant for preserving wealth under adverse conditions. Therefore, the LLC combines into one form the best elements from the corporation (limited liability for all of the owners) and the general partnership (absence of formalities, low costs, tax benefits). For most commercial real estate investors, this is probably the business form of choice.

It should be noted that while owners have "limited liability" in an LLC that limitation only means that the creditors of the corporation cannot go after the personal assets of the owner. To the extent that the owner has assets that remain in the LLC, those assets are not immune from the claims of creditors.

As LLCs are relatively new to the business arena, it is important to form the LLC in a state that follows the *Revised Uniform Limited Partnership Act* (RULPA) view in its LLC statutes.

C Corporation

Corporations are formally chartered at the state level and provide for a separation of ownership from management. They are more costly to establish and maintain that other business, but they provide unparalleled protection for the owners from claims against the business itself. Owners elect directors who have the formal responsibility for selecting and monitoring corporate management. C corporations are taxed as entities themselves and repatriate profits to their owners through dividends, which are then subject to the personal income tax (so-called *double taxation*).

It should be noted that while owners have "limited liability" in a C corporation, but that limitation only means that the creditors of the corporation can not go after the personal assets of the owner. To the extent that the owner has assets that remain in the corporation, those assets are not immune from the claims of creditors.

Subchapter S Corporations

Subchapter S corporations differ from C corporations only in that profits are not subject to a separate corporate tax and such profits are prorated to the various owners directly where they will be subject to the personal income tax. The term used to describe this is that Subchapter S corporations are treated as "conduits" for tax purposes.

Close Corporations (CC)

Close corporations have all the characteristics of a C corporation (double taxation, limited liability, etc.), but are less expensive to charter and maintain. Laws on this type of corporation vary considerable from state to state, however

- CCs generally are held by a single shareholder or closely knit group of shareholders.
- The corporation may be formed initially as a close corporation or may amend its articles of incorporation to include this statement.
- A CC's profits are taxed twice: once at the corporate level and again when profits are distributed as dividends to their shareholders. If a close corporation meets specific IRS requirements, a corporation can file for Subchapter S corporation status and generally avoid paying tax at the corporate level.
- The shareholders of a close corporation are personally liable for the debts and liabilities of the close corporation only to the extent of their capital contribution.
- There are no public investors, and its shareholders are active in the conduct of the business.
- Bylaws are not required if provisions, normally included in bylaws, are included in the shareholders' agreement.

Professional Corporations (PC)

These corporations are designed to meet the needs of groups of professionals (physicians, dentists, lawyers, etc.) who wish to practice together and wish to organize their business association in a corporate framework. (This will have advantages in transferring and valuing ownership, in the corporation's existence separate from the owners and an indefinite life, but will also include taxation at both the corporate level and the personal level.) Control will be vested in a board of directors that is elected by the shareholders. Costs of formal registration, filing, and reporting requirements vary from state to state.

Professional Associations (PA)

These corporations are designed to meet the needs of groups of professionals (physicians, dentists, lawyers, etc.) who wish to practice together and wish to organize their business association in a corporate framework. (This will have advantages in transferring and valuing ownership, in the corporation's existence separate from the owners and an indefinite life, but will also include taxation at both the corporate level and the personal level.) Control will be vested in a board of directors that is elected by the shareholders. Costs are formal registration, filing, and reporting requirements vary from state to state.

Service Corporations (SC)

Service corporations are corporations designed to meet the needs of groups of professionals (physicians, dentists, lawyers, etc.) who wish to practice together and wish to organize their business association in a corporate framework. (This will have advantages in transferring and valuing ownership, in the corporation's existence separate from the owners and an indefinite life, but will also include taxation at both the corporate level and the personal level.) Control will be vested in a Board of Directors who are elected by the shareholders. Cost of formal registration, filing and reporting requirements will vary from state to state.

Multiple Forms

It is possible to reap further advantages in term of minimizing taxes and minimizing liability by layering different business forms for holding an investment and operating the investment. Using different forms for holding and operating an investment involves using a two-entity structure. In this type of arrangement, an operating entity will carry out the actual business functions and a holding entity will own the major capital assets of the company, often including the operating entity itself. In this way, you can provide a nearly impermeable shield for your business assets against the claims of business and personal creditors. It is possible for business owners who desire a simplified structure to personally act as the holding entity, although in that case the liability shield will not be as strong.

The use of multiple business forms can be effective in protecting assets by minimizing the amount of vulnerable capital invested within the operating entity. Strategies that would accomplish this result would include:

- The owner personally owning and leasing assets to the operating entity.
- A strategic combination of equity and debt funding (debt funding for the operating entity, equity funding for the holding entity).
- Encumbering the operating entity's assets with liens that run in favor of the holding entity or owner.
- Systematic withdrawals of funds as they are generated.

To avoid the problem of the limited liability being challenged by charging orders, withdrawals of funds should be done on a regular basis, following due procedures. Such withdrawals could include the use of dividends, earned salary and wages to the owners, payments to the owners on leases of property or equipment held by the owner, and factoring account receivables.

Another advantage of a two-entity structure would be to allow for proper planning for *federal estate taxes*. This important issue is often overlooked in the hurley-burley context of business formation. Many commercial real estate investments thrive and grow to produce tremendous wealth for its owner. Yet, in the absence of effective estate planning, much of this wealth may be paid to the federal government in the form of estate taxes, rather than to the owner's family, when the business owner dies.

Franchiser or Franchisee

A franchise is a contractual arrangement between the owner (franchisor) of some property of type of business permits another (franchisee) to use that property or type of business. A franchise involves a relationship between the owner and the user. There are a number of situations in which a real estate investor would find it desirable to be either a franchisor or a franchisee. A real estate investor could function as a franchisor to use franchisees to provide capital for a business undertaking, provide entrepreneurship for a business, and to absorb the risk of loss. A real estate investor might wish to be a franchisee when experience or expertise in a particular business is needed, or when the franchisor's brand or goodwill is a valuable asset.

There are three basic types of franchises: (1) distributorships, (2) business systems, and (3) process systems. Distributorships involve licensing dealers to sell products such as Texaco gasoline stations. Business systems involve the use of a standard method of operation in conjunction with a brand name like Jiffy Lube. Process systems involve the ingredients and procedures used in making something like Pepsi Cola.

The relationship between the franchisor and franchisee is governed by a franchise agreement. As there is normally one large franchisor and many small franchisees, the franchisor usually has a franchise agreement prepared that is offered to prospective franchisees on a take-it-or-leave-it basis. Since franchisors have so much power relative to franchisees, courts will generally interpret any ambiguities in the franchisee agreement in favor of the franchisee. The courts will find the franchisor has an obligation of good faith in such an agreement and will generally not enforce any provision that is inherently unfair.

Entering into a franchisee agreement requires a good deal of disclosure about the nature of the franchise. Both state statute and Federal Trade Commission Rules generally requires such disclosure. Information is the commercial real estate investor's friend in considering the desirability of a franchise. It is important to evaluate all data associated with the franchise and to speak to existing franchisees about their experiences with the franchisor. Information collected should be subject to a thorough spreadsheet analysis of NOPAT (net income and cash flow) as have been applied to the various illustrations in this book.

SUMMARY

The choice of a business form offers greatest opportunities for the investor to control risk, maximize cash flow, and minimize taxes. While there are a variety of choices available, most small (< $1,000,000 equity) commercial real estate investors will want to choose a structure involving a limited liability company (LLC) or a Subchapter S corporation. Particular in combination, a Subchapter S corporation as the holding company and an LLC as the operating company form a great combination, offering the most effective protection for both personal assets outside the business and the investment in the business itself. Larger investors may well prefer the more formal setting of an LLC holding an operating, conventional C corporation.

APPENDIX

Operating Agreement for a Delaware LLC[1]

This sample operating agreement should not be used directly without consulting an attorney. This operating agreement for an LLC is presented as an example of how an LLC can be structure relative to a corporate form of organization. Perusing this agreement will allow the reader to see how various issues of control and liability are dealt with.

Sample Operating Agreement For _____, LLC
A Delaware Limited Liability Company
This Operating Agreement (the "Agreement") is made effective as of _____, by and among and those Persons (the "Members") identified in Exhibit A.

In consideration of the mutual covenants and conditions herein, the Members agree as follows:

ARTICLE I
ORGANIZATION
1.1 Formation and Qualification. The Members have formed a limited liability company (the "Company") under the Delaware Limited Liability Company Act (currently Chapter 18 of Title 6 of the Delaware Code) (the "Act") by filing Articles of Organization with the Delaware Secretary of State.

1.2 Governing Law. This Agreement shall be governed by and construed and interpreted in accordance with the laws of the State of Delaware, including the Delaware Limited Liability Company Act, (the "Act") as amended from time to time, without regard to Delaware's conflicts of laws principles. The rights and liabilities of the Members shall be determined pursuant to the Act and this Agreement. To the extent that any provision of this Agreement is inconsistent with any provision of the Act, this Agreement shall govern to the extent permitted by the Act.

1.3 Name. The name of the Company shall be "_____, LLC." The business of the Company may be conducted under that name or, on compliance with applicable laws, any other name that the Voting Members deem appropriate or advisable. The Voting Members on behalf of the Company shall file any certificates, articles, fictitious business name statements and the like, and any amendments and supplements thereto, as the voting Members consider appropriate or advisable.

---

[1] Reproduced with permission from CCH *Business Owner's Toolkit*™ (www.toolkit. cch.com), published and copyrighted by CCH Inc.

1.4 Term. The term of the Company commenced on the filing of the Articles of Organization and shall be perpetual unless dissolved as provided in this Agreement.

1.5 Office and Agent. The principal office of the Company shall be at such place or places of business within or without the State of Delaware as the Voting Members may determine. The Company shall continuously maintain a registered agent in the State of Delaware as required by the Act. The registered agent shall be as stated in the Certificate or as otherwise determined by the Voting Members.

1.6 Purpose of Company. The purpose of the Company is to engage in all lawful activities, including, but not limited to the following activities:

_____

_____

_____

ARTICLE II
MEMBERSHIP INTERESTS, VOTING AND MANAGEMENT
Section 2.1 Initial Members. The initial Members of the Company are the Members who are identified in Exhibit A.

Section 2.2 Classification of Membership Interests. The Company shall issue Class A Voting Capital ("Voting Capital"), to the Voting Members (the "Voting Members"). The Voting Members shall have the right to vote upon all matters upon which Members have the right to vote under the Act or under this Agreement, in proportion to their respective Percentage Voting Interest ("Percentage Voting Interest") in the Company. The Percentage Voting Interest of a Voting Member shall be the percentage that is derived when the Member's Voting Capital account is divided by the total of all of the Voting Capital accounts.

The Company may issue Class B, Nonvoting Capital ("Nonvoting Capital"). Members may own interests in both Voting Capital and Nonvoting Capital. Members who own interests only in Nonvoting Capital ("Nonvoting Members") shall have no right to vote upon any matters. Notwithstanding, to the extent otherwise permitted by this agreement, a Nonvoting Member shall have the right to file or participate in a mediation or an arbitration action, and shall be bound by an amendment to this agreement only if he signs such amendment.

Section 2.3 Percentage Ownership and Voting Interests. A Member's Ownership Interest ("Ownership Interest") is the total of his interests in Voting Capital and Nonvoting Capital, together with all of the rights, as a Member or Manager of the Company, that arise from such interests.

The Percentage Ownership Interest ("Percentage Ownership Interest") of a Member shall be calculated by adding together that Member's Voting Capital Account and Nonvoting Capital Account, and then dividing this sum by the total of all of the Member's Voting Capital and Nonvoting Capital Accounts.

The Members shall have the initial Ownership, Percentage Ownership and Percentage Voting Interests in the Company that are identified in Exhibit A, immediately following the making of the capital contributions set forth therein.

Section 2.4 Management by Voting Members. The Voting Members shall manage the Company and shall have the right to vote, in their capacity as Managers, upon all matters upon which Managers have the right to vote under the Act or under this Agreement, in proportion to their respective Percentage Voting Interests in the Company. Voting Members need not identify whether they are acting in their capacity as Members or Managers when they act.

The Nonvoting Members shall have no right to vote or otherwise participate in the management of the Company. No Nonvoting Member shall, without the prior written consent of all of the Voting Members, take any action on behalf of, or in the name of, the Company, or enter into any contract, agreement, commitment or obligation binding upon the Company, or perform any act in any way relating to the Company or the Company's assets.

Section 2.5 Voting. Except as otherwise provided or permitted by this Agreement, Voting Members shall in all cases, in their capacity as Members or Managers of the Company, act collectively, and, unless otherwise specified or permitted by this Agreement, unanimously. Except as otherwise provided or permitted by this Agreement, no Voting Member acting individually, in his capacity as a Member or Manager of the Company, shall have any power or authority to sign for, bind or act on behalf of the Company in any way, to pledge the Company's credit, or to render the Company liable for any purpose.

Unless the context requires otherwise, in this Agreement, the terms "Member" or "Members," without the qualifiers "Voting" or "Nonvoting," refer to the Voting and Nonvoting Members collectively; and the terms "Manager" or "Managers" refers to the Voting Members.

Section 2.6 Liability of Members. All debts, obligations and liabilities of the Company, whether arising in contract, tort or otherwise, shall be solely the debts, obligations and liabilities of the Company, and no Member shall be obligated personally for any such debt, obligation or liability of the Company solely by reason of being a Member.

Section 2.7 New Members. The Voting Members may issue additional Voting Capital or Nonvoting Capital and thereby admit a new Member or Members, as the case may be, to the Company, only if such new Member (i) is approved unanimously by the Voting Members; (ii) delivers to the Company his required capital contribution; (iii) agrees in writing to be bound by the terms of this Agreement by becoming a party hereto; and (iv) delivers such additional documentation as the Voting Members shall reasonably require to so admit such new Member to the Company.

Upon the admission of a new Member or Members, as the case may be, to the Company, the capital accounts of Members, and the calculations that are based on the capital accounts, shall be adjusted appropriately.

ARTICLE III
CAPITAL ACCOUNTS
3.1 Initial Capital Contributions. Each original Member to this Agreement shall make an initial Capital Contribution to the Company in accordance with Exhibit A, at the time of each Member's execution of this Agreement.

3.2 Capital Accounts. A separate capital account shall be maintained for each Member's ownership interest in Class A Voting Capital (the "Voting Capital Account") and Class B Nonvoting Capital (the "Nonvoting Capital Account").

The capital account of each Member shall be increased by (i) the amount of any cash and the fair market value of any property contributed to the Company by such Member (net of any liability secured by such contributed property that the Company is considered to assume or take subject to), (ii) the amount of income or profits allocated to such Member.

The capital account or accounts of each Member shall be reduced by (i) the amount of any cash and the fair market value of any property distributed to the Member by the Company (net of liabilities secured by such distributed property that the Member is considered to assume or take subject to on account of his ownership interest), (ii) the amount of expenses or loss allocated to the Member. If any property other than cash is distributed to a Member, the Capital Accounts of the Members shall be adjusted as if the property had instead been sold by the Company for a price equal to its fair market value and the proceeds distributed.

Guaranteed Payments ("Guaranteed Payments") for salary, wages, fees, payments on loans, rents, etc., may be made to the Members. Guaranteed Payments shall not be deemed to be distributions to the Members on account of their Ownership Interests, and shall not be charged to the Members' capital accounts.

No Member shall be obligated to restore any negative balance in his Capital Account. No Member shall be compensated for any positive balance in his Capital Account except as otherwise expressly provided herein. The foregoing provisions and the other provisions of this Agreement relating to the maintenance of Capital Accounts are intended to comply with the provisions of Regulations Section 1.704-1(b)(2) and shall be interpreted and applied in a manner consistent with such Regulations. The Members agree that the initial Capital Accounts of the Members on the date hereof are as set forth in Exhibit A.

3.3 Additional Contributions. If, at any time or times hereafter, the Voting Members shall determine that additional capital is required by the Company, the Voting Members shall determine the amount of such additional capital and the anticipated time such additional capital will be required; whether such additional capital shall be provided by the Members by way of additional Capital Contributions or by way of loans from Members; whether additional Capital Contributions, if any, shall be of in the form of Class A Voting Capital or Class B Nonvoting Capital. No Member shall be obligated, at any time, to guarantee or otherwise assume or become liable for any obligations of the Company or to make any additional Capital Contributions advances or loans to the Company, unless such obligations are specifically accepted and agreed to by such Member.

In the event that additional Class A Voting Capital is to be issued, the Voting Members who exist immediately prior to such issuance shall be provided written notice of this intent, and shall be offered in such notice the opportunity to make additional capital contributions in Class A Voting Capital in proportion to their respective Percentage Voting Interests; provided that this right, if not exercised within ninety (90) days after such notice is received, shall expire automatically, unless this period is extended by the Voting Members. Any loans or additional capital contributions shall be voluntary.

The capital accounts of the Members, and the calculations that are based on the capital accounts, shall be adjusted appropriately to reflect any transfer of an interest in the Company, distributions, or additional capital contributions.

ARTICLE IV
MANNER OF ACTING
4.1 Officers and Agents of the Company. The Voting Members may authorize any Member or Members of the Company, or other individuals or entities, whether or not a Member, to take action on behalf of the Company, as the Voting Members deem appropriate. Any Member may

lend money to and receive loans from the Company, act as an employee, independent contractor, lessee, lessor, or surety of the company, and transact any business with the Company that could be carried out by someone who is not a Member; and the Company may receive from or pay to any Member remuneration, in the form of wages, salary, fees, rent, interest, or any form that the Voting Members deem appropriate.

The Voting Members may appoint officers of the Company who, to the extent provided by the Voting Members, may have and may exercise all the powers and authority of the Members or Managers in the conduct of the business and affairs of the Company. The officers of the Company may consist of a President, a Treasurer, a Secretary, or other officers or agents as may be elected or appointed by the Voting Members. The Voting Members may provide rules for the appointment, removal, supervision and compensation of such officers, the scope of their authority, and any other matters relevant to the positions. The officers shall act in the name of the Company and shall supervise its operation, within the scope of their authority, under the direction and management of the Voting Members.

Any action taken by a duly authorized officer, pursuant to authority granted by the Voting Members in accordance with this Agreement, shall constitute the act of and serve to bind the Company, and each Member hereby agrees neither to dispute such action nor the obligation of the Company created thereby.

4.2 Meetings of Voting Members. No regular, annual, special or other meetings of Voting Members are required to be held. Any action that may be taken at a meeting of Voting Members may be taken without a meeting by written consent in accordance with the Act. Meetings of the Voting Members, for any purpose or purposes, may be called at any time by a majority of the Voting Members, or by the President of the Company, if any. The Voting Members may designate any place as the place of meeting for any meeting of the Voting Members. If no designation is made, the place of meeting shall be the principal place of business of the Company.

4.3 Notice of Meetings. In the event that a meeting of the Voting Members is called, written notice stating the place, day and hour of the meeting and the purpose or purposes for which the meeting is called shall be delivered not less than five nor more than sixty business days before the date of the meeting unless otherwise provided, either personally or by mail, by or at the direction of the Members calling the meeting, to each Voting Member. Notice of a meeting need not be given to any Voting Member who signs a waiver of notice or a consent to holding the meeting or an approval of the minutes thereof, whether before or after the meeting, or who attends the meeting without protesting, prior thereto or at its commencement, the lack of notice to such Voting Member.

4.4 Record Date. For the purpose of determining Voting Members entitled to notice of or to vote at any meeting of Voting Members or any adjournment thereof, the date on which notice of the meeting is provided shall be the record date for such determination of the Voting Members. When a determination of Voting Members has been made as provided in this Section, such determination shall apply to any adjournment thereof.

4.5 Quorum. Members holding at least 67% of the Voting Capital in the Company represented in person, by telephonic participation, or by proxy, shall constitute a quorum at any meeting of Voting Members. In the absence of a quorum at any such meeting, a majority of the Voting Members so represented may adjourn the meeting from time to time for a period not to exceed sixty days without further notice. However, if the adjournment is for more than sixty days, or if after the adjournment a new record date is fixed for another meeting, a notice of the adjourned meeting shall be given to each Voting Member. The Voting Members present at a duly organized meeting may continue to transact business only as previously provided on the agenda until adjournment, notwithstanding the withdrawal during such meeting of that number of Voting Members whose absence would cause less than a quorum.

4.6 Voting. If a quorum is present, a unanimous vote of the Voting Members so represented shall be the act of the Members or Managers, unless the vote of a lesser proportion or number is otherwise required by the Act, by the Certificate or by this Agreement.

ARTICLE V
ALLOCATIONS AND DISTRIBUTIONS
5.1 Allocations of Profits and Losses. Profits and Losses, after deducting Guaranteed Payments, shall be allocated among the Members in proportion to their Percentage Ownership Interests. Any special allocations necessary to comply with the requirements set forth in Internal Revenue Code Section 704 and the corresponding Regulations, including, without limitation, the qualified income offset and minimum gain charge-back provisions contained therein, shall be made if the Voting Members deem these actions to be appropriate.

5.2 Distributions. Subject to applicable law and any limitations elsewhere in this Agreement, the Voting Members shall determine the amount and timing of all distributions of cash, or other assets, by the Company. Except as otherwise provided in this Agreement, all distributions shall be made to all of the Members, in proportion to their Percentage Ownership Interests. Except as otherwise provided in this Agreement, the decision as to whether to make distributions shall be within the sole discretion of the Voting Members.

All such distributions shall be made only to the Members who, according to the books and records of the Company, are the holders of record on the actual date of distribution. The Voting Members may base a determination that a distribution of cash may be made on a balance sheet, profit and loss statement, cash flow statement of the Company or other relevant information. Neither the Company nor the Members shall incur any liability for making distributions.

5.3 Form of Distribution. No Member has the right to demand and receive any distribution from the Company in any form other than money. No Member may be compelled to accept from the Company a distribution of any asset in kind in lieu of a proportionate distribution of money being made to other Members except on the dissolution and winding up of the Company.

ARTICLE VI
TRANSFER AND ASSIGNMENT OF INTERESTS

6.1 Resignation of Membership and Return of Capital. For a period of one (1) year after the Articles of Organization for the Company are filed ("the filing"), no Member may voluntarily resign his membership in the Company, and no Member shall be entitled to any return of capital from the company, except upon the written consent of all of the other Voting Members. During the second year after the filing, a Member may voluntarily resign his membership, but such Member shall be entitled to receive from the Company only the book value of his Ownership Interest, adjusted for profits and losses to the date of resignation, unless otherwise agreed by written consent of all of the other Voting Members. Subsequent to the second year after filing, a Member may voluntarily resign his membership and shall be entitled to receive from the Company the fair market value of his Ownership Interest, adjusted for profits and losses to the date of resignation. Fair market value may be determined informally by unanimous agreement of all of the Voting Members, including the resigning Member. In the absence of an informal agreement as to fair market value, the Voting Members shall hire an appraiser to determine fair market value. The cost of any appraisal shall be deducted from the fair market value to which the resigning Member is entitled. The other Voting Members may elect, by written notice that is provided to the resigning Member within thirty (30) days after the resignation date, for the Company to purchase the resigning Member's Interest (whether the interest is being purchased at book value or fair market value) in four (4) equal annual installments, with the first installment being due sixty (60) days after the Member's resignation.

6.2 Death of a Member. Upon the death of a Member, the Member's estate or beneficiary or beneficiaries, as the case may be, shall be entitled to receive from the Company, in exchange for all of the deceased Member's Ownership Interest, the fair market value of the deceased Member's Ownership Interest, adjusted for profits and losses to the date of death. Fair market value may be determined informally by a unanimous good-faith agreement of all of the Voting Members. In the absence of an informal agreement as to fair market value, the Voting Members shall hire an appraiser to determine fair market value. The cost of any appraisal shall be deducted from the fair market value to which the deceased Member's estate or beneficiary or beneficiaries is or are entitled. The Voting Members may elect, by written notice that is provided to the deceased Member's estate or beneficiary or beneficiaries, within thirty (30) days after the Member's death, to purchase the deceased Member's Ownership Interest over a one-year (1 year) period, in four (4) equal installments, with the first installment being due sixty (60) days after the Member's date of death. Unless otherwise agreed unanimously by the Voting Members, prior to the completion of such purchase, the Member's estate or beneficiary or beneficiaries, shall have no right to become a Member or to participate in the management of the business and affairs of the Company as a Member or Manager, and shall only have the rights of an Assignee and be entitled only to receive the share of profits and the return of capital to which the deceased Member would otherwise have been entitled. The Company, or the other Voting Members, in its or their discretion, may purchase insurance on the lives of any of the Members, with the company or the purchasing Member named as the beneficiary, as the purchaser may decide, and use all or any of the proceeds from such insurance as a source of proceeds from which the deceased Member's Membership Ownership Interest may be purchased by the Company.

6.3 Restrictions on Transfer. Except (i) as otherwise provided in this Article or (ii) upon the unanimous consent of all of the other Voting Members, no Member shall sell, hypothecate, pledge, assign or otherwise transfer, with or without consideration, any part or all of his Ownership Interest in the Company to any other person or entity (a "Transferee"), without first offering (the "Offer") that portion of his or her Ownership Interest in the Company subject to the contemplated transfer (the

"Offered Interest") first to the Company, and secondly, to the other Voting Members, at the purchase price (hereinafter referred to as the "Transfer Purchase Price") and in the manner as prescribed in the Offer.

The Offering Member shall make the Offer first to the Company by written notice (hereinafter referred to as the "Offering Notice"). Within twenty (20) days (the "Company Offer Period") after receipt by the Company of the Offering Notice, the Company shall notify the Offering Member in writing (the "Company Notice"), whether or not the Company shall accept the Offer and shall purchase all but not less than all of the Offered Interest. If the Company accepts the Offer to purchase the Offered Interest, the Company Notice shall fix a closing date not more than twenty-five (25) days (the "Company Closing Date") after the expiration of the Company Offer Period.

In the event the Company decides not to accept the Offer, the Offering Member or the Company, at his or her or its election, shall, by written notice (the "Remaining Member Notice") given within that period (the "Member Offer Period") terminating ten (10) days after the expiration of the Company Offer Period, make the Offer of the Offered Interest to the other Voting Members, each of whom shall then have a period of twenty-five (25) days (the "Member Acceptance Period") after the expiration of the Member Offer Period within which to notify in writing the Offering Member whether or not he or she intends to purchase all but not less than all of the Offered Interest. If two (2) or more Voting Members of the Company desire to accept the Offer to purchase the Offered Interest, then, in the absence of an agreement between them, such Voting Members shall have the right to purchase the Offered Interest in proportion to their respective Percentage Voting Interests. If the other Voting Members intend to accept the Offer and to purchase the Offered Interest, the written notice required to be given by them shall fix a closing date not more than sixty (60) days after the expiration of the Member Acceptance Period (hereinafter referred to as the "Member Closing Date").

The aggregate dollar amount of the Transfer Purchase Price shall be payable in cash on the Company Closing Date or on the Member Closing Date, as the case may be, unless the Company or the purchasing Voting Members shall elect by written notice that is delivered to the Offering Member, prior to or on the Company Closing Date or the Member Closing Date, as the case may be, to purchase such Offered Interest in four (4) equal annual installments, with the first installment being due on the Closing Date.

If the Company or the other Voting Members fail to accept the Offer or, if the Offer is accepted by the Company or the other Voting Members and the Company or the other Voting Members fail to purchase all of the Offered Interest at the Transfer Purchase Price within the time and in the manner specified, then the Offering Member shall be free, for a period (hereinafter referred to as the "Free Transfer Period") of sixty (60) days from the occurrence of such failure, to transfer the Offered Interest to a Transferee; provided, however, that if all of the other Voting Members other than the Offering Member do not approve of the proposed transfer by unanimous written consent, the Transferee of the Offered Interest shall have no right to become a Member or to participate in the management of the business and affairs of the Company as a Member or Manager, and shall only have the rights of an Assignee and be entitled to receive the share of profits and the return of capital to which the Offering Member would otherwise have been entitled. A Transferee shall be admitted as a Member of the Company, and as a result of which he or she shall become a substituted Member, with the rights that are consistent with the Membership Interest that was transferred, only if such new Member (i) is approved unanimously by the Voting Members; (ii) delivers to the Company his required capital contribution; (iii) agrees in writing to be bound by the terms of this Agreement by becoming a party hereto.

If the Offering Member shall not transfer the Offered Interest within the Free Transfer Period, his or her right to transfer the Offered Interest free of the foregoing restrictions shall thereupon cease and terminate.

6.4 Involuntary Transfer of a Membership Interest. A creditor's charging order or lien on a Member's Membership Interest, bankruptcy of a Member, or other involuntary transfer of Member's Membership Interest, shall constitute a material breach of this Agreement by such Member. The creditor, transferee or other claimant, shall only have the rights of an Assignee, and shall have no right to become a Member, or to participate in the management of the business and affairs of the Company as a Member or Manager under any circumstances, and shall be entitled only to receive the share of profits and losses, and the return of capital, to which the Member would otherwise have been entitled. The Voting Members, including a Voting Member whose interest is the subject of the charging order, lien, bankruptcy, or involuntary transfer, may unanimously elect, by written notice that is provided to the creditor, transferee or other claimant, at any time, to purchase all or any part of Membership Interest that was the subject of the creditor's charging order, lien, bankruptcy, or other involuntary transfer, at a price that is equal to one-half (1/2) of the book value of such interest, adjusted for profits and losses to the date of purchase. The Members agree that such valuation is a good-faith attempt at fixing the value of the interest, after taking into account that the interest does not include all of the rights of a Member or Manager, and after deducting damages that are due to the material breach of this Agreement.

ARTICLE VII
ACCOUNTING, RECORDS AND REPORTING
7.1 Books and Records. The Company shall maintain complete and accurate accounts in proper books of all transactions of or on behalf of the Company and shall enter or cause to be entered therein a full and accurate account of all transactions on behalf of the Company. The Company's books and accounting records shall be kept in accordance with such accounting principles (which shall be consistently applied throughout each accounting period) as the Voting Members may determine to be convenient and advisable. The Company shall maintain at its principal office all of the following:

A current list of the full name and last known business or residence address of each Member in the Company set forth in alphabetical order, together with, for each Member, the Class A Voting Capital account and Class B Nonvoting Capital account, including entries to these accounts for contributions and distributions; the Ownership Interest, Percentage Ownership and Voting Interests; a copy of the Certificate and any and all amendments thereto together with executed copies of any powers of attorney pursuant to which the Certificate or any amendments thereto have been executed; copies of the Company's federal, state and local income tax or information returns and reports, if any, for the six most recent taxable years; a copy of this Agreement and any and all amendments hereto together with executed copies of any powers of attorney pursuant to which this Agreement or any amendments thereto have been executed; copies of the financial statements of the Company, if any, for the six most recent Fiscal Years; the Company's books and records as they relate to the internal affairs of the Company for at least the current and past four Fiscal Years; true and full information regarding the status of the business and financial condition of the Company; and true and full information regarding the amount of cash and a description and statement of the agreed value of any other property or services contributed by each Member and which each Member has agreed to contribute in the future, and the date on which each became a Member.

7.2 Inspection of Books and Records. Each Member has the right, on reasonable request for purposes reasonably related to the interest of the person as a Member or a Manager, to: (a) inspect and copy during normal business hours any of the Company's records described in Section 7.1; and (b) obtain from the Company promptly after their becoming available a copy of the Company's federal, state and local income tax or information returns for each Fiscal Year.

7.3 Accountings. As soon as is reasonably practicable after the close of each Fiscal Year, the Voting Members shall make or cause to be made a full and accurate accounting of the affairs of the Company as of the close of that Fiscal Year and shall prepare or cause to be prepared a balance sheet as of the end of such Fiscal Year, a profit and loss statement for that Fiscal Year and a statement of Members' equity showing the respective Capital Accounts of the Members as of the close of such Fiscal Year and the distributions, if any, to Members during such Fiscal Year, and any other statements and information necessary for a complete and fair presentation of the financial condition of the Company, all of which the Manager shall furnish to each Member. In addition, the Company shall furnish to each Member information regarding the Company necessary for such Member to complete such Member's federal and state income tax returns. The Company shall also furnish a copy of the Company's tax returns to any Member requesting the same. On such accounting being made, profits and losses during such Fiscal Year shall be ascertained and credited or debited, as the case may be, in the books of account of the Company to the respective Members as herein provided.

7.4 Filings. The Voting Members, at Company expense, shall cause the income tax returns for the Company to be prepared and timely filed with the appropriate authorities. The Voting Members, at Company expense, shall also cause to be prepared and timely filed with appropriate federal and state regulatory and administrative bodies amendments to, or restatements of, the Certificate and all reports required to be filed by the Company with those entities under the Act or other then current applicable laws, rules, and regulations. If the Company is required by the Act to execute or file any document and fails, after demand, to do so within a reasonable period of time or refuses to do so, any Member may prepare, execute and file that document with the Delaware Secretary of State.

7.5 Bank Accounts. The Company shall maintain its funds in one or more separate bank accounts in the name of the Company, and shall not permit the funds of the Company to be co-mingled in any fashion with the funds of any other Person.

7.6 Tax Matters Partner. The Voting Members may, in their exclusive discretion, appoint, remove and replace a Tax Matters Partner at any time or times. The Voting Members shall from time to time cause the Company to make such tax elections as they deem to be in the interests of the Company and the Members generally. The Tax Matters Partner, as defined in Internal Revenue Code Section 6231, shall represent the Company (at the Company's expense) in connection with all examinations of the Company's affairs by tax authorities, including resulting judicial and administrative proceedings, and shall expend the Company funds for professional services and costs associated therewith.

ARTICLE VIII
DISSOLUTION AND WINDING UP

8.1 Dissolution. The Company shall be dissolved, its assets shall be disposed of, and its affairs wound up on the first to occur of: the entry of a decree of judicial dissolution pursuant to the Act; or the unanimous approval of the Voting Members.

8.2 Winding Up. On the occurrence of an event specified in Section 8.1, the Company shall continue solely for the purpose of winding up its affairs in an orderly manner, liquidating its assets and satisfying the claims of its creditors. The Voting Members shall be responsible for overseeing the winding up and liquidation of Company, shall take full account of the assets and liabilities of Company, shall cause such assets to be sold or distributed, and shall cause the proceeds therefrom, to the extent sufficient therefor, to be applied and distributed as provided in Section 9.4. The Voting Members shall give written notice of the commencement of winding up by mail to all known creditors and claimants whose addresses appear on the records of the Company. The Members shall be entitled to reasonable compensation for such services.

8.3 Distributions in Kind. Any noncash assets distributed to the Members shall first be valued at their fair market value to determine the profit or loss that would have resulted if such assets were sold for such value. Such profit or loss shall then be allocated pursuant to this Agreement, and the Members' Capital Accounts shall be adjusted to reflect such allocations. The amount distributed and charged against the Capital Account of each Member receiving an interest in a distributed asset shall be the fair market value of such interest (net of any liability secured by such asset that such Member assumes or takes subject to). The fair market value of such asset shall be determined by the Voting Members, or if any Voting Member objects, by an independent appraiser (and any such appraiser must be recognized as an expert in valuing the type of asset involved) selected by a Majority of the Voting Members.

8.4 Order of Payment of Liabilities on Dissolution. After a determination that all known debts and liabilities of the Company in the process of winding up, including, without limitation, debts and liabilities to Members who are creditors of the Company, have been paid or adequately provided for, the remaining assets shall be distributed to the Members in proportion to their positive Capital Account balances, after taking into account profit and loss allocations for the Company's taxable year during which liquidation occurs.

8.5 Adequacy of Payment. The payment of a debt or liability, whether the whereabouts of the creditor is known or unknown, shall have been adequately provided for if payment thereof shall have been assumed or guaranteed in good faith by one or more financially responsible Persons or by the United States government or any agency thereof, and the provision, including the financial responsibility of the Person, was determined in good faith and with reasonable care by the Members to be adequate at the time of any distribution of the assets pursuant to this Section. This Section shall not prescribe the exclusive means of making adequate provision for debts and liabilities.

8.6 Compliance with Regulations. All payments to the Members on the winding up and dissolution of Company shall be strictly in accordance with the positive capital account balance limitation and other requirements of Regulations Section 1.704-1(b)(2)(ii)(d), as the voting Members deem appropriate.

8.7 Limitations on Payments Made in Dissolution. Except as otherwise specifically provided in this Agreement, each Member shall only be entitled to look solely to the assets of the Company for the return of such Member's positive Capital Account balance and shall have no recourse for such Member's Capital Contribution or share of profits (on dissolution or otherwise) against any other Member.

8.8 Certificate of Cancellation. The Voting Members conducting the winding up of the affairs of the Company shall cause to be filed in the office of, and on a form prescribed by the Delaware Secretary of State, a certificate of cancellation of the Certificate on the completion of the winding up of the affairs of the Company.

ARTICLE IX
EXCULPATION AND INDEMNIFICATION
9.1 Exculpation of Members. No Member shall be liable to the Company or to the other Members for damages or otherwise with respect to any actions taken or not taken in good faith and reasonably believed by such Member to be in or not opposed to the best interests of the Company, except to the extent any related loss results from fraud, gross negligence or willful or wanton misconduct on the part of such Member or the material breach of any obligation under this Agreement or of the fiduciary duties owed to the Company or the other Members by such Member.

9.2 Indemnification by Company. The Company shall indemnify, hold harmless and defend the Members, in their capacity as Members, Managers, or Officers, from and against any loss, expense, damage or injury suffered or sustained by them by reason of any acts or omissions arising out of their activities on behalf of the Company or in furtherance of the interests of the Company, including but not limited to any judgment, award, settlement, reasonable attorneys' fees and other costs or expenses incurred in connection with the defense of any actual or threatened action, proceeding or claim, if the acts or omissions were not performed or omitted fraudulently or as a result of gross negligence or willful misconduct by the indemnified party. Reasonable expenses incurred by the indemnified party in connection with any such proceeding relating to the foregoing matters may be paid or reimbursed by the Company in advance of the final disposition of such proceeding upon receipt by the Company of (i) written affirmation by the Person requesting indemnification of its good-faith belief that it has met the standard of conduct necessary for indemnification by the Company and (ii) a written undertaking by or on behalf of such Person to repay such amount if it shall ultimately be determined by a court of competent jurisdiction that such Person has not met such standard of conduct, which undertaking shall be an unlimited general obligation of the indemnified party but need not be secured.

9.3 Insurance. The Company shall have the power to purchase and maintain insurance on behalf of any Person who is or was a Member or an agent of the Company against any liability asserted against such Person and incurred by such Person in any such capacity, or arising out of such Person's status as a Member or an agent of the Company, whether or not the Company would have the power to indemnify such Person against such liability under Section 10.1 or under applicable law.

ARTICLE X
MISCELLANEOUS
10.1 Authority. This Agreement constitutes a legal, valid and binding agreement of the Member, enforceable against the Member in accordance with its terms. The Member is empowered and duly authorized to enter into this Agreement (including the power of attorney herein) under every applicable governing document, partnership agreement, trust instrument, pension plan, charter, certificate of incorporation, bylaw provision or the like. The Person, if any, signing this Agreement on behalf of the Member is empowered and duly authorized to do so by the governing document or trust instrument, pension plan, charter, certificate of incorporation, bylaw provision, board of directors or stockholder resolution or the like.

10.2 Indemnification by the Members. Each Member hereby agrees to indemnify and defend the Company, the other Members and each of their respective employees, agents, partners, members, shareholders, officers and directors and hold them harmless from and against any and all claims, liabilities, damages, costs and expenses (including, without limitation, court costs and attorneys' fees and expenses) suffered or incurred on account of or arising out of any breach of this Agreement by that Member.

ARTICLE XI
DISPUTE RESOLUTION

11.1 Disputes Among Members. The Members agree that in the event of any dispute or disagreement solely between or among any of them arising out of, relating to or in connection with this Agreement or the Company or its organization, formation, business or management ("Member Dispute"), the Members shall use their best efforts to resolve any dispute arising out of or in connection with this Agreement by good-faith negotiation and mutual agreement. The Members shall meet at a mutually convenient time and place to attempt to resolve any such dispute.

However, in the event that the Members are unable to resolve any Member Dispute, such parties shall first attempt to settle such dispute through a non-binding mediation proceeding. In the event any party to such mediation proceeding is not satisfied with the results thereof, then any unresolved disputes shall be finally settled in accordance with an arbitration proceeding. In no event shall the results of any mediation proceeding be admissible in any arbitration or judicial proceeding.

11.2 Mediation. Mediation proceedings shall be conducted in accordance with the Commercial Mediation Rules of the American Arbitration Association (the "AAA") in effect on the date the notice of mediation was served, other than as specifically modified herein, and shall be non-binding on the parties thereto.

Any Member may commence a mediation proceeding by serving written notice thereof to the other Members, by mail or otherwise, designating the issue(s) to be mediated and the specific provisions of this Agreement under which such issue(s) and dispute arose. The initiating party shall simultaneously file two copies of the notice with the AAA, along with a copy of this Agreement. A Member may withdraw from the Member Dispute by signing an agreement to be bound by the results of the mediation, to the extent the mediation results are accepted by the other Members as provided herein. A Member who withdraws shall have no further right to participate in the Member Dispute.

The Members shall select one neutral third party AAA mediator (the "Mediator") with expertise in the area that is in dispute. If a Mediator has not been selected within five (5) business days thereafter, then a Mediator shall be selected by the AAA in accordance with the Commercial Mediation Rules of the AAA.

The Mediator shall schedule sessions, as necessary, for the presentation by all Members of their respective positions, which, at the option of the Mediator, may be heard by the Mediator jointly or in private, without any other members present. The mediation proceeding shall be held in the city that is the company's principal place of business or such other place as agreed by the Mediator and all of the Members. The Members may submit to the Mediator, no later than ten (10) business days prior to the first scheduled session, a brief memorandum in support of their position.

The Mediator shall make written recommendations for settlement in respect of the dispute, including apportionment of the mediator's fee, within ten (10) business days of the last scheduled session. If any Member involved is not satisfied with the recommendation for settlement, he may commence an arbitration proceeding.

11.3 Arbitration. Arbitration proceedings shall be conducted under the Rules of Commercial Arbitration of the AAA (the "Rules"). A Member may withdraw from the Member Dispute by signing an agreement to be bound by the results of the arbitration. A Member who withdraws shall have no further right to participate in the Member Dispute.

The arbitration panel shall consist of one arbitrator. The Members shall select one neutral third party AAA arbitrator (the "Arbitrator") with expertise in the area that is in dispute. If an Arbitrator has not been selected within five (5) business days thereafter, then an Arbitrator shall be selected by the AAA in accordance with the Commercial Arbitration Rules of the AAA. The arbitration proceeding shall be held in the city that is the company's principal place of business or such other place as agreed by the Arbitrator and all of the Members. Any arbitrator who is selected shall disclose promptly to the AAA and to both parties any financial or personal interest the arbitrator may have in the result of the arbitration and/or any other prior or current relationship, or expected or discussed future relationship, with the Members or their representatives. The arbitrator shall promptly conduct proceedings to resolve the dispute in question pursuant to the then existing Rules. To the extent any provisions of the Rules conflict with any provision of this Section, the provisions of this Section shall control.

In any final award and/or order, the arbitrator shall apportion all the costs (other than attorney's fees which shall be borne by the party incurring such fees) incurred in conducting the arbitration in accordance with what the arbitrator deems just and equitable under the circumstances.

Discovery shall not be permitted in such arbitration except as allowed by the rules of arbitration, or as otherwise agreed to by all the parties of the Member Dispute. Notwithstanding, the Members agree to make available to one another and to the arbitrator, for inspection and photocopying, all documents, books and records, if determined by the arbitration panel to be relevant to the dispute, and by making available to one another and to the arbitration panel personnel directly or indirectly under their control, for testimony during hearings if determined by the arbitration panel to be relevant to the dispute. The Members agree, unless undue hardship exists, to conduct arbitration hearings to the greatest extent possible on consecutive business days and to strictly observe time periods established by the Rules or by the arbitrator for the submission of evidence and of briefs. Unless otherwise agreed to by the Members, a stenographic record of the arbitration proceedings shall be made and a transcript thereof shall be ordered for each Member, with each party paying an equal portion of the total cost of such recording and transcription.

The arbitrator shall have all powers of law and equity, which it can lawfully assume, necessary to resolve the issues in dispute including, without limiting the generality of the foregoing, making awards of compensatory damages, issuing both prohibitory and mandatory orders in the nature of injunctions and compelling the production of documents and witnesses for presentation at the arbitration hearings on the merits of the case. The arbitration panel shall neither have nor exercise any power to act as amicable compositeur or ex aequo et bono; or to award special, indirect, consequential or punitive damages. The decision of the arbitration panel shall be in written form and state the reasons upon which it is based. The statutory, case law and common law of the State of Delaware shall govern in interpreting their respective rights, obligations and liabilities arising out of or related to the transactions provided for or contemplated by this Agreement, including without limitation, the validity, construction and performance of all or any portion of this Agreement, and the applicable remedy for any liability established thereunder, and the amount or method of computation of damages which may be awarded, but such governing law shall not include the law pertaining to conflicts or choice of laws of Delaware; provided however, that should the parties refer a dispute arising out of or in connection with an ancillary agreement or an agreement between some or all of the Members which specifically references this Article, then the statutory, case law and common law of the State whose law governs such agreement (except the law pertaining to conflicts or choice of law) shall govern in interpreting the respective rights, obligations and liabilities of the parties arising out of or related to the transactions provided for or contemplated by such agreement, including, without limitation, the validity, construction and performance of all or any portion of such agreement, and the applicable remedy for any liability established thereunder, and the amount or method of computation of damages which may be awarded.

Any action or proceeding subsequent to any Award rendered by the arbitrator in the Member Dispute, including, but not limited to, any action to confirm, vacate, modify, challenge or enforce the arbitrator's decision or award shall be filed in a court of competent jurisdiction in the same county where the arbitration of the Member Dispute was conducted, and Delaware law shall apply in any such subsequent action or proceeding.

ARTICLE XII
MISCELLANEOUS

12.1 Notices. Except as otherwise expressly provided herein, any notice, consent, authorization or other communication to be given hereunder shall be in writing and shall be deemed duly given and received when delivered personally, when transmitted by facsimile if receipt is acknowledged by the addressee, one business day after being deposited for next-day delivery with a nationally recognized overnight delivery service, or three business days after being mailed by first class mail, charges and postage prepaid, properly addressed to the party to receive such notice at the address set forth in the Company's records.

12.2 Severability. If any provision of this Agreement, or the application of such provision to any Person or circumstance, shall be held by a court of competent jurisdiction to be invalid or unenforceable, the remainder of this Agreement, or the application of such provision to Persons or circumstances other than those to which it is held to be invalid or unenforceable, shall not be affected thereby.

12.3 Binding Effect. Subject to Article VII, this Agreement shall bind and inure to the benefit of the parties and their respective Successors.

12.4 Counterparts. This Agreement may be executed in one or more counterparts, each of which shall be deemed an original, but all of which together shall constitute one and the same instrument.

12.5 Entire Agreement. This Agreement contains the entire agreement of the parties and supersedes all prior or contemporaneous written or oral negotiations, correspondence, understandings and agreements between or among the parties, regarding the subject matter hereof.

12.6 Further Assurances. Each Member shall provide such further information with respect to the Member as the Company may reasonably request, and shall execute such other and further certificates, instruments and other documents, as may be necessary and proper to implement, complete and perfect the transactions contemplated by this Agreement.

12.7 Headings; Gender; Number; References. The headings of the Sections hereof are solely for convenience of reference and are not part of this Agreement. As used herein, each gender includes each other gender, the singular includes the plural and vice versa, as the context may require. All references to Sections and subsections are intended to refer to Sections and subsections of this Agreement, except as otherwise indicated.

12.8 Parties in Interest. Except as expressly provided in the Act, nothing in this Agreement shall confer any rights or remedies under or by reason of this Agreement on any Persons other than the Members and their respective Successors nor shall anything in this Agreement relieve or discharge the obligation or liability of any third Person to any party to this Agreement, nor shall any provision give any third Person any right of subrogation or action over or against any party to this Agreement.

12.9 Amendments. All amendments to this Agreement shall be in writing and signed by all of the Members to the agreement at the time of the amendment.

12.10 Attorneys' Fees. In any dispute between or among the Company and one or more of the Members, including, but not limited to, any Member Dispute, the prevailing party or parties in such dispute shall be entitled to recover from the non-prevailing party or parties all reasonable fees, costs and expenses including, without limitation, attorneys' fees, costs and expenses, all of which shall be deemed to have accrued on the commencement of such action, proceeding or arbitration. Attorneys' fees shall include, without limitation, fees incurred in any post-award or post-judgment motions or proceedings, contempt proceedings, garnishment, levy, and debtor and third party examinations, discovery, and bankruptcy litigation, and prevailing party shall mean the party that is determined in the arbitration, action or proceeding to have prevailed or who prevails by dismissal, default or otherwise.

12.11 Remedies Cumulative. Subject to Article XI, remedies under this Agreement are cumulative and shall not exclude any other remedies to which any Member may be lawfully entitled.

12.12 Jurisdiction and Venue/Equitable Remedies. The Company and each Member hereby expressly agrees that if, under any circumstances, any dispute or controversy arising out of or relating to or in any way connected with this Agreement shall, notwithstanding Article XI, be the subject of any court action at law or in equity, such action shall be filed exclusively in the courts of the State of _____ or of the United States of America located in the counties of _____ or _____, as selected by the Member that is the plaintiff in the action, or that initiates the proceeding or arbitration. Each Member agrees not to commence any action, suit or other proceeding arising from, relating to, or in connection with this Agreement except in such a court and each Member irrevocably and unconditionally consents and submits to the personal and exclusive jurisdiction of such courts for the purposes of litigating any such action, and hereby grants jurisdiction to such courts and to any appellate courts having jurisdiction over appeals from such courts or review of such proceedings. Because the breach of the provisions of this Section would cause irreparable harm and significant injury to the Company and the other Members, which would be difficult to ascertain and which may not be compensable by damages alone, each Member agrees that the Company and the other Members will have the right to enforce the provisions of this Section by injunction, specific performance or other equitable relief in addition to any and all other remedies available to such party or parties without showing or proving any actual damage to such parties. Members will be entitled to recover all reasonable costs and expenses, including but not limited to all reasonable attorneys' fees, expert and consultants' fees, incurred in connection with the enforcement of this Section.

IN WITNESS WHEREOF, this Limited Liability Company Operating Agreement has been duly executed by or on behalf of the parties hereto as of the date first above written.

_____   _____

_____   _____

_____   _____

_____   _____

_____   _____

CHAPTER 5

Buying versus Leasing

Leasing is a very common practice in commercial real estate. Leasing is an alternative to financing with debt, and sometimes with equity as well. Real estate investors often have opportunities to either be a lessor or lessee. When properly used, either role can enhance the profit from an investment and reduce the risks of that investment. The advantages of leasing from either side have to do with taxes and access to capital. As a lessor the investor may effectively provide the financing for a property and reap the advantages of the depreciation cash flow and interest tax offset. As a lessee the investor may gain a greater tax shield (the lease rents themselves) and access to capital that would otherwise be denied.

This chapter addresses the questions:

- When is it good to buy?
- When is it good to lease?
- When is it more desirable to lease a property than sell it?
- What factors contribute to the advantages of leasing over buying or vice versa?
- What are the mechanics of evaluating a lease versus buy situation?

The answer to these questions depend on:

- The differing tax situation between the lessor and lessee. In general, where the lessor has a lower tax rate than the lessee, this favors leasing, rather than buying.
- The different cost of debt to the lessor and lessee. Where the lessor has lower costs of capital than the lessee does, this favors leasing, rather than buying.

■ The timing of cash flows. Where the lessor has a lower WACC than the lessee and cash flows are weighted toward the end of the leasing period, this situation favors leasing over buying.

■ The length of the lease. Generally shorter lease times decrease the leasing costs for both the lessor and lessee, but have the effect of increasing the riskiness of the investment for the lessor.

■ Differing access to capital between the lessor and lessee. Where the lessor has greater creditworthiness than the lessee does, this favors leasing over buying.

The general approach to evaluating a lease versus buy situation requires contrasting the viewpoints of the lessor and lessee. In general, the potential lessee has made the decision to go ahead with a capital acquisition. The question before the lessee is how to finance that capital acquisition. The answer to the lessee is thus, "The decision that costs the least." Least in this situation involves minimizing the present value of all cash flows associated with the acquisition.

The approach of the potential lessor is quite different. The decision to lease involves a capital expenditure that is evaluated on the basis of the cash flows it is expected to generate. The idea is to maximize the difference between the present value of those cash flows and that capital expenditure. This is the definition of *net present value* (NPV.) The decision of the lessor to lease is made on the relative magnitude of that value.

It is not realistic to generalize that in a particular situation an investor should lease (or buy). Generalizations are precluded by the interaction of the different relevant variables in a given situation (tax rates, interest rates, timing of cash flows, length of life of the lease, terminal value, risk, and ability to raise capital). Lease versus buy needs to be approached on a case-by-case basis.

An approach to this problem can be seen in the circumstances of Johnstone's Pharmacy.

ILLUSTRATION # 1: JOHNSTONE'S PHARMACY— TEN YEAR HOLDING PERIOD

Charlie Johnstone owns a successful pharmacy. But he is unhappy with its inner-city location. He wishes to move the pharmacy to a more suburban location to give better service to his customers. He would also like to enlarge his pharmacy to better compete with the large national pharmacy chains moving into the metropolitan area. He has found what he believes to be an excellent location at the intersection of high traffic volume, Rt. 24 and Rt. 31, in the middle of the suburbs about a half-mile away from a large hospital. Charlie knows his business and feels absolutely certain that whatever the cost of this location; his new pharmacy at this location would be a smashing success.

The lot is good sized (300 ft. by 400 ft.) and would provide him with ample room to build a super-sized (12,000 sq. ft.) pharmacy. The large size of the lot would mean no problem in observing zoning setback and parking regulations and has good access from the two highways. The lot is available for $300,000. Charlie has talked with a local contractor and estimates he could build exactly the type of building he wants for $100 per sq. ft. and that various soft costs (legal and accounting fees, landscaping, lights, and a parking lot) would add another $20 per sq. ft. to the cost. Thus, Charlie anticipates a total cost of $1,740,000 ($1,440,000 for the building and $300,000 for the land).

Charlie has also talked with his local banker. The local banker would be willing to lend Charlie $1,200,000 for an interest-only bridge loan at 10%, while the project is under construction, and roll that over into a conventional 10% fixed-rate, 20-year mortgage when the building is complete. This poses a problem for Charlie. Coming up with the equity of $540,000 takes everything that Charlie has been able to save from 20 years of work and his wife's 401k, a second mortgage on his home; and he and his wife will have to personally sign for the loan. This effectively leaves Charlie with no cash reserves. In addition, Charlie's $540,000 of investments in various financial securities has yielded an average of 10% over the last 12 years. Charlie feels that he can finance this new building if it is absolutely necessary, but he wonders if there is an alternative.

Charlie discusses this situation with the owner of the land, Bill Bolton, whom he knows slightly as a well-thought-of developer in town. Bill suggested that Charlie should allow him to build-to-suit lease rather than Charlie buying the land and building the store himself. That way Charlie would not have to come up with any cash and would get exactly the type of building he desired. Of course, Charlie and his wife would have to personally sign on the lease and pledge some of their assets to secure the lease, but there would be no cash crunch. Bill offers Charlie a triple-net, 10-year lease at $125,000 per year with an option to renew for another 10 years on the same terms.

Charlie wonders if this is a good deal.

Analysis

In a lease-versus-buy analysis, the perspectives of the lessor and lessee always differ. The lessee is assumed to have made the decision to invest. The NPV is sufficiently high to overcome all concerns about the desirability

of the investment. The question now confronting the lessee is how to minimize the cost of the investment. The answer to this question can be determined by comparing the present values of the cash flows associated with the
leasing decision and the buying decision. These cash flows represent the
differing costs of the two alternatives. The idea is to choose that method of
financing that cost the least when all relevant factors are considered.

In contrast, the lessor looks at the lease as an investment much as
any other capital budgeting decision. The lease generates a certain
amount of revenue and against these are arrayed a variety of expenses.
Noteworthy among these are interest expense and depreciation. These
are noteworthy because they represent tax-deductible expenses to the
lessor. This explains the sensitivity of the relative desirability of the
lease-versus-buy decision to interest and tax rates from both the perspectives of the lessee and the lessor. As with any capital investment, the
lessor's criteria of desirability will be a positive NPV that covers both
the cost of capital and any perceived risk.

To the lessee, the lease-versus-buy decision is really a matter of
choosing the method of financing a project. The method selected normally has substantial implications for the overall success of the project.

The context in which this decision takes place is indicated in Table
5.1. Note that Bolton (the potential lessor) has better access to capital than
Johnstone (mortgage rates of 9.5% versus 10% as well as a WACC of
8.5% versus 9%.) Also, Bolton can get better terms (more financial leverage) than Johnstone can. Bolton only needs $140,000 of equity, whereas
Johnstone requires $540,000. It can further be seen that Johnstone has
higher tax exposure than Bolton.

To compare the advantages of leasing versus buying, it is necessary
to compare apples to apples and oranges to oranges. Therefore the costs
of building to both Johnstone and Bolton will be the same (Table 5.2.)

Note that the interest on the bridge loan is not capitalized, but
expensed, because income taxes are higher than capital gain taxes. If it
is assumed that Charlie desires a 10-year holding period, then the terminal value of the building will depend on its market value at that time.
The assumption in Table 5.3A is that the building will be sold for
$2,000,000 in 10 years. Tables 5.3A and 5.3B indicate that with a 10%
fixed rate mortgage for $1,200,000 the terminal cash flow from the sale
to Charlie Johnstone will be $977,358.

The $977,358 registers as a gain in the 10th year. Prior to that time,
Charlie will experience net cash outflows ranging from $606,510 to
$120,356 (Table 5.4). It should be noted that these cash flows take as a
credit the tax savings from depreciation, but depreciation itself does not
register as either a cash inflow or cash outflow, because it is a noncash
expense. Further, the after-tax gains Charlie would be presumed to have

TABLE 5.1   Johnstone and Bolton Assumptions

Johnstone's Assumptions:	Values
Mortgage rate	10.00%
Personal tax rate	27.00%
Pharmacy tax rate	35.00%
WACC	9.00%
Initial capital required	
Equity	$540,000
Debt	$1,200,000

Bolton's Assumptions	
Mortgage rate	9.50%
Tax rate	25.00%
WACC	8.50%
Initial capital required	
Equity	$140,000
Debt	$1,600,000

TABLE 5.2   Johnstone's Pharmacy, Initial Cash Flows Build

Cash Outflows:	
Purchase of land	$300,000
Construction of pharmacy	1,440,000
Interest on bridge loan[a]	72,000
Total cash out	1,812,000

Cash Inflows	
Loan from bank	1,200,000
Equity from C. Johnstone[b]	612,000
Total cash in	1,812,000

[a] The loan is drawn down over the year, and interest is paid on only the funds used.
[b] The $72,000 interest is expensed.

TABLE 5.3A Johnstone's Pharmacy, Tax Consequences of Sale of Property, 10-Year-Holding Period

Sale of building		$2,000,000
Fixed plant and improvements	$1,440,000	
Less accumulated depreciation	454,356	
Net-fixed plant and improvements		985,644
Cost of land		300,000
Gain on sale		714,356
Capital gains tax (15%)		107,153
After-tax gain on sale		607,202

TABLE 5.3B Johnstone's Pharmacy, Cash Gain from Sale of Property

Sale of property	$2,000,000
Less:	
Tax liability	107,153
Loan balance	915,489
Cash gain from sale	977,358

made on his $540,000 investments portfolio is included as a debit, because it represents a real opportunity cost to Charlie, even though it is not a cash expenditure per se. Mortgage principal payments are seen as a cash outflow even though they do not constitute an expense for income tax purposes. These are recaptured at the time of sale (Table 5.3B.) The net effect of these cash flows is to generate a cost of building to Charlie Johnstone whose present value is $920,545 (Table 5.4.)

This present value can be readily translated to the cost of a comparable lease. That is done by calculating the value of an annuity (constant flow of cash) each year over the 10-year period that would have a present value equal to $920,545. The value of that *equivalent annual annuity* (EAA) would be $143,439. However, since that lease payment would be tax deductible, the EAA that is really comparable to $143,439 would be $220,676. That is, equal to $143,439/(1 − 0.35), where 0.35 is Johnstone's tax rate. Thus, if the lease offered to Johnstone is above $220,676, it would be to his advantage to build. If the lease offered is below $220,773, it is to Johnstone's advantage to lease. The lease offer on the Table is $125,000, well below Johnstone's buy-lease threshold. On this basis, he should lease. The advantage to him is seen in Table 5.5.

TABLE 5.4 Johnstone's Pharmacy Build Decision, Building Costs and Cash Flows[a]

After-Tax Mortgage Interest Payments[b]	Mortgage Principle Payments	After-Tax Interest Opportunity Costs[c]	Building Depreciation[d]	Improvements Depreciation[e]	Depreciation Tax (Savings)	Equity Contribution	Cash (Gain) on Sale[f]	Total Cash Flows Out[g]
$46,800	$20,952	$19,710	$15,385	$12,000	$9,585	$540,000		$606,510
78,000	23,047	39,420	30,769	22,800	18,749			128,787
76,638	25,351	39,420	30,769	20,520	17,951			120,356
75,140	27,887	39,420	30,769	18,480	17,237			121,960
73,492	30,675	39,420	30,769	16,632	16,590			123,562
71,680	33,743	39,420	30,769	14,952	16,002			125,184
69,686	37,117	39,420	30,769	14,160	15,725			126,846
67,492	40,829	39,420	30,769	14,160	15,725			128,304
65,080	44,912	39,420	30,769	14,184	15,734			129,603
62,426	44,912	39,420	30,769	14,184	15,734			131,024
59,507	49,403	39,420	30,769	14,160	15,725		$977,358	–844,754

[a] Note that maintenance, insurance, and taxes are not included. Because this is a triple-net lease, they will be the same, whether the building is owned or leased, and thus do not affect the comparison.

[b] An 8% fixed-rate, 20-year conventional mortgage.

[c] Although this does not represent an actual expenditure, the investment of $540,000 has an opportunity cost (10%), which is adjusted for Johnstone's personal tax rate.

[d] $1,200,000 depreciated over 39 years, using the half-year convention.

[e] Land improvements (streets, blacktop, sidewalk, drainage ditches, etc.) have a recovery period of 15 years and are depreciated 150% declining balance using the half-year convention.

[f] From Table 5.2B.

[g] Cash flow out includes tax-adjusted interest payments and principal payments less the depreciation of tax savings and cash gain on sale. Note depreciation costs themselves do not influence cash flows, because they do not represent a cash expenditure.

TABLE 5.4   (Continued)

Present value of cash flows	$920,545
Discount rate	9.00%
Equivalent annual annuity	$143,439
Tax-adjusted EAA	$220,676

Note: This is the nominal lease payment that makes the lessee indifferent between leasing and buying.

TABLE 5.5   Johnstone's Pharmacy, After-Tax Lease Cost

Year	Lease	Tax Savings	After-Tax Lease Cost
1	$175,000	$61,250	$113,750
2	175,000	61,250	113,750
3	175,000	61,250	113,750
4	175,000	61,250	113,750
5	175,000	61,250	113,750
6	175,000	61,250	113,750
7	175,000	61,250	113,750
8	175,000	61,250	113,750
9	175,000	61,250	113,750
10	175,000	61,250	113,750
PV of lease cost	$730,009		
Equivalent annual annuity			$113,750

The question then becomes is this a lease that would be profitable to Bill Bolton to offer? This question is addressed in Table 5.6. The pattern of cash flows for Bill generated by the lease is negative except for the last year. This would normally ring alarm bells for Bill, except that the cash payments are small and a substantial portion of which represents equity payments on the mortgage. Further, the estimated $2,000,000 sale price of the building at the end of 10 years does not seem unduly optimistic. This represents an average annual appreciation of only 1.4%. Consequently, the project is seen as profitable for Bill Bolton at a lease rate of $75,000. Of course, because a little analysis will show Bill Bolton that Charlie is willing to lease at a rate up to $220,676, he could safely charge a higher rate. As can be seen from Table 5.7, a lease rate of $200,000 is still profitable for Charlie, but much more profitable for Bill. Of course Charlie might counteroffer with a lease rate of $55,500 to Bill. As seen in Table 5.7, this lease rate would just be barely profit-

TABLE 5.6 Bill Bolton Developments, Pharmacy Cash Flow Analysis, 10-Year-Holding Period

Year	Lease Revenue	Depreciation[a]	Administrative Costs	Interest	EBT	Taxes	Net Income	Depreciation	Principal Payments	Cash Gain on Sale	Equity Contribution	Cash Flow
0			$2,000	$72,000	-$74,000	-$18,500	-$55,500	$27,385	$29,563		-$140,000	-$195,500
1	$175,000	$27,385	2,000	152,000	-6,385	-1,596	-4,788	53,569	32,371			-6,967
2	175,000	53,569	2,000	149,192	-29,761	-7,440	-22,321	51,289	35,446			-1,123
3	175,000	51,289	2,000	146,116	-24,406	-6,101	-18,304	49,249	38,814			-2,461
4	175,000	49,249	2,000	142,749	-18,998	-4,750	-14,249	47,401	42,501			-3,813
5	175,000	47,401	2,000	139,062	-13,463	-3,366	-10,097	45,721	46,539			-5,197
6	175,000	45,721	2,000	135,024	-7,745	-1,936	-5,809	44,929	50,960			-6,626
7	175,000	44,929	2,000	130,603	-2,532	-633	-1,899	44,929	55,801			-7,930
8	175,000	44,929	2,000	125,762	2,309	577	1,732	44,929	61,102			-9,140
9	175,000	44,953	2,000	120,460	7,586	1,897	5,690	44,953	66,907			-10,459
10	175,000	44,929	2,000	114,656	13,415	3,354	10,061	44,929		$977,358		965,441

[a] From Table 5.4.

NPV = $588,672
Discount rate = 8.50%

89

TABLE 5.7   Johnstone and Bolton Outcomes

Lease	$200,000	$125,000	$55,500
Bolton's NPV	711,443	342,368	357
Johnstone's PV cost of building	920,545	920,545	920,545
The EEA of Johnstone's PV cost of building	143,439	143,439	143,439
Johnstone's tax-adjusted EEA of building[a]	220,676	220,676	220,676

[a] The EEA is the Equivalent Annual Annuity. It represents that constant flow of cash whose PV over the period is equal to the PV of the cost of building. Since qualifying lease payments are tax deductible, the nominal lease that is the same as the EEA would be the EEA/$(1 - Tx)$.

able for Bill. The eventual lease price agreed on would depend on the negotiating power of the two parties. (Charlie can always go to another developer for a better lease rate.) The lease will ultimately end up somewhere between $55,500 and $220,676. This may be referred to as the "zone" of negotiation.

ILLUSTRATION #2: 20-YEAR-HOLDING PERIOD

In this illustration the assumptions and initial cost structure assumed earlier are continued in this analysis of a 20-year holding period.

The initial effect of the longer holding period is to increase the cash gain from the sale to $2,018,277 (Tables 5.8A and Tables 5.8B.) For the most part, this reflects the build-up of equity in the property compared to the 10-year scenario described in Tables 5.3A and 5.3B as the mortgage is paid off.

A change also takes place in the cost structure of the property over the longer time horizon. The effect of delaying the sale of the property another 10 years (Table 5.9) results in a substantial increase in the cost (PV of cash flows) of the property to $1,330,464 for Charlie Johnstone. This effectively raises Johnstone's EAA to $207,313 and the nominal break of his buy-lease threshold to $318,943. Johnstone's rise in the EAA largely reflects the steady diminution of the tax depreciation and interest shields that occur over time in addition to the effect of delaying the sale of the property.

TABLE 5.8A Johnstone's Pharmacy, Tax Consequences of Sale of Property, 20-Year-Holding Period

Sale of building[a]		$2,298,315
Fixed plant and improvements	$1,440,000	
Less accumulated		
depreciation	454,356	
Net-fixed plant and improvements		985,644
Cost of land		300,000
Gain on sale		1,012,671
Capital gains tax (15%)		151,901
After tax gain on sale		860,770

[a] Represent annual appreciation of 1.4% over cost.

TABLE 5.8B Johnstone's Pharmacy, Cash Gain from Sale of Property

Sale of property	$2,298,315
Less:	
Tax liability	151,901
Loan balance	128,138
Cash gain from sale	2,018,277

This same effect occurs for Bill Bolton as a lessor. Table 5.10 shows that much larger lease revenues are now required to make the project viable. The effect, depicted in that table, shows even a $125,000 lease generates a negative NPV of –$46,122 for Bill Bolton. In contrast, over the shorter time horizon (Table 5.7) the same lease of $125,000 generates an NPV of $342,368 for Bill Bolton. As can be seen from Table 5.11, any lease revenue below $107,000 over the 20-year time horizon will result in a negative NPV for the lessor in this situation.

It thus can be concluded that longer lease times increase leasing costs for both the lessor and the lessee. While shorter leasing terms might be more desirable for the lessee, shorter leasing times for the lessor may increase the lessor's risk, because of the increasingly larger importance of the terminal value of the property. The zone of negotiation over the 20-year time period will be between $107,000 and $220,000.

TABLE 5.9   Johnstone's Pharmacy, 20-Year Build Decision, Building Costs and Cash Flows[a]

Year	After-Tax Mortgage Interest Payments[b]	Mortgage Principle Payments	After-Tax Interest Opportunity Costs[c]	Building Depreciation[d]	Improvements Depreciation[e]	Depreciation Tax (Savings)	Equity Contribution	Cash (Gain) on Sale[f]	Total Cash Flows Out[g]
0	$46,800	$20,952	$19,710	$15,385	$12,000	$9,585	$540,000		$606,510
1	78,000	23,047	39,420	30,769	22,800	18,749			128,787
2	76,638	25,351	39,420	30,769	20,520	17,951			120,356
3	75,140	27,887	39,420	30,769	18,480	17,237			121,960
4	73,492	30,675	39,420	30,769	16,632	16,590			123,562
5	71,680	33,743	39,420	30,769	14,952	16,002			125,184
6	69,686	37,117	39,420	30,769	14,160	16,002			126,846
7	67,492	40,829	39,420	30,769	14,160	15,725			128,304
8	65,080	44,912	39,420	30,769	14,160	15,725			129,603
9	62,426	49,403	39,420	30,769	14,184	15,734			131,024
10	59,507	54,343	39,420	30,769	14,160	15,725			132,604
11	56,296	59,777	39,420	30,769	14,184	15,734			134,325
12	52,763	65,755	39,420	30,769	14,160	15,725			136,235
13	48,878	72,330	39,420	30,769	14,184	15,734			138,319
14	44,604	79,563	39,420	30,769	14,160	15,725			140,629
15	39,902		39,420	30,769	14,184	15,734			143,152

TABLE 5.9 (Continued)

Year	After-Tax Mortgage Interest Payments[b]	Mortgage Principle Payments	After-Tax Interest Opportunity Costs[c]	Building Depreciation[d]	Improvements Depreciation[e]	Depreciation Tax (Savings)	Equity Contribution	Cash (Gain) on Sale[f]	Total Cash Flows Out[g]
16	$34,731	$87,520	$39,420	$30,769	$7,080	$13,247			$148,423
17	29,042	96,272	39,420	30,769		10,769			153,964
18	22,784	105,899	39,420	30,769		10,769			157,334
19	15,901	116,489	39,420	30,769		10,769			161,040
20	8,329	128,138	39,420	30,769		10,769		$2,018,277	-1,853,159

[a] Note that maintenance, insurance, and taxes are not included. Because this is a triple-net lease, they will be the same, whether the building is owned or leased, and thus do not affect the comparison.

[b] An 8% fixed-rate, 20-year conventional mortgage.

[c] Although this does not represent an actual expenditure, the investment of $540,000 has an opportunity cost (10%), which is adjusted for Johnstone's personal tax rate.

[d] $1,200,000 depreciated over 39 years, using the half-year convention.

[e] Land improvements (streets, blacktop, sidewalk, drainage ditches, etc.) have a recovery period of 15 years and are depreciated 150% declining balance using the half-year convention.

[f] From Table 5.2B.

[g] Cash flow out includes tax-adjusted interest payments and principal payments less the depreciation of tax savings and cash gain on sale. Note depreciation costs themselves do not influence cash flows because they do not represent a cash expenditure.

Present value of cash flows = $1,330,464
Discount rate = 9.00%
Equivalent annual annuity = $207,313
Tax-adjusted EAA = $318,943

TABLE 5.10   Bill Bolton Developments, Pharmacy Cash Flow Analysis, 20-Year Holding Period

Year	Lease Revenue	Depreciation	Administrative Costs	Interest	EBT	Taxes	Net Income	Depreciation	Principal Payments	Cash Gain on Sale	Equity Contribution	Cash Flow
0			$2,000	$72,000	-$74,000	-$18,500	-$55,500				-$140,000	-$195,500
1	$125,000	$27,385	2,000	152,000	-56,385	-14,096	-42,288	$27,385	$29,563			-44,467
2	125,000	53,569	2,000	149,192	-79,761	-19,940	-59,821	53,569	32,371			-38,623
3	125,000	51,289	2,000	146,116	-74,406	-18,601	-55,804	51,289	35,446			-39,961
4	125,000	49,249	2,000	142,749	-68,998	-17,250	-51,749	49,249	38,814			-41,313
5	125,000	47,401	2,000	139,062	-63,463	-15,866	-47,597	47,401	42,501			-42,697
6	125,000	45,721	2,000	135,024	-57,745	-14,436	-43,309	45,721	46,539			-44,126
7	125,000	44,929	2,000	130,603	-52,532	-13,133	-39,399	44,929	50,960			-45,430
8	125,000	44,929	2,000	125,762	-47,691	-11,923	-35,768	44,929	55,801			-46,640
9	125,000	44,953	2,000	120,460	-42,414	-10,603	-31,810	44,953	61,102			-47,959
10	125,000	44,929	2,000	114,656	-36,585	-9,146	-27,439	44,929	66,907			-49,416
11	125,000	44,953	2,000	108,300	-30,253	-7,563	-22,690	44,953	73,263			-51,000
12	125,000	44,929	2,000	101,340	-23,269	-5,817	-17,452	44,929	80,223			-52,746
13	125,000	44,953	2,000	93,718	-15,672	-3,918	-11,754	44,953	87,844			-54,645
14	125,000	44,929	2,000	85,373	-7,302	-1,826	-5,477	44,929	96,190			-56,737
15	125,000	44,953	2,000	76,235	1,812	453	1,359	44,953	105,328			-59,016
16	125,000	37,849	2,000	66,229	18,922	4,730	14,191	37,849	115,334			-63,293
17	125,000	30,769	2,000	55,272	36,958	9,240	27,719	30,769	126,290			-67,802
18	125,000	30,769	2,000	43,275	48,956	12,239	36,717	30,769	138,288			-70,802
19	125,000	30,769	2,000	30,137	62,093	15,523	46,570	30,769	151,425			-74,086
20	125,000	30,769	2,000	15,752	76,479	19,120	57,359	30,769	165,811	$2,018,277		1,940,594

NPV = ($46,122)
Discount rate = 0.085

TABLE 5.11   Johnstone and Bolton, 20-Year Outcome

Lease	$300,000	$125,000	$107,000
Bolton's NPV	1,370,706	128,643	888
Johnstone's PV cost of building	1,330,766	1,330,766	1,330,766
EAA of Johnstone's PV cost of building	207,360	207,360	207,360
Johnstone's tax-adjusted EAA of building[a]	319,016	319,016	319,016

[a] The EAA is the equivalent annual annuity. It represents that constant flow of cash whose PV over the period is equal to the PV of the cost of building. Because qualifying lease payments are tax deductible, the nominal lease that is the same as the EAA would be the EAA/(1 − Tx).

ILLUSTRATION #3: VARIATIONS IN TAX RATES

The relative importance of a tax differential between the lessor and lessee can be seen in Table 5.12. The effect of relatively higher taxes on the potential lessee (or where the tax rate spread between the lessor or lessee becomes larger) is to increase the desirability of leasing, other factors remaining constant. The greater the tax disparity between the lessee and lessor, the larger will be the zone of negotiation and the greater the advantage to the lessor. Note that the advantage to the lessor comes from

TABLE 5.12   Johnstone and Bolton, 20-Year Outcome Zone of Negotiation, Sensitivity to Tax Differential

Tax spread[a]	−10.00%	−5.00%	0.00%	5.00%	10.00%
Zone of negotiation:					
Bolton's minimum lease rate[b]	$107,000	$107,000	$107,000	$107,000	$107,000
Johnstone's tax adjusted EAA[c]	$288,880	$295,001	$301,939	$309,867	$319,016

[a] The tax spread is Johnstone's Pharmacy rate minus Bolton's rate. These are set at 15–25%, 20–25%, 25–25%, 30–25%, and 35–25% respectively.
[b] This is the lowest lease at which Bolton will have a positive NPV, given his tax rate of 25%.
[c] The EAA is the equivalent annual annuity. It represents that constant flow of cash whose PV over the period is equal to the PV of the cost of building. Because qualifying lease payments are tax deductible, the nominal lease that is the same as the EEA would be the EEA/(1 − Tx).

his or her relatively lower tax rate. The reason a high tax rate favors leasing for the lessee is that the entire cost of the lease is tax deductible.

SUMMARY

The Johnstone Pharmacy example gives insight into what makes for a buying situation or a leasing situation and how it can be evaluated. Perhaps the most important pragmatic factor is access to capital. In this example, Charlie Johnstone was barely able to contemplate financing the new building himself. A more expensive building, or fewer assets in his possession, would not have been practical. Perhaps next in importance is the length of the lease. In general, shorter lease terms favor leasing over buying, although this will be constrained by any resultant increase in risk to the lessor. The differing tax situation between the lessor and lessee will also effect the desirability of leasing versus buying. Where the lessor has a lower tax rate than the lessee, leasing, rather than buying, is favored. The different cost of debt to the lessor and lessee may also be important, although such differences will not be as important as the preceding factors. Where the lessor has lower costs of capital than the lessee does, this favors leasing rather than buying. The timing of cash flows also may play a role in this decision. Where the lessor has a lower cost of capital than the lessee and cash flows are weighted toward the end of the leasing period, this situation favors leasing over buying.

In summary, the role of a lessor or lessee may well suit an investor in commercial real estate. Because of the nature of tax laws and imperfections in capital markets leasing often results in a potential win-win situation for both participating parties.

CHAPTER 6

Residential Real Estate

Investing in residential real estate provides a high-return, low-risk approach to creating substantial wealth, especially for the small investor or the investor new to real estate. There are pitfalls, however. We have all seen the headlines and infomercials that blare "A Geek like Me Made $250,000 in Three Weeks," "Bankrupt and in Debt, I Made $75,000 a Month Working 15 Minutes a Day," "Be Independent and Wealthy Working Weekends." These are appeals to the gullible, lazy, and ignorant. There is no easy path to riches, buying and selling real estate, or any other way.

However, diligence, hard work and energy can be applied to real estate investing to create substantial personal wealth for yourself and your family. Furthermore, you don't have to be rich to do it. Individuals with modest, even humble, financial resources can make remarkable amounts of money investing in residential real estate. Every region, every state, and every locality abounds with opportunities.

Buying a residential property, renting it out, and selling it is a great way to make money, especially for those with limited resources. Residential property includes single-family homes, duplexes, triplexes and fourplexes. As a result of social policy in the United States directed towards encouraging home ownership, the government facilitates the financing of such properties and allows them substantial tax breaks. This is even truer for the investor in rental properties than it is for the homeowners themselves.

There are two basic ways to make money in residential real estate: (1) buying at market value and reaping profits over the long haul; and (2) buying below the market for a fast turnaround ("flipping"). Buying at the market to make money requires patience, hard work, and time, lots of time. While buying at the market may be a slow way to create wealth, it is relatively certain and risk free if done right. Flipping properties basically involves taking advantage of market imperfections, other people's misfortunes, or other people's ignorance. If flipping does not involve outright fraud (for which it is not uncommon to go to jail), it is a lot like tightrope walking. While it looks easy, it is hard to do in fact—and very dangerous.

BUYING AT THE MARKET

The Formula for Success

If there is magic in real estate, it lies in the power of compound interest. The basic formula for successful investing in residential real estate is (1) buy the right property; (2) use lots of leverage with a fixed rate mortgage; (3) allow your rents to rise over time with inflation; (4) allow the property to appreciate over time; (5) sell that property, and start over with (1) again. This process works especially well because (1) it is possible to substitute sweat equity for cash; (2) the tax laws favor you in this process; and (3) the social imperative of fostering home ownership for everyone result in capital being available to you as an investor on excellent terms.

One of the great things about the housing market is that it is always in flux, creating a continuous stream of new opportunities. Between 6 and 7 million new and existing homes are sold each year. There is no shortage of housing options, but with so many choices the challenge becomes finding the property that best meets your needs. The housing market is complicated because the stock of homes for sale is always changing. If it were possible to have a complete list of every home for sale at this very moment in a given community, such a list would become obsolete within seconds as new homes become available and properties now for sale are put under contract.

The basic idea behind this formula is that you buy a property for a fixed amount of cash (a little bit of your cash and lots of others' cash) and watch your costs go up slower than your revenues. The high degree of leverage magnifies your gain and you come out way ahead.

An example of how this can work is presented in Tables 6.1 and 6.2. This is an idealized and simplified situation, where everything goes right. In this case, an investor locates a house with curb appeal in a good neighborhood of a city with a growing economic base. The investor is able to buy the house at a fair market value for $102,500. (A fair market value means you could turn around and sell it for $102,500 as easy as you bought it.) If there is a real estate commission to be paid,

TABLE 6.1 Generic Residential Investment, NOPAT

Year	Net Rental Income[a]	Taxes and Insurance[b]	Maintenance	Depreciation[c]	EBIT	Taxes (20%)	NOPAT (EBIT (1 − tx))
1	$12,000	$2,400	$1,000	$3,000	$5,600	$1,120	$4,480
2	12,720	2,448	1,020	3,000	6,252	1,250	5,002
3	13,483	2,497	1,040	3,000	6,946	1,389	5,557
4	14,292	2,547	1,061	3,000	7,684	1,537	6,147
5	15,150	2,598	1,082	3,000	8,469	1,694	6,776
6	16,059	2,650	1,104	3,000	9,305	1,861	7,444
7	17,022	2,703	1,126	3,000	10,193	2,039	8,155
8	18,044	2,757	1,149	3,000	11,138	2,228	8,910
9	19,126	2,812	1,172	3,000	12,143	2,429	9,714
10	20,274	2,868	1,195	3,000	13,210	2,642	10,568

[a] Rental income per month is 1% of property value, increasing at 6% annually.
[b] Taxes are $100 per month; mortgage and hazard insurance are each $50 per month, bringing the total PITI (principal, interest, taxes, insurance) to $832.07 per month.
[c] Depreciated over 25.5 years, no half-year convention. Land value is $20,000.

TABLE 6.2 Generic Residential Investment, Net Income

Year	EBIT[a]	Interest[b]	EBT	Taxes (20%)	Net Income
1	$5,600	$6,467	−$867	−$173	−$694
2	6,252	6,392	−140	−28	−112
3	6,946	6,312	633	127	507
4	7,684	6,227	1,457	291	1,166
5	8,469	6,136	2,333	467	1,867
6	9,305	6,039	3,266	653	2,613
7	10,193	5,936	4,258	852	3,406
8	11,138	5,825	5,313	1,063	4,250
9	12,143	5,707	6,435	1,287	5,148
10	13,210	5,582	7,629	1,526	6,103

[a] From Table 6.1
[b] On a 30-year conventional fixed rate mortgage at 6.5%.

this represents a service paid for and does not directly represent the value of the property). The investor then qualifies for an FHA mortgage, where only $2,500 is needed to close on the property. The investor is able to obtain a fixed rate 30-year mortgage for 6.5% with no points. The large amount of debt on this house will require the investor to purchase mortgage insurance for another $50 a month along with taxes ($100) and hazard insurance ($50), this raises his or her monthly outlays, *principal, interest, taxes, and insurance* (PITI), to $832.

The power of leverage to the investor is seen from the fact that as the house appreciates 6% the first year, this represents an immediate paper return of $6,000 on the $2,500 investment. However, in this example, what determines the profitability of the investment is not the appreciation of the house, which is good because future appreciation is always tinged with uncertainty. The profitability of this investment is determined by the fact that the house is immediately rented out for a monthly rate equal to 1% of its total value and remains fully rented out over the entire 10-year holding period. Furthermore, during this holding period, maintenance expenses remain minimal (no roof, heating system, and the like to replace) and interest rates are low.

This basically means the project will generate positive cash flow from the beginning (except for the initial injection of capital). In other words, the investment is fundamentally profitable by itself, as an income generating entity.

This can be seen from the strong NOPAT (Table 6.1) consequent on these assumptions. Given the fact that a low interest rate of 6.5% was secured, net income is also strong for this investment (Table 6.2). Under these circumstances, if the house can be expected to appreciate 6% per year, it can be sold in 10 years for $183,562 (Table 6.3A). This will generate an after-tax cash gain of $78,580 (Table 6.3B.)

TABLE 6.3A   Generic Residential Investment, Tax Consequences of Sale of Property, 10-Year Holding Period

Sale of building[a]	$183,562
Less accumulated depreciation	30,000
Cost of land	20,000
Gain on sale	133,562
Capital gains tax (15%)	20,034
After-tax gain on sale	113,528

[a] Property appreciates at 6% per year.

TABLE 6.3B Generic Residential Investment, Cash Gain from Sale of Property

Sale of property	$183,562
Less:	
Tax liability	20,034
Loan balance	84,948
Cash gain from sale	78,580

TABLE 6.4 Generic Residential Investment, Cash Flow Statement

Year	Net Income	Depre- ciation	Less Equity Payments	Less Initial Cash	Plus Cash Gain from Sale[a]	Net Cash Flows	Net Cash Flows W/O Sale
1	-$694	$3,000	$1,118	$2,500		-$1,311	-$1,311
2	-112	3,000	1,193			1,695	1,695
3	507	3,000	1,272			2,234	2,234
4	1,166	3,000	1,358			2,808	2,808
5	1,867	3,000	1,449			3,418	3,418
6	2,613	3,000	1,546			4,067	4,067
7	3,406	3,000	1,649			4,757	4,757
8	4,250	3,000	1,760			5,491	5,491
9	5,148	3,000	1,877			6,271	6,271
10	6,103	3,000	2,003		78,580	85,679	7,100

[a] From Table 6.3B.

NPV at 12% with sale = $41,772
NPV at 12% without sale = $16,472

IRR with sale = 158.10%
IRR without sale = 156.51%

Taking into consideration the required initial startup cost of $2,500, first-year cash flow is negative (-$1,311), but turns positive in the second year and grows strongly throughout the entire 10-year holding period (Table 6.4). There are two ways to evaluate the performance of this investment. The first is to examine the present value of these cash flows. Without the sale of the property, the present value of the investment is $16,472. Because this number is discounted to its present value, it can be directly compared to the investors net outlay of $1,311 in the first year. This means the investor has a 12-fold return after taking account of the normal 12% his or her funds would otherwise earn. If the sale of the property is taken into account, the present value of $41,772 represents a more than 30-fold increase to the investor!

The other way to look at the performance of the investment is to judge its success on the basis of its internal rate of return. Note from Table 6.4, both with and without the realization of the sale of the property,[1] that the return on the investor's net $1,311 investment is over 150% annually. Now that is a strong return.

This is the kernel of truth upon which the "sucker ads" are based. Real estate investing, especially residential real estate investing, is a path that can lead to substantial wealth creation. However, it should be noted that everything went right in this example. Did things go well for the investor because he or she was lucky, or did things go well because the investor worked hard and diligently put forth the effort to make things go right? The authors can personally testify that good tenant relations, for example, are never a matter of luck. Good luck commeth to him or her who "worketh like hell" is a true aphorism.

For those with little capital starting out, a particularly attractive variant of the strategy of buying at the market is buying a duplex, triplex, or fourplex and living in one of the units while renting the others out. This is a great strategy since it will be your own residence, where financing is normally easier and cheaper to come by. Living next to your tenants allows you to monitor their behavior and thus lessens the chance of the tenants engaging in destructive behavior. Also, as neighbors, you can develop a relationship with the tenant that increases their chances of paying the rent in a timely fashion. Furthermore, when the window breaks, the toilet clogs, the oven will not heat, and the like, you can be "Johnny-on-the-Spot" and fix it quickly and inexpensively yourself. Quick responsive personal care of your tenants is a great way to build goodwill and ensure the all-important timely payment of rents.

If being called by your tenant at 9:30 at night, when you were just settling down, because their toilet is leaking and you have to go fix it is not your cup of tea, then the strategy of investing in residential real estate is not for you. If you do not fix the toilet and allow it to leak, you will have much more expensive problems to deal with in terms of tile, rug, wood, and mold damage. In addition you will have a tenant who thinks, "Hey, he doesn't care about me. Why should I go the extra mile to see he gets paid on time—or even at all!" Deciding to call a professional plumber to go there at that time of night will get you a $250 bill to replace a $2.00 wax seal. Over time, you will find that sort of behavior will consume any potential profits in the property.

---

[1] The small difference between the two IRRs reflects the tendency of this technique to severely devalue far-out cash flows like the cash realized from the gain on sale. The meaning of these figures is that this investment is going to be highly profitable, whatever the disposal of the property at the end of 10 years.

One hears talk of being able to hire an independent "utility man" who will be happy to come to your property and do efficient, quality repairs at any hour of the day or night for $10. We have never encountered such a person. We think he is mythical. One can hire a professional property manager who will find tenants, collect rents, and see to problems that arise. They charge 10% to 20% of gross rents and when the toilet breaks down at 9:30 P.M. they will call that plumber and send you the $250 bill.

Unlike investing in apartments, where the size of the operation (economies of scale) permits you, as the investor, to hire professional help and to not involve yourself in day-to-day problems, investing in residential real estate requires a "hands on" commitment. If you are not willing to make that commitment, this is not the area for you.

Buying Below the Market

Buying below the market is a slippery slope. The appeal of this strategy lies in our own greed. We would all like something for nothing. The notion that the elderly widow Jones in her residence worth $100,000 (with $50,000 equity) is going to fall behind in her payments and, in danger of being foreclosed by the bank, will panic and sell the property to us for $60,000 appeals to our avaricious side, despite the shameful nature of the deed (no pun intended). Alternatively, a bungling Federal bureaucracy has seized a six-acre, $200,000 farmstead for failure to pay taxes, and is now going to auction it off to the low bidder and you, as an investor, will have the opportunity to buy the property for $40,000. This is the stuff of pipe dreams. It is not likely to happen.

Markets tend to be efficient because there are many participants, both on the buy and sell side. All participants are trying to maximize what is good for them. Where there are numerous buyers and all buyers have the same information, then the property will sell for its true value. If not all buyers have the same amount of information, then there is the possibility of exceptional gain. The question under these circumstances is why you, as an investor, should have more and better information than the other potential buyers?

The authors have stood out in the rain on a cold, nasty November morning, on the county courthouse steps, waiting for the county clerk to begin the sale of tax delinquent properties. We were but one of perhaps 20 participants, bundled against the cold, under umbrellas in the misting, cold rain, waiting for a chance to buy below market. Properties with assessed valuations of $100,000, which were probably worth $100,000 (one can never be sure), began bidding at $40,000, but quickly rose to the low 90s and were sold there. The differential between the supposed value of $100,000 and the $93,000 bid reflected the possibility that the roof leaked, the furnace did not work, lead was in the paint, asbestos was insulating the pipes, and hazardous chemical were stored in basement. Where a $100,000 property was sold for $40,000 it was invariably because there was a serious crack in the foundation, mold problem, water infiltration problem or some other major defect in the property. Some of the group had that information and so they bid cautiously. If you were not possessed of that information, you were likely to go home a "winner." Being a winner means that you paid $49,000 for a house assessed at $100,000 that was probably worth $40,000 and, perhaps, less as you found out exactly what you bought. ("What! Termites have eaten through the main structural supports. So that's why the house has a slight sag.")

This is not to say that it is impossible to buy below the market. There certainly appear to be lots of opportunities available. Distressed property comes in many forms, such as preforeclosures, REO (real-estate owned) or bank owned properties, real estate auctions, probate properties, properties whose owners are going through divorce, and abandoned properties. Opportunities can arise, but they are the exception, not the rule. In any area, there are numerous opportunities to purchase residences that are in various stages of foreclosure, have been seized by creditors, have been seized by the government, or whose owners want to get rid of them quickly. It may be that among the chaff, there is a nugget of grain, but the investor will have to expend considerable effort to find it. The market for distressed properties is crowded with opportunists looking for the same thing. So there will be competition. With hard work and diligence, it may be possible to find a great buy, but it will not be easy. If it was easy, there would be lots of buyers and the price would be pushed up to market value

The authors have worked hard to find what appeared to be a gem (a property truly available below its market price). Every time, when we went to buy that gem at the auction, our "discovery" turns out to have been discovered by others as well. Oftentimes the competition for that property is so fierce, we never even get to bid. One reason for this is that there are individuals who try to make a profession of finding, buying, and flipping properties that they can buy below market value. These are hard-working professionals who treat this activity as a full time job. They are smart, experienced, and, over the years, have developed all sorts of informal contacts and sources of information. If you ask one, "How are you doing?" we have never heard an individual respond "Hey, I made $250,000 in a month working 15 minutes a day." What they say is, "I spend so much time on various properties that don't work out, this is barely worth my time!"

The difficulties in implementing a successful buying-below-market strategy do not deter the writers of books or providers of information on this subject.[2] The Internet is full of sites by successful "experts" in this area who will be happy to share their "secrets" with you of how to do this for $995. Perhaps this is a validation of what P. T. Barnum had to say about the public.

A variant of buying below the market involves buying a deteriorated property. One that has been so physically damaged, it is selling at a severe discount to comparable properties. This is buying a "fixer upper." If you are handy with building skills (carpentry, masonry, electrical work, and plumbing) or have relatives and friends who are, this can be an excellent way to begin a career in real estate investing. Success will basically come through "sweat equity." As long as you understand there will be sweat, and it will be your sweat, that is okay.

The way this works is that there is a house in a good stable neighborhood where there are clear comparables for value that indicate that the house should be worth $100,000. The owner has tried to sell the house first at $100,000, then at $90,000, then at $80,000. No buyer will touch it because of water accumulation problem in the basement. There is serious structural damage to the house frame; and the electrical and heating systems are shot. In addition, there is a serious mold problem that would make it unhealthy for anyone to live there while the house is in that condition. Further, all the appliances are deteriorated and the kitchen cabinets are distressed. Prospective buyers, who have inquired from licensed contractors about fixing it up, have received estimates ranging for $60,000 to $100,000.

You make an offer to buy it from the owner (the house is in such poor condition, it will not pass an FHA inspection and no bank will finance it) for $35,000 with him or her financing it for $2,000 down and a conventional 10-year note on the balance at 5%. You buy it and take eight months to fix the water problem in the basement, gut the house, put up new drywall and paint, and replace everything that has to be replaced. Your direct costs for materials, supplies and appliances are $35,000. You did all the labor yourself, working weekends and evenings. The house looks like new and sells quickly for $100,000. Your basis was $70,000 ($35,000 for the house and $35,000 to fix it up), so

---

[2] For example, William Bronchick and Robert Dahlstrom, *Flipping Properties: Generate Instant Cash Profits in Real Estate* (Chicago: Dearborn, 2001); Diane Kennedy, Robert T. Kiyosaki, and Garrett Sutton, *Real Estate Loopholes: Secrets of Successful Real Estate Investing* (New York: Warner Books, 2003); Kevin C. Myers, *Buy It, Fix It, Sell It: Profit!* (Chicago: Dearborn, 1998); Suzanne P. Thomas, *Rental Houses for the Successful Small Investor* (Boulder, CO: Gemstone House, 1999); Mike Summey and Roger Dawson, *The Weekend Millionaire's Secrets to Investing in Real Estate: How to Become Wealthy in Your Spare Time* (New York: McGraw-Hill, 2003).

your profit is $30,000 before tax. The question becomes "Was this house really bought below the market, or was it bought at the market for what it really was worth?" The "profit" really should be considered as a payment for your labor.

Again, there is not likely to be a situation where a $100,000 house just looks distressed and can be bought for $60,000. The buyer spends $3,000 on new paint and $2,000 on new rugs and flips the now "good looking" house for $100,000, clearing a fast $35,000 profit. Who would be so stupid to sell such a house for $60,000? Why aren't your competitors clamoring to buy the house at that price? Why doesn't the competition bid the price up to $95,000? There are two possibilities. One is that the competitors will soon be along to bid up the price of the house. The other is that someone out there knows something about the house that you don't!

Potentially fertile grounds for finding properties "below the market" are those properties acquired by financial institutions and various government agencies as a result of defaulted debt or liens and are being liquidated. Although most financial institutions and government agencies make an effort to sell such property at its market value (and appear to do a good job at it), there may be occasional exceptions to this. It may be that you "happen to be in the right place at the right time." Banks should be your number one lead for properties that have been repossessed. In addition, there may be an array of state and municipal agencies that liquidate properties on a regular basis. On the Federal level, there are many agencies holding properties and looking to liquidate them (most of these agencies have online sites detailing the properties offered.) These would include:

- Bureau of Land Management
- Federal Deposit Insurance Corporation
- General Services Administration
- Internal Revenue Service
- U.S. Marshals Service
- National Park Service
- Small Business Administration
- Fannie Mae
- Federal Deposit Insurance Corporation
- Housing and Urban Development (HUD)
- The Department of Veterans Affairs
- The U.S. Army Corps of Engineers
- U.S. Customs
- Department of Agriculture, Rural Development

DETERMINING THE VALUE OF REAL ESTATE

Whether you are "buying at market" or "below market," knowing the value of a property is critical to making a wise investment decision. The market value of any property is never exact. There is always a haze of ambiguity surrounding that value until a transaction takes place. Then the property is worth what someone has paid for it. If buying at the market, then the investor needs to be sure they have not, in fact, paid in excess of market value. If buying below the market, the investor needs to make sure that is, in fact, the case.

Value is measured by price, but how is price determined? Price is determined by the "open outcry" of buyers and sellers. Sellers want to be paid a higher price; buyers want to pay a lower price. At any point in time, in any market, there are always some unsatisfied buyers and sellers. We know they are unsatisfied because they have not bought or sold yet. Where the needs of a single buyer meet up with the needs of a single seller, a transaction will take place. That price marks the spot where supply meets demand, that price determines value. That is, value is not determined from bid prices or from ask prices, but from the price at which transactions actually take place. When real estate markets are "tight," prices rise as demand exceeds supply and the bid ask spreads narrows. As markets weaken, the bid ask spread expands. A good index of the bid-ask spread in any real estate market id the "average days on the market." When the average house on the market takes 180 days to sell, you can bet prices are falling. When the average time on the market is 25 days, prices will be spiraling up.

One nonmarket approach to determining market value is through the appraisal process. An appraised value is not exactly the same thing as a market value, but under many circumstances it is a close approximation. Both sellers and buyers use appraised values in pricing properties. Banks always require an appraisal when they are considering a mortgage application. Appraisers try to determine market value, which they define as the most probable price at which a property will sell (1) in a competitive market under all conditions requisite to a fair sale; (2) with the buyer and seller each acting prudently, knowledgeably and for self-interest; and (3) with neither party under undue duress.[3] Where a reasonable time is allowed for exposure in the open market—approximately 12 months to effect a sale of the property. Price is identified apart from special financing amounts and/or terms, services, fees, costs, or credits incurred in the transaction. The words "most probable price" reflect the facts that, because every parcel of property is unique, fixed prices do not exist (such as those for stocks and bonds).

---

[3] *The Appraisal of Real Estate,* 12th ed. (Chicago: Appraisal Institute, 2003).

The three traditional approaches used to determine the market value of a property are the comparables or sales approach, the cost approach, and the income approach. While one or another of the approaches may be suitable for a particular property, a professional appraiser will normally reach a value estimate by melding the results of all three approaches.

Comparables (Sales) Approach

The "comps" approach to determine value is based on the principle of substitution (i.e., a given property is worth approximately the same as another one offering similar benefits or utility). This approach can be used for all types of property, whether commercial or residential. The first step is to locate data of recent sales of other properties comparable to the property to be valued. Next, the key features or characteristics of each comparable property are compared to the subject property and any differences noted. Differences may be negative (an older or smaller structure) or positive (better location or more amenities). Finally, the sale price of each comparable property is adjusted up or down to reflect both the positive and negative differences between it and the subject property. The estimated value of the subject property then will be in the range of the two or three most comparable properties.

Cost Approach

The cost approach is based on the common-sense notion that a buyer will not pay more for improved real estate than the cost to acquire a site and construct an improvement of equal utility. However, this approach is severely limited by that fact that each parcel of land is made unique by its physical location. Therefore, it cannot be duplicated.

The cost approach involves the following four steps. First, an estimate is made of the cost to reproduce the existing improvements on the subject property. Second, because the existing improvements on the subject property have incurred some loss of value due to depreciation, the accrued depreciation must be estimated and then deducted from the reproduction cost new. Third, the value of the underlying land (as unimproved) must be estimated. Since this cannot be done by the cost approach, the land value must be determined by using the sales approach. Fourth, the value of the subject property, then, is determined by adding together the depreciated cost of the improvements and the land value. Because the cost approach is considered the least precise of all three approaches, it is usually given the least weight in reaching a final determination of value. The cost approach, however, is often the sole method used in valuing public and religious properties, where the income approach cannot be used and for which comparable sales are often not available.

Discounted Cash Flow (Income) Approach

In valuing commercial property, the income approach plays the most prominent role because the buyer's object is the maximum return on investment. The income return involves two steps. The first is to determine the amount and degree of certainty of the future flow of income from the property. The second is to apply an appropriate capitalization rate to annual projected income in order to determine future return on investment.

One often encounters problems when determining the most appropriate measure of "income." The most common measure of income used in the appraisal process is net income. Net income is determined from the property's historical pattern of generating net income, as well as from the terms of current leases. From an investor's perspective, cash flow provides a better measure of value. Thus, the investor must translate net income to a cash flow measure.

The second step in this approach involves determining an appropriate discount rate. This calls for both knowledge of current capital market conditions as well as any risk factors associated with the property whose value is being estimated. The most common formulation of this ratio takes the form of the net income divided by the discount rate. Therefore, if a property had a net income of $10,000 and the appropriate discount rate was 10%, then this approach to determining value would yield a value of $100,000.

A more complex form of income capitalization is yield capitalization, which looks further into the future and attempts to estimate return over a projected holding period (typically 10 years). Yield capitalization involves the concept of a discount rate, defined as a rate used to convert future cash flow into present value. Under this method, cash inflows and outflows are projected for each year during the estimated holding period. Then the annual net cash flows are converted to a present value equal to the purchase price of the property. The discount rate that does this, represents the return of investment (just as the discount rate does in direct capitalization). In addition, since it is assumed that the property is sold at the end of the holding period, yield capitalization usually involves the use of a terminal discount rate. This allows a terminal value for the property to be defined.

ILLUSTRATION #1: THE FOXBOROUGH'S DUPLEX

John Foxborough had worked for six years as a mechanic for a local automobile dealer and currently makes $21 an hour (annual take home pay was around $40,000.) He, his wife, and their three toddlers live in a three-bedroom apartment near the dealership where John works. John's wife Cindy could not work because of a disability, but she took care of John and the kids just fine. John and his wife had saved $3,800 and Cindy's father said he would give them $5,000 toward a new home. Unfortunately, the homes in the area in which they wanted to live (close to John's work) were expensive, and they found they could not afford the mortgage payment on any house they wanted to buy. FHA rules require that the mortgage payment cannot be greater than 29% of take-home pay; so, in John's case, the biggest mortgage payment they could afford would be $997. However, they were not discouraged and kept looking.

One day their real estate agent wanted to show them a "very special" property. A duplex located in a good area in a neighborhood of single-family homes. One side of the duplex was in good shape; the other side had been trashed. John and Cindy liked where the property was, but were dismayed by the side of the duplex that they toured. But the entire property was for sale with a price tag of $200,000. "I can't possible afford that," said John.

Then the real estate agent explained that this property would normally be worth $240,000, but because one side of the duplex was torn up, the price had been lowered. The real estate agent explained that, in addition to the need for some new paint, the plumbing, electrical, and heating systems did not work properly. The problems could be expensive to take care of. "Heck, I can fix that. I can fix anything!" said John. The real estate agent further explained that the good side of the duplex currently had a tenant on a month-to-month lease following the expiration of a year's lease for $1,000 a month. The agent explained, under FHA rules, you can count 70% of that rent toward your payment. "You will have no trouble qualifying to make your payment."

John was able to buy the property with FHA financing for $6,000 down. He met the income qualification on his mortgage of $197,000 (closing costs were $3,000) between his income and the expected rent. John got a little less than the "best" interest rate because part of the property was rented out, but he did get a 30-year conventional mortgage at 8.5% plus two points. They closed on the house in January. John's family stayed in the apartment that first month while he renovated his half of the duplex. By February 1, it was not great, but it was livable and they moved in. John continued to work on the duplex and had it in great shape by June, spending a total of $1,400 for parts and materials. In August, John's tenant moved out. In September, spending $600 John refurbished, repaired and painted that side of the duplex and rented it out to an elderly couple in October for $1,100 a month. In January, three years later, John rented the duplex out to a young professional couple for $1,200 a month, after installing new carpet for $1,600. They stayed and three years later, John raised their rent to $1,300. During this time, John was very quick to remedy any complaints the tenants had and would periodically repaint their quarters. John kept both units in top working order.

As a landlord, John operated as a sole proprietor. However, he kept meticulous records, a separate checking account for everything having to do with the rental business, and allocated all joint expenses on a 50-50 basis. That way, he would always know if his business as a real estate investor was making a profit or losing money.

The first year was the roughest for John and Cindy. Aside from the fact they lost one full month of rent (September), they had heavy outlays for necessary repairs and refurbishing, it seemed like John was working day and night, either fixing up their side of the duplex or their tenant's side. The only way they got through was by putting about $4,000 on their charge cards. However, they did have their "dream house" and they liked the neighborhood and the schools.

NOPAT started fairly strong and got better (Table 6.5), but the property was so highly leveraged that net income (Table 6.6) was very negative that first year and didn't break out of the red until the fifth year. It helped a lot in that first year that they received almost $1,000 credit on their income tax. Even so, there were substantial first year losses to deal with.

TABLE 6.5   Foxborough's Duplex, NOPAT

Year	Net Rental Income[a]	Taxes and Insurance[b]	Mainte- nance	Depre- ciation[c]	EBIT	Taxes (20%)	NOPAT (EBIT $(1 - tx)$)
1	$11,300	$1,950	$800	$2,909	$5,641	$1,128	$4,513
2	13,200	1,989	210	2,909	8,092	1,618	6,474
3	13,200	2,029	214	2,909	8,048	1,610	6,438
4	14,400	2,069	1,850	2,909	7,572	1,514	6,057
5	14,400	2,111	225	2,909	9,155	1,831	7,324
6	14,400	2,153	230	2,909	9,108	1,822	7,287
7	15,600	2,196	234	2,909	10,261	2,052	8,209
8	15,600	2,240	239	2,909	10,212	2,042	8,170
9	15,600	2,285	244	2,909	10,163	2,033	8,130
10	15,600	2,330	248	2,909	10,112	2,022	8,090

[a] In Year 1 rental income was 8 × $1000 + 3 × 1,100; in Year 4 rent goes to $1,200; and in Year 7 rent goes to $1,300 per month.
[b] Taxes are $200 per month; hazard and mortgage insurance are 125 per month; and both are estimated to rise 3% annually. (50% allocation to rental property.)
[c] The land was valued at $40,000, so the building was valued at $160,000: $832.07 per month, depreciated over 27.5 years, full-year convention.

TABLE 6.6   Foxborough's Duplex, Net Income

Year	EBIT[a]	Interest[b]	EBT	Taxes (20%)	Net Income
1	$5,641	$10,314	–$4,673	–$935	–$3,738
2	8,092	8,278	–186	–37	–149
3	8,048	8,206	–159	–32	–127
4	7,572	8,129	–557	–111	–446
5	9,155	8,044	1,112	222	889
6	9,108	7,951	1,157	231	926
7	10,261	7,851	2,410	482	1,928
8	10,212	7,741	2,471	494	1,977
9	10,163	7,622	2,540	508	2,032
10	10,112	7,493	2,619	524	2,096

[a] From Table 6.5.
[b] On a 30-year conventional fixed rate mortgage at 8.5%. The two points paid on the mortgage are expensed the first year.

After 10 years of being constantly on call to "fix this" or "fix that," John was ready for a break. Cindy wanted to move to a conventional single-family home further out in the suburbs. Over the decade, they found that their house had appreciated 6% a year and sold for $358,170 (Table 6.7A). Furthermore, this sale price translated into a cash gain of $139,984 (Table 7.7B). Their payoff for the years of hard work and sacrifice had arrived. This gain allowed them to put a substantial amount of money down on their new home, and they wound up with a much nicer home with about the same PITI.

John's original investment of $6,600 had wound up generating a present value of $49,972, an incredible 49% annual return on his investment (Table 6.8). John and Cindy had pride in their accomplishment and while they were pleased with the outcome, felt they had not taken to big a risk. (The negative cash flow that first year was a big hurdle for them to overcome.) "Even if the house didn't sell for a big gain, we still would have made 25% a year on our investment," said John. "Sure beats what we would have earned at the bank."

ILLUSTRATION #2: KAI'S MANSION

Kai Wei Nit had graduated from the local state college as a computer programmer and web designer. To his chagrin, he found there were no jobs to be had. All the big firms had outsourced their IT jobs overseas,

TABLE 6.7   Foxborough's Duplex, Tax Consequences of Sale of Property, 10-Year Holding Period

Sale of building[a]	$358,170
Less accumulated depreciation	29,091
Cost of land	40,000
Gain on sale	289,079
Capital gains tax (15%)	43,362
After-tax gain on sale	245,717

[a] Property appreciates at 6% per year.

TABLE 6.7B   Foxborough's Duplex, Cash Gain from Sale of Property

Sale of property	$358,170
Less:	
Tax liability	43,362
Loan balance	174,823
Cash gain from sale	139,984

TABLE 6.8   Foxborough's Duplex, Cash Flow Statement

Year	Net Income	Depre- ciation	Less Equity Payments	Less Initial Cash1	Plus Cash Gain from Sale[a]	Net Cash Flows	Net Cash Flows w/o Sale
1	-$3,738	$2,909	$745	$6,600		-$8,174	-$8,174
2	-149	2,909	810			1,950	1,950
3	-127	2,909	882			1,900	1,900
4	-446	2,909	960			1,503	1,503
5	889	2,909	1,045			2,753	2,753
6	926	2,909	1,137			2,698	2,698
7	1,928	2,909	1,238			3,599	3,599
8	1,977	2,909	1,347			3,539	3,539
9	2,032	2,909	1,466			3,475	3,475
10	2,096	2,909	1,596		$139,984	143,393	3,409

[a] $6,000 and $600 for painting.

NPV at 12% with sale = $49,972
NPV at 12% without sale = $4,901

IRR with sale = 49.07%
IRR without sale = 25.40%

which flooded the market with their ex-employees. Every time he had an interview, he was up against five or six individuals 10 years' older than he, who had more experience, and were, in fact, better programmers. The only thing Kai knew for sure was that he did not want to work in his father's grocery store.

Kai took a job as a mortgage consultant with a local mortgage broker. Kai had a good personality, learned fast, and soon was quite successful. In his job as a mortgage broker, Kai became very familiar with the real estate market. Basically, this West Coast metropolitan area was growing leaps and bounds and houses had historically appreciated 5% to 10% a year. This had put house prices up to what many considered absurd levels. Yet, Kai saw that there was no limit in sight for the housing boom. In fact, because of increasing environmental restrictions on the use of land and the increasing cost of building, it looked to Kai as if prices would go up even faster in the future.

Kai lived in a downtown condo that he liked. He had bought it for $200,000 four years ago and now it was worth close to $500,000. Kai wanted more of that! Kai thought the real estate market in his town had unlimited potential. Kai enjoyed working, but wanted to do some investing that would make him "big time" money.

Kai knew of a spectacular 6,000 sq. ft. Japanese-style home on a mountaintop overlooking the most scenic valley in the area. This place had it all: sunken tubs, waterfalls, koi pond, even a mushroom garden. Although this particular location was subject to danger from forest fire, earthquakes, and mudslides, "What the heck!" thought Kai. Houses like this are prime. They do not usually come on the market. The only reason this one was being sold is that it was a fighting point in a particularly nasty divorce.

Kai wondered about the potential return and risk associated with such a large investment. The house was appraised for $1.8 million (land value was $500,000) and Kai only made $110,000 a year (putting him in the 40% tax bracket.) Kai had $20,000 cash in the bank and he could raise another $250,000 with a second mortgage on his condo, but that would be stretching it. Kai felt sure he could lease the Japanese-style property for $10,000 a month to one of the many dot-com executives who were always buzzing in and buzzing out of town. The fact that the property was an easy run of six miles to the airport did not hurt its appeal either. Kai did not want to live on the property, although he loved it. He wanted it strictly as an investment. He was thinking about taking a shot it and making an offer of $1.5 million. However, first he would "run the numbers."

Kai found he could take second mortgage on his condo for 9% and two points. He also arranged for a preapproved alternative (nonstandard) mortgage of $1.3 million. The mortgage would be in a conventional format with a 30-year payment schedule of fixed interest and principal, but would balloon in 10 years. The rate for this was 8% with 6 points. Closing costs would be $75,000. Kai knew the investment had to be long-term, because there are lots of short-term ups and downs in the residential real estate market, so he decided to look at the investment over a 10-year time horizon.

When Kai looked at NOPAT (Table 6.9) he found that over the ten-year holding period it ran from –$32,018 to $28,671—not very strong to carry a high degree of leverage. Then Kai looked at net income (Table 6.10) and his suspicions were confirmed. With the mortgage under consideration, net income would be negative throughout the holding period. Kai made the aggressive assumption that the value of the house would appreciate 10% annually and thus generate a selling price of $3,890,614 (Table 6.11A). This would create a cash gain from the sale of $2,514,717 (Table 6.11B). The result of all this was a cash flow (Table 6.12) that was negative the first three years of the holding period, then negligible positive the remaining seven years. Kai concluded, "This project is on thin ice."

Kai loved the house, but felt the whole investment was too risky for him. The potential gain (NPV) of $529,459 was attractive, but too dependent on the appreciation of the house. What if the house could not be sold at the end of the holding period? He was looking at a big loss! The potential gain of 25% annually on his investment in this highly leveraged deal was not worth the risk for him.

Kai decided to look elsewhere.

ILLUSTRATION #3: 118 TURTLEDOVE DR.

Driving to work, John Bigalow had noticed that the house at 118 Turtledove Dr. in his well-kept suburban neighborhood had been put up for auction in two weeks. This was only two blocks from where he lived. This surprised John as houses in this middle-class part of the city turned over pretty quickly. "Sold" signs quickly replaced the "For Sale" signs which were put up in a week or two. "Why would anybody want to auction off a house around here?" John wondered. He decided to investigate. He went and talked to the neighbors and found that an elderly widow, who had dementia, had lived in the home the past five years. The property had been trashed and was unappealing. So, it had to be auctioned off, rather than sold through a real estate listing. The neighbors thought the house was actually in fine shape, all it needed was a good cleaning and fresh paint.

TABLE 6.9 Kai's Mansion, NOPAT

Year	Net Rental Income[a]	Taxes and Insurance[b]	Closing costs	Maintenance	Depreciation[c]	EBIT	Taxes (40%)	NOPAT (EBIT(1 − tx))
1	$100,000	$36,000	$75,000	$6,000	$36,364	−$53,364	−$21,345	−$32,018
2	120,000	36,720		6,180	36,364	40,736	16,295	24,442
3	120,000	37,454		6,365	36,364	39,817	15,927	23,890
4	135,000	38,203		6,556	36,364	53,877	21,551	32,326
5	135,000	38,968		6,753	36,364	52,916	21,166	31,749
6	135,000	39,747		6,956	36,364	51,934	20,774	31,160
7	135,000	40,542		7,164	36,364	50,930	20,372	30,558
8	135,000	41,353		7,379	36,364	49,904	19,962	29,943
9	135,000	42,180		7,601	36,364	48,856	19,542	29,314
10	135,000	43,023		7,829	36,364	47,784	19,114	28,671

[a] In Year 1 rental income was 8 × $1000 + 3 × 1,100; in Year 4 rent goes to $1,200; in Year 7 rent goes to $1,300 per month.

[b] Includes taxes and hazard and mortgage insurance that are boht estimated to rise 3% annually. (50% allocation to rental property.)

[c] The land was valued at $500,000, so the building was valued at $1 million, which is depreciated over 27.5 years, full-year convention.

TABLE 6.10 Kai's Mansion, Net Income

Year	EBIT[a]	Interest[b]	EBT	Taxes (40%)	Net Income
1	-$53,364	$173,308	-$226,671	-$90,668	-$136,003
2	40,736	93,717	-52,981	-21,192	-31,789
3	39,817	91,995	-52,179	-20,871	-31,307
4	53,877	90,130	-36,253	-14,501	-21,752
5	52,916	88,110	-35,194	-14,078	-21,117
6	51,934	85,922	-33,988	-13,595	-20,393
7	50,930	83,553	-32,623	-13,049	-19,574
8	49,904	80,987	-31,083	-12,433	-18,650
9	48,856	78,208	-29,352	-11,741	-17,611
10	47,784	75,199	-27,415	-10,966	-16,449

[a] From Table 6.9.
[b] On a 30-year conventional fixed rate mortgage at 8%. The six points paid on the mortgage are expensed the first year. The monthly P&I payment will be $9,539.

TABLE 6.11 Kai's Mansion, Tax Consequences of Sale of Property, 10-Year Holding Period

Sale of building[a]	$3,890,614
Less accumulated depreciation	363,636
Cost of land	500,000
Gain on sale	3,026,977
Capital gains tax (15%)	454,047
After-tax gain on sale	2,572,931

[a] Property appreciates at 10% per year.

TABLE 6.11B Kai's Mansion, Cash Gain from Sale of Property

Sale of property	$3,890,614
Less:	
Tax liability	454,047
Loan balance	921,850
Cash gain from sale	2,514,717

TABLE 6.12 Kai's Mansion, Cash Flow Statement

Year	Net Income	Depreciation	Less Equity Payments	Less Initial Cash[a]	Plus Cash Gain from Sale	Net Cash Flows	Net Cash Flows w/o Sale
1	-$136,003	$36,364	$9,580	$200,000		-$309,219	-$309,219
2	-31,789	36,364	10,375			-5,800	-5,800
3	-31,307	36,364	11,236			-6,180	-6,180
4	-21,752	36,364	12,169			2,443	2,443
5	-21,117	36,364	13,179			2,068	2,068
6	-20,393	36,364	14,272			1,698	1,698
7	-19,574	36,364	15,457			1,333	1,333
8	-18,650	36,364	16,740			974	974
9	-17,611	36,364	18,129			623	623
10	-16,449	36,364	19,634		$2,514,717	2,514,997	281

[a] $6,000 and $600 for painting.

NPV at 12% with sale = $529,459

NPV at 12% without sale = -$280,213

IRR with sale = 26%

John made $70,000 a year as an estimator for a regional contractor. His wife earned $45,000 as a department manager at an upscale department store. They had no children and two dogs (daschunds). There home had an appraised value of $225,000, and they owed $80,000 on the mortgage. He had about $100,000 in the bank in CDs. He had not put his money in the stock market because so many of his friends had been burned there. John did not like to take unnecessary risks. If I could buy this house at the right price, there would be no risk, thought John.

John wondered what the house would sell for. He called the auction house and arranged for an inspection with a friend who had some experience as a remodeler. The inspection revealed the house was a real mess. His friend thought the electrical, plumbing, and heating systems were sound, but the roof looked a little "iffy." The friend was also suspicious of a crack that had opened up in the kitchen wall. There was no time for a more thorough follow-up inspection.

John thought this might be an ideal way for him to invest his money. He could buy the house and quickly resell it. Depending on what he paid for it, he might make a big profit. I'll be a "flipper," he thought. John found he could get a second mortgage on his house for $100,000, and with his CDs he could buy the house outright.

Prior to the auction, John had a real estate salesrep show him the "comps" for the house. It was very clear that the market value of this house was about $200,000. John thought the house looked so bad, even though that was superficial, that he might be able to buy the house for $120,000 or $125,000 for a good profit. Armed with this information John showed up at the auction with a cashiers check for $25,000 in his suit coat pocket.

There were about 15 bidders at the auction, which took place on the lawn at 118 Turtledove. John recognized about half of them as neighbors. The auctioneer talked about the terms and conditions of the sale, noted the excellent neighborhood and location of the property, and then announced the sale was "as is, where is" with no guarantees or warranties whatsoever.

The auctioneer opened the bid at $200,000; there were no takers. He dropped it to $150,000 still no takers. He dropped it to $120,000 and someone bid. The auctioneer then ran it up to $135,000 in $5,000 increments. John then bid $136,000. Someone in the back bid $140,000 and the race was on. In two minutes John won the bidding at $149,000.

John completed the formalities of the transaction and then closed on the house in two weeks (out-of-pocket closing costs to John were $3,500). John's first move was to hire a junk dealer to clean all the junk out of the house—that was $1,000. Then John had the roof examined and found that the roof indeed needed to be replaced. Also, water leakage through the roof required some of the underlying plywood to be replaced. The new roof was $3,500 and $1,000 for repairs. John then had the house painted and the crack in the kitchen plastered over ($4,500 and new carpeting throughout ($6,000). John also decided the house needed more curb appeal, so he had some landscaping done ($1,000). All that work took about a month and cost John a total of $19,500.

John thought he would try to make a few extra bucks, so he tried selling it *FSBO* (For Sale by Owner). John spent a month fooling around showing the property to those who were obviously unqualified (would not meet the income test for buying the house), those who were just shopping, and those who didn't keep their appointments. After that month, John found a good real estate agent (based on the recommendation of another friend) who listed the property through her brokerage for 6.5% plus a $500 listing fee.

Three weeks later, John received an offer for the house at $198,000 subject to inspection. John accepted on that basis. The inspector found that fireplace chimney lining had been cracked and needed to be replace, that there were cracks in the front sidewalk that were in violation of the county code, and termite damage in the walls on the back side of the house. The fireplace lining cost $2,500 to repair, the sidewalk $3,000, the termite damage cost $1,700, but, in the process of correcting this damage, the contractor found why there was a crack in the kitchen wall. The metal and wood beams underlying the first floor had been improperly attached and the whole house was sagging into the middle. Correcting that problem cost $5,650. After another month, all these repairs were completed and John had a closing on the house. Fees and return of escrows at closing netted John $750.

The costs to John associated with buying the property were $47,653 (Table 6.13). As a result, John cleared $1,347 (Table 6.14) on his investment. While this was a positive return and better than he would have earned depositing his money in a bank, John was not sure this return was enough to justify the two months of constant worry, tension, and aggravation he encountered. At one point, the inspector thought the furnace was faulty and would need to be replaced for $5,000. Fortunately that had turned out not to be the case; but John had night sweats just thinking about the close call. Summing up this experience, John thought, Never again!

ILLUSTRATION #4: 2415 MULBERRY STREET

Carlos Erjcito and his wife owned a townhouse at 2415 Mulberry Street in a rehabbed area of a large metropolitan area. Carlos had long been

TABLE 6.13   Costs to Bigelow for 118 Trutledove Dr.

Application for second mortgage	$350
Interest on second mortgage	
8% annual for two months.)	1,333
Closing costs on purchase	3,500
Junk removal	1,000
Roof and repairs	4,500
Carpeting	6,000
Painting	4,500
Landscaping	1,000
Fireplace lining	2,500
Termite damage	1,700
Sidewalk repair	3,000
Beam repair	5,650
Real estate commission	13,370
Closing fees and escrow recovery	−750
Total costs	47,653

TABLE 6.14   Profit Statement

Sale price	$198,000
Cost of property	149,000
Costs of	
refurbishing	47,653
Gain (loss)	1,347

active in community affairs and had seen a great improvement in the neighborhood over time. He had rented his townhouse for two years before he bought it from the owner for $35,000. Over the 10 years he had owned the townhouse, he had seen its value rise from $35,000 to $70,000, both because of improvements he had made and the general improvement in the neighborhood. He currently owed $20,000 on his mortgage. Carlos liked his community. He thought it provided a good environment for his four children. It seemed like it was a great community for individuals looking for starter homes.

Although most homes on his street were in good shape, the town-house directly across from him at 2418 Mulberry had long been a distressed eyesore in the community. Recently, vandals had started a fire there, completely destroying the interior of the building. The city could not tear down the building because that would weaken the occupied structures on each side.

The city had a building reclamation program in which a person could buy a house like this for $1 and pay no taxes for three years if they lived in the house for two years following renovation. Such buildings were widely available in the city, but most such buildings were located in areas so bad, no one wanted to live there. The councilman in Carlos's district suggested he purchase this house. The city had a special $50,000 mortgage available for renovations of this type and the councilman would see to it that Carlos would get the mortgage. The mortgage was for 30 years at 2% and the city paid all closing costs. The councilman suggested that by buying the house, Carlos would help his community and help himself.

Carlos was a mason and had many friends in the building trades. He thought he could do a lot of the work himself or use his friends. He decided to take a chance and bought the house for $1.

The terms of the mortgage were that it gave the mortgagee an initial $5,000 to defray additional front-end costs. Subsequent disbursements from the mortgage were tied to specific renovations of the building (e.g., the installation of floors and drywall, the installation of a HVAC (Heating, Venting, and Air Conditioning system). Construction had to be completed in one year. Carlos thought the total cost of renovation would top $85,000. Carlos figured he would work on renovating the townhouse until it was finished, and then he would move into it with his family. He planned to rent out his current house for $400 a month.

The first thing the house needed was to have its masonry structure strengthened. Carlos worked on it himself and in a month (and for $3,000) had completed the work. Next he had some of his friends who were carpenters come in and do the joists, framing, and floors. Next came the installation of the electrical and plumbing systems. Progress was made with remarkable speed because Carlos was always at the house and worked with every subcontractor, often doing some of the work himself. The project had started in January and was 75% completed in June when Carlos had drawn down the whole $50,000 mortgage. Carlos then got a second mortgage on his own home for $35,000 at 6% and began to use that money to finish the house at 2418 Mulberry. In November, the house was completely rehabbed for a total of $79,000. Carlos and his family moved in and rented the old house to a second cousin and her family, newly arrived from Mexico, for $400 a month.

This situation continued for 10 years when Carlos sold both properties, took his profits, and returned to Mexico a comparatively rich man.

How this worked exactly can be seen from Tables 6.15 through 6.16.

The financial data in the tables does not carry the normal meaning because of a variable not included. Carlos's explicit cost of living in 2418 Mulberry is the $185 monthly payment on the $50,000, 2% mortgage. If the opportunity cost of him living there is $400 (what he is charging his cousin living in 2415 Mulberry), then there is a $215 a month (or $2,580 a year) profit he is reaping that is not recorded in this analysis. Thus, both the positive NOPAT (Table 6.15) and the negative net income (Table 6.16) understate the performance of the rental for Carlos and his family.

Assuming the neighborhood continues to improve as a desirable place to live, the houses can be expected to appreciate at 3% annually. This would give them both a sale value of $106,169 (Tables 6.17A, 6.17B, 6.17C, and 6.17D). As Carlos goes to sell both houses, this leads to a big payday for him in the 10th year. It should be remembered that the negative cash flows leading up to that point are not really negative when the opportunity cost of renting 2418 Mulberry is taken into account.

TABLE 6.15   2415 Mulberry, NOPAT on Rental House

Year	Rental Income	Taxes and Insurance[a]	Mainte-nance	Depre-ciation[b]	EBIT	Taxes (10%)	NOPAT (EBIT $(1 - tx)$)
1	$0	$0	$0	$0	$0	$0	$0
2	4,800	265	103	1,636	2,796	559	2,237
3	4,800	273	106	1,636	2,785	557	2,228
4	4,800	425	109	1,636	2,629	526	2,103
5	5,400	438	113	1,636	3,213	643	2,571
6	5,400	451	116	1,636	3,197	639	2,557
7	5,400	464	119	1,636	3,180	636	2,544
8	5,400	478	123	1,636	3,162	632	2,530
9	6,000	493	127	1,636	3,744	749	2,995
10	6,000	507	130	1,636	3,726	745	2,981

[a] Taxes step up in the 4th year because the first three years are tax-free.
[b] The presumed land value is $25,000, so the depreciable basis is $45,000.

TABLE 6.16   2415 Mulberry Street, Net Income

Year	EBIT[a]	Interest[b]	EBT	Taxes (10%)	Net Income
1	$0	$4,613	–$4,613	–$461.34	–$4,152
2	2,796	4,472	–1,676	–168	–1,508
3	2,785	4,319	–1,535	–153	–1,381
4	2,629	4,156	–1,527	–153	–1,374
5	3,213	3,981	–767	–77	–691
6	3,197	3,792	–596	–60	–536
7	3,180	3,590	–410	–41	–369
8	3,162	3,358	–196	–20	–176
9	3,744	3,123	621	62	559
10	3,726	2,871	855	86	770

[a] From Table 6.15.
[b] Interest includes the original mortgage on this property, which was for $32,000 at 9% for 30 years, and the interest on the second mortgage, which was for $35,000 for 15 years at 6%.

TABLE 6.17A   2418 Mulberry Street, Tax Consequences of Sale of Property, 10-Year Holding Period

Sale of building[a]	$106,169
Original cost	$79,001

[a] Original cost of $79,000 appreciating at 3% per year.

TABLE 6.17B   2418 Mulberry Street, Cash Gain from Sale of Property

Sale of property[a]	$106,169
Less:	
Loan balance[b]	36,656
Cash gain from sale	69,514

[a] Original cost of $79,000 appreciating at 3% per year.
[b] On the subsidized mortgage. Because this is a primary residence, not a rental property, there will be no taxable gain.

TABLE 6.17C   2415 Mulberry Street, Tax Consequences of Sale of Property, 10-Year
Holding Period

Sale of building[a]	$106,169
Less accumulated	
depreciation	$14,727
Cost of land	25,000
Gain on sale	66,442
Capital gains tax (15%)	9,966
After-tax gain on sale	56,476

[a] Original cost of $79,000 appreciating at 3% per year.

TABLE 6.17D   2415 Mulberry Street, Cash Gain from Sale of Property

Sale of property[a]	$106,169
Less:	
Tax liability	9,966
Loan balance[b]	17,384
Cash gain from sale	78,819

[a] Property comparable to 2418 Mulberry.
[b] From both the first and second mortgages.

Even without that rental income, the cash flows resulting from Carlos' investment are highly profitable (Table 6.18). The NPV of the investment is $32,049 and the return on capital is 31%. This performance reflects the high degree of leverage and low interest rates Carlos is able to obtain. Thus, his effective initial investment of $1,572 compounds at 31% a year, over 10 years, plus the benefit of reduced rents over that same period. Thanks to his investing in residential real estate, Carlos will go back to Mexico with capital adequate to securing him the good life.

ILLUSTRATION #5: REGINA'S PROPERTIES

Regina Stillworth, took early retirement as an administrator with the police department. She liked the city and owned a condo in the downtown business district. She also owned 12 garages that she rented out in a poor area of the inner city. Only 48, she meant to enjoy a long retirement and travel the world. Regina was single and lived frugally. Over time she had accumulated about $125,000 in diversified mutual funds

TABLE 6.18 2415 Mulberry Street, Cash Flow Statement

Year	Net Income	Depreciation	Less Equity Payments[a]	Less Initial Cash[b]	Plus Cash Gain from Sale[c]	Net Cash Flows
1	−$4,152	$0	$2,021	$1,572		−$7,745
2	−1,508	1,636	2,162			−2,034
3	−1,381	1,636	2,315			−2,060
4	−1,374	1,636	2,478			−2,216
5	−691	1,636	2,653			−1,708
6	−536	1,636	2,842			−1,741
7	−369	1,636	3,044			−1,777
8	−176	1,636	3,276			−1,816
9	559	1,636	3,511			−1,315
10	770	1,636	3,763		$148,333	146,976

[a] First year's equity is on the condo's second mortgage. Second and subsequent equity payments are for the resort property.
[b] This represents the first year's negative net income less the opportunity cost of rent.
[c] From Table 6.13B and 6.13D.

and her condo with an appraised vale of $150,000 was almost entirely paid for. She had about $10,000 in her savings account. The garages had taken a lot of effort to manage, and she now wanted to turn these over to a professional manager. She figured that, after the management fees, her net on the garages would be about $15,000 a year. Added to her $42,000 pension from the police department and $2,000 in dividends from her mutual funds, she had just enough to live on and do the kind of traveling she had always wanted to do.

Regina was worried about the future. While she had hopes that the value of her mutual funds would grow over time, she knew she could not count on that as a future source of income. Stocks were as likely to go down as up, she thought. She expected the value of her garages would remain about the same over time. They produced a good income stream that gave them value, but they were located in a very dangerous and deteriorating section of the city. She didn't expect her condo to increase in value over time either. There was an awful lot of condo construction going on in the city, and she figured the market was going to be saturated for a long time.

Regina was worried about inflation in the future. She saw clearly that the price level was going to rise a lot faster than her income in future years. Regina expected to live at least another 30 years and she knew that if prices increased an average of even 3% over the increases in her income, the effect of compounding that differential in 20 years would be to reduce the purchasing power of her income by 46%. She certainly did not want to be forced back into the labor market in her sixties!

Regina thought she might solve the problem by investing in a single-family home in a nearby expensive resort area. She thought she could get good financing if she bought it as an owner-occupied residence and lived there for a few years. After that she would return to the city and live in her condo. Regina had observed that property values in this ocean resort always went up. Sometimes they went up faster, sometimes slower. The resort area she was thinking of was located adjacent to a pristine beach and was famous for the quality of its water and general beauty. People came from all over the world to vacation there. Regina's hope was that a property in this area would generally increase its value faster than the general inflation rate. Further, that such a property would prove highly desirable as a rental unit and rents of that type were generally inflation proof as well. It seemed to Regina that the financial leverage possible with such an investment would allow her to do what she otherwise could not.

Regina spent considerable time looking for the right property at that resort. She found a small ranch (1,800 sq.ft. on a slab) that seemed to be in good shape. It was located in an excellent section of the resort, but looked dowdy and unattractive from the curb because its shutters were flaky, its paint was peeling, and its shrubbery was overgrown with weeds. Regina felt that at $400,000 the house was overpriced, but she knew that was the market for this house. In this resort, the average price of a single-family home sold in the past year had been over $750,000, but most of those were big gaudy affairs.

Regina wanted to remain diversified, so she only sold off $25,000 of her mutual fund portfolio. She took a 15-year second mortgage on her condo for $100,000 at 6.5% and gave a year's lease on it for $1,250 a month. She bought the ranch house for $400,000 and secured a $275,000 first mortgage for 6.25% and 2 points using the $125,000 as a down payment.

She quickly found that the monthly P&I payment of $1,693, along with another $430 a month for taxes and insurance, was too rich for her blood. She couldn't afford to live there. What was really good, though, was that the demand for rental properties was very strong (as she had thought), and she found a property manager who could rent the property out continuously on a month-to-month basis for an average of $2,200 a month. At the end of the year, Regina moved back to her old condo.

How this worked out for Regina is revealed in Tables 6.19 through 6.23.

TABLE 6.19 Regina's Properties, NOPAT

Year	Condo Income[a]	Shore Income[b]	Taxes and Insurance[c]	Maintenance[d]	Depreciation[e]	EBIT	Taxes (20%)	NOPAT (EBIT(1 − tx))
1	$15,000	$0	$430	$800	$3,636	−$4,866	−$973	−$3,893
2		27,000	443	210	3,636	22,711	4,542	18,169
3		28,350	456	214	3,636	24,043	4,809	19,235
4		29,768	470	218	3,636	25,443	5,089	20,354
5		31,256	484	223	3,636	26,913	5,383	21,530
6		32,819	498	227	3,636	28,457	5,691	22,765
7		34,460	513	232	3,636	30,078	6,016	24,062
8		36,183	529	236	3,636	31,781	6,356	25,425
9		37,992	545	241	3,636	33,569	6,714	26,856
10		39,891	561	246	3,636	35,448	7,090	28,358

[a] Condo rent, net of condo fees, is $1,250 per month.

[b] In Year 1 monthly rental income was $2250 and increases 5% annually following the first year.

[c] Taxes and insurance are $430/month, the first year's increasing 3% annually thereafter.

[d] An initial expenditure of $1,800 at the resort property was required. This is not tax deductible, because the property was not rented the first year. Thereafter, maintenance on the resort property falls to $210, increasing 2% annually, and is tax deductible.

[e] First year depreciation is for the condo. Second and subsequent years is for the resort property. For depreciation purposes, land is valued at $300,000 and property at $100,000. Depreciation is over 27.5 years, full-year convention. The depreciable basis of the condo is $100,000 with a life of 27.5 years as well.

128

TABLE 6.20   Regina's Properties, Net Income

Year	EBIT[a]	Interest[b]	EBT	Taxes (20%)	Net Income
1	-$4,866	$6,380	-$11,246	-$2,249	-$8,997
2	22,711	16,889	5,822	1,164	4,657
3	24,043	16,668	7,375	1,475	5,900
4	25,443	16,434	9,009	1,802	7,207
5	26,913	16,184	10,729	2,146	8,583
6	28,457	15,918	12,539	2,508	10,031
7	30,078	15,635	14,443	2,889	11,555
8	31,781	15,333	16,448	3,290	13,158
9	33,569	15,013	18,557	3,711	14,845
10	35,448	14,671	20,776	4,155	16,621

[a] From Table 6.19.
[b] First year's interest is on the condo's second mortgage. Second and subsequent interest is for the resort property. Two points are expensed the first year on the resort property, because Regina lives there that year.

TABLE 6.21   Regina's Properties, Tax Consequences of Sale of Property, 10-Year Holding Period

Sale of building[a]	$716,339
Less accumulated	
depreciation	36,364
Cost of land	300,000
Gain on sale	379,975
Capital gains tax (15%)	56,996
After-tax gain on sale	322,979

[a] Resort property appreciates at 6% per year.

TABLE 6.21B   Regina's Properties, Cash Gain from Sale of Property

Sale of property	$716,339
Less:	
Tax liability	56,996
Loan balance	232,138
Cash gain from sale	427,205

As a result of living at the resort property the first year, Regina found it was simply too expensive, however enjoyable, for her budget at that time. NOPAT (Table 6.19) was –$3,893 with net income also negative at (Table 6.20) –$8,997. The first year consumed almost all her savings to make up the necessary cash flow deficit. This problem is rectified when she switches back to living in the condo the second year and renting the resort property out. NOPAT then turns positive and continues to grow through the 10th year as rents at the resort property rise 5% each year. Net income follows a similar pattern rising from –$8,997 in Year 1 to 16,621 in Year 10.

Although it is likely she will hold onto the resort property for the rental income (given her need for this investment), for purposes of figuring out where she stands, the resort property will be assumed to be sold in the 10th year after appreciating 6% annually. This generates a sales price of $716,339 (Table 6.21A) and a net cash gain of $427,205 (Table 6.21B.)

This may be seen to generate her a net present value on her investment of $58,267 or an IRR of 18% (Table 6.22). Will this return be adequate to allow her to "beat" inflation? The annual return of 18% certainly suggests that.

Another way to look at her gain is to identify her changes in assets over the 10-year holding period. It can be seen from Table 6.23 that her assets will appreciate 13%, when she purchases the resort property, compared to 3% when she does not. This is testimony to the combined power of leverage and the compound increases of property rents and property value. If the rate of inflation were 5% over this 10-year period, without this investment Regina would lose 2% (5 – 3%) of her assets. However, by investing in the resort property the real purchasing power associated with her assets would increase more than 8% on an annual basis.

SUMMARY

There is substantial money to be made in real estate, either buying at market value and reaping profits over the long haul, or buying below the market for a fast turnaround (flipping). As a general rule, buying at the market and riding the compounding earnings up over time provides a steady path to the accumulation of real wealth. Buying at the market to make money requires patience, hard work, and time, lots of time. While buying at the market may be a slow way to create wealth, it is relatively certain and risk free if done right.

TABLE 6.22 Regina's Properties, Cash Flow Statement

Year	Net Income	Depreciation	Less Equity Payments[a]	Less Initial Cash[b]	Plus Cash Gain from Sale[c]	Net Cash Flows	Future Value of Cash Flows[d]
1	-$8,997	$3,636	$4,073	$125,000		-$134,434	
2	4,657	3,636	3,430			4,864	$5,699
3	5,900	3,636	3,650			5,886	6,761
4	7,207	3,636	3,885			6,959	7,837
5	8,583	3,636	4,135			8,085	8,926
6	10,031	3,636	4,401			9,266	10,030
7	11,555	3,636	4,684			10,507	11,150
8	13,158	3,636	4,985			11,809	12,286
9	14,845	3,636	5,306			13,176	13,439
10	16,621	3,636	5,647		$427,205	441,815	441,815

[a] First year's equity is on the condo's second mortgage. Second and subsequent equity payments are for the resort property.
[b] Includes closing costs.
[c] From Table 6.16.
[d] The future value of cash flows at the end of year 10, appreciated at 2% per year.

NPV at 12% = $58,267

IRR = 17.67%

131

TABLE 6.23   Regina's Assets

With Resort Property:

	Original Time	Time Plus 10 Years
Cash[a]	$566	$690
Condo[b]	150,000	182,849
Mutual funds[c]	100,000	162,889
Cash gain on income and sale of resort property[d]		517,944
Total	250,566	864,372
Annual gain	13.18%	

Without Resort Property:

	Original Time	Time Plus 10 Years
Cash[1]	$10,000	$12,190
Condo[2]	150,000	182,849
Mutual funds[3]	125,000	203,612
Total	285,000	398,651
Annual gain	3.41%	

[a] The first year's cash flow was negative $9,434, more than the $125,000 generated from the sale of mutual funds and the second mortgage. This money came from savings, which are assumed to appreciate at 2% annually.
[b] The condo is also assumed to appreciate at 2% annually.
[c] Mutual funds are assumed to appreciate at 5% annually.
[d] The positive cash flows of Years 2–10 in Table 6.18 are brought forward to the 10th year assuming 2% appreciation. See Tables 6.21A and 6.21B.

Making a fast buck by flipping properties is largely a "will o' the wisp." Buying below the market involves taking advantage of market imperfections, and property owner's misfortunes or ignorance. The fast buck in real estate is a lot like tightrope walking. It looks easy, but it is hard to do in fact—and often very dangerous.

The formula for success in real estate does not require rocket science to master. Success lies in the combination of using the widely available capital available for purchasing homes and taking that capital up in a fixed rate mortgage. Over time, rents and property values will appreciate, but your largest cost will not. This is a great way to avoid the ravages of inflation. This process is especially favorable to the beginning real estate investor because it is possible to substitute sweat equity for cash, the tax laws favor the investor in this process, and the social imperative of fostering home ownership for everyone, results in capital being available to investors on excellent terms. In the investment arena, this is a hard combination to beat.

Additionally, there is always opportunity in the housing market. The market is always in flux as a result of changing population or changing land use patterns. Thus, continuous streams of new opportunities are always being created for the astute investor.

CHAPTER 7

Apartments

The historically low interest rates, which began with the turn of the millennium, at first lowered the demand for apartments. This is due to the fact that many potential renters were able to buy housing, because the decline in interest rates translated to a lower monthly principal and interest payment. However, this greater demand for single-family housing quickly translated itself into much higher housing prices. Paradoxically, this increase in demand for housing has created a tremendous demand for rental units.

This is because the result of higher housing prices was to price many potential purchasers out of the housing market, even after being helped by lower interest rates. Thus, because they could not afford to buy a home, they were forced into the rental market, driving rents up. In the short run, supply for both apartments and residential housing is quite inelastic (insensitive to price) because of the time necessary to get planning approval, building permits and do the construction. In the longer run, the supply of apartments is still inelastic because government officials often discourage the building of apartments because of fears of excessive demands on schools, roads, and other municipal services.

Investing in apartments generally produces better returns and less risk than investing in residential real estate. This is because apartments are less costly to construct, operate, and maintain on a per unit basis. In addition, apartments do not get caught up in the amenity value issues that characterize single-family homes. Apartments are bought and sold strictly on the basis of their economic value, which is determined by their ability to produce a net cash flow now and in the future. Apartments also have the advantage for investors that they do not require the personal attention of the investor. All areas have professional rental management companies who are willing to relieve the investor of the day-to-day responsibilities of managing the property. Moreover, apartments usually have enough economies of scale to make this cost feasible.

135

THE MARKET FOR APARTMENTS

As with all real estate, location is always a key factor in determining value. Location is important because it will impact the demand for the apartments. Location is not a single force, but rather a mosaic of factors that impact the demand for an apartment. Locate next to a university and you have student demand. Locate next to interstate access and you have commuter demand. It matters whether the location has good access to municipal services (schools, libraries, etc.), good access to traffic pathways, and whether the area is attractive.

Generally, apartment complexes can be classified as one of three types: garden, midrise, and high-rise apartments. Garden apartments have from one to three levels and normally contain large balconies or patio areas. Midrise apartment complexes range from four levels to six levels. Anything higher than six levels would be classified as high-rise. Typically zoning laws or the value of the underlying land determines the particular type of apartment to be constructed in a given location. An apartment complex developed downtown adjacent to a central business district is typically going to be a high-rise to amortize the high price of the underlying land. Apartment complexes in suburbia are usually garden apartments, because they are perceived to better fit into their surroundings aesthetically and to make fewer demands on municipal services. This is likely to be forced by zoning laws even where there is an economic incentive to build midrise or high-rise complexes. As a general rule, the cost of constructing apartment units rises more than proportionately as height rises.

The demand for apartments of all types grows long term in our society. Cyclical variations in apartment demand do occur. However, in terms of the risk-return outcomes the strong long-term fundamentals in this market tend to make apartments a good investment opportunity. This growth is driven by an expanding population resulting from in-migration, the life cycle of young adults leaving home and renting before they are ready for the responsibilities of home ownership, the transitory housing needs of an increasingly mobile society, and the graying of the baby boom population, whose members increasingly find renting preferable to home ownership. The supply of apartments is fairly inelastic in the short run (anything under one year), but more elastic (sensitive to price) in the long run (that period of time it takes to develop new apartment properties and bring them to the market).

The combination of inelastic short run supply and more elastic long run supply can create the "boom" and "bust" cycle that frequently occurs in office buildings and shopping centers. What can happen is that at some point in time where the demand for apartments exceeds the supply, rentals rise dramatically. This rise in rentals makes it profitable for investors and developers to bring units on the market. Since numerous investors and developers make this decision independently, there is a tendency for so many units to arrive simultaneously on the market that suddenly supply exceeds demand and rentals fall precipitously.

While this cyclical effect for apartments is not as pronounced as it is for office buildings and shopping centers, it does exist. As long as the investor is aware of the potential existence of such a cycle, it may be used to identify good opportunities for unusual profits. Buying when rents are down is a good thing (as long as falling rents do not signal problems such as a declining neighborhood in which the apartment is located or a significant fall in the area's economic base) and selling when rents are high is similarly a good thing. Investors in apartments are further advantaged by the existence of a clear index of excess demand or excess supply. This index is the vacancy rate in apartments (an easily obtainable, locally published figure). Where the relevant vacancy rate is above 20%, there is a significant excess supply of apartments in the market and rents will be heading down. When the vacancy rate is under 5%, then one can confidently look toward rapidly rising rents. An important caveat should be noted here. The vacancy rate must be relevant to the specific market the apartment property under consideration serves. It may be that the citywide vacancy rate is 25%, signaling an overbuilt situation. However, if the apartment under consideration is located on the suburban fringe in an area considered highly desirable and has a rapidly expanding population, then that 25% vacancy rate may not be relevant to that particular apartment.

A particularly attractive approach to developing apartments in recent years has involved conversions of properties designed for other purposes to apartments (or condos). School buildings, factories, office buildings, warehouses, and department stores have all been profitably converted into apartments. This is because these properties were obtainable for a relatively low cost, having been devalued when their historical purpose became obsolete or redundant. Furthermore, these facilities were often located in an area that was ideal for apartment dwellers. All that was necessary to turn such properties into successful investments was "thinking outside the box."

MEASURES OF APARTMENT VALUE

There are a number of formulas frequently used to determine the value and desirability of an apartment from an investor's perspective. These would include the price earnings approach, the discounted cash flow approach, the price earnings approach, the gross rent approach, the 20% Rule, and the cost-per-unit statistic. All of these rules reflect different perspectives of the same thing. Namely, that the value of an apartment facility is a function of the amount of cash it throws off on a net basis. The desirability of the investment is then determined by the size of the investment relative to its cash flow.

Discounted Cash Flow

The apartment unit may throw off a certain net cash flow per year. Note that this is not net income. Net cash flow would be the sum of net income and depreciation less any equity payments on a mortgage necessary and required capital expenses. This cash flow normally is presented for a number of years (5 and 10 years being very common formulations) and includes a "terminal vale." The cash flow in each of these years is then discounted back to its present value using some kind of discount rate. The terminal value of the cash flow is found by dividing the cash flow in the last year by the "capitalization (cap) rate."

The discount rate and the cap rate are determined by taking an appropriate rate of interest (usually defined in terms of the opportunity cost of a similar investment plus some additional risk premium) and using that to discount the cash flows back to their present value. The cap rate may or may not be the same as the discount rate (although they normally are the same), but they are determined by the same factors.

An example of this would be as shown in Table 7.1.

Here are seen irregular cash flows extending over a five-year time horizon. These cash flows may reflect actual estimates of what the forecaster expects to happen. The cash flows are discounted on the basis of an opportunity cost (17% and a risk factor of 5%). Both of these estimates are subjective and depend on the experience and perception of the individual developing the forecast. The cap rate used in this example to determine a terminal value is the same as the discount rate. It is possible for the cap rate to differ from the discount if that future period of time is expected to have a different interest rate structure or have greater uncertainty than the next five years.

Price-Earnings Ratio (P/E Ratio)

The price-earnings approach is a very common way of expressing the value of apartment facilities. The primary appeal of this methodology is its simplicity. Obviously, the discounted cash flow methodology is not for everyone. The price-earnings approach is based directly on the discounted cash flow approach, but is simplified and expressed much more succinctly. The simplifying assumptions made are that the net cash flow is either a perpetual constant or a perpetual constant growing at a constant rate.

An example of this would be as shown in Table 7.2.

TABLE 7.1 Discounted Cash Flow Example

Given	Year 1	Year 2	Year 3	Year 4	Year 5	Terminal Cash Flow[a]
Net cash flow estimate	$250,000	$263,000	$268,000	$272,000	$275,000	$1,250,000
Discounting[b] to present value	$\dfrac{250,000}{(1 + 0.22)}$	$\dfrac{263,000}{(1 + 0.22)^2}$	$\dfrac{268,000}{(1 + 0.22)^3}$	$\dfrac{272,000}{(1 + 0.22)^4}$	$\dfrac{275,000}{(1 + 0.22)^5}$	$\dfrac{1,250,000}{(1 + 0.22)^5}$
Present value	$204,918	$176,700	$147,589	$122,781	$101,750	$462,499
Value of the apartment facility (Sum of present values)	$1,216,237					

[a] The terminal value was found by dividing the terminal cash flow of $279,000 by the cap rate of 22% (the same rate as the discount rate).
[b] The discount rate was found by taking the opportunity cost of the investment of 17% and adding to that a risk adjustment factor of 5%.

TABLE 7.2   Price-Earnings Ratio Example

Given (a perpetual constant)	Year 1	Year 2	.....	Year n
Net cash flow estimate	$250,000	$250,000	.....	$250,000
Discounting[a] to present value	250,000/0.22			
Present value	1,136,363.636, which may be expressed as $1,136,364 = 1/0.22 ($250,000) or			
Price = 1/0.22 Earnings, or Price = 4.5 Earnings				

Given (a perpetual constant growing at a constant rate)	Year 1	Year 2	.....	Year n
Cash flow estimate	$250,000(1.06)	$250,000(1.06)^2$	.....	$250,000(1.06)^n$
Discounting[a] to present value	1,562,500			
Present value	1,562,500 which may be expressed as $1,562,500 = 1/(0.22 − 0.06) ($250,000) or			
Price = 1/0.16 Earnings, or Price = 6.25 Earnings				

[a] The discount rate was found by taking the opportunity cost of the investment of 17% and adding to that a risk adjustment factor of 5%.

When the net cash flow is treated as a constant, it is possible to speak of price (value) as a multiple of earnings. A multiple of 4.5 will be used in the first illustration (Table 7.2). Allowing for the possibility of growth (as in the second illustration in this table) creates a higher earnings multiple. Thus, we will use a 6.25 multiple in this illustration.

The most common way used to express apartment value is the price-earnings ratio. The problem with this approach is that it contains a lot of ambiguity. For example where a buyer offers five times earnings for an apartment and the seller demands seven, what could account for such a difference in perceived value? They may well be talking about apples and oranges.

The first problem encountered is to define the term earnings. For example, does it mean net income? Net income incorporates a capital structure (amount and cost of debt) into its expenses. This might not be relevant to the buyer. For example, a different capital structure could well result in a different net income. Also, using net income precludes the issue of depreciation. Depreciation may be large or small. It makes a heck of a difference in the determination of the value of the apartment facility.

Another issue concerns the growth factor built into price earnings. The future is always tinged with uncertainty. This is the most difficult component of value to assess. The seller may well project a high future growth rate. The buyer, being cautious in the face of uncertainty, may well project a lower growth rate.

The third problem is what is the appropriate discount rate to use. *Opportunity cost* refers to the next best use of the capital employed. How does one know what "the next best use" is? The next best use could be putting the funds in a FDIC-insured bank and earning 3%. The next best use could be buying stock in a REIT that specializes in apartments and is projected to yield 8%. The next best yield could be what a competitor is currently earning. Even when the answer to that part of the discount rate is clear, how is one to judge a "risk" factor? Risk, like beauty, is always in the eye of the beholder. This is a purely judgmental component of value.

Gross Rent Multiple (GRM)

It is not uncommon for the value of an apartment to be characterized this way. "That apartment complex is worth 2.5 times earnings." "This apartment complex is worth 2 times earnings." This is a very rough "rule of thumb" approach to determining value. On its face, it should not be particularly accurate because expenses will vary from apartment type to apartment type. New apartments (with low maintenance and upkeep requirements) that are desirable (and thus have low vacancy rates, low turnover, and little trouble attracting new tenants) will typically have operating expense ratios from 30% to 40%. Apartments that have been in existence for a decade or longer, but have been well maintained and are still in demand by the relevant population, will tend to have an operating expense ratios from 45% to 55%. Older building (20 years and more) with outdated and worn facilities, which are located in areas obviously past their prime as desirable places to live, can have operating expense ratios in the 65% to 75% range. Obviously, if there were three apartments, each of them a different "type" as above, they could not all be worth the same gross multiple of revenues.

The 20% Rule

In commercial real estate, this rule is occasionally applied to determine the maximum price that will be paid for an apartment. The rule is basically stated in this fashion: If the price paid for the apartment does not have a cash flow 20% above the sum of operating expenses and loan payments, then it is a bad buy. If the price paid does generate a cash flow 20% or more above the sum of operating expenses and loan payments, then it is a good buy. The 20% Rule incorporates both profit and what buyers consider a necessary safety margin for their investment.

Note that the 20% rule is based on cash flow. It does not consider net income. Thus, depreciation should be counted as part of income. Furthermore, this calculation is before taxes. In terms of the analytical framework used in this book, that means the EBIT together with whatever mortgage payment (P&I) exists should be 80% or less than cash flow plus taxes.

One of the chief problems with this rule is that it only looks at value from the perspective of a single year. An advantage of this rule is that it does take into consideration cash flow and EBIT, thus allowing the potential investor to use an optimized capital structure in their calculations.

Cost Per Unit

It is not uncommon for investors in comparing apartment complexes to say that Complex A, with 40-units, is selling for $275,000 and Complex B, with 28 units, is selling for $185,000. A's cost is, therefore, $6,875 per unit and B's cost is $6,607. If the two apartment complexes are otherwise perfectly comparable, then clearly B is the more preferable of the two. Of course, two apartment complexes are never perfectly comparable. They are likely to differ both in revenue potential and cost of operation. It is quite possible to find an apartment complex, where the cost per unit is $20,000 and the investor stands to make a ton of money. In contrast, one can find an apartment complex that can be purchased for

$2,000 a unit that is going to be nothing but trouble and a big disappointment for the investor.

In summary, determining the value of an apartment complex from the perspective of an investor is not about cost, not about revenue (GRM), not even about the relationship between the two (the P/E ratio.) All of the above may be commonly used as rough measures to determine a project's potential, but the fact of the matter is you cannot tell what you have until you run the numbers in a discounted cash flow analysis.

ILLUSTRATION #1: QUEENSBURY MANOR

Suburban development tracked relentlessly northwest of the large metropolitan area following the path of a heavily used major interstate highway. The population had exploded, but the pattern of growth had been erratic and hop-scotched over various parcels of land. Most of the development had been in single-family residential developments that functioned as bedroom communities for the larger metropolitan area. There had also been considerable number of strip shopping centers and small regional malls constructed. Municipal services (water, sewer, and schools) had been stretched to capacity for a decade in the small townships that comprised this corridor.

This particular piece of property is 5-acre tract of land that had been zoned for high density residential. It is located at the intersection of two busy state roads just off a major interstate. It was undeveloped despite three separate development proposals being presented to the planning commission. This location has "success" as a location for an apartment complex written all over it.

First Order was a small local REIT that wanted to develop the property very badly. They had successfully developed five other apartment complexes in this region. They felt they had the resources, the experience, and the marketing "oomph" to make this project go. They thought that the appeal of their project to the local planning board would lie in their contribution to the county's tax base and that they would reserve part of their complex for housing for the elderly. This would be their biggest project.

Acquisition Phase

The plan they brought to the county planning commission called for 1,100 units in 15 buildings called "Queensbury Manor." The buildings would be a mix of garden and midrise units. Two of the midrise units were reserved for the elderly. Altogether there would be 880,000 sq. ft. of living space (this was a lot to crowd into 5 acres and required zoning variances). First Order though they could bring the entire project in for $70 million, which included the cost of the land and $10 million in necessary parking lots, access roads, lighting, and landscaping. This gave First Order an embedded total cost of about $80 a sq. ft. of living space.

First Order had financing lined up. They would put $7 million equity directly into the project, finance remaining startup costs from their cash flow, and get a bridge loan from an insurance company that they had worked with for $63 million at 10% and two points. That loan would then roll over into a conventional 25-year mortgage at 9% and another two points.

First Order felt that they could easily get a 60% occupancy rate that first year with an average monthly rent of $950. First Order already had the staff in place to market and manage the property. All they needed was planning commission approval (and a variance from the Zoning Board) and they were good to go. First Order was so enthusiastic because the numbers looked great.

To get the project started, First Order would be directly injecting $7 million of equity and financing an array of startup costs totaling $6,552,000. The initial cash flows are depicted in Table 7.3.

NOPAT is seen to start off positive and progress to almost $8 million in 10 years (Table 7.4.) In contrast, owing to the high degree of leverage employed, net income (Table 7.5) remains in the red for the first three years, but then turns positive and reaches $2,650,225 by year 10.

TABLE 7.3 Queensbury Manor, Acquisition Period Cash Flows

Uses:	
Hard and soft costs for buildings	$58,000,000
Building improvements	10,000,000
Points on bridge loan	126,000
Points on first mortgage	126,000
Bridge loan interest	6,300,000
Land	2,000,000
Total cash out	76,552,000
Sources:	
Mortgage loan	63,000,000
Equity	7,000,000
Total cash in	70,000,000
Cash balance[a]	–6,552,000

[a] Financed out of REIT cash flow.

TABLE 7.4 Queensbury Manor, Holding Period NOPAT, Net-Operating Profits after Taxes

Year	Revenues[a]	Property Management[b]	REIT Overhead	Depreciation[c]	Property Taxes[d]	EBIT	Taxes (40%)	NOPAT EBIT(1 − tx)
1	$7,524,000	$902,880	$50,000	$2,984,091	$2,340,000	$1,247,029	$249,406	$997,623
2	10,032,000	1,203,840	52,000	3,022,091	2,410,200	3,343,869	668,774	2,675,095
3	11,913,000	1,429,560	54,080	2,930,091	2,482,506	5,016,763	1,003,353	4,013,410
4	12,627,780	1,515,334	56,243	2,848,091	2,556,981	5,651,131	1,130,226	4,520,905
5	13,385,447	1,606,254	58,493	2,774,091	2,633,691	6,312,919	1,262,584	5,050,335
6	14,188,574	1,702,629	60,833	2,708,091	2,712,701	7,004,320	1,400,864	5,603,456
7	15,039,888	1,804,787	63,266	2,699,091	2,794,082	7,678,662	1,535,732	6,142,930
8	15,942,281	1,913,074	65,797	2,700,091	2,877,905	8,385,415	1,677,083	6,708,332
9	16,898,818	2,027,858	68,428	2,699,091	2,964,242	9,139,199	1,827,840	7,311,359
10	17,912,747	2,149,530	71,166	2,700,091	3,053,169	9,938,792	1,987,758	7,951,033

[a] Reflects an average monthly rent of $950 with an occupancy rate of 60% the first year, 85% the second year, and 95% the third year. Thereafter, rents rise 3% annually.
[b] Borrowing from their existing staff and facilities, First Order estimated management expenses would run 12% of revenues.
[c] The $58 million buildings are depreciated over 27.5 years, full-year convention, the $10 million improments are depreciated over 15 years, double-declining balance, midquarter convention.
[d] Property taxes rise 3% annually.

TABLE 7.5 Queensbury Manor, Income Statement

Year	Revenues[a]	Property Management[a]	REIT Overhead[a]	Depreciation[a]	Property Taxes[a]	Interest[b]	Earnings before Taxes	Taxes (40%)	Net Income
1	$7,524,000	$902,880	$50,000	$2,984,091	$2,340,000	$6,391,636	−$5,144,607	−$2,057,843	−$3,086,764
2	10,032,000	1,203,840	52,000	3,022,091	2,410,200	6,327,578	−2,983,708	−1,193,483	−1,790,225
3	11,913,000	1,429,560	54,080	2,930,091	2,482,506	6,257,113	−1,240,350	−496,140	−744,210
4	12,627,780	1,515,334	56,243	2,848,091	2,556,981	6,179,602	−528,470	−211,388	−317,082
5	13,385,447	1,606,254	58,493	2,774,091	2,633,691	6,094,339	218,580	87,432	131,148
6	14,188,574	1,702,629	60,833	2,708,091	2,712,701	6,000,551	1,003,769	401,508	602,262
7	15,039,888	1,804,787	63,266	2,699,091	2,794,082	5,897,383	1,781,279	712,512	1,068,767
8	15,942,281	1,913,074	65,797	2,700,091	2,877,905	5,783,899	2,601,516	1,040,606	1,560,910
9	16,898,818	2,027,858	68,428	2,699,091	2,964,242	5,659,066	3,480,132	1,392,053	2,088,079
10	17,912,747	2,149,530	71,166	2,700,091	3,053,169	5,521,751	4,417,041	1,766,816	2,650,225

[a] From Table 7.4.
[b] The $63 million loan at 10% results in an annual principal and interest payment of $6,940,589. The two points on both the bridge loan and the first mortage are straight-line depreciated over the life of the property (27.5 years.) The interest on the bridge loan is expensed in Year 0.

TABLE 7.6A   Queensbury Manor, Tax Consequences of Sale of Property

Sale of building		$70,000,000
Fixed plant and improvements	$68,000,000	
Less accumulated depreciation	28,064,909	
Net fixed plant and improvements		39,935,091
Cost of land		2,000,000
Gain on sale		28,064,909
Capital gains tax (15%)		4,209,736
After-tax gain on sale		23,855,173

TABLE 7.6B   Queensbury Manor, Cash Gain from Sale of Property

Sale of property	$70,000,000
Less:	
Tax liability	4,209,736
Loan balance	54,301,143
Cash gain from sale	$11,489,121

First Order intends to hold the property for at least 30 years. However, in computing the potential return from the property, they assume the property's value at the end of 10 years will be equal to its original cost. This assumption is made in Tables 7.6A and 7.6B with the result that the "sale" will generate a cash flow of $11,489,121 at that time.

The net result of these projections for First Order was that although cash flow was negative in the first year of operating Queensbury Manor, it turns positive in the second year and continues to increase hitting $4,787,170 in its 10th year (Table 7.7.) This has the effect of generating a net present value of $3,930,227 for First Order that represents an annual return on their investment of 17%. First order is pleased with that result, because they feel the risk associated with Queensbury Manor is negligible. Furthermore, this return makes no allowance for any appreciation in the property. Finally, the trends at the end of the decade speak for even better results in the following years.

The planning commission, unfortunately, did not accept First Order's proposal. Although they liked the increase in the tax base and the provision for housing for the elderly, there was substantial opposition from neighbors who thought the project was "too big" and nearby merchants who feared traffic congestion (too much of a good thing.) The formal reasons given by the planning commission for rejecting the project were (1)

TABLE 7.7 Queensbury Manor, Cash Flow Statement

Year	Net Income[a]	Depreciation[a]	Equity Payments	Capital Contributions[b]	Gain on Sale of Land[c]	Net Cash Flows
0	$0	$0		$13,552,000		$13,552,000
1	-3,086,764	2,984,091	$640,589			-102,673
2	-1,790,225	3,022,091	704,647			1,231,866
3	-744,210	2,930,091	775,112			2,185,881
4	-317,082	2,848,091	852,623			2,531,009
5	131,148	2,774,091	937,886			2,905,239
6	602,262	2,708,091	1,031,674			3,310,352
7	1,068,767	2,699,091	1,134,842			3,767,858
8	1,560,910	2,700,091	1,248,326			4,261,001
9	2,088,079	2,699,091	1,373,158			4,787,170
10	2,650,225	2,700,091	1,510,474		$11,489,121	16,839,437

[a] From Table 7.5.
[b] Includes purchase of land for $60,000 in year 5.
[c] From Table 7.6BB.

NPV at 12% = $3,930,227
IRR = 16.65%

there were concerns that the township could not absorb such a large, abrupt increase in population; (2) the proposals were fought by existing neighbors as not fitting into the context of the neighborhood; and (3) a small Missawak Indian graveyard was on the site as a result of that property being used during the Revolutionary War as a fort. (The area was known locally as Fort Henry.) The descendants of the local Indians did not want the site disturbed for religious reasons.

ILLUSTRATION #2: FORT HENRY PARK

This illustration represents the next phase in the development of the above property.

Carl Willoughby was a successful local developer who had been semiretired for five years. Each week of the season he and three long-time friends (a physician, a banker, and the owner of a local pipe manufacturing company) played golf. Their talk focused on this property (which was also adjacent to their golf course) and how it was a shame that it was just sitting there, used as a dumping grounds for local scofflaws and a meeting place for romantic trysts. They all agreed that First Order's attempt to develop the project was "all wrong,"

Carl thought the right kind of proposal might be successful in getting an apartment project approved for that site. He proposed that they each put up $50,000 to form the Fort Henry LLC that would make such a proposal. If the proposal was successful, each of the partners would put up another $2 million to develop the property. Carl felt that the total project would come in around $22 million. Carl thought the $8 million equity should be sufficient to allow the LLC to get the remaining funds it needed on the basis of its own credit. That way, the four participants would have their personal liability limited to the $2,000,000 that they each invested in the LLC. The four men agreed to do this and had a law firm draw up the necessary papers with each of them having equal ownership in the property. The owners elected Carl Willoughby President and General Manager of the LLC.

Acquisition Period

Carl had a vision for a less-dense apartment complex than had been proposed by First Order. He knew this would increase his costs per unit, but felt that the market would support premium rents for a well-done property at this location. He commissioned an architect to design an apartment complex that would become a unique community resource and do so in collaboration with local community groups (including the

Missawak Indians). The architect developed a plan for a "Fort Henry Park" where six 24-garden units would be built in a "Colonial" style on 3.5 acres of the property. This meant that the community would house about 430 people. The remainder of the property would be dedicated to a formal Indian gravesite (with a small monument detailing the history of the Missawaks) and a park that would be open to the community.

The apartment size would average 1,000 sq. ft. Therefore, there would be 144,000 square foot of construction that would cost $100 per sq. ft. or a total of $14.4 million. Building improvements (sidewalks, walkways, parking lots, access roads, lighting, and landscaping), the Missawak monument, and park facilities would add another $5 million to the cost.

Fort Henry LLC was able to secure a bridge loan for the $15.4 million from a local bank using their $4 million as equity. The bridge loan was interest only and carried an interest rate of 11% and 3 points. When the project was completed, the bank would roll over the loan into a 20-year conventional mortgage for 2 points and a 9.5% interest rate.

The resultant cash flows from this activity are depicted in Table 7.8.

The apartments took a year to construct and open for business. Demand for the apartments was brisk—apartment rentals averaged $1,250 per month—and within six months 80% were rented. Carl had hired the Bronwitz Property Management Company to solicit tenants, manage tenant rolls, and take care of maintenance problems for 15% of gross revenues.

TABLE 7.8   Fort Henry Park, Acquisition Period Cash Flows

Uses:	
Architectural drawings and plans	$50,000
Legal and accounting fees	50,000
Points on bridge loan	462,000
Points on first mortgage	308,000
Bridge loan interest	847,000
Construction costs	14,400,000
Building improvements	5,000,000
Land	2,000,000
Total cash out	23,117,000
Sources:	
Mortgage loan	15,400,000
Equity	8,200,000
Total cash in	23,600,000
Cash balance	483,000

Holding Period

NOPAT began negative ($85,533), which was not a good sign for the future (Table 7.9). NOPAT then increased steadily to $1,334,336 over the 10-year horizon. This portends trouble, because this NOPAT is clearly not going to be sufficient to support the high degree of financial leverage envisioned for the project. This is confirmed by the fact that net income remains negative for the first six years of the project's life and then finally turns positive—but is only able to climb to an anemic $292,599.86 by Year 10 (Table 7.10).

Note that the Fort Henry LLC generates significant tax credits while it runs a loss. Because the project is organized as an LLC, these losses pass to the owners. If the owners are individuals, they will only be able to use $25,000 of these passive losses as income offsets. This would significantly diminish the attractiveness of the investment. However, the owners of the LLC can be any other business entity: a C corporation, an S corporation, an LLP (except sole proprietorships and regular partnerships) and capture all these benefits. For example, if the interests of the pipe company owner are represented by a C corporation as an owner of the LLC, those tax losses will come dollar for dollar over into his corporation as a charge against income.

Given the assumption in Tables 7.11A and 7.11B, that the project could sell for its original cost in its 10th year, then cash flows are positive in every year of operation except the first.

However, Table 7.12 reveals the cash flows are small relative to the investment in the LLC and consequently the net present value of the project is negative: –$1,140,853. However, there is actually a positive return to the LLC of 10%. The negative NPV reflects the fact that the investment did not recover its risk-adjusted cost of capital.

It should be noted that Table 7.11B shows the market value of Fort Henry Park as being $21.5 million. That is a stretch. It is likely that this property would have a market value of five to six times earnings. In its 10th year that gives Fort Henry Park a market value of $2.6 million (6 × 438,900 = $2,633,399). Factoring this value into the cash flow statement, presented in Table 7.13, yields a negative NPV of –$3,673,686 and an annual return on their investment of 1%. Clearly this is unsatisfactory from an investment perspective.

In retrospect, it appears that First Order had the more viable business plan. From an economic perspective, this 5-acre project needed more intense development to allow its investors to capture the potential economies of scale. Not only did Fort Henry LLC not do that, but they overspent on improvements and building design. Each proposed unit would have cost First Order $64,000. Fort Henry's cost per unit was $155,000. The higher rents that Fort Henry charged were not sufficient to cover this huge difference in expense.

TABLE 7.9 Fort Henry Park, Holding Period NOPAT, Net-Operating Profits after Taxes

Year	Revenues[a]	Property Management	LLC Overhead[b]	Depreciation[c]	Property Taxes[d]	EBIT	Taxes (40%)	NOPAT EBIT$(1 - tx)$
1	$1,503,360	$225,504	$30,000	$964,773	$390,000	-$106,917	-$21,383	-$85,533
2	2,129,760	319,464	31,200	983,773	401,700	393,623	78,725	314,899
3	2,380,320	357,048	32,448	937,773	413,751	639,300	127,860	511,440
4	2,523,139	378,471	33,746	896,773	426,164	787,986	157,597	630,389
5	2,674,528	401,179	35,096	859,773	438,948	939,531	187,906	751,625
6	2,834,999	425,250	36,500	826,773	452,117	1,094,360	218,872	875,488
7	3,005,099	450,765	37,960	822,273	465,680	1,228,422	245,684	982,737
8	3,185,405	477,811	39,478	822,773	479,651	1,365,693	273,139	1,092,554
9	3,376,529	506,479	41,057	822,273	494,040	1,512,680	302,536	1,210,144
10	3,579,121	536,868	42,699	822,773	508,862	1,667,919	333,584	1,334,336

[a] Reflects an average monthly rent of $1,450 with an occupancy rate of 60% the first year, 85% the second year, and 95% the third year. Thereafter, rents rise 3% annually.
[b] LLC overheads inflates 4% annually.
[c] The $14.5 million building is depreciated over 27.5 years, full-year convention; the $5 million improments are depreciated over 15 years, double-declining balance, midquarter convention.
[d] Property taxes rise 3% annually.

TABLE 7.10 Fort Henry Park, Income Statement

Year	Revenues[a]	Property Management	LLC Overhead	Depre-ciation[a]	Property Taxes	Interest[b]	Earnings before Taxes	Taxes (40%)	Net Income
1	$1,503,360	$225,504	$30,000	$964,773	$390,000	$1,403,864	-$1,510,780	-$604,312	-$906,468
2	2,129,760	319,464	31,200	983,773	401,700	1,368,710	-975,086	-390,035	-585,052
3	2,380,320	357,048	32,448	937,773	413,751	1,330,216	-690,916	-276,366	-414,550
4	2,523,139	378,471	33,746	896,773	426,164	1,288,066	-500,080	-200,032	-300,048
5	2,674,528	401,179	35,096	859,773	438,948	1,241,911	-302,380	-120,952	-181,428
6	2,834,999	425,250	36,500	826,773	452,117	1,191,372	-97,012	-38,805	-58,207
7	3,005,099	450,765	37,960	822,273	465,680	1,136,031	92,391	36,956	55,434
8	3,185,405	477,811	39,478	822,773	479,651	1,075,433	290,260	116,104	174,156
9	3,376,529	506,479	41,057	822,273	494,040	1,009,078	503,602	201,441	302,161
10	3,579,121	536,868	42,699	822,773	508,862	936,420	731,500	292,600	438,900

[a] Refer to Table 7.9.
[b] Interest on a conventional 20-year mortgage , with an interest rate of 9.5% and an annual payment of $1,747,541, plus 5-point depre-ciated straight line over the life of the property.

TABLE 7.11A   Fort Henry Park, Tax Consequences of Sale of Property

Sale of building		$21,500,000
Fixed plant and improvements	$19,500,000	
Less accumulated depreciation	8,759,727	
Net fixed plant and improvements		10,740,273
Cost of land		2,000,000
Gain on sale		8,759,727
Capital gains tax (15%)		1,313,959
After-tax gain on sale		7,445,768

TABLE 7.11B   Fort Henry Park, Cash Gain from Sale of Property

Sale of property	$21,500,000
Less:	
Tax liability	1,313,959
Loan balance	9,579,538
Cash gain from sale	10,606,503

TABLE 7.12   Fort Henry Park, Cash Flow Statement

Year	Net Income[a]	Depre- ciation[a]	Equity Pay- ments	Capital Contri- butions[b]	Gain on Sale of Land[c]	Net Cash Flows
0	$0	$0	$0	$8,200,000		−$8,200,000
1	−906,468	964,773	370,041			58,305
2	−585,052	983,773	405,195			398,721
3	−414,550	937,773	443,689			523,223
4	−300,048	896,773	485,839			596,725
5	−181,428	859,773	531,994			678,345
6	−58,207	826,773	582,533			768,566
7	55,434	822,273	637,874			877,707
8	174,156	822,773	698,472			996,929
9	302,161	822,273	764,826			1,124,434
10	438,900	822,773	837,485		$10,606,503	11,868,176

[a] From Table 7.10.
[b] From Table 7.8.
[c] 6 × earnings.

NPV at 12% = −$1,140,853
IRR = 9.68%

TABLE 7.13 Fort Henry Park, Cash Flow Statement

Year	Net Income[a]	Depre- ciation[a]	Equity Payments	Capital Contri- butions[b]	Gain on Sale of Land[c]	Net Cash Flows
0	$0	$0	$0	$8,200,000		−$8,200,000
1	−906,468	964,773	370,041			58,305
2	−585,052	983,773	405,195			398,721
3	−414,550	937,773	443,689			523,223
4	−300,048	896,773	485,839			596,725
5	−181,428	859,773	531,994			678,345
6	−58,207	826,773	582,533			768,566
7	55,434	822,273	637,874			877,707
8	174,156	822,773	698,472			996,929
9	302,161	822,273	764,826			1,124,434
10	438,900	822,773	837,485		$2,633,399	3,057,586

[a] From Table 7.10.
[b] From Table 7.8.
[c] 6 × earnings.

NPV at 12% = −3673686.467
IRR = 0.013876141

Carl Willoughby was wise to propose the business organization in the form of an LLC. This format restricted the potential loss for the owners to their initial investment. As it turned out, over the 10-year time horizon, the LLC did not default on its debt, so this was not an issue. However, it could have. Suppose at the time the Fort Henry project was begun when several other nearby apartment complexes were put up. This would result in a glut to the market. Under those circumstances, Fort Henry would not have been able to charge its premium rents. If competitive pressures restricted their average rent to $900, then a disaster would have occurred

Tables 7.14, 7.15, and 7.16 show the impact of this type of competitive market to be unsustainable for Fort Henry LLC. NOPAT, Net Income, and Cash flow are all substantially negative. Were this situation to persist through the end of the decade, present value of the losses to Fort Henry LLC would be over $4 million. Furthermore (from Table 7.16), this does not address any loss consequent on a default on the mortgage and subsequent liquidation. As the book value of the land and building is shown as $12 million (Table 7.11A) and the outstanding loan balance at that point being almost $10 million, one would expect the loan to be in default as the market value of the property would be a

TABLE 7.14 Fort Henry Park, Holding Period NOPAT, Net Operating Profits after Taxes (under competitive conditions)

Year	Revenues[a]	Property Management	LLC Overhead[b]	Depreciation[c]	Property Taxes[d]	EBIT	Taxes (40%)	NOPAT EBIT$(1 - tx)$
1	$933,120	$139,968	$30,000	$964,773	$390,000	-$591,621	-$118,324	-$473,297
2	1,321,920	198,288	31,200	983,773	401,700	-293,041	-58,608	-234,433
3	1,477,440	221,616	32,448	937,773	413,751	-128,148	-25,630	-102,518
4	1,492,214	223,832	33,746	896,773	426,164	-88,300	-17,660	-70,640
5	1,507,137	226,070	35,096	859,773	438,948	-52,751	-10,550	-42,201
6	1,522,208	228,331	36,500	826,773	452,117	-21,512	-4,302	-17,210
7	1,537,430	230,614	37,960	822,273	465,680	-19,097	-3,819	-15,278
8	1,552,804	232,921	39,478	822,773	479,651	-22,018	-4,404	-17,614
9	1,568,332	235,250	41,057	822,273	494,040	-24,288	-4,858	-19,430
10	1,584,016	237,602	42,699	822,773	508,862	-27,920	-5,584	-22,336

[a] Reflects an average monthly rent of $900 with an occupancy rate of 60% the first year, 85% the second year, and 95% the third year. Thereafter, rents rise 1% annually.
[b] LLC overheads inflates 4% annually.
[c] The $14.5 million building is depreciated over 27.5 years, full-year convention; the $5 million improments are depreciated over 15 years, double-declining balance, midquarter convention.
[d] Property taxes rise 3% annually.

TABLE 7.15   Fort Henry Park, Income Statement (under competitive conditions)

Year	Revenues[a]	Property Management[a]	LLC Overhead[a]	Depreciation[a]	Property Taxes[a]	Interest[a]	Earnings Before Taxes	Taxes (40%)	Net Income
1	$933,120	$139,968	$30,000	$964,773	$390,000	$1,403,864	–$1,995,484	–$798,194	–$1,197,291
2	1,321,920	198,288	31,200	983,773	401,700	1,368,710	–1,661,750	–664,700	–997,050
3	1,477,440	221,616	32,448	937,773	413,751	1,330,216	–1,458,364	–583,346	–875,018
4	1,492,214	223,832	33,746	896,773	426,164	1,288,066	–1,376,366	–550,546	–825,819
5	1,507,137	226,070	35,096	859,773	438,948	1,241,911	–1,294,662	–517,865	–776,797
6	1,522,208	228,331	36,500	826,773	452,117	1,191,372	–1,212,884	–485,154	–727,731
7	1,537,430	230,614	37,960	822,273	465,680	1,136,031	–1,155,128	–462,051	–693,077
8	1,552,804	232,921	39,478	822,773	479,651	1,075,433	–1,097,451	–438,980	–658,471
9	1,568,332	235,250	41,057	822,273	494,040	1,009,078	–1,033,366	–413,346	–620,020
10	1,584,016	237,602	42,699	822,773	508,862	936,420	–964,340	–385,736	–578,604

[a] From Table 7.14.

157

TABLE 7.16 Fort Henry Park, Cash Flow Statement (under competitive conditions)

Year	Net Income[a]	Depre-ciation[a]	Equity Payments	Capital Contributions[b]	Net Cash Flows
0	$0	$0	$0	$8,200,000	–$8,200,000
1	–1,197,291	964,773	370,041		–602,559
2	–997,050	983,773	405,195		–418,473
3	–875,018	937,773	443,689		–380,934
4	–825,819	896,773	485,839		–414,886
5	–776,797	859,773	531,994		–449,018
6	–727,731	826,773	582,533		–483,491
7	–693,077	822,273	637,874		–508,678
8	–658,471	822,773	698,472		–534,169
9	–620,020	822,273	764,826		–562,573
10	–578,604	822,773	837,485		–593,316

[a] From Table 7.15.
[b] From Table 7.8.

NPV at 12% = –$4,053,401

few million at most. (Remember, even NOPAT is negative at that point.) So the potential loss is several million dollars to Fort Henry LLC, but the liabilities against the LLC owners will be zero.

ILLUSTRATION #3: THE GOLDEN ARMS

The industrial district (locally known as "Hobo Yards") at the edge of the city's central business district (CBD) had its glory days far behind it. For the most part, it was an area of deteriorated and abandoned factories, warehouses, and railyards. Its chief architectural characteristic was broken windows and piles of rusting junk. However, the city itself remained vibrant. The finance, insurance and real estate sectors flourished, creating demand for retail, office, and living space.

There was a lot of interest in developing this area, both by a variety of city and state agencies and by the local business community. The EPA had been through the area and cleaned out or neutralized the various pockets of chemical and biological hazards. Although many investors were considering a number of possible uses for the different parcels of land, no one had yet committed themselves.

Stan Goldstein had grown up in the city. His father had established a chain of automobile dealerships in the city that now extended far into the suburbs. Stan owned these dealerships through an interest in a holding company that was shared equally among his two brothers and two sisters. Stan took no part in the management of the dealerships. Stan was 30 years old, very well off financially, had two MBAs and two ex-wives; however, he had yet to make his mark as a businessman. Stan had occupied himself by directing some local charities, but felt it was time to get serious.

Sam thought he saw an opportunity for a successful business venture. There was an old apparel factory sitting right between the CBD and "Hobo Yards." This building was four stories, all brick, and seriously dilapidated. In addition, it had a 40,000 sq. ft. footprint and local furniture company was using the lower floor as a warehouse. Sam thought this building had a great deal of potential if converted to apartments. Sam was able to buy the building for $500,000, after agreeing to "hold harmless" the current owner for any residual environmental hazards. At that price, Sam thought he couldn't lose money.

An engineering survey revealed contamination with lead paint and asbestos that did not deter Sam at all. He hired a first-class architectural firm to design a modern "life style" building that might prove attractive to young, affluent urbanites. "Life style" translated into an apartment building that included a large atrium, common areas for exercising and social gatherings, and retail space for two small restaurants and a coffee bar. The architect's plan allowed for 132 spacious apartments in addition to the retail space. The building was designed so that each apartment on the upper two floors had a spectacular view.

Acquisition Stage

Sam estimated that cleaning up the environmental problems, shoring up the old brickwork, and refurbishing the interior would cost about $11.2 million ($70 sq. ft. times 160,000 sq., ft,). Another $4 million would be needed for elevators, escalators, and interior finishes. Sam arranged a bridge loan with a local bank for $13.2 million, planning to put in $2 million in equity himself.

As one of the first to proceed with actually renovating a "Hobo Yards" property, Sam received some property tax incentives from the city. Sam's apartments were to be forgiven 100% of its property taxes the first two years of operation and then pay only 25% of its assessed taxes the next two years, then 50% for the next four years, and then 75% for the next three years. Thereafter, taxes were to be 100%.

TABLE 7.17   Golden Arms, Acquisition Period Cash Flows

Uses:	
Architectural drawings and plans	$200,000
Legal and accounting fees	50,000
Points on bridge loan	660,000
Bridge loan interest	1,320,000
Construction costs	13,900,000
Building improvements	6,400,000
Land	500,000
Total cash out	23,030,000
Sources:	
Mortgage loan	13,200,000
Equity	10,000,000
Total cash in	23,200,000
Cash balance	170,000

As the renovation and construction proceeded, Sam became personally involved with the work and was present on the jobsite everyday. As Sam became more involved in the project, he asked for "change orders" and extras that eventually put the total cost of the project up to $20 million. (Sam put in the additional money from his personal funds.) When the apartment was finished, it was a showplace. Sam named the apartment the "Golden Arms."

The bridge loan Sam arranged carried a 10% interest rate and 5 points. This would be rolled over into a 15-year conventional mortgage at 8.5% when the project was completed. The initial cash flows associated with the Golden Arms are depicted in Table 7.17.

It can be seen, that as a result of Sam "customizing" the finishing touches on the building and more-expensive-than-estimated lead paint abatement, Sam's equity in the project ballooned to $10 million. Sam then decided he would not get personally involved in operating the Golden Arms. Consequently, he hired a local property management firm to perform the necessary management function. The cost of this service was to be 18% of gross revenue.

Holding Stage

The Golden Arms was well received by its intended audience. Within six months the building was half rented (its occupancy rate for the first year was 63%) at rents ranging from $750 per month for apartments on the bottom floors to $2,250 for the "penthouse" apartments. The average rental was $1,380. Within two years the occupancy rate was holding steady at 95%. The Golden Arms normally had a waiting list of six months for new tenants.

The impact of the use of excessive financial leverage can be seen from a comparison of Tables 7.18 and 7.19. Table 17.18 reveals a healthy and growing NOPAT over the life of the project, suggesting the fundamental business soundness of the project. The result of the large interest expenditures in Table 7.17 turn net income negative in all but the eighth and 10th years. This indicates the critical role of developing an appropriate capital structure for the project.

Disposal Stage

By the 10th year, Hobo Park has been mostly redeveloped and land has appreciated in value. Sam receives an offer from a national REIT who wished to purchase his apartment building to convert it into an office building. They offer $30 million and Sam accepts. This generates after tax cash for Sam of $20,168,698 (Tables 7.20A and 7.20B.)

The resultant cash flows are depicted in Table 7.21. The result of the cash flows is a very small positive NPV. This means that Sam Goldstein barely earns the cost of his capital. Given that there is some degree of risk associated with this venture, that is not reflected in the cost of capital, Sam's return did not justify the risk taken. This is especially true since this more-or-less favorable outcome is heavily influenced by the sale of the property at a hefty profit. Without that profit, Sam's return would be well below that cost of capital (Table 7.22). However, it should be noted that Sam's return as an investor would have been much better if the initial cost overruns could have been avoided.

SUMMARY

Apartments make excellent real estate investments as a general rule. Per dollar of revenue, apartments require less fixed costs than other types of real estate investments. Apartment valuations are not difficult to establish because apartments are bought and sold on the basis of their economic value, which is determined by their ability to produce a net cash flow now and in the future. When the apartment complex is larger than four units, there will be sufficient economies of scale to permit hiring professional management so that the investor does not have to become personally involved in their management.

TABLE 7.18 Golden Arms, Holding Period NOPAT, Net Operating Profits after Taxes

Year	Revenues[a]	Property Management[b]	Depreciation[c]	Property Taxes[d]	EBIT	Taxes (40%)	NOPAT EBIT$(1 - tx)$
1	$1,505,270	$270,949	$1,074,205	$0	$160,117	$32,023	$128,094
2	2,073,610	373,250	1,098,905	0	601,455	120,291	481,164
3	2,226,624	400,792	1,039,105	500,000	286,727	57,345	229,382
4	2,404,754	432,856	985,805	500,000	486,094	97,219	388,875
5	2,597,134	467,484	937,705	1,000,000	191,946	38,389	153,556
6	2,804,905	504,883	894,805	1,000,000	405,218	81,044	324,174
7	3,029,297	545,274	888,955	1,000,000	595,069	119,014	476,055
8	3,271,641	588,895	889,605	1,000,000	793,141	158,628	634,513
9	3,533,372	636,007	888,955	1,500,000	508,411	101,682	406,729
10	3,816,042	686,888	889,605	1,500,000	739,550	147,910	591,640

[a] Reflects an average monthly rent of $1,380 with an occupancy rate of 62% the first year, 88% the second year, and 95% the third year. Thereafter, rents rise 8% annually. This also includes lease revenue from the restaurants and coffee shop.
[b] Property management fee is 18% of gross revenue.
[c] The $13.9 million building is depreciated over 27.5 years, full-year convention; the $6.5 million improments are depreciated over 15 years, double-declining balance, midquarter convention.
[d] Property taxes rise 3% annually.

TABLE 7.19 Golden Arms, Income Statement

Year	Revenues[a]	Property Management[a]	Depreciation[a]	Property Taxes	Interest[b]	Earnings before Taxes	Taxes (40%)	Net Income
1	$1,505,270	$270,949	$1,074,205	$0	$1,146,000	–$985,883	–$394,353	–$591,530
2	2,073,610	373,250	1,098,905	0	1,106,258	–504,803	–201,921	–302,882
3	2,226,624	400,792	1,039,105	500,000	1,063,138	–776,411	–310,565	–465,847
4	2,404,754	432,856	985,805	500,000	1,016,353	–530,260	–212,104	–318,156
5	2,597,134	467,484	937,705	1,000,000	965,592	–773,646	–309,458	–464,188
6	2,804,905	504,883	894,805	1,000,000	910,515	–505,298	–202,119	–303,179
7	3,029,297	545,274	888,955	1,000,000	850,757	–255,688	–102,275	–153,413
8	3,271,641	588,895	889,605	1,000,000	785,920	7,221	2,889	4,333
9	3,533,372	636,007	888,955	1,500,000	715,571	–207,160	–82,864	–124,296
10	3,816,042	686,888	889,605	1,500,000	639,243	100,307	40,123	60,184

[a] From Table 7.18.
[b] The interest on a 15-year mortgage for $13.2 million at 8.5%, includes 5 point, straight-lined depreciation over 27.5 years.

163

TABLE 7.20A   Golden Arms, Tax Consequences of Sale of Property

Sale of building		$30,000,000
Fixed plant and improvements	$20,300,000	
Less accumulated depreciation	9,587,645	
Net fixed plant and improvements		10,712,355
Cost of land		2,000,000
Gain on sale		17,287,645
Capital gains tax (15%)		2,593,147
After tax gain on sale		14,694,499

TABLE 7.20B   Golden Arms, Cash Gain from Sale of Property

Sale of property	$30,000,000
Less:	
Tax liability	2,593,147
Loan balance	7,238,155
Cash gain from sale	20,168,698

TABLE 7.21   Golden Arms, Cash Flow Statement

Year	Net Income[a]	Depreciation[a]	Equity Payments	Capital Contributions[b]	Gain on Sale of Land[c]	Net Cash Flows
0	$0	$0	$0	$10,000,000		−$10,000,000
1	−591,530	1,074,205	467,550			482,675
2	−302,882	1,098,905	507,292			796,023
3	−465,847	1,039,105	550,412			573,258
4	−318,156	985,805	597,197			667,649
5	−464,188	937,705	647,958			473,517
6	−303,179	894,805	703,035			591,626
7	−153,413	888,955	762,793			735,542
8	4,333	889,605	827,630			893,937
9	−124,296	888,955	897,979			764,658
10	60,184	889,605	974,307		$20,168,698	21,118,487

[a] From Table 7.18.
[b] From Table 7.8.
[c] From Tables 7.20A and 7.20B.

NPV at 12% = $210,180
IRR = 12.32%

TABLE 7.22 Golden Arms, Cash Flow Statement (without land sale)

Year	Net Income[a]	Depreciation[a]	Equity Payments	Capital Contributions[b]	Net Cash Flows[c]
0	$0	$0	$0	$10,000,000	–$10,000,000
1	–591,530	1,074,205	467,550	0	482,675
2	–302,882	1,098,905	507,292	0	796,023
3	–465,847	1,039,105	550,412	0	573,258
4	–318,156	985,805	597,197	0	667,649
5	–464,188	937,705	647,958	0	473,517
6	–303,179	894,805	703,035	0	591,626
7	–153,413	888,955	762,793	0	735,542
8	4,333	889,605	827,630	0	893,937
9	–124,296	888,955	897,979	0	764,658
10	60,184	889,605	974,307	0	–24,518

[a] From Table 7.18.
[b] From Table 7.8.
[c] From Tables 7.20A and 7.20B.

NPV at 12% = –$5,867,929
IRR = –8.88%

The ability of an apartment complex to generate cash flow has to do with location. As with all real estate, location is always a key factor in determining value. Location is important because it will impact the demand for the apartments. Location is multidimensional and can impact a complex's cash in many different ways.

The long-term demand for apartments grows in our mobile, dynamic, and transient society. In terms of the risk-return outcomes, the strong long-term fundamentals in this market tend to make apartments a good investment opportunity. This is true even when cyclical variations in apartment demand occur. This growth is driven by an expanding population resulting from (1) immigration; (2) the life cycle of young adults leaving home and renting before they are ready for the responsibilities of home ownership; (3) the transitory housing needs of an increasingly mobile society; and (4) the graying of the baby boom population whose members increasingly find renting preferable to home ownership. These strong fundamentals will tend to counter cyclical fluctuations in the housing rental market.

Attractive risk-return outcomes can often be found in the rental housing market by "thinking outside the box." School buildings, factories, office buildings, warehouses, and department stores have all been profitably converted into apartments in recent years. Such properties may frequently be acquired at a low cost because they have been devalued in terms of their traditional uses. Often such properties offer excellent locations, but have not been thought of in terms of their potential for rental housing.

CHAPTER 8

Condominiums

Physically, condos are individually owned units in an apartment-style building, but condominiums are really about lifestyle choices. This is true in two senses. First, the condo represents an alternative lifestyle choice to a traditional single-family residence. "Residential condos" cost less to build, usually cost less to maintain, often offer an automatic sense of community and there is no lawn to mow! Secondly, there is a "destination condo" syndrome that conceptually is related to timeshare properties, but takes the ownership form of a condominium. A condo in Hawaii, the Barbados, Orlando, Palm Springs, wherever; like timeshares, this is the stuff from which dreams are made. Own a little bit of paradise, who can resist?

From an investment perspective, opportunities may be found in both types of condos. However, "proceed with caution!" Although condos (compared to single-family residences) are less costly to build, may be less costly to maintain, and often do not require the personal involvement that renting a single-family residence does, there is a potential drawback. Condos historically are often slower to appreciate than single-family residences in boom times and depreciate faster than single-family residences in bad times. While the market cycle pricing of condos may inhibit their desirability as an investment property, condos have countervailing advantages: ease of maintenance and upkeep, less administrative input from the investor, and greater liquidity in buying and selling (because of the homogeneous properties of condominium properties.) It is an axiom in real estate that all real property is unique, because its physical location is unique. Condominiums may prove an exception to that because other properties in the condominium association are excellent substitutes for any give property within that condominium.

Alternatively, much of the "destination condo" market is a rather poor investment. That is, these properties are marketed with intense selling pressure on the basis of an emotional appeal and thus are overpriced as an investment. An exception to this caveat would, of course, be buying a destination condo on the secondary market at a steep discount.

RESIDENTIAL CONDOS

Condominiums may be described as a hybrid form of real estate ownership. Condo owners hold a deeded title to the specific area occupied by their unit, not to the land beneath. As a result, condos are characteristically built to maximize the value of the land underneath them. Large, multistoried buildings composed on many individual units are commonplace. The owners of the different condo units jointly own the common areas such as the ground, pool, walkways, recreational areas, elevators, and the like. If the condo owner finances the property, the unit will have a separate mortgage, will pay a property tax on the unit and a pro rata share of the common area, and pay a monthly maintenance fee to the condo association for common expenses. A board of directors elected by the condo owners will govern the complex, making a set of rules controlling the usage of the individual units and common areas and will assess each unit a maintenance fee.

When a condo is being considered as an investment, the purchaser should evaluate the more than the specific unit under consideration. Because the investor is buying into the whole of the condo association, the costs, risks, and nuances should be carefully evaluated as well. Condo associations can and do make rules about whether or not units can be rented and, if allowed, the terms under which the units they can be rented. The condo associations make rules about the use of the common area (no softball on the lawn) and individual units (no hanging towels on the balcony). Consequently, the policy of the condo association towards landlords and tenants should be thoroughly explored by the investor.

The existence of a common interest has financial implications as well. The financial health of the condo should be investigated. Are all owners current in their condo fees? Are any "special assessments" likely? What does the condo budget look like? Find out if there are any liens outstanding against the condominium association. Is there any existing litigation (or threat of litigation) against the condo association? Is it structurally sound? Are there any environmental concerns such as the presence of lead paint or asbestos? Obtain a certificate of insurance showing how much the condo board has purchased to cover damages to the common areas. Get a statement of the percentage of occupancy of the condominium complex. This may alert you to potential problems if the occupancy rate is low.

Condominiums are sometimes confused with townhouses and cooperatives. These two forms of ownership share the ownership of "commons" as condo owners, but differ in other respects. *Townhouses* are usually a series of single-story or multistory units that are linked to each other horizontally by common walls. Townhouse owners hold title to their units and the land beneath them, so townhouse units cannot be stacked on top of each other. All townhouse owners own common areas jointly. Townhouse owners pay property taxes on their individual units. A property owners' association usually manages the townhouse complex and collects fees from all owners in order to maintain common areas. *Cooperatives* (co-ops) are formed by cooperative arrangement. A corporation holds title to all associated real estate. Buyers purchase stock in the co-op corporation and are considered shareholders, not owners of real property. Each shareholder holds a lease to his unit that runs for the life of the corporation. The corporation pays taxes. Any mortgages are normally held and paid by the corporation. All costs to operate the property are shared by shareholders. An administrative board must usually approve new cooperative shareholders.

A positive attribute of investing in residential condos is that this form of ownership appears to be increasingly conducive to modern lifestyles. Baby boomers who have raised their children in the traditional single-family home now want a smaller, more compact home. A home without maintenance responsibilities that offers an instant sense of community is doubly attractive. Young professional couples (Dinks: Double income no kids), who have delayed the child bearing decision, find condos offer exactly the type of life style they are seeking. Young unmarried professionals either living together or singly, often have an affinity for the carefree lifestyle condominiums afford. The fit between these individuals and the lifestyles they prefer has increased the demand for condominiums.

Twenty years ago, condominiums carried the connotation of a residence somewhat inferior to the traditional single-family home. No more. Today condos are universally accepted on a par with single-family residences. Condos are scattered throughout the urban and suburban landscape. Condos are available at every level of luxury and finish that could be desired.

The wide acceptance of condos, indeed the preference for condos, has created increasing demand for this type of residence. This demand is both for ownership and rentals. Normally, this would bode well for the investor, implying the likelihood of higher rents and property values.

The fly in the ointment is the rather elastic supply of condos. When condo prices rise and it becomes profitable to build more, developers flood in, resulting in increasing supply. This leads to a glut the market causing prices and rents to decrease. The cobweb effect of less short-run supply, higher prices, more long-run supply, and lower prices is common to many areas of real estate, but none more than condos.

Investors need to be cautious about the market's stage in this cycle when considering investing in a residential condo. Obviously, the investor would do well to buy when the market has excess supply. (When condos are a drug on the market and the conventional wisdom says never invest in a condo.) The investor should also consider selling that condo when there are conditions of excess demand (When it is hard to find a condo to buy or rent. When the conventional wisdom is that condos are the way to turn lead into gold.)

A powerful investment strategy for condos involves the conversion of hotels and apartment buildings into condominiums. Particularly in urban areas, a hotel or apartment may have deteriorated over the years and is no longer attractive for its original function. Such properties are often not profitable and even if they are profitable, they do not generate sufficient capital to put into refurbishing the property to increase its attractiveness. Even if they produced such capital, the market they serve is not sufficiently attractive to warrant the expenditure.

Such properties are often ripe for conversion to condos. As long as such properties are well located they have potential for success in the condo market, even though they did not have success as hotels or apartments. Their lack of success in the old format usually means they can be acquired cheaply. As long as the building is structurally sound, apartment and hotel design is usually amenable to a condo format. The costs of redesigning and refurbishing the interior of the building are often much less than the cost of new construction. Selling the condos means the investor can expect a quick return on his or her money.

DESTINATION CONDOS

There is currently a boom in destination condos. The effect of the tragedy of 9/11 was to reduce the desire of many individuals and families to vacation internationally. Thoughts turned to the possibilities of vacationing domestically or within "safe" areas such as Mexico or the Caribbean. The focus of individual's vacation or "getaway" desires centered on attractive destinations that were unaffected by terrorism or the threat of war. The desirability of destinations market was further increased by the first baby boomers reaching retirement age. They too desired a "dream" destination to escape the cares and worries of their lives.

This desire was at first met by timeshares, which prospered by offering a portion of a property during a particular time period in a high-pressure, emotionally charged atmosphere. Timeshares were wildly successful (for the sellers) and prospered. They prospered by basically selling a dream in a context that was not price sensitive (see Chapter 11). Is price really a consideration when one has a chance to achieve paradise?

However, timeshares could not reach a significant part of that "destination" market because many people were suspicious of the timeshare format. After all, what does one really own when one "owns" two weeks at a particular property? There is no deed in the traditional sense. This concern effectively cut off timeshares from a significant part of the destination market.

It did not take timeshare developers long to realize how they could access this larger market. Thus, the concept of the "destination condo" was born. The same sales techniques that were so successful with timeshares were brought over to the destination condo market. Developers worked very hard to build condos in attractive settings and provide amenities in the common areas that were highly desirable. Such attractive properties were wrapped in a "hard sell."

Developers of destination condos offer contests in which the "winners" win a free weekend at this wonderful condominium, where they will be exposed to a high-powered sales pitch. Or developers may offer a valuable prize to individuals willing to come to the condominium, where they will be exposed to exceptional sales pressure. Many succumb to this effort and live to regret the day. Not because the condominium is less than what was promised (although this does happen) in the sales effort, but because the price paid was way above the "market" price of the property. The market price for a destination condo is determined in the resale market by the forces of supply and demand in a context in which the emotional appeal of a particular condo is ruthlessly reduced to its value in economic terms. As a result, the secondary market for a given condo, no matter how desirably located or well appointed, is almost always priced well below its price on the primary market (when bought directly from the developer) with discounts running to 30% not uncommon.

This means the wise investor would never buy from a developer, but will always look to the resale market for a purchase.

Selling practices on the secondary market are a far cry from the selling blitz the developer puts on. Condos in the resale market are generally listed with real estate agents and become part of the generalized supply of available residential housing. Some real estate brokers specialize in condos, or even condos from a particular condominium complex, if it is large enough. However, they are generally not aggressive sellers. Basically, the buyers must come to them.

A second issue determining the value of the condo has to do with the condo fee. The condo association through its governing board sets the condo fee. Condo owners elect the governing board. However, as a condominium is developed and has not yet "sold out" or finished its final phase, the developer will own most of the condo units and therefore control the governing board. It is not unheard of for the governing board under these circumstances to award generous maintenance contracts to a management company owned by the developer. Thus, the developer not only profits from the sale of the condos, but from the continuance of the condo association. To the extent that such excessive condo fees are "locked in" they can further depress the resale market for the condos.

Another problem from an investment perspective is that the supply of destination condos in the long run is highly elastic. If, as a result of a region's popularity as a destination, demand increases pushing up condo prices, more destination condos will be built causing price to fall. The Orlando, Florida market provides a good example of increased demand inducing an overbuilt supply of condos, depressing condo prices excessively.

In all fairness to the possibility of a destination condo being constructed in a truly unique location, where replication is not possible, then the supply of condos would be highly inelastic. If demand were to increase rapidly, prices might increase even faster because supply was unable to keep pace.

Flipping Destination Condos

A particular type of "investing" in destination condos has become an easy path to riches in some circles. It is asserted that flipping "preconstruction" condos can make "big bucks." This opportunity is created when developers offer the lowest prices to buyers before the condos are completed (or even before they are begun). Some purchasers buy with only the thought of selling as the condo nears completion or is finished for a quick profit. Thus, the condos are flipped.

Consider a hypothetical condominium apartment that is expected to sell for $225,000, but have a preconstruction price of $175,000. An investor, who expects the value to increase, signs a contract agreeing to purchase the condo when it is completed for $175,000, arranges for a mortgage and puts $2,000 down as a binder. When the investor's unit is ready, he does a "double closing," taking title to the property from the developer and immediately reselling it to another buyer for $225,000. Sometimes double closings can be avoided, and costs lowered, when developers agree to waive clauses in condo purchase contracts that bar investors from assigning the contracts to another buyer. Some condo developers charge nothing to waive clauses barring purchase contract assignments; others do so for a fee. Without the double closing, the $2,000 up-front reaps a quick $50,000 on the flip! If the double closing is necessary, of course the profit would be reduced by legal fees and other closing-related costs the investor would pay, but these will be minor compared to the gain.

The risk in all this is that the condo price does not rise or, even worse, that the investor may not be able to find a buyer at all and have to take possession and live in it or sell the condo at a fire sale price.

Selling a lot of units "preconstruction" to investors often benefits the builder. Developers usually have to presell a certain percentage of units in order to qualify for a loan to finance construction. Also, the early sales can be used as evidence of strong demand to prospective buyers. Some developers even make contractual commitments to raise prices when predetermined sales thresholds are passed—a major motivation for bargain hunters to put down deposits in the earliest stages of a development. Contractual commitments to raise unit prices then promotes the appreciation that can make flipping profitable.

Aside from the risk to the investor that the market for condos will fall before getting a chance to flip the property, where the relationship between the investor and the developer is anything but arm's length, the relationship between the developer and the "preconstruction" investor may appear questionable to the bank that finances the developer or to the eventual buyers. Of course, such concerns are unlikely if the market stays strong and all participants come away satisfied. The problem is that condo markets are inherently volatile (at least more so than residential housing). If the developer winds up defaulting because of a spike in interest rates, some economic calamity, or simple overbuilding in that particular market, you can bet that the aggrieved parties will be looking for someone to blame.

ILLUSTRATION #1: SEDGEWICK CONDOS

The Sedgewick Arms had been a small four-story hotel with 20 rooms located adjacent the city's business district for 70 years. At one time, it had the reputation of being one of the best places to stay in town. Sadly, that day has long gone. The hotel had antiquated plumbing, no air conditioning (and this was a town that became hot in the summer), a quaint, but excruciatingly slow elevator, and had become generally dingy over the years. The hotel had been allowed to deteriorate because it was caught up in a contested estate for years and no one took responsibility for running it properly. Once the title was clear, the hotel was sold to Betty and Bob James for $2.2 million. Betty and Bob had an idealistic vision of turning the hotel into an executive urban bed and breakfast. They spent considerable money renovating the first two floors along the lines of what they imagined an "English Country House" would look like. Two hard years, of trying unsuccessfully to make that business work, left them worn out, dispirited, and broke. They wanted out. They were eager sellers, but there was no around one who wanted to buy the hotel/bed and breakfast.

Hector Paniagua was an entrepreneur who had an MBE (minority business enterprise) construction company. Hector got a fair amount of work from the city renovating schools and other municipals, but he had not made a lot of money doing that work. He had just finished constructing eight townhomes on the edge of the city and was amazed by the strong demand for these properties. He had made more money on that project than he had made in the previous three years of business.

Acquisition Stage

Hector had heard about the Sedgewick Arms and thought he might be able to convert that property into a condominium. He investigated the property and found that he could purchase it for $1.8 million. That was a lot of money, but Hector felt that good building locations in the city were few and far between. Hector found the building structurally sound, but in need of substantial upgrading. Hector thought that his hard costs for converting the building into 12 modest, 1,800-square-foot condominiums would be about $40 per square foot. That would cost $864,000 in total. He asked some more experienced developers about the soft costs in this type of project. They had told him that condo conversions required a lot of legal work and his soft cost could easily run to 25% of the project costs. Hector decided to budget $400,000 for soft costs.

It was Hector's impression that there had been a number of luxury condos brought to the market in that city over the past year for prices ranging from $700,000 to $1.2 million, but nothing was being built for middle-class people. Hector thought if the Sedgewick Arms condominiums were priced at $320,000, they would sell like hotcakes. At that price the numbers looked good to Hector. Hector talked to his banker, who liked his plan and agreed to an interest only loan of $2.3 million for 18 months at 12% for Hector's project, but did not want to lend him more than that. Hector would secure this loan personally and a first mortgage on the property. Hector then found that the City's Economic

Development Committee would lend him $600,000 to do the project because it constituted a "civic improvement." The loan would also be an interest only loan for 18 months at 14% and they wanted a second mortgage on the building. This loan meant that Hector would have to put about $250,000 of his own money into the project and that would take all of Hector's capital. Hector decided to take the risk.

The resultant cash flows for the Sedgewick Arms conversion are presented in Table 8.1. As can be seen, the hard costs Hector anticipated came in on budget. The soft costs were higher than anticipated, both the legal cost of creating a condominium and the marketing of his projects. Towards the end of the first year, when the project was almost completed, Hector saw that he would soon run out of cash. He decided to sell two

TABLE 8.1 Sedgewick Condos, Acquisition Period Cash Flows

	Year 1	Year 2
Uses:		
Architectural drawings and plans	$35,000	$0
Legal and accounting fees	50,000	200,000
Bank loan interest[a]	138,000	138,000
Econ. development loan interest[b]	42,000	42,000
Construction costs[c]	864,000	0
Selling and marketing costs	0	75,000
Building and land[d]	1,800,000	0
Total cash out	2,929,000	455,000
Sources:		
Bank mortgage loan	2,300,000	0
Economic development loan	600,000	0
Equity[e]	250,000	234,000
Preconstruction sales	500,000	0
Total cash in	3,650,000	234,000
Cash balance	721,000	–221,000

[a] The loan balance is drawn down evenly over the first year and only used for six months the second year.
[b] The loan balance is drawn down evenly over the first year and only used for six months the second year.
[c] Construction costs = $40 per sq. ft. × 1,800 sq. ft. × 12.
[d] The building has a value of $800,000, the underlying land $1 million.
[e] The equity in the second year is effective equity provided by preconstruction sales of $500,000.

units on a "preconstruction" basis for $250,000 each. He found another local investor who believed in his project and thought the opportunity to purchase the two condominiums below the market was a good deal. Hector insisted that part of the deal was the investor actually close on the properties immediately and pay for them. This the investor did, and Hector raised another $500,000 to finance the projects expenses with.

Hector found that his assessment of the market was correct. Within three months he had sold the remaining 10 condos for $320,000 each, and within six months he had closed on them. As can be seen from Tables 8.2A this generated total sales of $3.7 million. Given his expenses and tax liabilities, Hector's gain from the renovating the Sedgewick Arms into the Sedgewick Condominiums is $268,600 dollars (Table 8.2B.) Hector earned an excellent return on his initial investment of $250,000.

TABLE 8.2   Sedgewick Condos, Profit and Loss Statement

Sale of condos[a]	$3,700,000
Cost of building	1,800,000
Constructions costs	864,000
Miscellaneous costs[b]	360,000
Interest costs	360,000
Gain on sale	316,000
Income tax[c]	47,400
After-tax gain on sale	268,600

[a] Two condos were sold at the end of the first year at a preconstruction price of $250,000 each. The remaining 10 condos were sold for an average of $320,000 each in the first six months of the second year.
[b] Architectural, legal, accounting and sales costs.
[c] This project qualifies for capital gains treatment, although the first year there was a loss generating a tax credit. The tax is net over two years.

TABLE 8.2B   Sedgewick Arms, Cash Gain from Sale of Property

Sale of property	$3,700,000
Less:	
Tax liability	47,400
Loan balance	2,900,000
Equity contribution	$484,000
After-tax gain on sale	268,600

It should be noted that high return is always associated with high risk. Hector earned this outstanding return by taking on substantial risk. In the first place, Hector was only marginally capitalized. When his expenses ran a little higher than anticipated, the whole project could have well foundered on a lack of liquidity had Hector been unable to sell the two condominium units. In addition, Hector could have encountered expensive hidden structural defects in the building during the renovation process. This could easily have increased his costs to the point where the project was not profitable. In the third place, Hector could have misjudged the market for the type of condominiums he developed or, even though he judged the market correctly when the project began, market conditions had changed and were no longer favorable. In either case he may not have found a ready market for the condominiums. With his limited financing, Hector could not have afforded to hold onto those units until market conditions improved. They would have to have been sold at fire sale prices resulting in a substantial loss for Hector.

ILLUSTRATION #2: SEDGEWICK ARMS WITH PRECONSTRUCTION INVESTMENT

Juan Mendoza was a successful restaurateur in the city where Hector did the Sedgewick Arms conversion. He owned three prosperous restaurants that were managed by his children and he was semiretired. Juan knew Hector Paniagua socially. When he heard about Hector's cash flow problems, he thought he could help Hector (and himself) by purchasing the two preconstruction condos Hector was offering for sale. Juan was able to secure conventional 15-year mortgages on each of the two properties for $220,000 at 7.25% and two points. Each of the properties has closing costs of $6,500 of which $3,000 were escrows monies. Juan bought the properties in December and resold them in May (Table 8.3)

The resultant cash flows from these transactions are depicted in Tables 8.4A and 8.4B. In order to accomplish this investment, Mr. Mendoza was required to put up equity of $109,700. After selling the condos at the expected price of $320,00 each, Mr. Mendoza reaped an after tax gain of $42,581. Certainly, this was not a bad return on his investment of $109,700 for five months. To be sure, Mr. Mendoza experienced less risk than Hector Paniagua because he had a shorter holding period. However, if the market for condos had soured during this five-month period, Juan was on the hook for $500,000 worth of condos. Had interest rates spiked violently during this period of time, Mr. Mendoza may well have experienced a very painful loss.

TABLE 8.3 Sedgewick Condos Preconstruction Investment,[a] Cash Flows Out

Item	December	January	February	March	April	May	Total Cash Flows
Interest points[b]	$17,600						$17,600
Interest payments[c]	0	$0	$0	$0	$0	$0	0
Equity payments[c]	0	0	0	0	0		0
Closing costs, except escrows	3,500						3,500
Escrows	3,000					−3,000	0
Legal fees	1,500						1,500
Real estate sales commission[d]						44,800	44,800
Initial equity	85,600						85,600

[a] On the purchase of two condos for $250,000 each and their subsequent sale for $320,000 each.
[b] Two points.
[c] On two $220,000 15-year mortgages at 7.25% with a total monthly payment of $4,017.
[d] 7%.

TABLE 8.4   Sedgewick Condos Preconstruction Investment, Profit and Loss Statement

Sale of condos[a]	$640,000
Sales commission[b]	44,800
Interest costs	33,426
Miscellaneous costs[c]	5,000
Cost of condos	500,000
Gain on sale	56,774
Income tax[d]	14,194
After-tax gain on sale	42,581

[a] Two condos were sold for $320,000 each.
[b] From Table 8.3.
[c] Closing costs other than escrow and legal fees.
[d] This investment did not qualify for capital gains treatment because it was not held for 6 months. Mr. Mendoza's effective tax rate is 25%.
Note: Depreciation was not charged since investment was for five months.

TABLE 8.4B   Sedgewick Condos Preconstruction Investment, Cash Gain from Sale of Property

Sale of property	$640,000
Less:	
Tax liability	14,194
Loan balance	0
Equity contribution[a]	1,500
After-tax gain on sale	42,581

[a] The initial equity contribution plus P&I payments on the mortgages.

ILLUSTRATION #3: SWISS ALPS CONDOS

The small city renowned for its beauty was nestled beneath majestic snow-capped mountains. The town was also the home of a large university, several prestigious research institutes, and a few small, but rapidly expanding high tech companies. The town residents were so enamored of the way the town was that they passed a series of "green belt" statutes. These statutes created a perpetual no-development zone for three miles around the city and prohibited new construction within the city. The effect of this legislation was to fix the supply of housing. As the university continued to grow and the various businesses that were in town continued to expand, the cost of housing soared. (The average price of a single-family residence in the city had skyrocketed to $500,000.) While no new buildings were permitted, conversion of existing structures was permitted by exception when deemed advantageous to the community.

Joe Dow was a graduate of the university. Unable to find a job in his specialty (German history), Joe became an entrepreneur and started a landscaping company. Over time, the landscaping company grew to have $3 million sales and was quite profitable. Joe was well aware of the shortage of housing in town, especially for university students.

Joe was aware of what had once been a Victorian mansion two blocks from the university. The old house was currently cut up into nine shabby student apartments and had become increasingly dilapidated over the years. The neighbors considered it an eyesore. The apartments generated a cash flow of $100,000 per year and the owner had put the property up for sale with an asking price of $1.2 million. The real estate community considered the price outrageous. Joe wondered if the property might be worth more if it was converted to a condominium. He thought that condos could be offered to professors and administrators at the university for a price comparable to single-family housing and that the location of the property would guarantee strong demand.

Joe secured a six-month option to purchase the property for $1.2 million for $10,000. During this time, he hired an architect to prepare a plan for renovating the structure into five separate condominiums and submitted that plan to the local planning board. The plan called for exterior renovations that would transform the building into a "Swiss chalet" like structure with five interior condo units ranging in size from 1,100 sq. ft. to 2,000 sq. ft. Joe had secured a local contractor who was willing to do the renovations for $560,000 (8,000 sq. ft. at $70 per sq. ft.). The neighbors thought this plan would represent a definite improvement in the property and so the local planning board approved it. Joe would call the condominium the "Swiss Alps Condos."

Joe figured the entire project would take a year to complete and cost around $1.9 million. Joe found a local banker willing to give him an 11% building loan for $1.5 million and 3 points, which Joe had to secure with his personal residence and business. Joe had $200,000 in savings and thought he could get the remainder by taking out a secured loan for $200,000 against his landscaping equipment. On that basis he obtained a conventional five-year loan from a different bank for $200,000 at 12% plus 1 point.

As can be seen from the data presented in Table 8.5, Joe's cost estimate turned out to be about $150,000 too low and he started to run out of cash about three-fourths of the way through the year. Joe asked his bank for an additional loan who refused. This situation was remedied by accelerating his sales by one unit that was sold—to the banker's son—for $400,000. The remaining four units were sold almost immediately upon completion for an average of $500,000 a unit. (Joe literally had buyers lined up at his office to be sure of getting a unit.)

The result of this development was to generate an after-tax profit of $281,496 (Tables 8.6A and 8.6B). This represented a more than doubling of Joe's $200,000 investment. Of course, Joe mortgaged himself up to his neck to do the condo conversion. Had the market fallen apart on Joe, the outcome would be very different and much less satisfactory. Although, given the context of such a limited supply of housing, and constantly increasing demand for housing, there does not appear much risk of the market going bad for Joe.

TABLE 8.5   Swiss Alps Condos, Acquisition Period Cash Flows

	Year 1
Uses:	
Property option	$10,000
Architectural drawings and plans	85,000
Legal and accounting fees	55,000
Bank loan interest[a]	112,500
Business equipment loan interest[b]	2,000
Business equipment loan equity[b]	0
Construction costs[c]	560,000
Selling and marketing costs	22,000
Building and land[d]	1,200,000
Total cash out	2,046,500
Sources:	
Bank mortgage loan	1,500,000
Business equipment loan	200,000
Equity	200,000
Preconstruction sales[e]	400,000
Total cash in	2,300,000
Cash balance	253,500

[a] The loan balance of $1.5 million is drawn down evenly over the first year plus 2 points.
[b] Represents 12 months of P&I payments on a conventional 5 year loan for $200,000.
[c] Construction costs = $40 per sq. ft. × 1,800 sq.ft. × 12.
[d] The Building has a value of $400,000, the underlying land $800,000.
[e] One unit was sold preconstruction for $400,000 in order to augment cash flow.

TABLE 8.6   Swiss Alps Condos, Profit and Loss Statement

Sale of condos[a]	$2,400,000
Cost of building	1,200,000
Constructions costs	560,000
Miscellaneous costs[b]	172,000
Interest costs	114,500
Gain on sale	353,500
Income tax[c]	53,025
After-tax gain on sale	300,475

[a] Two condos were sold at the end of the first year at a preconstruction price of $250,000 each. The remaining 10 condos were sold for an average of $320,000 each in the first six months of the second year.
[b] Option, architectural, legal, accounting and sales costs.
[c] This project qualifies for capital gains treatment with an effective rate of 15%.

TABLE 8.6B   Swiss Alps Condos, Cash Gain from Sale of Property

Sale of property	$2,400,000
Less:	
Tax liability	53,025
Loan balance	1,500,000
Equity contribution	200,000
After-tax gain on sale	300,475

ILLUSTRATION #4: GOLDEN PALMS CONDOS

Jenny VanderValk and Eileen Cocoran had taught together in public schools for 25 years. For years they had vacationed at the "Golden Isles" resort community that was in commuting distance from where they lived. They thought they would take the generous retirement package the school system offered them and live in the "Golden Isles" forever. However, they could not afford to do so and give up work entirely, so they bought a 14-unit motel, "The Golden Palms," to augment their pension.

Over the past ten years, they had been able to extract a good living from the motel. Jenny and Eileen were the office staff and the maid service. They did it all themselves. The motel had a loyal following of vacationers who returned year after year. The Golden Palms had a great location, right on the major highway leading into town and two blocks from the ocean.

Jenny and Eileen had paid off their mortgage and owned the Golden Palms outright. Although they were now comfortable financially, the years had taken its toll on them and they were ready to give up the hard physical labor that operating a motel meant. They were ready to really retire this time. They had bought the Golden Palms tens years ago for $112,000. They were stunned then, when an offer came in from a big motel chain to buy their property for $1.5 million.

They were thinking this offer over and discussing it with their friends, when one of their "regulars" said she wished she could buy the motel unit she normally stayed in because she loved it so much. This got Jenny and Eileen thinking. They knew that many of the new resort buildings in town were "condos," but they were not sure exactly what that meant and they wondered if they could convert their motel to a condo and sell the units to their loyal and faithful customers. They called a lawyer friend and she assured them that it could be done.

The procedures for converting a standard titled real property in that state to a condominium regime were relatively simple. The lawyer though she could create 14 separate condos out of the 14 units and the office area, parking lot, swimming pool, and recreational area would be owned in common by all condo unit owners. The lawyer thought this would take about three months and $200,000.

A construction friend offered to remodel each of the units for $15,000 so that they would be easier to sell. Jenny and Eileen thought that would not be necessary, as they had a ready market for these units from their many customers. They knew that "ocean side" properties in the new big condos closer in to the heart of town sold in the $250,000–$400,000 range. These properties differed from their motel units in that they were generally much larger and had more amenities. However, these new resort condos had stiff condo maintenance fees (typically $3,000–$4,000 a year.).

They thought they would send a mailing to their customer list detailing their intentions to create a condominium and sell the 14 units for $279,000 each. They were very surprised when, within two weeks, they received 36 replies from families who said they were definitely interested. Jenny and Eileen then created the condominium and sold 13 units (reserving one for themselves) to their former customers within two months. To conform to the requirements of the law though, they had to "sell" their unit to themselves.

The financial outcome of this decision is detailed in Tables 8.7, 8.8A, and 8.8B. Jenny and Eileen did far better converting their motel to a condo than they would have done selling out to the large motel chain. They were able to sell their motel as condo units for a gross of $3,906,000 from which they netted $3,108,081.

TABLE 8.7   Golden Palms Condos, Cash Flows

	Year 1
Uses:	
Legal fees	$200,000
Total cash out	200,000
Sources:	
Equity[a]	200,000
Total cash in	200,000
Cash balance	0

[a] The conversion occurred so quickly that legal expenses were treated as an account payable and paid from cash received from condo sales.

TABLE 8.8   Golden Palms Condos, Profit and Loss Statement

Sale of condos[a]	$3,906,000
Fixed plant and equipment[b]	80,000
Depreciation	62,566
Net fixed plant and equipment	17,434
Land	32,000
Legal fees	200,000
Gain on sale	3,656,566
Capital gains tax[c]	548,485
After-tax gain on sale	3,108,081

[a] Fourteen condos at $279,000 each.
[b] The motel was initially purchased for $112,000: $32,000 for land and $80,000 for building and fixtures.
[c] This project qualifies for capital gains treatment with an effective rate of 15%.

TABLE 8.8B   Golden Palms Condos, Cash Gain from Sale of Property

Sale of property	$3,906,000
Less:	
Tax liability	548,485
Equity	249,434
After-tax gain on sale	3,108,081

ILLUSTRATION #5: PLEASURE WORLD CONDOS

Richard James had immigrated to America 30 years ago. Through hard work and luck, Richard had become one of the larger landlords in Tampa Bay, Florida. Essentially, Richard lived frugally, and invested everything he earned back into his business of renting homes. He owned 11 apartments with 130 separate tenants and 15 single-family homes. He worked to keep his homes in tip-top shape and gave good service to his tenants. He was proud that his four sons worked for him, along with half-dozen fellow countrymen. His business generated a cash flow of over a million dollars a year, and he estimated his net worth at $10 million. He was proud of the fact that in all his years he had never missed a mortgage payment or defaulted on a debt. In the business community, he was respected as a man of his word.

Richard was always on the lookout for a bargain. He loved a chance to buy distressed or undervalued properties. One day he received a call from a business acquaintance he knew from Tampa, but had moved to Orlando some years ago. His friend told him that he had become a developer of destination condos in the Orlando area. He told Richard "The Orlando market is crazy. People come from all over the world to visit Disney World. Many of those who come here are eager to buy a home here. It's a prestige thing. They pay for the address. Condos work well for them because, unlike a home, they don't have to be maintained and can be easily rented out. Demand is unlimited. Last year I built a small condominium for $2 million and sold it out in three weeks for $3 million. Soon I'll be as rich as you!"

Richard was impressed because he respected his friend as an honest person. His friend continued, "Right now I'm in the middle of building a $25 million condo, a hundred units. I've got a $20 million loan from a syndicate of insurance companies, but it's not enough. We had a strike, then a shortage of pipes, and then a shortage of roofing materials. We are way behind schedule. I'm running out of money. The project itself is golden. These units will sell like hot cakes for $400,000 apiece. Our cost will be $250,000. It's a regular gold mine. What I am going to do is sell some of these units on a preconstruction basis below market price to my friends. I'm going to sell these units at my cost of $250,000. In six months, you can turn around and flip these units for $400,000. You can't lose. Further, I'll allow you to sell the unit without actually taking possession. All you have to do is to make a commitment to buy the unit. When the units are finished a buyer will come along and he buys your right to buy the unit. You have almost no costs because you don't take title and you don't actually have to finance the properties." It's good for me because I can take your commitment to the bank and borrow money on that.

All this sounded pretty interesting to Richard. He knew people in Miami who had done exactly this and made some big bucks. "Why not?" thought Richard. This should be easy money. He told his friend he would commit for five units. Within a month Richard James had signed the contracts that committed him to purchasing five condo units at "Pleasure World" for $250,000 each when they were completed, or in six months, whichever came first.

Unfortunately, his friend ran into additional construction problems. He could not get an agreement with the Florida Department of the Environment over his drainage and use of Pleasure World's waterfront. Six months flew by and the condos were still not completed. Richard James was consequently forced to close on the units, even though they were not ready for occupancy. The close was "dry," with money to change hands when the units were completed. Richard arranged for individual mortgages of $200,000 on each unit (conventional 30-year fixed rate at 7% with 4 points) and put $250,000 of his own money into the units plus closing costs ($30,000). Two months later, the condos were completed.

Unfortunately, the bottom had just suddenly dropped out of the condo market. One month it was great, the next month kaput! The market succumbed to a sudden rise in interest rates, higher energy costs (which reduced the number of travelers), and a very large number of condo projects coming to the market at the same time. Richard received a few desultory offers for his units from "bottom feeders" which he rejected out of hand. "I'm not going to sell these units for $200,000!" he shouted at his now ex-friend.

Richard decided to dig his heels in and rent the units until the market revived. He hooked up with a foreign travel agent that specialized in bringing groups in from Hungary, Poland, and Romania. He leased the five units to the agency for a year for $1,200 a month per unit. At the end of the first year the market had still not improved and he rolled the lease over with the same travel agency for $1,250 per month. By the end of the second year, the market was slowing slight signs of recovery. Richard found another travel agency that catered to the Japanese and were willing to pay $1,400 per month. At the end of third year the market was definitely looking stronger, but had not yet recovered to previous highs. Richard listed his units (for a 6% sales commission) with a local real estate agent and sold all five units within one month for an average of $289,000 apiece.

Being forced to close on the properties moved Richard's equity contribution from virtually nothing to $340,000 (Table 8.9.) Even if all goes well subsequently, this will certainly reduce the relative return on his investment. If things do not go well, he will suffer a significant loss of capital.

As can be seen from Table 8.10, NOPAT is positive but small. Once the interest charges hit that cash flow, net income will turn substantially negative (Table 8.11.) Leverage is so high that he is unlikely to be able to make a profit unless rents are very, very strong. If rents were that strong however, he would probably not have a problem selling the condo units at a profit.

At this point it is very clear that Richard needs to cut his losses. There is a time not to throw good money after bad. Richard struggled, trying to avoid his initial losses consequent on the collapse of the condo market. However, at this point it is clear that staying in the market longer is likely to only lead to more red ink. Selling the condos at $289,000 stops the bleeding and ultimately generates $114,238 (Tables 8.12A and 8.12B).

TABLE 8.9 Pleasure World Condos, Acquisition Period Cash Flows

Uses:	
Closing costs	$30,000
Loan points	40,000
Legal expenses	20,000
Purchase condos[a]	1,250,000
Total cash out	1,340,000
Sources:	
Mortgage loan	1,000,000
Equity	340,000
Total cash in	1,340,000
Cash balance	0

[a] Each $250,000 condo is $200,000 improvements and $50,000 land.

TABLE 8.10 Pleasure World Condos, Holding Period NOPAT, Net-Operating Profits after Taxes

Year	Revenues[a]	Condo Fees[b]	Depreciation[c]	Property Taxes	EBIT	Taxes (40%)	NOPAT EBIT $(1 - tx)$
1	$54,000	$13,500	$28,790	$10,000	$1,710	$342	$1,368
2	$75,000	13,500	$36,364	$10,000	15,136	3,027	12,109
3	$84,000	15,120	$36,364	$10,000	22,516	4,503	18,013

[a] First year rents were $1,200 for nine months. Subsequent rents were for 12 months at $1,250 and $1,400 respectively.
[b] Condo fees are $300 per month.
[c] Straight line 27.5 years midmonth convention in third month. Depreciated over 15 years, double-declining balance, midquarter convention.

TABLE 8.11 Pleasure World Condos, Income Statement

Year	Revenues[a]	Condo Fees	Depreciation[a]	Property Taxes	Interest[b]	Earnings before Taxes	Taxes (40%)	Net Income
1	$54,000	$13,500	$28,790	$10,000	$109,678	-$107,968	-$43,187	-$64,781
2	75,000	13,500	36,364	10,000	68,944	-53,808	-21,523	-32,285
3	84,000	15,120	36,364	10,000	68,156	-45,640	-18,256	-27,384

[a] From Table 8.10.
[b] Interest on a $1 million mortgage for 30 years at 7% plus 4 points expensed in the first year.

TABLE 8.12 Pleasure World Condos, Tax Consequences of Sale of Condos

Sale of condos		$1,156,000
Less sales costs[a]		72,360
Net gain from sale		1,083,640
Building	$1,000,000	
Less accumulated Depreciation	101,517	
Net fixed plant and improvements		898,483
Cost of land		250,000
Gain on sale		7,517
Capital gains tax (15%)		1,128
After-tax gain on sale		6,390

[a] 6% sales commissions and $2,000 closing costs.

TABLE 8.12B   Pleasure World Condos, Cash Gain from Sale of Property

Net sale of condos	$1,083,640
Less:	
Tax liability	1,128
Loan balance	968,274
Cash gain from sale	$114,238

TABLE 8.13   Pleasure World Condos, Cash Flow Statement

Year	Net Income[a]	Depre- ciation[a]	Equity Pay- ments	Capital Contri- butions[b]	Gain on Sale of Land[c]	Net Cash Flows
0				$340,000		–$340,000
1	–$64,781	$28,790	$10,158			–46,149
2	–32,285	36,364	10,892			–6,813
3	–27,384	36,364	11,680		$114,238	111,538

[a] From Table 8.11.
[b] From Table 8.9.
[c] From Table 8.12B.

NPV at 12% = –$345,211

    The damage is totaled up in Table 8.13. Signing the contract to purchase the five condos at Pleasure World leads to a present value loss of $345,211. Flipping condos does not always go as planned. There are two ways to learn this lesson. One is from experience.

ILLUSTRATION #6: CROOKED KEY CONDO

Anne Smyth loved the ocean. She particularly loved visiting Crooked Key Island on Florida's Gulf Coast. She felt she could spend her whole life wandering through the huge nature preserve on Crooked Key. Crooked Key Island had the look of an undeveloped island, but was honeycombed with homes, cottages and occasional unobtrusive condominiums. Every year while she vacationed on the island she thought she would love to live there. She feared it would be impossible for she knew property on the island was frightfully expensive.

    At 50, Anne was twice divorced, no children, worked for an advertising agency in Los Angeles for $90,000 a year and had about

$100,000 in the bank. She lived in an apartment that she hated in Los Angeles. She knew even a small condo on Crooked Key cost upwards of $400,000. She wondered if the tax advantages of home ownership and the effect of financial leverage could give her an edge in affording such a home.

Anne searched the island and was fortunate to find the "dream" condo that she had always longed for. It was $489,000. She thought she might be able to buy it as a personal residence and then convert it into rental property. The renters would help to finance the property through their rents, and, eventually, she would be able to afford to live there herself—she hoped to be able to retire at 62, 12 years away. She decided to make an offer on the property at $489,000 with the sellers picking up all closing costs, subject to her being able to attain financing.

Financing this expensive a condo was a problem. Anne knew that her income alone would not support the necessary mortgage. She found a local bank that was willing to work with her. The $100,000 savings would only give her equity in the home of 20%. The bank had told her that if she could put 25% down on the house, they would count 75% of a lease towards her capacity to carry the mortgage. She borrowed $25,000 on a personal note to her brother. The bank treated this loan as a "gift" from her brother and allowed her to use it as a down payment. (Although her brother would actually gift her the money, she insisted that she would pay 6% interest on the loan if he would let her pay back the principle after 12 years.) That enabled her to put $125,000 down on the condo. She found a local rental agent who was able to get a year lease on the property for $1,800 a month ($1,440 after his 20% for managing the property.) The bank had offered a conventional 30-year $364,000 mortgage for 7% with the 25% equity. That mortgage would generate a monthly principle and interest payment of $2,422. That constituted 32% of her gross income, a figure the bank said was too high. However, the bank took 75% of her net rental income of $1,440 ($1,080) and subtracted that from the $2,422 P&I payment. That left $1,342, only 15% of her gross income. A figure the bank was comfortable with. Anne was able to buy the house. Now, she had to live with it.

The flow of NOPAT over a 12-year time horizon for Anne is weak (Table 8.14). This amount is certainly not large enough to carry the substantial interest charges. So net income (Table 8.15) starts out negative (at −$20,524) and by the 12th year is still negative (−$9,482.) On her $90,000 salary, what with the expenses of living in LA, she could not carry this charge. Note also, that net income would be another 25% worse if it were not for the substantial tax break she will earn. However, Ann thought the project was "doable" even though the cash flow was negative. Table 8.16 shows that cash flow in the first year will be −$14,150 and fall slowly to –$6,941 in the twelfth year. This is possible, though difficult, for Anne to do. It means 12 years of sacrifice, 12 years of self-denial, and 12 years of scrimping and saving. However, it can be done, and that, to Anne, is what is important.

After the 12th year she can return to Crooked Key and live year round in her own condo. At this point her mortgage balance will be $297,644. If she were able to refinance over another 30 years at the same rate, her payment would fall to $1,980. Between her pension and social security, that should afford a comfortable retirement for Anne.

However, a lot may happen over the 12-year period. It is certainly possible interest rates will fall and she could refinance saving considerable money. Another possibility is that rents on Crooked Key rise at more than 5%. This can happen either because Crooked Key continues to grow in popularity among renters or because there is a larger inflation in the overall economy. In either case it will benefit Anne as her mortgage is a fixed rate and she will continue to pay if off in cheaper and cheaper dollars. Better a debtor be...

TABLE 8.14 Crooked Key Condo, Holding Period NOPAT, Net Operating Profits after Taxes

Year	Revenues[a]	Property Manage-ment[b]	Depre-ciation[c]	Property Taxes[d]	EBIT	Taxes (20%)	NOPAT EBIT $(1 - tx)$
1	$21,600	$4,320	$10,072	$6,000	$1,208	$242	$967
2	22,680	$4,536	10,509	6,180	1,455	291	1,164
3	23,814	$4,763	10,509	6,365	2,177	435	1,741
4	25,005	$5,001	10,509	6,556	2,938	588	2,351
5	26,255	$5,251	10,509	6,753	3,742	748	2,993
6	27,568	$5,514	10,509	6,956	4,589	918	3,672
7	28,946	$5,789	10,509	7,164	5,483	1,097	4,387
8	30,393	$6,079	10,509	7,379	6,426	1,285	5,141
9	31,913	$6,383	10,509	7,601	7,421	1,484	5,937
10	33,509	$6,702	10,509	7,829	8,469	1,694	6,775
11	35,184	$7,037	10,509	8,063	9,575	1,915	7,660
12	36,943	$7,389	10,509	8,305	10,740	2,148	8,592

[a] Assumes an initial rent of $1,800 that appreciates 5% annually.
[b] Property management fee is 20% of gross revenue, but includes normal maintenance.
[c] Straight-line depreciation for 27.5 years, midmonth convention for the first month.
[d] Increase 3% annually.

TABLE 8.15 Crooked Key Condo, Income Statement

Year	Revenues[a]	Property Management[a]	Depreciation[a]	Property Taxes	Bank Interest[b]	Brother's Interest[c]	Earnings before Taxes	Taxes (20%)	Net Income
1	$21,600	$4,320	$10,072	$6,000	$25,363	$1,500	-$25,655	-$5,130.90	-$20,524
2	22,680	4,536	10,509	6,180	25,096	1,500	-25,141	-5,028.13	-20,113
3	23,814	4,763	10,509	6,365	24,809	1,500	-24,132	-4,826.45	-19,306
4	25,005	5,001	10,509	6,556	24,502	1,500	-23,063	-4,612.66	-18,451
5	26,255	5,251	10,509	6,753	24,172	1,500	-21,930	-4,386.05	-17,544
6	27,568	5,514	10,509	6,956	23,819	1,500	-20,729	-4,145.85	-16,583
7	28,946	5,789	10,509	7,164	23,440	1,500	-19,456	-3,891.26	-15,565
8	30,393	6,079	10,509	7,379	23,033	1,500	-18,107	-3,621.41	-14,486
9	31,913	6,383	10,509	7,601	22,598	1,500	-16,677	-3,335.40	-13,342
10	33,509	6,702	10,509	7,829	22,131	1,500	-15,161	-3,032.27	-12,129
11	35,184	7,037	10,509	8,063	21,630	1,500	-13,555	-2,710.98	-10,844
12	36,943	7,389	10,509	8,305	21,092	1,500	-11,852	-2,370.45	-9,482

[a] From Table 9.14.
[b] The interest on a 30 year conventional mortgage at 7%.
[c] Interest only at 6%.

TABLE 8.16 Crooked Key Condo, Cash Flow Statement

Year	Net Income[a]	Depreciation[a]	Bank Equity Payments	Net Cash Flows
1	–$20,524	$10,072	$3,698	–$14,150
2	–20,113	10,509	3,965	–13,568
3	–19,306	10,509	4,251	–13,048
4	–18,451	10,509	4,559	–12,500
5	–17,544	10,509	4,888	–11,923
6	–16,583	10,509	5,242	–11,316
7	–15,565	10,509	5,621	–10,677
8	–14,486	10,509	6,027	–10,004
9	–13,342	10,509	6,463	–9,295
10	–12,129	10,509	6,930	–8,550
11	–10,844	10,509	7,518	–7,853
12	–9,482	10,509	7,968	–6,941

[a] From Table 8.15.

SUMMARY

Condos are an up and coming area in real estate, but an area of limited potential for real estate investors. Increasing affluence, a desire to live in exotic getaway destinations, the desire for a "leisure" lifestyle, and retiring baby boomers drive demand for condos. On the other hand, condos compared to single-family residences are often slower to appreciate than single-family residences in boom times and depreciate faster than single-family residences in bad times.

Many real estate markets are cyclical. This is certainly true for the condo market. Wise investors always want to be sure they are buying at the bottom of the cycle, not the top. While condos do have some properties that make them desirable passive investment vehicles (ease of maintenance and upkeep, less of an administrative burden on the investor, and greater liquidity in buying and selling resulting from the homogeneous nature of properties within a condominium community), the investor pays for much of that with a condo maintenance fee.

Investors should especially be wary of the emotional appeal of the destination condo market, which works much the same as the market for timeshares (Chapter 9). That is, these properties are marketed with intense selling pressure on the basis of an emotional appeal and, thus, are overpriced as an investment. A preferred strategy would involve buying a destination condo on the secondary market at a steep discount.

Timeshares

A s a general rule, timeshares are not about making money. Timeshares are about fulfilling dreams. Timeshares are about pride of ownership Timeshares are about getting away to a place of beauty, relaxation, and pleasure in a world filled with problems and troubles. Timeshares are about a sense of predictability and permanence in an uncertain, chaotic world. Timeshares represent a significant and growing sector of the real estate market.

The timeshare industry is fast growing and worldwide. The concept of property as timeshares (that is, the ownership of a time interval at a particular piece of property) was originated in the French Alps in the 1970s. These property owners' primary desire was to trade the vacation they could have on their own property for a vacation on another property in a different location. The motivation was to be able to vacation in different parts of the world.

Today more than 3 million households own vacation intervals at nearly 4,500 resorts located in 81 countries. Vacationers around the world are turning to vacation ownership resorts as their preferred travel destination, with timeshare owners hailing from 174 countries. North America remains the global leader with nearly half of all the resorts and approximately two million owners. Europe is the second most dominant region for vacation ownership, with approximately 22% of owners worldwide and more than 1,000 resorts. Although timeshares are often bought on the basis of the ambiance and attributes of a particular property, only 2% of timeshare owners normally return to the same location at the same time each year.

This fact has important implications for investing in a timeshare. For reasons developed in this chapter, timeshares purchased directly from a developer are much more expensive than timeshares purchased as closeouts or resales. The timeshare is often purchased not for the particular amenities

195

of that timeshare, although they are frequently sold on that basis, but as a vehicle to trade for other timeshares. The key to successfully investing in a timeshare is then to purchase the highest quality unit (in terms of geographic location and time of the year) at the lowest price. Most first-time timeshare buyers do so before they understand the nature of the industry. This mistake is not only frequently made, but quite expensive!

THE TIMESHARE CONCEPT

The concept of a *timeshare* may be represented by the ownership of a particular piece of real estate for a particular time interval. (There are many different variations in this general concept.) The idea is you do not need to buy a condo in Orlando when you only plan to use it a week every spring. Instead of buying the whole condo, you buy that condo for a specific week of the year. This makes "ownership" much more affordable and available to a wider group of people. Quality timeshares (in terms of season and location) at the beginning of 2003 average $4,000 to $8,000 for a week's ownership at even the most desirable resorts.

With ownership you have the right to use that particular property during that particular week. While a given property might cost $240,000 to own entirely, one may be able to buy that particular week for $8,000. (Depending on variations in supply and demand, different weeks will have different prices.) From this perspective, the cost savings are obvious.

The immediate alternative to buying a timeshare is renting. A simple comparison of the costs of timesharing versus renting may be made as follows:

Cost of timeshare	$8,000
Opportunity cost of $8,000 @ 10%	800
Timeshare maintenance fee	500
Total cost of timeshare	1,300
Cost of renting equivalent property	1,500
Cost advantage to timeshare	+ 200

However, determining the relative desirability of timeshare ownership is more complex than this simple analysis suggests. Different real properties are never equivalent. Each parcel of real estate is differentiated by its location. "Here" is not the same as "there." In addition, timeshares are frequently located in resorts that offer a unique set of amenities. Individual tastes and preferences may well dictate that a particular timeshare by virtue of its uniqueness has no good substitute. The perception may well be that a particular timeshare has no peer and is therefor of great value.

Timeshare owners are attracted to this form of vacation primarily by the high standards of quality accommodations and services available at the resorts that they own and exchange. It is felt that these properties are better maintained and staffed than are properties that are merely rented. In addition, the location of these properties is felt to be superior to those available through the rental market. The leading industry association, the American Resort Developers Association (ARDA), asserts that over a third of initial timeshare buyers eventually purchase additional timeshare units.

While timeshares are literally located everywhere, many timeshares are in properties with stunning, highly desired locations. The heart of London, Paris, Tokyo, New York City all have timeshares. If the beach is your thing, from the pounding surf at Waikiki to the French Riviera, timeshare are there. Practically anywhere one could imagine as a desirable vacation destination will have timeshare properties located there. Timeshare resort amenities rival those of other top-rated resort properties and may include swimming pools, tennis, Jacuzzis, golf, bicycles, and exercise facilities. Also featured may be boating, ski lifts, restaurants, and equestrian facilities. Most timeshare resorts offer a full schedule of onsite or nearby sporting, recreational, and social activities for adults and children. The resorts are often staffed with well-trained hospitality professionals. Many timeshare resorts offer concierge services for assistance with visiting area attractions.

The attractions of timeshare ownership have an economic dimension. Timeshares offer individuals the opportunity to purchase fully furnished vacation accommodations for only a percentage of the cost of full ownership. For a one-time purchase price and payment of a yearly maintenance fee, purchasers own their property in perpetuity. The fact that owners share both the use and costs of upkeep of their unit and the common grounds of the resort property ensure that the property will be well maintained over time.

Unlike a hotel room or rental cottage, which requires payment for each use with rates that usually increase each year, ownership at a timeshare property enables vacationers to enjoy a resort, year after year. Timeshare owners may look forward to a lifetime of ownership with minimal exposure to inflation. Costs may be expected to only rise by the increase in maintenance costs.

Another dimension in determining the relative desirability of timeshare is the advantage of flexibility. An individual who rents a property for a vacation or getaway has wide latitude in determining where and when they will rent. Of course this latitude may be circumscribed by the need to reserve a property in advance or the absolute availability of desirable property ("Sorry, we are all full up"). In contrast, with a timeshare your access to the property during the defined time period is certain. If skiing is your thing and you have a strong desire to ski Vail every Christmas week, then a timeshare may well serve better than renting just to give assurance of an available property. Of course with a timeshare, if the kids are sick, a job crisis occurs, or Aunt Maude is dying, you may not be able to take advantage of your fixed time slot and the property would go unutilized.

As the original spur to create timeshares was to increase flexibility, not reduce it, there is a very large market for exchanging timeshares. There are two major exchange companies, Resort Condominiums International (RCI); and Interval International (II). Both companies link timeshare resorts together worldwide. When a timeshare owner desires to exchange their property for another, the exchange company is contacted and a request submitted. You offer the exchange company (there is a small fee to belong to an exchange company and a larger fee to actually make an exchange) your property and get the opportunity to use another property. Whether or not another timeshare owner takes your property, you get the opportunity to select and use an equivalent property.

There are certain controls to ensure that the exchange is fair. An off-season week somewhere generally cannot be exchanged for a prime time week elsewhere. It must be exchanged for an off-season week. This process is facilitated by the exchanges that publish full-color catalogs showing the various timeshare resorts worldwide. They then color code the various weeks of the year for each resort. RCI uses red, white, and blue. II uses red, yellow, and green. A red week with either RCI or II designates a week that is highly demanded. This might be winter at a ski resort or summer at a beach resort. A blue, or green, time is the off-season. This would be the opposite of the above example: summer at the ski resort and winter at the beach resort. White or yellow weeks are in between; not really prime season and not really the dead season. Obviously off-season weeks cost less to purchase. Prime season weeks cost more.

The exchange system works on what is known as a value-for-value system. Want the best weeks at the nicest resorts in the most sought after locations? Own something similar to exchange. Think this way: off-season gets off-season, prime season (red weeks) gets you the best.

A large factor in this equation is pride of ownership. In our culture, there is a significant difference between being an owner and a renter. Ownership implies personal and economic stability. Ownership implies being a good citizen, one who is committed to the community. Ownership implies economic success. Renting implies more transience and less stability: "Here today and gone tomorrow." Renting suggests a degree of impermanence, of less attachment to the community, of a more marginalized individual. While such stereotypes may not be accurate, they certainly exist and do affect behavior.

THE PRIMARY MARKET FOR TIMESHARES

Timeshares are originally offered to the market by a developer who has created a resort especially for that purpose or has converted a real estate property (usually a hotel) to that purpose. The advantages to the developer of creating timeshares are usually significant. Efficient markets in equilibrium bring price down to cost. The primary timeshare market does not appear to be efficient in that sense. The reason for that is the demand for timeshares tends to be a function of emotion and the ambiance offered by the property. "Oh, isn't this wonderful? Wouldn't you like to spend the rest of your life here?"

Developers work very hard to create an environment where the amenities offered by the timeshare stimulate demand. Developers of timeshares are given to having contests in which the "winners" win a free weekend in this fabulous resort where they will be exposed to a high-powered sales pitch. Or developers may offer a valuable prize to individuals willing to come to the resort where they will be exposed to exceptional sales pressure. Many succumb to this effort and live to regret the day. Not because the resort or timeshare is less than what was promised (although this does happen), but because the price paid was way above the "market" price of the property. The market price for a timeshare is determined in the secondary market by the forces of supply and demand in a context in which the emotional appeal of a particular timeshare is ruthlessly reduced to its value in economic terms. As a result, the secondary market for a given timeshare is almost always priced well below its price on the primary market with discounts running to 40% not uncommon.

THE SECONDARY MARKET FOR TIMESHARES

The secondary market for timeshares is not well centralized. Sometimes the resort in which the timeshare is located will maintain a secondary market for its timeshares. Some real estate brokers specialize in timeshares; other real estate brokers will list such properties, but do not make a special effort to do so. The Internet provides a medium for a significant part of the timeshare secondary market. The companies that facilitate timeshare exchanges offer listings for timeshare properties for sales (and rent as well). A number of timeshare owners associations (most notably the ARDA) also support an active secondary market for timeshares.

INVESTMENT POTENTIAL

From a buyer's perspective, timeshares have historically had little upside. This reflects the fact that, when bought from a developer, most timeshares are overpriced. As the timeshare owners become disillusioned with the timeshare, sooner or later they are dumped on the secondary market, depressing price in that market. On the secondary market, the price of timeshares is almost always below their replacement cost. At least this has been the experience of the last 30 years of this market.

Another problem from an investment perspective is that the supply of timeshares in the long run is highly elastic. If, as a result of a region's popularity or amenities demand increases, pushing up timeshare price, more timeshares are built when price exceeds costs, in turn causing price to fall as additional supply comes onto the market.

The Orlando, Florida market is a classical case of increased demand inducing an overbuilt supply in the timeshare market depressing timeshare prices. Timeshares became so popular in Orlando, because so many individuals were attracted by Disney World and other resorts located there, that many developers jumped into the market at the same time, building a tremendous supply of timeshares. This had a disastrous affect on the secondary market for timeshares in Orlando. If supply is not elastic because of environmental or other restriction on further construction, then it would be possible for increasing demand to push up price, but this requires a very special set of circumstances.

TIMING IN THE TIMESHARE MARKET

In the first decade of the 21st century, it appears that if the timeshare market were to ever have any investment appreciation potential, now is the time. This is possible because of the impact of 9/11 and the demographics of the U.S. population. The effect of 9/11 was to reduce the desire to travel, especially for travel by air and even more so for travel by air internationally. This reduced the demand for timeshare exchanges on both sides of the Atlantic and brought forth a large increase in timeshares on the market by owners anxious to avoid the carrying costs of timeshares they were not going to use. This situation had depressed the price of timeshares in general by 2003. This may reflect a temporary disequilibrium in the timeshare market that will dissipate as travel fears subside. If this occurs, timeshare prices might well rise in the near future.

The timeshare market is very attractive to retirees and in the United States the baby boomers are nearing that stage of their life. If the beginning of the baby boom may be reckoned as 1945, then the fist baby boomers will hit 65 in 2010. While some retirees will wait until that time to look into the timeshare market, it is not unlikely that some retirees will begin to plan for their future before they actually retire. The baby boomer group (those born between 1945 and 1955) now constitutes the largest single demographic force in the population. If these individuals enter the timeshare market in large numbers, then prices are sure to escalate as long as supply does not increase correspondingly.

THE EXCHANGE PROCESS

As indicated above, most timeshares are purchased with a view towards being able to exchange that timeshare for others. This opportunity is one of the most attractive features of owning timeshares. For this reason, the exchange power of a timeshare unit is one of the most important factors in determining its value.

While exchanges may be arranged privately on a one-to-one basis, independent companies that specialize in that business arrange most exchanges. The two largest and most reputable are Resort Condominiums International (RCI) and Interval International (II). Most timeshares use one or the other of these firms, while some use both. In addition there are numerous small exchange companies that specialize in particular types of resorts or regions, as well as major resort companies (e.g., Marriott International) that develop timeshare resorts and maintain a "private" internal exchange system.

As can be seen in the data in Table 9.1, RCI is the larger of the two companies.

TABLE 9.1   RCI and II Compared

	RCI	II
Resorts serviced	3,700	1,900
Participants	3,500,000	1,300,000
Confirmed exchanges (2001)	2,000,000	669,000
Exchange fee (2003)		
Domestic	$129	$107
International	$169	$129
Annual membership fee	$89	$79

Exchanges at both companies may be deposited—this creates the sup-ply—two years to two weeks in advance. Exchanges may be requested—this creates the demand—from two years to two days at RCI and two years to one day at II. Membership may be purchased independently, but are frequently part of the package when one buys a timeshare.

For your dues, you get a travel magazine and a large catalog ("wish book") with the pictures and descriptions of the various resorts. The wish book will usually list the occupancies of the units, the seasonal designations, amenities, and other attributes of the resort. To obtain an exchange, you must first deposit your timeshare (Spacebank) with the exchange company (with II this is not necessarily true, but is with RCI). Once you do this, the exchange company is free to give it to somebody else, and you cannot get it back, so be sure you want to let it go, and are not going to use it for the year you give them.

Once you have spacebanked, you may make a request. When you make the request, if it is not immediately confirmed (most are not), you must pay a refundable deposit equal to the fee for the week in order for the search to continue. The best way to obtain a desirable property is to be as early and as general in your request as you are comfortable with. If possible, give a range of dates to look for (usually a month) and an area or a list of at least several timeshares that you would stay at. If possible, you should make this request a year in advance, since the most space-bankings are done either just under a year in advance or when mainte-nance is paid (which will be around the first of the year for many).

Following the request, you ask them to "call to confirm," and then they will have to contact you to see if the unit is what you want. When this happens, it is your right to ask for a 24-hour hold while you con-firm the destination with your family and/or investigate other details (such as air fair.) If you do not call back within 24 hours, you lose the right to that particular timeshare. As a result of unforeseen circum-stances, if you need to cancel your exchange, RCI allows a grace period of 24hrs to cancel exchanges without penalty. There is a charge of $75 if the exchange date is 60 days or more away. No refunds for cancellations are allowed less than 60 days away.

TAX IMPLICATIONS OF TIMESHARES

If the timeshare is owned personally, then certain continuing expenses associated with the timeshare may be tax deductible. Chief among these would be interest on a mortgage for the timeshare (ownership in the timeshare must be deeded) and any property taxes associated with the timeshare. General maintenance expenses and any assessed capital improvement fees would not be tax deductible.

If the timeshare is owned personally, and sold at a profit, the difference between your cost, or depreciated basis if you have been renting, and the net selling price would be subject to the capital gains tax. If the timeshare is sold at a loss, that loss will not be deductible unless it offsets other capital gains taken during the same period.

If the timeshare is owned as a business, then all continuing expenses associated with the timeshare would be deductible as a business expense. If the timeshare is sold for a profit, the difference between the net selling price and your cost (or depreciated basis if you have been renting) would be subject to the capital gains tax. If the timeshare is sold at a loss, when it is a business that loss may be used to offset other revenue in the business.

Many timeshare owners, when faced with the prospect of selling at a loss, convert the business to a rental property, thus qualifying the timeshare as a business and enabling a more favorable tax treatment. If you use your timeshare for both rental (not using the vacation home rules) and personal use, you must allocate the original cost of the timeshare to business and other use when computing the taxable gains and losses.

If you convert property from personal use to business use, the basis for determining gain is cost where the basis for loss is the lower of cost or fair market value on the date of conversion. Your cost is generally your original cost, plus additions for the following items: (1) closing costs incurred when you purchased your timeshare; (2) the portion of your annual maintenance fee (for all years owned) allocated to capital reserves or used specifically for capital improvements (such as a new roof); and (3) any special assessments for capital improvement purposes which you paid. This amount should be reduced by any depreciation expense in years you rented the timeshare. *Fair market value* (FMV) is the price a reasonable buyer and seller would agree upon in an open market.

In the face of a loss in selling the timeshare, many owners consider giving it to charity. The question really under consideration here is whether or not the tax saving would exceed the selling price of the property. This generally will not be the case because where one is donating a "deeded" timeshare, the contribution amount will be based on the FMV on the date of donation. That's the amount an arms-length buyer/seller would pay for it. And, if the FMV exceeds $5,000 the IRS requires a written appraisal.

This advice is not intended as a substitute for that of your personal tax advisor. The tax consequences of any financial decision are often affected by the unique circumstances of the taxpayer. Make sure you get professional advice when preparing your tax return. The tax implications of the following examples are not explored because (1) they are unlikely to affect the basic viability of the investment and (2) they vary so much from individual to individual.

ILLUSTRATION #1: HIDDEN HILLS ORLANDO

This is an example of when things go wrong. While the situation depicted is fictional, there are tens of thousands of timeshare owners out there who can relate to this situation.

Abby and John Jefferson received a telemarketer phone call that seemed too good to be true. Abby does not usually talk to telemarketers, but Abby's uncle had given this company their name. Hidden Hills Orlando was a timeshare resort located in Orlando, Florida only a quarter mile from Disney World. Hidden Hills wanted Abbey and John and their two children to come for a fabulous weekend at their resort for free. In addition, Hidden Hills would give them each a $100 voucher towards airfare. All Abby and John had to do was attend a two-hour presentation where the advantages of timeshare living would be explained. They were under absolutely no obligation to buy anything. As Abbey and John lived in Toledo, Ohio and it was February, this sounded like a wonderful idea.

So Abby, John and their two children scheduled a "magical" weekend. They arrived in Orlando after an uneventful flight, and took the Hidden Hills bus to the resort site. It was beautiful with palm trees and the warm sun. What a change from Toledo! They were given a beautifully decorated spacious two-bedroom apartment overlooking the fourth hole of the most attractive golf course that John had ever seen. On the evening that they arrived, they were personally welcomed by their Hidden Hills Associate, Fred, and escorted to a free buffet with an open bar! Fred was very nice and quite friendly. Many other couples were there like themselves, and everybody was excited by how beautiful the resort was.

They made an appointment to see Fred the next morning at 9:00 A.M. Fred gave them a tour of the grounds; three acres of beautifully manicured lawns, tropical flowers, and palm trees, the swimming pool, the health club, the tennis courts, the library, the kids' game room, and three onsite restaurants, one of which had a five-star chef. Then Fred took them to the "Presentation Room" where he discussed the history of the resort (it was built two years ago) and how they hoped to make it a first-class destination in Orlando. Fred told them "Nearby condos in buildings or resorts not half as beautiful as ours sell for $500,000." Abby and John believed that and knew that such a property was well beyond their means.

Then Fred explained, "Timesharing is magic because it means you don't have to buy the whole condo. You can buy just a week of it! In fact, this third week in February is available for the very apartment you are staying in. It can always be yours for that week. You can own it. You even get a deed for the property and it can be financed with a mortgage just like any other real estate you would care to buy. Furthermore, because the firm that has developed the resort is eager to finish with it, they have arranged for special financing at a below-market rate. You can buy this property today for $24,000 with nothing down (although you do have to pay closing costs of $1,200) and get a 30-year fixed-rate mortgage at 5%. That's a deal!"

"Further," Fred told them, "if you ever get tired of visiting this beautiful resort, you can trade your week through our exchange company for a week in the Vail, the Swiss Alps, Monte Carlo, Paris, or anywhere else in the world you want to go at any time of the year, depending on availability. You can't lose."

The principle and interest on the rate offered worked out to $128.84 per month. Fred explained that there was a $400 maintenance fee associated with their unit ("Its important to keep the place up"), but that this could be paid monthly. Along with taxes and insurance their cost would be $170 per month. Fred pointed out that while that came to $2,040 a year, to rent a condo in Orlando that was not even as nice as this would cost at least $2,500. Moreover, every year rents tended to rise 5% or 10%, but if they bought now, their mortgage would never rise. Also, if they rented, "poof" that money was gone forever, but here they were investing. Every mortgage payment they made built equity. Someday the property would be paid off free and clear. They could leave it to their kids or grandkids.

Now Abby and John loved Hidden Hills. This was a vacation they dreamed about. They thought they could never afford such luxury. It was so nice there. However, John made $60,000 per year and Abby made $30,000, and that did not go real far in Toledo raising two children. They could do it, but it would be a great strain on their budget. Before they had left Toledo, they made a pact with each other that come what may, they would not buy anything while they were down in Orlando. They did not want to be pressured.

Fred was not using high pressure, he was just educating them in a friendly way. The arguments he made were powerful and well received by Abby and John. Abby and John were sorely tempted. It was so beautiful here. After much hemming and hawing, they explained to Fred that although they really loved Hidden Hills, they did not feel they could commit to such a large purchase right away; they would need time to think about it. Fred was not put out by their decision. He remained charming and friendly and said that he certainly understood their situation. He had kids of his own. They wished each other well and Abby and John left to take the kids to Disney World.

Of course, the kids loved it and had the time of their lives. They kept saying, "They wished this could go on forever." That resonated with Abby and John, and they talked seriously about taking Fred up on his offer. However, they did not make a decision and decided this could be put off to later.

The next morning Fred called them up and said that he had exciting news. Could he meet with them for just half an hour. Well, Fred had been so charming and they had enjoyed their vacation so much, how could they refuse? When they met with Fred, the exciting news was that the partnership, which had developed the resort, was thinking about breaking up and the sales staff had been ordered to liquidate as many units as possible immediately. Fred explained that he had just been authorized to sell the very unit they were in for that February week for $12,000. But it had to be done today. Tomorrow would be too late. This offer would never be repeated!

Abby and John nearly fell out of their chairs. They could scarcely believe their good fortune. They looked at each other and then at Fred and said, "We'll do it." Before they left on the plane for Toledo, it was done. All the papers had been signed. There was even a clause that would allow them to rescind the deal within the next 36 hours. As if! Abby and John knew a good deal when they saw it. They had purchased their "Garden of Eden" for a principle and interest payment of $64.42 per month or $113 per month overall (with the condo fee, taxes, and insurance included.) They spent the next 36 hours telling all their friends and relatives the good news.

They went to Hidden Hills the next year and found it as beautiful as ever, although the airfare and incidental costs did make a dent in their budget. They had a great time, but perhaps not quite as fabulous as the first time. They went the third year also. Again, Hidden Hills had lost none of its beauty and attractiveness, and they had a good time. However, they had a feeling of *deja vû* and thought they would try another resort the next time. Abby and John signed up with their resort's exchange company and found that their timeshare did not have a high trading value. It seemed that while there was a strong demand for timeshares in Orlando, demand was not particularly strong in the middle of February (because most kids were going to school). Also, because of the popularity of timeshares in Orlando, the market had been heavily overbuilt.

Abby and John never did find another timeshare that suited them as to time and place. The fourth year they were going to go, but their youngest child was down with the flu and so the family was going nowhere then. During that winter their car broke down and the roof leaked. Abby and John bought a new car and fixed the roof, but now their budget was sadly out of wack. They began to feel like that $113 payment was killing them. They decided to put the timeshare on the market. They even thought that they might make a profit because they had gotten such a good price when they bought it.

Abby and John were sadly disillusioned when they talked to an Orlando real estate firm that specialized in timeshares. The real estate person told them the best they could hope for was $2,000 and even at that, "Don't expect a quick sale." John could not believe it. He checked timeshare sales on the Internet and found a dozen two-bedroom apartments for sale at Hidden Hills, some as low as $1,500 with a more desirable time slot than the middle of February! "What was he thinking!"

As a practical matter, to sell their unit, John and Abby would have to pay off that $12,000 mortgage, which meant that they would have to put about $10,000 on the table. Abby and John did not have $10,000!

Since John and Abby did not have the $10,000, they decided to stick it out. Maybe prices would improve in the future. Sadly, while their principle and interest payment remained constant at $64.42 a month. The cost of maintenance, taxes, and insurance did move up. After four years, their monthly payment was up to $165. Worse yet, in the fifth year the timeshare owners' association charged for a special $1,000 assessment to fix a perennial utility problem at the property. John and Abby visited the property twice more. Each time, the timeshare was as physically attractive as when they first saw it. Despite the continuing beauty of Hidden Hills, the visits were despoiled by a sense of remorse. In the 10th year, they sold the property for $3,500. They had visited their timeshare five times, allowed relatives to use it twice, and left it unused three times. They were never able to exchange it for what they considered a comparable timeshare.

Surprisingly, the financial result of this purchase need not be a debacle. Table 9.2 shows the cash flows associated with the timeshare resulting in a positive NPV and a IRR of 8%. This outcome assumes that the imputed rents are true opportunity costs—that is, they would have gone to Orlando and paid that rent if they did not own the timeshare—if the imputed rent associated with the use of the timeshare reflects actual value for the Jefferson's family. If this was the case, the timeshare was a good deal. Also, delaying recognition of that loss for 10 years (at 10%, a nominal loss of $9,454 in ten years is really only a loss of $3,645 now) reduces the overall timeshare loss. This analysis also avoids the issue of travel costs associated with the use of the timeshare as well as the fact that undoubtedly the Hidden Hills timeshare could have been exchanged for some other timeshare and that, presumably, has economic value which is unrecognized here.

TABLE 9.2 Cash Flow Analysis, Hidden Hills Orlando

Year	Mortgage Payment	Closing Costs	Maintenance Taxes and Insurance[a]	Special Assessment	Loss on Mortgage Loan	Tax Savings on Mortgage Interest[b]	Imputed Rent[c]	Sale Price	Net Cash Flow
1	$773.04	$1,200.00	$665.04			$178.79	$2,500.00		$41
2	773.04		684.99			176.08	2,575.00		1,293
3	773.04		705.54			173.22	2,652.25		1,347
4	773.04		726.71			170.22			−1,330
5	773.04		748.51	$1,000.00		167.06	2,813.77		459
6	773.04		770.96			163.74	2,898.19		1,518
7	773.04		794.09			160.26	2,985.13		1,578
8	773.04		817.92			156.59	3,074.68		1,640
9	773.04		842.45			152.74			−1,463
10	773.04		867.73		$9,761.05	148.69		$3,500.00	−7,753

[a] Assumed to rise 3% per year.
[b] The Jeffersons are assumed to be in a 30% tax bracket.
[c] Assumed to rise 3% per year.

NPV at 10% = $317

IRR = 8.05%

If the imputed rent is not counted in this analysis as an opportunity cost, then the financial outcome for the Jeffersons is much more bleak.

Table 9.3 illustrates that in the absence of the impact of imputed rent as a cash offset, the timeshare generates a $12,426 loss for the Jeffersons. An outcome that would be a financial disaster for the family.

This analysis points out that even where a lot goes wrong, timeshares do have investment potential, but everything cannot go wrong! The key to recognizing that potential is to buy at the right price and to buy quality (timeshare property in a desirable location at a desirable time.) Consumer studies show that the demand for timeshares in the secondary market is dependent on time and place, not on the amenity value of the timeshare.

This attribute of timeshares is illustrated in the following situation.

ILLUSTRATION #2: CHRISTMAS AT VAIL

Jane and Henry Roberts are approaching retirement and wish to travel worldwide. They are interested in timeshares because from talking with their friends they feel that timeshares are generally of better quality than comparable rental properties. They also have studied the primary and secondary timeshare markets and have investigated exactly how the timeshare exchanges work.

Because Jane and Henry wish to travel widely and often, they feel it important to buy a timeshare that is in high demand so that they will have the widest possible exchange opportunities. Jane and Henry are not skiers, but they have determined that the highest demand exists for ski related timeshares during the Christmas holidays. They searched for three months on the Internet, examining all the major ski destinations. They find the last two weeks of December and the first week of January for sale at a beautiful resort located next to the largest ski run in Vail, Colorado. These timeshares were sold four years earlier by the developer for $25,000 apiece. The Roberts are able to purchase them through an Internet broker for $15,000 apiece, with $400 per week maintenance and closing costs of $1,500 per unit. Jane and Henry recognize these units are pricey (the average timeshare sells between $4,000 and $8,000), but they certainly are prime. Henry, an-about-to-retire executive in the oil industry, finances the $49,500 by withdrawing from his 401k. Henry figures this is a lot cheaper than a RV and he does not have to drive!

Immediately after buying these properties, they offer them up for exchange a year in advance. In their first year they are able to exchange

TABLE 9.3 Cash Flow Analysis, Hidden Hills Orlando

Year	Mortgage Payment	Closing Costs	Maintenance Taxes and Insurance[a]	Special Assessment	Loss on Mortgage Loan	Tax Savings on Mortgage Interest[b]	Sale Price	Net Cash Flow
1	$773.04	$1,200.00	$665.04			$178.79		-$2,459
2	773.04		684.99			176.08		-1,282
3	773.04		705.54			173.22		-1,305
4	773.04		726.71			170.22		-1,330
5	773.04		748.51	$1,000.00		167.06		-2,354
6	773.04		770.96			163.74		-1,380
7	773.04		794.09			160.26		-1,407
8	773.04		817.92			156.59		-1,434
9	773.04		842.45			152.74		-1,463
10	773.04		867.73		$9,761.05	148.69	$3,500.00	-7,753

[a] Assumed to rise 3% per year.
[b] The Jeffers are assumed to be in a 30% tax bracket.

NPV at 10% = ($12,426)

210

for magnificent timeshares in Paris (the first week in June), Munich (the second week in October for the Oktoberfest), and St. Maartens (the second week of January). In each of the following four years they are able to exchange their timeshares for the most desirable worldwide properties.

After five years of world travel, the Roberts' health begins to deteriorate and they sell their timeshares. To their surprise and delight, they find that an economic boom during this period has caused the price of the most desirable timeshares to rise 8% per year.

The cash flow implication of this investment is depicted in Table 9.4. As things have worked out for the Roberts, they have not only gotten their hearts desire of traveling worldwide, but have done so in such a manner as to earn a substantial positive return on their timeshare purchase.

The Roberts' success in this endeavor reflected the fact that they entered the timeshare market as knowledgeable consumers. Their strategy of buying right and buying quality earned them a 20% return on their investment as well as affording them travel opportunities not otherwise available.

SUMMARY

The timeshare market is best entered not as an investor looking for an economic return, but as a consumer who is expecting to reap both psychic and economic income from their investment. To be successful in this quest it is important to understand the difference between the primary and secondary timeshare markets. This understanding will probably result in the successful timeshare investor *never* buying in the primary timeshare market. The second key to success as an investor in the timeshare market is to understand the need to buy quality timeshares. Quality timeshares are not characterized by the amenities or beauty of a property, but by their (desirable) location and (desirable) time slot. Buying quality timeshares allows the investor to maximize his psychic income by affording the best possible exchange opportunities and will function to maintain (or increase) the value of the timeshare unit over time. No matter how cheap a timeshare in Kansas City in January is, it is not worth it. Who would want to go to Kansas City in January?

TABLE 9.4 Cash Flow Analysis, Christmas at Vail

Year	Initial Funds	Opportunity Cost of Funds[a]	Maintenance Taxes and Insurance[b]	Imputed Rent[c]	Tax Savings on Mortgage Interest[d]	Gain on Sales[e]	Net Cash Flow
1	-$49,500	-$4,950	$2,400	$6,000			-$46,050
2		-4,500	2,472	6,480			4,452
3		-4,500	2,546	6,998			5,045
4		-4,500	2,623	7,558			5,681
5		-4,500	2,701	8,163		66,120	72,484

[a] It is assumed the $49,500 would earn 10% if left in the 401k.
[b] Maintenance costs of $400 per unit are expected to be matched by taxes and insurance and increase 3% per year.
[c] Rents are expected to increase 8% per year.
[d] There are no tax savings because the Roberts' used their own funds to finance the purchase.
[e] The Vail properties are expected to appreciate 8% per year.

NPV at 10% = $15,942

IRR = 20%

212

CHAPTER 10

Undeveloped Land

Undeveloped land frequently exerts an emotional appeal on an investor. "Falling in love with the land" can and does happen. However, purchasing undeveloped land, because the beauty of the forest casts a spell on one, is a far different behavior than purchasing the land as an investment. The strong emotional appeal of a property can cloud the business sense of an investor. Buying undeveloped land is usually easy; selling undeveloped land is usually hard. More than one investor, who has been taken with the attractiveness of undeveloped property, has bought high and then, in the absence of buyers, sold low.

There are two kinds of undeveloped land:

- Raw land
- Developing land

Raw land tends to be located in rural areas, far from existing patterns of development. Developing land is located in areas that are transitioning from a rural environment to a suburban or urban environment. The two types of undeveloped land have differing investment characteristics, but share the disadvantages of the lack of a depreciation tax shield, little opportunity for leverage, and a negative cash flow.

Considerable difficulties are encountered in trying to determine the value of undeveloped land for reasons discussed below. However, an excellent source of data on current development potential is available from *Emerging Trends in Real Estate*, an annual study by the Real Estate Research Corporation (www.rerc.com). This publication examines development potential in different areas from the perspective of existing price trends, existing business locations, demographic projections, and the attitude of local government towards development.

GENERAL INVESTMENT CHARACTERISTICS

Appreciation from Shifting Land Use

Patterns of economic growth in the United States dictate a general shift from less intensive land use to more intensive land use over time. However, this pattern is heterogeneous, partly as a natural consequences of market forces, partly as a result of governmental land use controls (e.g., zoning, water and sewer service, historical designations, etc.). In any given geographical area, considerable variation in the intensity of land use may be found. Residential homes juxtaposed to industrial properties. Commercial areas side by side with residential areas. Undeveloped patches of land located in areas of suburban homes, industrial properties, and commercial districts. Office and professional buildings located in the middle of what appears to be nowhere.

Land development is driven by a complex array of forces. Prime among these would be changes in the existing transportation infrastructure. Old roads enlarged, new roads, new entrances and exits off of limited access highways all bring with them the potential for changes in land use. However, by itself transportation factors do not determine land use. Zoning restrictions are always important in determining land use, but zoning restrictions are not always absolute. Zoning laws can be changed or variances granted. Demographic patterns can be a factor as well. An area of single-family residential with an older population may be ripe for conversion to condominiums or apartment homes. Ethnicity also impacts land use. A small immigrant population may locate in a particular area by happenstance. However, their presence attracts immigrants of a shared ethnicity. Quite suddenly, the demand for housing and appropriate infrastructure in that area soars and land use patterns change.

Nearby land use is often an important factor in determining the use of particular piece of property. A manufacturing facility springing up in a cornfield in a rural county may soon be followed by other manufacturing facilities. Fast-food stores that convert that residential property to a more intense use may soon join a fast-food store located along a busy highway that has grown up next to a residential area. Suburban development, in heretofore agricultural areas, not only spawns similar suburban residential areas, but supporting commercial facilities as well.

Inflation

There is an appeal in purchasing undeveloped land as a hedge against inflation. Where wealth is held in the form of money or near-money, inflation (the general rise in prices) erodes that wealth. The idea is that land is in fixed supply and as the general population increases and level of economic activity rises, the price of land shall rise proportionately. Unfortunately, the demand for all undeveloped land does not rise proportionately.

Since 1960, the Consumer Price Index has increased 125%. Some undeveloped land during those 43 years has increased far more in value. Some undeveloped land has declined in value. The reasons for such variation in the price appreciation of undeveloped land may be found in local or regional conditions having to do with changing demographics, changing land use patterns, shifts in industrial activity or composition, changes in the transportation system, changing land use regulations, changes in public services, and the changing tastes and preferences of the population.

In addition, there appears to be a random factor affecting patterns of land use. Land use is rarely homogeneous. Incongruities occur even in what appears to be highly uniform suburban areas as prior land uses are grandfathered in the face of development. In highly developed urban land, one may always find the occasional undeveloped property and certainly incongruous land uses that defy rational explanation. Why one piece of property is intensively developed and another bypassed often appears to be the result of happenstance.

These factors make determining the future value of undeveloped land difficult. Even where long term trends appear to be strong, well settled and predictable, the unexpected is likely to occur. As holding undeveloped land for price appreciation requires a very long holding period, the uncertainty inherent in this type of investment activity is magnified.

Speculation

Volatility in the price of undeveloped land is occasionally fueled by speculative fever. Before we had stock markets as a social institution to absorb speculative fervor, land booms served this function. Land booms are characterized by rapidly rising land prices unrelated to the use of the underlying land. Speculators bid up the price of land, not to use the land themselves, but because they feel a "greater fool" will shortly come along and pay an even higher price for the land. Engaging in this strategy, especially as a relatively unsophisticated investor, is obviously dangerous and to be avoided.

Carrying Costs

As a general rule, investments in undeveloped land generate a negative cash flow. Not only must the investor bear explicit carrying costs such as property taxes and financing costs, but also the opportunity cost of having invested elsewhere. Rarely can any significant revenue be derived from the undeveloped property. Thus, in investing in undeveloped land the investor faces the certain prospects of a negative cash flow for an indeterminate period of time against the possibility of a big payoff in the distant future. That certainly sounds more like gambling than investing.

Leverage

In most real estate investments the potential return is significantly enhanced by opportunities for leverage. Apartments, office buildings, parking lots, and the like tend to generate a reliable positive cash flow. From a banker's perspective, this makes such investments desirable loan prospects. The investor can then combine equity and debt in a manner which substantially enhances the return on equity to the investor.

In the case of developing land, no such positive cash flow exists. Bankers are generally loath to lend on such property unless otherwise secured. Even where such loans are possible the loan-to-value ratio will be low compared to that available for other real estate properties. Thus, the investor in undeveloped land loses the opportunities associated with leveraging their own money.

Taxes

One of the advantages associated with investments in commercial real estate is the opportunity to generate a tax shield by depreciating the property improvements. However, raw land cannot be depreciated.

Furthermore, the gains associated with investing in undeveloped land will invariably be treated for income tax purposes as capital gains. The current favorable treatment in tax law afforded to this source of income is an advantage to this type of investing.

RAW LAND

> For Sale: 60 Acres on West Virginia mountain top, 5-mile view, mature trees and meadows, borders trout stream, and 500,000-acre state forest. $30,000.

The acquisition of raw land for its potential appreciation is often overlaid with an emotional attraction. The ownership of raw land may yield investors psychic income having to do with "owning" a piece of America, or dreams of an idyllic retirement far removed from the stresses of the urban environment. This appeal is dangerous to an investor. The advertisement may have great emotional appeal to the investor who can almost hear the birds sing and the rustle of squirrels high in the oak trees. However, beauty is in the eye of the beholder. While the supply of raw land in general is quite large, each specific parcel is uniquely defined

FIGURE 10.1 Supply and Demand for Raw Land

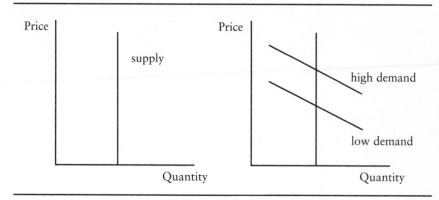

by its location and particular attributes. Effectively, the supply of that piece of land is perfectly inelastic. Demand for that piece of land may be non-existent (Figure 10.1), low or high.

The high demand represents a potential purchaser who just happens to "love" that property. Where such a purchaser exists, the property will sell for a high price. However, given that there is a lot of raw land out there, if the owner wants to sell and no particular purchaser who "loves" that land is present, there will be no buyers. If the land cannot be sold on the basis of its location or attributes, then it must be sold on the basis of price. It may take a low price indeed to cause a purchaser to be willing. It may even be that there is no purchaser at any price! This potential lack of liquidity of such a property should be a concern to a potential investor.

It should also be noted that occasionally areas of raw land become "hot". This can create a buying frenzy among purchasers that quickly evolves into outright speculation. Such waves of speculative interest in raw land are not uncommon and invariably yield the same result: a disastrous collapse in values.

A variation of this theme is found in various "land scams," which take the form of selling property one does not actually own or selling non-existent property. This is not uncommon where the buyer is buying on the basis of emotion that can be easily manipulated. A good first step in determining whether or not a property can be legitimately offered for sale is by checking with the Interstate Land Sales Division (ISLD) of the Office of Consumer and Regulatory Affairs at the federal Department of Housing and Urban Development (accessible at www.hud.gov). The ISLD report covers zoning restrictions, tax assessments, title characteristics, road access, the availability of utilities and available local services. If the property developer is not regulated at the federal level, try the local State Office of Consumer affairs or its equivalent.

Additional factors that must be investigated in connection with purchasing raw land would include any environmental or zoning regulations that affect the lands potential for development. Of particular concern in this area are the Clean Water Act's strictures against the use of wetlands. While it might be thought that wetlands can be easily identified by the existence of wet and swampy ground that is not the case. The nature of "wetlands" is defined in a set of complex bureaucratic codes. Designated wetlands are identified by the U.S. Geological Service and identified on special wetland maps (available at www.usgs.gov/esic/ esic.html). No development of wetlands is permitted without the express permission of the U.S. Corps of Engineers and the Environmental Protection Agency. In addition, the purchaser must investigate state and local government codes in this area.

If raw land is desirable from the point of view of an individual on the basis of its amenity value alone, then the property should be purchased. If the potential for resale is going to be a factor in the decision, it would be advisable to purchase property that is unique in some special sense or has a distinguishing feature that differentiates it from nearby properties. If purchasing from a developer's inventory be sure to check the resale market. Where the motivation for purchasing raw land is primarily emotional, such a purchase is more akin to an act of consumption than an act of investment.

Investing in raw land combines a potential for high returns with high risk. Under the right circumstances buying raw land low and selling it high can be very rewarding. The prospects for investing successfully in raw land are enhanced by the fact that it is in fixed supply. There are only so many mountain tops, beach fronts, and the like. The United States has 50 billion acres of land, about 22 acres per person. Of these 22 acres, only about three are available for development.

A second factor auguring higher prices for raw land is the demographic structure of the United States. The biggest cohort purchasing raw land is a affluent couple close to retirement age. At the turn of the millennium, this translates into the baby boomer generation. Born between 1945 and 1955, the average baby boomer turns 55 in 2005. Consequently, 2005 to 2015 should be prime years for the appreciation of raw land real estate.

Although some concerns are manifesting themselves about the phenomena of deflation (generally falling prices) in the current post-Iraq economic environment, the two dominant macroeconomic trends over the past half-century have been economic growth and inflation. The Gross Domestic Product rose from $275 billion in 1950 to $10.6 trillion at the end of 2002, an average annual increase of 7.2%. Real economic growth during this period was 3.5%, with the difference being an average inflation of 3.8%. Both of these factors may impact the price of raw land. There is no reason why an increase in real income would not have a more than proportionate impact on the prices of raw land given that raw land as a luxury good having a high degree of income elasticity. As a commodity in fixed supply, it also follows that inflation may have a proportionate impact on the value of raw land. Thus, it may be that an investment in raw land would prove to be more than an inflation hedge over time.

The underlying economics of investing in raw land are not as favorable as the other types of real estate discussed in this book. The reason for this lies in the fact the raw land cannot be depreciated. Thus, the tax shield that is available to those purchasing real estate containing depreciable facilities is not available to the purchasers of raw land. In addition, raw land will generally not generate revenue during its holding period. However, the land may well be subject to taxes and necessary expenses (e.g., liability insurance) creating a negative cash flow during the holding period.

Furthermore, the return to the investor even when successful will be lower than for other types of real estate investments. The reason for this is that it is difficult to generate much financial leverage for this type of investment. Bankers are well aware of the potential price volatility inherent in raw land. In addition, they generally do not like to extend credit in circumstances, where they see a negative cash flow with certainty offset only by the potential for price appreciation.

An exception to the difficulties of leveraging raw land purchases can be found when the buyer obtains seller financing. Seller financing is relatively common for raw land properties. While this may appear like an attractive option for the buyer, it would be reasonable to ask why the seller is agreeing to supply the financing. A common answer to this question is, "Because they couldn't sell it otherwise!" Because raw land typically lacks liquidity, and is an asset whose sale awaits the fortuitous confluence of a buyer who "loves" the property and has the money to buy it, sellers frequently are forced to eliminate the second qualifier by supplying the necessary financing. This in all likelihood means that when a buyer goes to sell the property, he also must expect to offer financing to another prospective buyer. This also means that cash buyers will expect substantial discounts.

Break-even analysis for raw land suggests a similar caution for investors. Investing in raw land is all about fixed costs. The initial cost of the land, any financing costs, any carrying costs (e.g., taxes) are all unrelated to the ability of the property to generate revenue. This means the greatest possible amount of operating leverage is obtained. Combined with the fact that the revenue associated with raw land is both problematic and likely to be in the distant future, the high fixed costs suggest a lack of flexibility from the investment perspective.

In conducting a break-even analysis for developing land, one must be careful to adjust for the rate of inflation. This is necessary because over time the true return on an investment is the nominal (paper) rate of return less the rate of inflation. If one invests $500,000 in raw land and 20 years later sells the land for $500,000, the investor would not be said to "break-even." Rather there would be a loss. Had inflation averaged 3% during this period, the original $500,000 is now worth only $277,000, a real loss of $223,000.

An investment which return a nominal 12% over a period of years during which inflation averaged 4% would be better said to have earned a return of 8% (12% – 4% = 8%).

RAW LAND EXAMPLE

Acquisition Phase

A businessman goes on a duck hunting trip to a lake in rural Virginia. He feels "This is the life!" and falls in love with 25 lakefront acres in rural Virginia. He seeks out the owner of the land and purchases the property from him directly. The property is purchased for $90,000, with $40,000 up front and $50,000 in five years with no interest. The purchaser spends and additional $10,000 on acquiring a clear title and making sure the land is free of liens and environmental problems.

Holding Phase

The individual plans to use the land for duck hunting and camping with his family for 20 years. He feels that this expenditure cannot be justified unless he sees a positive return on his investment. The individual recognizes that the property will have tax and insurance costs that increase an average of 3% per year. The property is expected to appreciate at a fantastic 10.6% annually over a 20-year holding period.

Disposal Phase

The individual no longer hunts and his family is grown and lives in other parts of the country. The lake area has become increasingly popular as a site for vacation homes and a local developer offers him a cash sale of $750,000 for the property.

The analysis in Table 10.1shows the outcome if the property appreciates at the optimistic rate 10.6% annually. Even though the property increases in value 750%, the toll of the negative cash flow on profitability is significant. The net result (given an opportunity cost of funds of 8%) is a nominal gain of $35,541 and an internal rate of return of 10.16%. If inflation had averaged just 3% during this time period, the real NPV to the individual would be a negative $14,064 and an internal rate of return of 6.82%.

TABLE 10.1 Duck Hunter's Paradise, Raw Land Analysis with No Investment Expense Writeoff

Year	Costs and Revenues	Property Taxes	Insurance	Taxes[a]	Net Cash Flow	Inflation Adjusted Net Cash Flows
1	($50,000)	($600)	($450)	$0	($51,050)	($49,518.50)
2		(618)	(464)	0	(1,082)	(1,017.58)
3		(637)	(477)	0	(1,114)	(1,016.67)
4		(656)	(492)	0	(1,147)	(1,015.75)
5	(50,000)	(675)	(506)	0	(51,182)	(43,951.54)
6		(696)	(522)	0	(1,217)	(1,013.92)
7		(716)	(537)	0	(1,254)	(1,013.01)
8		(738)	(553)	0	(1,291)	(1,012.10)
9		(760)	(570)	0	(1,330)	(1,011.19)
10		(783)	(587)	0	(1,370)	(1,010.28)
11		(806)	(605)	0	(1,411)	(1,009.37)
12		(831)	(623)	0	(1,453)	(1,008.46)
13		(855)	(642)	0	(1,497)	(1,007.55)
14		(881)	(661)	0	(1,542)	(1,006.65)
15		(908)	(681)	0	(1,588)	(1,005.74)
16		(935)	(701)	0	(1,636)	(1,004.84)
17		(963)	(722)	0	(1,685)	(1,003.93)
18		(992)	(744)	0	(1,735)	(1,003.03)
19		(1,021)	(766)	0	(1,788)	(1,002.13)
20	750,000	(1,052)	(789)	(150,000)	598,159	325,275.38

[a] Assumed capital gain rate of 20%.

Nominal	
Net present value at 8%	$35,540.92
IRR	10.13%

Inflation adjusted	
Net present value at 8%	($14,064.09)
IRR	6.82%

If the investor has positive net income from other investments, the various expenses associated with the investment (including the cost of financing) may be written off producing a tax saving that can reduce the negative cash flow associated with the investment. This analysis is undertaken in Table 10.2. The tax offset raises the nominal NPV to

TABLE 10.2   Duck Hunter's Paradise, Raw Land Analysis with Investment Expense Writeoff

Year	Costs and Revenues	Property Taxes	Insurance	Taxes[a]	Net Cash Flow	Inflation Adjusted Net Cash Flows
1	($50,000)	($600)	($450)	($420)	($51,470)	($49,925.90)
2		(618)	(464)	(433)	(1,514)	(1,424.62)
3		(637)	(477)	(446)	(1,560)	(1,423.33)
4		(656)	(492)	(459)	(1,606)	(1,422.05)
5	(50,000)	(675)	(506)	(473)	(51,654)	(44,357.47)
6		(696)	(522)	(487)	(1,704)	(1,419.49)
7		(716)	(537)	(502)	(1,755)	(1,418.22)
8		(738)	(553)	(517)	(1,808)	(1,416.94)
9		(760)	(570)	(532)	(1,862)	(1,415.67)
10		(783)	(587)	(548)	(1,918)	(1,414.39)
11		(806)	(605)	(564)	(1,976)	(1,413.12)
12		(831)	(623)	(581)	(2,035)	(1,411.85)
13		(855)	(642)	(599)	(2,096)	(1,410.58)
14		(881)	(661)	(617)	(2,159)	(1,409.31)
15		(908)	(681)	(635)	(2,224)	(1,408.04)
16		(935)	(701)	(654)	(2,290)	(1,406.77)
17		(963)	(722)	(674)	(2,359)	(1,405.51)
18		(992)	(744)	(694)	(2,430)	(1,404.24)
19		(1,021)	(766)	(715)	(2,503)	(1,402.98)
20	750,000	(1,052)	(789)	149,263.53	897,422	488,013.20

[a] Assume investor tax bracket of 40%. Assume capital gain rate of 20%.

Nominal
Net present value at 8% $94,760.37
IRR   12.53%

Inflation adjusted
Net present value at 8% $68,245.13
IRR   15.25%

$94,760. with an internal rate of return of 12.53%. The real NPV rises to $68,245 with a 15.25% rate of return.

The favorable outcome suggested in Tables 10.1 and 10.2 is predicated on the assumption of a consistent rate of appreciation in the property's value of 10.6% over a 20-year period. While such a rate of appreciation is certainly possible, it is not certain. The question becomes what risk is associated with this return.

It is possible that sometime during the 20-year period, the lake would be found to have been contaminated by PCBs, or the State had passed environmental laws restricting development of this type of property. Such occurrences would necessarily reduce the value of the property, perhaps, to even below its initial cost. Alternatively, it may be that this area becomes less popular, reducing the anticipated rate of property appreciation, or the relative price of gasoline may significantly increase making this location prohibitively expensive to use. In either case, the vale of the property would be substantially diminished, resulting in substantial losses to the investor.

While, there may be a investment rational that justifies the purchase of this "Duck Hunter's Paradise" an unemotional perspective would likely conclude that the risk relative to the return does not make this property an attractive investment vehicle. To buy this land, the individual should like duck hunting a whole lot!

Break-Even Analysis

As almost all costs associated with investing in raw land are fixed, the potential return on the investment is entirely dependent on the estimate of future land value. This implies the highest degree of risk. Worse yet, the estimate of future land value is often made for the distant future, further increasing the uncertainty of the investment.

DEVELOPING LAND

Unlike raw land, developing land has little amenity value and a much more predictable future. Developing land is in a transitional area, between raw land and developed land. A classic investment in developing land might be 25 acres of farmland, but zoned for residential development, and located just outside the suburban fringe or a three-acre parcel located just off the exit and entry ramps for an interstate highway that is planned to begin building in three years. The future value of such developing land is far more predictable than that of raw land, but still not known with certainty.

Appreciation in the value of developing land results from shifting land use patterns. The trends toward more roads, increasing suburban spread, and economic growth in general are well established in our society. It is certainly conceivable that within a span of 50 years a property could have gone from agricultural cultivation along a dirt road, to residential homes along a paved two-lane road, to a strip shopping center along a four-lane highway. The difficulty of successfully investing in developing lands is that the exact pattern and timing of those shifts is very difficult to predict.

The level of economic activity or the pace of development in a geographic region is subject to the vagaries of unpredictable events. The oil crisis of the 1970s sparked a movement of population out of the Northeast and Midwest to the Sunbelt. Land values crashed in Boston in the early 1980s and suburban development came to a dead halt. The fall in fuel oil prices in the late 1980s caused a disastrous fall in land values in Colorado and Texas. Boeing shifts its headquarters from Seattle to Chicago. The automotive industry decides to shift its production facilities from Detroit and other traditional northern areas to rural Midwest and southern communities. The Corps of Engineers decides to reverse its policy of draining the Everglades. The impact of the Cuban population on land use in Florida has been profound. Las Vegas redefines itself as a mecca for retirees. All of these events were essentially unpredictable and all had substantial impact on the pattern of shifting land use in their region.

Whatever the overall trends in a particular region, considerable variation from that trend will be observed in specific localities. Such variation may reflect specific land use regulations, zoning laws, road patterns, the availability of public utilities (water lines, sewer districts, etc.), the availability of public services (parks, hospitals, etc.) and prior land use patterns. Predicting how those patterns will affect a specific parcel of land is difficult.

Even within a narrowly defined locality, considerable variation in land-use patterns may be observed. Vacant lots on otherwise fully developed highways. Apple orchards in the midst of residential neighborhoods. Apartment buildings abutting industrial sites. Vacant land scattered all about with no apparent rhyme or reason. All of which work top make investing in developing land a risky enterprise.

An added danger to investing in developing land is the potential liability associated with land contaminated by hazardous waste. Under the 1980 Superfund Law, a property owner of contaminated lands (or even an ex-property owner) may be liable for clean up costs, even if they had nothing to do with the contamination. Buying a 20-acre parcel for a shopping center, when it is currently largely undeveloped, but does have a few old shacks on the land, can be risky! It could turn out that one of those shacks 30 years ago was used as a foundry to make brake shoe moldings and the land is thoroughly contaminated by lead and asbestos. Developing land should always be checked against the Comprehensive Environmental Response Compensation and Liability Information (CERCLIS) list that is maintained by the federal Environmental Protection Agency (www.epa.gov/superfund/sites/query/basinstr.htm.). Each state has its own environmental protection agency that should also be contacted in this matter as they will be most familiar with the environmental issues in a specific locality.

In this contemporary word, property owners may also be beset by all manner of stakeholder claims. A 50-acre site with an old farmhouse on it is purchased to create an office park, but the farmhouse cannot be torn down because it has local historical significance. Or, as the ground is prepared for construction, a human skeleton is unearthed. It is determined that the site contains a hitherto unknown Indian graveyard. Representatives of a local Indian tribe file suit to halt construction. The possibilities are endless, overlaying all development activities with a rich layer of uncertainty.

The underlying economics of investing in developing land are not as favorable as for the other types of real estate discussed in this book. The reason lies in the fact the vacant land cannot be depreciated. Thus, the tax shield that is available to those purchasing real estate containing depreciable facilities is not available to the purchasers of developing land. In addition, developing land will generally not generate revenue during its holding period. However, the land may well be subject to taxes and necessary expenses (e.g., taxes, preparing a land-use plan,) creating a negative cash flow during the holding period. Leverage is somewhat easier to obtain for developing land because creditors can be more certain of the land's value with actual development a close proximity.

DEVELOPING LAND EXAMPLE

Acquisition Phase

An investor learns that the state plans to build a new limited-access highway in six years for 200 miles between two regional urban centers. The land between the two urban centers has historically been used for agricultural purposes and has seen little development owing to its rugged topography. The investor obtains a map of the project and locates the site of an on-off ramp located about midway between the two urban centers. The investor surveys the real estate available and finds a 50-acre parcel just off the ramp that would be an excellent location for a gas station, motel, convenience store, and a couple of fast-food restaurants. This parcel is currently used for farming. The offering price for the parcel is $500,000 and the investor learns that the property was bought four years earlier for $100,000. He attempts to negotiate a lower price, but the seller tells him there are other willing buyers with ready cash to buy at $500,000. The property also has some zoning problems and an environmental problem, where a farmer had used a pit on the property to dump excess pesticides over the years. The investor estimates it will take $50,000 in legal feels to acquire the property, an additional $100,000 to clear the zoning problems, and an additional $50,000 to rectify the environmental problem.

Holding Phase

The investor purchases the property for $500,000 having secured a $400,000 mortgage from a local bank with 12% interest only payment for four years and a balloon payment at the end of the fifth year. Initial property taxes of $2,000 per year and liability insurance of $3,000 per year are expected to increase at 5% annually during the holding period. In the first four years of ownership, the investor rectifies the zoning and environmental issues associated with the property. At the end of five years, the property is appraised for $800,000 and the investor secures a another 12% interest only loan for five years to finance the principal payment on the first balloon note.

Disposal Phase

At the end of nine years, the road is completed and traffic is flowing. The investor sells the property in the tenth year to an REIT for $2,000,000 that wishes to develop its commercial potential.

An analysis of this situation is presented in Table 10.3.

In this example, the price of the property is seen to escalate 26% a year over a 10-year period. While this astounding rate of growth may occur in the circumstances described, it also may not. Road construction may be delayed for a number of years. The zoning problems that were thought to be resolvable are not. The environmental cleanup is much more extensive and expensive than originally thought. Land on the other access and egress points of the highway interchange may also be on the market with aggressive sellers. The REIT may play off one property owner against the other, driving the price down. The REIT and/or other buyers may decide that other interchanges are more desirable. It may not be possible to sell for cash. The buyer may require

TABLE 10.3 Highway Interchange Analysis with Investment Expense Writeoff

Year	Costs and Revenues[a]	Property Taxes	Insurance	Interest	Taxes[b]	Net Cash Flow	Net Cash Flows
1	($550,000)	($2,000)	($3,000)	($60,000)	($26,000)	($589,000)	($571,330.00)
2	–50,000	(2,100)	(3,150)	(60,000)	(26,100)	(89,150)	(83,881.24)
3	–50,000	(2,205)	(3,308)	(60,000)	(26,205)	(89,308)	(81,508.54)
4	–50,000	(2,315)	(3,473)	(60,000)	(26,315)	(89,473)	(79,209.69)
5		(2,431)	(3,647)	(60,000)	(26,431)	(39,647)	(34,045.81)
6		(2,553)	(3,829)	(60,000)	(26,553)	(39,829)	(33,176.31)
7		(2,680)	(4,020)	(60,000)	(26,680)	(40,020)	(32,335.71)
8		(2,814)	(4,221)	(60,000)	(26,814)	(40,221)	(31,523.18)
9		(2,955)	(4,432)	(60,000)	(26,955)	(40,432)	(30,737.94)
10	5,000,000	(3,103)	(4,654)	(60,000)	972,897	3,959,346	2,919,717.28

[a] $550,000 initial acquisition costs, zoning, and environmental expenditures the first three years.
[b] Assumes a 40% tax on income and a 20% tax on capital gains.

Nominal
Net present value at 8% $958,091.06
IRR   18.56%

Inflation adjusted
Net present value at 8% $533,191.63
IRR   15.00%

227

owner financing or prefer a lease arrangement. The property is highly illiquid and at the mercy of the buyers. In the event the seller unexpectedly needs to liquidate, the liquidating price could be abnormally low. The desirability of the investment is highly dependent on the selling price of the property.

Within the example presented in Table 10.3, it can be seen that the assumed exceptional appreciation of the acquired property results in only moderate profits for the investor. The nominal net present value of $958,091. This is not bad on a financial commitment of $750,000, but this reflects only an annual gain of 18.56%. While this is nothing to sneeze at, the question may be raised: "Is it worth the risk?" On an inflation adjusted basis, the returns are even more modest. The expected NPV is $533,191, with an IRR of 15%.

The reason for the relatively modest profit level compared to the risk shouldered in this type of investment is (1) the relatively long holding period and (2) the negative cash flows occurring throughout that period.

Break-Even Analysis

In the above example, all costs are fixed. Return is purely a function of the anticipated future value of the property. While this future value may be more certain than that of raw land, considerable variance in outcome is possible. Whether or not investing in developing land is potentially profitable, the requirement for such fixed costs ensures a high degree of risk.

SUMMARY

Stripped of its emotional content, investing in undeveloped land is generally going against the odds from an investor's point of view. To be sure, there may be exceptions to this conclusion, but they will be exceptions to the general rule. The underlying circumstances that mitigate against success in undeveloped real estate compared to other types of real estate are (1) the dependence on a highly uncertain future payoff; (2) the burden of carrying a negative cash flow over a long period of time; and (3) the comparative advantage depreciable real estate has over undeveloped land in generating a valuable tax shield.

As an investor, if you feel compelled to invest in undeveloped real estate, be sure to do your homework. Make certain the seller has a deliverable title to the property, that the property value is not, will not be, compromised by existing or future land use regulation and that you are not paying too much for the property. The first point above can be addressed through a good lawyer or title company. The second point can be addressed by talking with local persons (neighbors, the agricultural extension person, local officials) who would know about the circumstances of the parcel of land under consideration and checking the local resale market. Analyzing the price will require talking with local developers, bankers, real estate salespersons, and checking the resale market.

Investors in undeveloped real estate will generally benefit from tempering their enthusiasm for a property with the recognition that the investment is basically not liquid and represents a long-term commitment to an assets subject to considerable price volatility.

CHAPTER 11

Self-Storage Facilities

Self-storage facilities represent a burgeoning opportunity in real estate investment. The demand for such facilities is on the rise from both individuals and small businesses. In an increasingly affluent and materialistic society, individuals increasingly have more "stuff" than they can reasonably accommodate in their present residence. In an increasingly mobile society, individuals in transition need to places to store their possessions temporarily. Small, and even some large, businesses have found self-storage facilities cost-effective ways to store their records, inventory, extra equipment, and seasonal goods.

There are currently about 30,000 self-storage facilities (SSF) located throughout the United States.[1] The rapid growth of the industry has resulted in progressive and accelerating change as to the function of such facilities. Self-storage facilities offer the financial leverage, tax advantages, and cash flow characteristics that characterize other commercial real estate properties. The industry began in the 1960s with properties that offered little in the way of location, convenience, and amenities such as air conditioning, heating, and 24-hour secure access. Basically, these were the equivalent of C-type office buildings. Today's self-storage facilities have evolved into centrally located facilities with elaborate amenities. The equivalent of A-type office facilities. In many locations, the demand for facilities of this type appears to be strong and will support a rate structure that makes developing such properties profitable.

SSFs are rented for the exclusive purpose of storing personal property and the care, custody, and the renter maintains control of property placed in self storage. Self storage is, therefore, not warehousing and presumes no possession of customers' goods. The fundamental aspect of

---

[1] www.selfstorage.org.

self storage is that it is a "self-service" operation and consumers/tenants retain the "care, custody, and control" of their personal property. The definition of "personal property" is vast and regulations in this country typically focus on prohibited properties that may be stored as opposed to permitted properties. Prohibited properties typically include hazardous materials, perishable foods, and ammunition.

Early SSFs largely consisted of low, flat, one-story buildings typically located in lower-density suburban areas. Such facilities were generally not heated or air conditioned and were of starkly functional design. These units were originally thought of as "mini-warehouses" and often restricted by zoning ordinances to commercial and industrial zones as a result.

Modern SSFs are being built as much larger multistoried buildings with heating, air conditioning, and often offering a wide array of complimentary services. These SSFs are often designed to fit into the existing architectural setting. Increasingly such units are being located in residential areas because they do not generate much traffic, are not noisy, do not create pollution, and place a very light burden on municipal services.[2] These facilities are designed to meet the need for easily accessible, small-scale storage space. A typical SSF covers two to three acres and consists of five to six buildings, each containing approximately 10,000 square feet of storage space. The size of the storage units can range from 25 square feet to 600 square feet. Internal driveways provide access and parking at individual storage units.

Successful SSFs require a location well served by major highways. Well traveled routes between commercial and residential districts, adjacent to interstate highways, major thoroughfares abutting commercial and residential areas all show potential for this type of facility. Successful modern SSFs are typified by a wide assortment of amenities and services that increase their value for their customers. The two absolutely critical elements for a successful SSF are that it provides good security and convenience.

Good security is provided by the sturdy construction of individual storage areas, strong doors, and door casings, locks typically supplied by the renter of the unit (to control access), door alarms, a perimeter fence, controlled access through the perimeter fence, a resident manager, bright lights, and 24/7 video and electronic surveillance of the grounds, an accurate record of individuals entering and leaving the premises.

Convenience involves 24/7 access for renters and their associates; an arrangement of facilities that facilitates access, egress, loading, and unloading; automatic interior lighting where appropriate; available loaner

<hr>

[2] *American Planning Association's Planning Advisory Service Report Number 396, September, 1986.*

dollies and hand trucks; available packing, moving, mailing, and storage supplies (including tape, bubble wrap, boxes, furniture covers, etc.); outside storage for autos, trucks, RVs, boats, and equipment to compliment the available inside storage; an adequate selection of different size storage units; and lean rest-room facilities.

Another approach to SSFs gaining popularity involves the conversion of industrial or commercial property to SSFs. Depending upon the area, such facilities may be conveniently located for this purpose. The property may be inexpensive because it is no longer being used for its original purpose. Thinking "outside the box" can prove rewarding in this situation. Where the facility already has heating and air conditioning facilities, partitioning the interior can be relatively inexpensive and lead to excellent rental revenues.

ILLUSTRATION #1: THAD AND JENNY RIDGELY

Thad Ridgely had been the manager and 10%-owner of a Pizza Hut for ten years in a small midwestern town. His Pizza Hut had been sold out to make way for a new highway coming through town. From his years of work, Thad had saved $100,000. He wanted to use that money to establish his own business. He wanted a business in which he could work with his wife Jenny and two teen-aged boys—a business with growth potential; a business where he could be in control. Thad was well thought of in town and had established good relations with the local bank.

The highway that had taken his Pizza Hut was an extension of an existing highway that would now connect two small growing cities that were 50 miles apart. Much of the area along this highway was still farmland, although here and there were scattered gas stations, convenience stores and fast-food restaurants. Thad thought the land along this highway would see increasing traffic and growth.

Acquisition Period

Thad had read about the growth in the self-storage industry and this type of enterprise appealed to him. Thad had a vision for a self-storage facility called Macomb Self-Store (after the county in which he was located). Thad found a farmer close to town who would lease him five acres of land, which had an old farmhouse on it, situated on the highway for $5,000 a year with an option to buy the land for $60,000 at the end of five years. The farmhouse was dilapidated, but inhabitable. Thad then found a construction firm that agreed to construct a chain-link fence around two acres directly behind the farmhouse in exchange for the right to park its construction equipment and truck on the unfenced portion of the land for the next five years. Thad and the construction firm agreed that this would be an exchange of services valued by each at $20,000. The result was that neither would have to put forth any cash for the services that they had exchanged. Thad found another contractor to build two storage buildings 50 ft. by 220 ft. on cement slabs that were each partitioned into 2 units 30 ft. by 25 ft., 10 units 20 ft. by 25 ft., 6 units 10 ft. by 25 ft., and 10 units 6 ft. by 12 ft. All units had sturdy outside overhead roll down doors, electric lights and outlets, but no heating and air conditioning. The areas around the building were not blacktopped to save expenses, rather the area was filled with crushed stone.

The contractor agreed to construct these buildings for $146,000 (22,000 sq. ft. at $65 per sq. ft. Thad financed this building with a $80,000 mortgage by the local bank that gave him a 15-year conventional mortgage at 10%. Thad converted the front room in the old farmhouse into an office that was stocked with boxes, bubble wrap, tape, locks, and a variety of moving supplies. Thad also entered into an arrangement with the local U-Haul dealer to store some of his unrented vehicles along the highway on Thad's land. Thad would get 25% of any rental contract he would write for the U-Haul dealer.

Holding Period

The first year was rough for the Ridgelys. As can be seen from Table 11.1, the completion of the self store facility took almost all of Thad's

TABLE 11.1   Macomb Self-Store, Acquisition Period Cash Flows

Uses:	
Land lease	$5,000
Building	146,000
Inventory	5,000
Accounting and legal expenses	4,200
Mortgage payment	
Interest	0
Principal	0
Total cash out	160,200
Sources:	
Mortgage loan	80,000
Equity	100,000
Total cash in	180,000
Cash balance	19,800

savings. A second factor was that the first quarter of the first year was eaten up in construction of the storage buildings and fence. Once the business was up and running, there was a slow process for customers becoming aware of the services they offered. A key to attracting the attention of customers turned out to be the joint effort with the U-Haul dealer. Many customers drove into town in a U-Haul and naturally stored their stuff at Macomb Self-Store while they looked for a permanent residence. Also, there was an unexpected demand for parking trucks, boats, campers, RVs, and the like on the unfenced portion of its property. However, sales of their basic storage bins were slow to develop. The net effect of all this on sales was a relatively low utilization rate that let to inadequate sales levels that first year (Table 11.2).

The second year brought a substantial improvement in utilization rates that continued into the third year and then stabilized. The increased utilization rates, along with increases in their ancillary business lines, brought about steadily increasing NOPAT (Table 11.3). By the end of the fifth year, the business was producing enough revenue that Thad felt comfortable exercising his option on the underlying land for $60,000.

Because the mortgage on the property was relatively small (with an annual P&I payment of $10,518), interest charges were not great. Thus, as can be seen from Table 11.4, NOPAT and net income tracked each other fairly closely.

The task of managing the Macomb Self-Store was basically 24/7 in order to service the customers. Although Thad and Jenny had both been able to draw a modest salary from the business, and they did get to use the farmhouse as their residence, they worked excessive hours. Also, their boys, who had been teenagers when they started the business and a great help, were now gone. As the land along the highway had been increasingly developed, the value of their property increased correspondingly. When a developer offered Thad and Jenny $300,000 for their land (to be used as a strip shopping center), they jumped at the opportunity.

Disposal Stage

The sale of the property for $300,000 can be seen to generate an after-profit gain for the Ridgely's of $105,732 (Table 11.5A). Furthermore, this sale resulted in a $235,530 gain in cash (Table 11.5B).

Table 11.6 reveals that for the return on their initial investment of $100,000 and their subsequent investment of $60,000), the Ridgelys garnered an NPV of $140,312 that represented an annual return of 28%. Whether this endeavor was considered successful by the Ridgelys would depend on how they weighed the return received, plus the opportunity they had "to be their own boss," against all the hours they put in.

TABLE 11.2 Macomb Self-Store, Revenue Structure[a]

Storage Bins	Number	Monthly Rates	Utilization			Revenue		
			Year 1	Year 2	Year 3	Year 1	Year 2	Year 3
30 ft. by 25 ft.	2	$250	50%	75%	75%	$750	$1,125	$1,125
20 ft. by 25 ft.	20	200	50%	75%	90%	600	900	1,080
10 ft. by 25 ft.	12	140	40%	80%	90%	269	538	605
6 ft. by 12 ft.	30	90	45%	80%	90%	219	389	437
Supplies						1,000	3,000	4,000
U-Haul						1,500	3,000	3,200
Outside storage						2,000	4,000	5,000
Miscellaneous[b]						20,000		
Total revenue						26,338	12,951	15,447

[a] Revenues after the third year increase at 8% per year.
[b] Represents a noncash transaction.

236

TABLE 11.3 Small Office Building Conversion, Macomb Self-Store, Holding Period NOPAT, Net-Operating Profits after Taxes

Year	Revenues	Legal and Accounting Expenses[a]	Salary[b]	Depreciation[c]	Utilities, Taxes, and Other Overhead[d]	EBIT	Taxes (20%)	NOPAT EBIT $(1 - tx)$
1	$74,144	$4,200	$60,000	$3,205	$6,350	$389	$78	$311
2	92,548	1,200	60,000	6,232	6,668	18,448	3,690	14,758
3	107,204	1,236	60,000	5,901	7,001	33,066	6,613	26,453
4	115,780	1,273	60,000	5,613	7,351	41,543	8,309	33,235
5	125,043	1,311	60,000	5,364	7,718	50,649	10,130	40,519
6	135,046	1,351	60,000	5,148	8,104	60,443	12,089	48,355
7	145,850	1,391	60,000	4,961	8,510	70,989	14,198	56,791
8	157,518	1,433	60,000	4,798	8,935	82,352	16,470	65,881
9	170,119	1,476	60,000	4,658	9,382	94,604	18,921	75,683
10	183,729	1,520	60,000	4,536	9,851	107,822	21,564	86,258

[a] Increases reflect a 3% annual increase.
[b] $60,000 for Thad Ridgely and $20,000 for Jenny Ridgely.
[c] Depreciation would consist of the original building ($146,000) depreciated over 39 years using the half-year convention and the improvements (fence at $20,000) depreciated over 15 years using the double-declining balance with half-year convention.
[d] Annual increase of 5%.

TABLE 11.4 Macomb Self Store, Income Statement

Year	Revenues[a]	Legal and Accounting Expenses[a]	Salary[b]	Depreciation[c]	Utilities, Taxes, and other Overhead[d]	Interest[e]	Earnings before Taxes	Taxes (20%)	Net Income
1	$74,144	$4,200	$60,000	$3,205	$11,350	$8,000	-$12,611	$0	-$12,611
2	92,548	1,200	60,000	6,232	11,668	7,748	5,700	1,140	4,560
3	107,204	1,236	60,000	5,901	12,001	7,471	20,595	4,119	16,476
4	115,780	1,273	60,000	5,613	12,351	7,167	29,377	5,875	23,501
5	125,043	1,311	60,000	5,364	12,718	6,831	38,818	7,764	31,054
6	135,046	1,351	60,000	5,148	8,104	6,463	53,981	10,796	43,185
7	145,850	1,391	60,000	4,961	8,510	6,057	64,931	12,986	51,945
8	157,518	1,433	60,000	4,798	8,935	5,611	76,740	15,348	61,392
9	170,119	1,476	60,000	4,658	9,382	5,121	89,483	17,897	71,587
10	183,729	1,520	60,000	4,536	9,851	4,581	103,241	20,648	82,593

[a] Increases reflect a 3% annual increase.

[b] $60,000 for Thad Ridgely and $20,000 for Jenny Ridgely.

[c] Depreciation would consist of the original building ($146,000) depreciated over 39 years using the half-year convention and the improvements (fence at $20,000) depreciated over 15 years using the double-declining balance with half-year convention.

[d] Includes the land lease the first five years. All other factor increase annually at 5%.

[e] Based on an annual payment of $10,514 representing a self-amortizing 15-year mortgage for $80,000 at 10%.

TABLE 11.5A   Macomb Self-Store, Tax Consequences of Sale of Property

Sale of building		$300,000
Fixed plant and improvements	$166,000	
Less accumulated		
depreciation	480,000	
Net fixed plant and improvements		−314,000
Cost of land		60,000
Gain on sale		554,000
Capital gains tax (15%)		83,100
After-tax gain on sale		470,900

TABLE 11.5B   Macomb Self-Store, Cash Gain from Sale of Property

Sale of property	$300,000
Less:	
Tax liability	83,100
Loan balance	0
Cash gain from sale	216,900

TABLE 11.6   Macomb Self-Store, Cash Flow Statement

Year	Net Income[a]	Depre- ciation[a]	Equity Payments	Capital Contri- butions[b]	Gain on Sale of Land[c]	Net Cash Flows
1	−$12,611	$3,205	$2,518	$100,000		−$109,406
2	4,560	6,232	2,770			10,792
3	16,476	5,901	3,047			22,377
4	23,501	5,613	3,351			29,114
5	31,054	5,364	3,686	60,000		−23,582
6	43,185	5,148	4,055			48,332
7	51,945	4,961	4,461			56,906
8	61,392	4,798	4,907			66,191
9	71,587	4,658	5,397			76,244
10	82,593	4,536	5,937		$235,530	322,658

[a] From Table 11.4.
[b] Includes purchase of land for $60,000 in year 5.
[c] From Table 11.5B.

NPV at 12% = $140,312
IRR = 28.41%

Break-Even Analysis

Because the Ridgelys used family labor at the Macomb Self-Store, there are no variable costs! This creates a situation in which once the fixed costs are covered by revenues, any additional revenue is 100% profit (at least, prior to taxes). If Macomb Self-Store fixed costs are $88,700— $60,000 for salary, $1,200 for legal, $5,000 for depreciation, a land lease of $5,000, utilities of $7,000, and a mortgage payment of $10,500 (strictly speaking, only the interest component of a mortgage payment is an expense)—then any revenue in excess of that amount is profit. Thus, we see from Table 11.4 that, with revenues in the first year of $74,000, the Ridgelys suffered a $12,000 loss; but in the second year, with revenues of $92,000, the Ridgelys emerged with a $5,000 gain.

ILLUSTRATION #2: THE PAISLEY BROTHERS' "TAJ MAHAL"

Richard and Bill Paisley were brothers who had extensive experience investing in commercial real estate throughout their metropolitan area. Some of their investments had worked out well, some had not. The present situation in their town was the glut of office buildings. The market had been severely overbuilt during the last five years, and the area had lost its largest employer to a corporate reorganization.

Richard and Bill held a 3-acre parcel one block from the intersection of a major highway and interstate. They had intended to build a 6-story office at that site because of its good access and its proximity to large up-scale neighborhoods and apartment complexes. Location, aside, now was clearly not the time to build an office building. Richard and Bill had paid $500,000 for that parcel in better times and now its value had fallen considerably. On the market it would only bring $200,000, and they did not want to take the loss.

Bill could not see turning the property into a small strip shopping center, a motel, a gas station, or a restaurant. The whole metropolitan area (and particularly this locality) seemed awash in these types of properties. Richard had read about the increasing popularity of self-storage facilities. With a little bit of research, he found that his area had relatively few self-storage facilities. Moreover, no one had yet built one of the large, attractive, multistory buildings that seemed to be in the forefront of the industry. An even more auspicious sign was that the nearest self-storage facility to their property site was five miles away. In doing their research, Bill and Richard had found that one of the reasons for the lack of self storage facilities was their county had restricted them to purely industrial and commercial districts. As most of the land around their site was used for residential purposes, they thought this might be a barrier to developing a self-storage facility. They talked with a lawyer specializing in such matters, and he thought that they would be successful obtaining a change in the law or getting a variance for their property. Of the two approaches, the lawyer thought obtaining a variance would be cheaper and faster. On this basis, Richard and Bill thought they would try to do the project.

Acquisition Stage

Getting a zoning variance proved to be more difficult than they thought. The zoning committee definitely did not like the idea of a fence of any type around the property and thought that a "warehouse" would detract from the general appearance of the area (a fear of the many nearby residents who attended the zoning meeting). However, Richard and Bill overcame these objections by having a notable local architect design a three-story building that looked like (in Richard's words) the "Taj Mahal." and would even have a glass front and an atrium. The building would have a footprint of 300 ft. by 200 ft. or 180,000 sq. ft. and have 187,200 sq. ft. are for storage. The building would also have a dedicated "manager's apartment" and an office for selling supplies and administrative functions. Construction would cost $120 per sq. ft. with another $20 per sq. ft. for soft costs. The total price tag on the building would be $25,200,000. Richard and Bill wondered if the facility could do enough business to justify that expenditure.

Richard and Bill employed a consultant to do some market research for this service in this location. The consultant found tremendous latent demand for self storage at this location if it was strictly first class. The need of the population segment most likely to be using self storage was for relatively small spaces. So Richard and Bill had the architect design 1,400 6 ft. by 10 ft., 500 12 ft. by 10 ft., and 300 12 ft. by 12 ft. storage areas. A front desk 24/7 would monitor entrance into the facility. Entrance into the facility would only be allowed to those who had an electronic pass. Each door to a unit was keyed individually (a $25 charge). The entrance and all hallways were monitored continuously by video.

Richard and Bill went to their favorite bank that offered to lend $22 million for the project. This would be structured as a bridge loan for one year at 12% interest only and then rolled over into a conventional 20-year mortgage at 10.5%. The net effect of these activities was that Bill and Richard had to invest $6,450,000 to make the project go (Table 11.7). They could have built an office building for less! However, their perception of the market was that this was a better way to go.

TABLE 11.7 Paisley Brothers Enterprises, Acquisition Period Cash Flows

Uses:	
Land[a]	$200,000
Building	25,500,000
Inventory	50,000
Accounting and legal expenses	45,000
Interest	2,640,000
Total cash out	28,435,000
Sources:	
Mortgage loan	22,000,000
Equity	6,450,000
Total cash in	28,450,000
Cash balance	15,000

[a] Land is valued at $200,000 because that is its market value at the time the project is initiated.

Holding Stage

The market research Richard and Bill paid off with an accurate assessment of demand. Consumers welcomed their large facility with a pent up desire for self storage. Richard and Bill were pleased that they could fill almost half their building that first year. Their customers ranged from the traditional transitional householder who needed a place to store furniture, while looking for a permanent residence, to a painting contractor who needed a place to store his ladders and scaffolding (but no paint or flammable liquid). Utilization rates climbed steadily the first three years and then stabilized at a level that allowed for normal turnover. The impact upon revenues may be seen in Table 11.8

The first year of operations generated significant NOPAT ($1,200,320), even with almost half the storage facility's capacity unutilized. As can be seen from Table 11.9, NOPAT climbs steadily throughout the 10-year holding period to $4,064,839 in the 10th year.

Because of the large mortgage ($22.5 million) being carried, the mortgage payment of $2,672,852, with its $2,310,000 interest component, was large enough to drive net income into the red in the first year of operation. It is true that Richard and Bill could have cut down a bit on the labor and overhead expense (Table 11.10), and probably broke even for that first year, but they felt that, since they were charging such premium rates, they ought to provide premium service to maintain their customer base. Their judgment of the market proved correct after reaching capacity; they are able to increase revenue 8% a year through rate increases. In the 10th and final year of their planned holding period, net income rose to $2,884,614.

TABLE 11.8 Paisley Brothers Enterprises, Revenue Structure

Storage Bins	Number	Monthly Rates	Utilization			Revenue		
			Year1	Year 2	Year 3	Year1	Year 2	Year 3
6 ft. ×10 ft.	1,400	$140	50%	75%	90%	$420	$630	$756
12 ft. ×10 ft.	500	185	50%	75%	90%	555	833	999
12 ft. ×12 ft.	290	215	50%	75%	90%	645	968	1,161
Supplies						66,000	87,000	104,000
Moving equipment						45,000	64,000	77,000
Total revenue						112,620	153,430	183,916

TABLE 11.9   Paisley Brothers Enterprises, Holding Period NOPAT, Net-Operating Profits after Taxes

Year	Revenues[a]	Legal and Accounting Expenses[b]	Salary and Wages[c]	Depreciation[d]	Utilities, Taxes, and other Overhead[b]	EBIT	Taxes (32%)	NOPAT EBIT$(1 - tx)$
0		$45,000	$40,000	$326,923	$25,000	-$110,000	-$35,200	-$74,800
1	$2,216,100	8,000	80,000	653,846	36,000	1,765,177	564,857	1,200,320
2	3,308,650	8,400	82,400	653,846	37,800	2,526,204	808,385	1,717,819
3	3,970,180	8,820	84,872	653,846	39,690	3,182,952	1,018,545	2,164,407
4	4,287,794	9,261	87,418	653,846	41,675	3,495,595	1,118,590	2,377,004
5	4,630,818	9,724	90,041	653,846	43,758	3,833,449	1,226,704	2,606,745
6	5,001,283	10,210	92,742	653,846	45,946	4,198,539	1,343,532	2,855,006
7	5,401,386	10,721	95,524	653,846	48,243	4,593,052	1,469,776	3,123,275
8	5,833,497	11,257	98,390	653,846	50,656	5,019,348	1,606,192	3,413,157
9	6,300,177	11,820	101,342	653,846	53,188	5,479,981	1,753,594	3,726,387
10	6,804,191	12,411	104,382	653,846	55,848	5,977,704	1,912,865	4,064,839

[a] After the third year, revenues increase 8% a year.
[b] Increases reflect a 5% annual increase.
[c] Salaries for a resident manager and four part-time employees.
[d] Depreciation would consist of the original building ($25,500,000) depreciated over 39 years using the half-year convention.

TABLE 11.10 Paisley Brothers Enterprises, Income Statement

Year	Revenues[a]	Legal and Accounting Expenses[b]	Salary[c]	Depreciation[d]	Utilities, Taxes, and other Overhead[b]	Interest[e]	Earnings before Taxes	Taxes (32%)	Net Income
0	$0	$45,000	$40,000	$0	$25,000	$2,640,000	-$2,750,000	-$880,000	-$1,870,000
1	2,216,100	8,000	80,000	326,923	11,350	2,310,000	-520,173	-166,455	-353,718
2	3,308,650	8,400	82,400	653,846	11,668	2,271,901	280,436	89,739	190,696
3	3,970,180	8,820	84,872	653,846	12,001	2,229,801	980,840	313,869	666,971
4	4,287,794	9,261	87,418	653,846	12,351	2,183,280	1,341,638	429,324	912,314
5	4,630,818	9,724	90,041	653,846	12,718	2,131,875	1,732,613	554,436	1,178,177
6	5,001,283	10,210	92,742	653,846	8,104	2,075,073	2,161,308	691,619	1,469,689
7	5,401,386	10,721	95,524	653,846	8,510	2,012,306	2,620,479	838,553	1,781,926
8	5,833,497	11,257	98,390	653,846	8,935	1,942,949	3,118,120	997,799	2,120,322
9	6,300,177	11,820	101,342	653,846	9,382	1,866,309	3,657,479	1,170,393	2,487,085
10	6,804,191	12,411	104,382	653,846	9,851	1,781,622	4,242,079	1,357,465	2,884,614

[a] After the third year, revenues increase 8% a year.
[b] Increases reflect a 5% annual increase.
[c] Salaries for a resident manager and four part-time employees.
[d] Depreciation would consist of the original building ($25,500,000) depreciated over 39 years using the half-year convention.
[e] Consequent on a 20-year loan for $22 million at 10.5%, generating an annual payment of $2,672,852.

245

Disposal Stage

To exit from the business, Richard and Bill tried to sell their property by capitalizing its income stream. Although there were no comparable local sales, equivalent self-storage facilities in other cities normally traded at four to six times earnings. As this facility had achieved such a dominant position in its market, Richard and Bill were able to get top dollar for it at six times earnings. That translated into a sales price of $17,307,684. This meant they took a loss of $2,480,777 on the property, generating a tax credit of $372,117 (Table 11.11A). The net result of this sale was a modest cash gain of $711,974 (Table 11.11B).

The cash flows resulting from this project over the holding period are presented in Table 11.12. It can be seen that, when all was said and done, their NPV was a little less than a $1 million and they earned a meager 14% on their investment. Considering the size of the project and the risks associated with entering a new market, this return appears to not compensate Richard and Bill for the risk to which they were exposed.

Perhaps the problem here lies in the "Taj Mahal" approach undertaken to developing the facility. A more conservative approach to constructing and operating the facility could have produced for Richard and Bill a much more substantial return.

TABLE 11.11A   Paisley Brothers Enterprises, Tax Consequences of Sale of Property

Sale of building		$17,307,684
Fixed plant and improvements	$25,500,000	
Less accumulated depreciation	6,211,538	
Net fixed plant and improvements		19,288,462
Cost of land[a]		500,000
Gain on sale		-2,480,777
Capital gains tax (15%)		-372,117
After-tax gain on sale		-2,108,661

[a] The market value at the beginning of the project was $200,000, but since the original cost was $500,000, this would be used to calculate the taxable gain.

TABLE 11.11B   Paisley Brothers Enterprises, Cash Gain from Sale of Property

Sale of property	$17,307,684
Less:	
Tax liability	-372,117
Loan balance	16,967,826
Cash gain from sale	711,974

TABLE 11.12   Paisley Brothers Enterprises, Cash Flow Statement

Year	Net Income[a]	Depreciation[a]	Equity Payments	Capital Contributions[b]	Gain on Sale of Land[c]	Net Cash Flows
0	-$1,870,000			$6,450,000		-$8,320,000
1	-353,718	$326,923	$362,852			-26,794
2	190,696	653,846	400,951			844,542
3	666,971	653,846	443,051			1,320,818
4	912,314	653,846	489,572			1,566,160
5	1,178,177	653,846	540,977			1,832,023
6	1,469,689	653,846	597,779			2,123,536
7	1,781,926	653,846	660,546			2,435,772
8	2,120,322	653,846	729,903			2,774,168
9	2,487,085	653,846	806,543			3,140,932
10	2,884,614	653,846	891,230		711,974	4,250,435

[a] From Table 11.4.
[b] Includes purchase of land for $60,000 in year 5.
[c] From Table 11.5B.

NPV at 12% = $985,376
IRR = 14.22%

Break-Even Analysis

As the Paisley's self-store facility is much larger than the Ridegely self-store facility, there will be some small variable cost for both labor and utilities. However these variable costs will be small (5% for labor and 2% for utilities.) Given fixed costs of $3,471,000 for the "Taj Mahal"—legal $10,000, salaries $90,000, depreciation $653,000, utilities $45,000, and a mortgage payment of $2,673,000—total costs will thus be:

$$TC = FC + VC$$

$$TC = \$3,471,000 + 0.07\ S$$

Thus, the breakeven point requires that $S = \$3,471,000 + 0.07\ S$, Therefore the breakeven point is $3,732,000. After adjustments for rounding, this is why Paisley Brothers Enterprises does not make a profit until year 2 (Table 11.10).

ILLUSTRATION #3: AN ALTERNATIVE TO THE "TAJ MAHAL" APPROACH

If the Paisleys had taken a bare-bones approach to constructing their self-storage facility, they could probably have done it for $90 a sq. ft. for construction and $10 a sq. ft. for soft costs. That would have reduced the cost of the building from $25.5 million to $18 million. The bank would have lent them $15 million of this, substantially cutting their own equity required. See Table 11.13 for their cash requirements under this scenario.

Other opportunities to reduce expenses lie in the reduction of operating costs. Perhaps 24/7 is not necessary. Perhaps 6:00 A.M. to 10:00 P.M. is enough to meet 99% of customer's needs. Perhaps a less expensive system to control access and provide surveillance would be appropriate. These changes can have a significant impact on NOPAT as can be seen from Table 11.14. NOPAT is much higher than under the "Taj Mahal" scenario rising to $4,214,191 in the 10th year.

A corresponding pattern can be seen in net income (Table 11.15). The combination of lower costs, lower depreciation, and lower interest rates practically eliminates the first year's loss in net income. Net income is able to climb steadily to $3,248,965 by the 10th year.

This higher net income will, of course, translate into a higher sales price of $19,493,791 (Table 11.16A) and a larger cash gain from the sale of $4,804,263 (Table 11.16B). Note that this is more than quadruple the gain under the "Taj Mahal" scenario.

TABLE 11.13   Paisley Brothers Enterprises, Acquisition Period Cash Flows

Uses:	
Land[a]	$200,000
Building	18,000,000
Inventory	50,000
Accounting and legal expenses	45,000
Interest	1,800,000
Total cash out	20,095,000
Sources:	
Mortgage loan	15,000,000
Equity	5,125,000
Total cash in	20,125,000
Cash balance	30,000

[a] Land is valued at $200,000 because that is its market value at the time the project is initiated.

TABLE 11.14 Paisley Brothers Enterprises, Holding Period NOPAT, Net Operating Profits after Taxes

Year	Revenues[a]	Legal and Accounting Expenses[b]	Salary and Wages[c]	Depreciation[d]	Utilities, Taxes, and other Overhead[b]	EBIT	Taxes (32%)	NOPAT EBIT(1 − tx)
0		$45,000	$30,000	$230,769	$20,000	−$95,000	−$30,400	−$64,600
1	$2,216,100	8,000	65,000	461,538	31,000	1,881,331	602,026	1,279,305
2	3,308,650	8,400	66,950	461,538	32,550	2,739,212	876,548	1,862,664
3	3,970,180	8,820	68,959	461,538	34,178	3,396,686	1,086,939	2,309,746
4	4,287,794	9,261	71,027	461,538	35,886	3,710,081	1,187,226	2,522,855
5	4,630,818	9,724	73,158	461,538	37,681	4,048,717	1,295,589	2,753,127
6	5,001,283	10,210	75,353	461,538	39,565	4,414,617	1,412,677	3,001,940
7	5,401,386	10,721	77,613	461,538	41,543	4,809,970	1,539,191	3,270,780
8	5,833,497	11,257	79,942	461,538	43,620	5,237,140	1,675,885	3,561,255
9	6,300,177	11,820	82,340	461,538	45,801	5,698,677	1,823,577	3,875,101
10	6,804,191	12,411	84,810	461,538	48,091	6,197,340	1,983,149	4,214,191

[a] After the third year, revenues increase 8% a year.
[b] Increases reflect a 5% annual increase.
[c] Salaries for a resident manager and two part-time employees.
[d] Depreciation would consist of the original building ($18,000,000) depreciated over 39 years using the half-year convention.

TABLE 11.15 Paisley Brothers Enterprises, Income Statement

Year	Revenues[a]	Legal and Accounting Expenses[b]	Salary[c]	Depreciation[d]	Utilities, Taxes, and Other Overhead[b]	Interest[e]	Earnings before Taxes	Taxes (32%)	Net Income
0	$0	$45,000	$30,000	$0	$20,000	$1,800,000	−$1,895,000	−$606,400	−$1,288,600
1	2,216,100	8,000	65,000	230,769	11,350	1,890,000	10,981	3,514	7,467
2	3,308,650	8,400	66,950	461,538	11,668	1,858,828	901,266	288,405	612,861
3	3,970,180	8,820	68,959	461,538	12,001	1,824,382	1,594,480	510,234	1,084,246
4	4,287,794	9,261	71,027	461,538	12,351	1,786,320	1,947,297	623,135	1,324,162
5	4,630,818	9,724	73,158	461,538	12,718	1,744,262	2,329,417	745,414	1,584,004
6	5,001,283	10,210	75,353	461,538	8,104	1,697,787	2,748,291	879,453	1,868,838
7	5,401,386	10,721	77,613	461,538	8,510	1,646,432	3,196,572	1,022,903	2,173,669
8	5,833,497	11,257	79,942	461,538	8,935	1,589,685	3,682,140	1,178,285	2,503,855
9	6,300,177	11,820	82,340	461,538	9,382	1,526,980	4,208,117	1,346,597	2,861,519
10	6,804,191	12,411	84,810	461,538	9,851	1,457,691	4,777,890	1,528,925	3,248,965

[a] After the third year, revenues increase 8% a year.
[b] Increases reflect a 5% annual increase.
[c] Salaries for a resident manager and four part-time employees.
[d] Depreciation would consist of the original building ($25,500,000) depreciated over 39 years using the half-year convention.
[e] Consequent on a 20-year loan for $18 million at 10.5%, generating an annual payment of $2,186,879.

TABLE 11.16A   Paisley Brothers Enterprises, Tax Consequences of Sale of Property

Sale of building		$19,493,791
Fixed plant and improvements	$18,000,000	
Less accumulated depreciation	4,384,615	
Net fixed plant and improvements		13,615,385
Cost of land[a]		500,000
Gain on sale		5,378,407
Capital gains tax (15%)		806,761
After-tax gain on sale		4,571,646

[a] The market value at the beginning of the project was $200,000, but since the original cost was $500,000, this would be used to calculate the taxable gain.

TABLE 11.16B   Paisley Brothers Enterprises, Cash Gain from Sale of Property

Sale of property	$19,493,791
Less:	
Tax liability	806,761
Loan balance	13,882,767
Cash gain from sale	4,804,263

The net effect of a less-costly building, lower expenses, and a smaller bank loan has an exceptional effect on the profitability of the venture. As can be seen from Table 11.17, the NPV of the project rises by a factor of five to $4,965,730 and the IRR increases from 14% to 24%. Such gains are surely not spectacular, but they do seem to line up more appropriately the risk and the reward inherent in the project.

Given the two different scenarios, it would appear the latter is more desirable from the investor's point of view.

Break-Even Analysis (Paisley II)

The scaled-back version of the Paisley self-storage facility will have the same variable costs as the "Taj Mahal," but a significantly lower level of fixed costs. Fixed costs now will be $2,794,000—with legal $10,000, salaries $90,000, depreciation $462,000, utilities $45,000, and a mortgage payment of $2,187,000. This represents a reduction of $679,000 from the "Taj Mahal" scenario. Total costs will thus be:

$$TC = FC + VC$$

$$TC = \$2,794,000 + 0.07\ S$$

TABLE 11.17   Paisley Brothers Enterprises, Cash Flow Statement

Year	Net Income[a]	Depre- ciation[a]	Equity Payments	Capital Contri- butions[b]	Gain on Sale of Land[c]	Net Cash Flows
0	-$1,288,600			$5,125,000		-$6,413,600
1	7,467	$230,769	$296,879			238,236
2	612,861	461,538	328,051			1,074,400
3	1,084,246	461,538	362,496			1,545,785
4	1,324,162	461,538	400,559			1,785,700
5	1,584,004	461,538	442,617			2,045,542
6	1,868,838	461,538	489,092			2,330,376
7	2,173,669	461,538	540,447			2,635,207
8	2,503,855	461,538	597,194			2,965,393
9	2,861,519	461,538	659,899			3,323,058
10	3,248,965	461,538	729,188		$4,804,263	8,514,767

[a] From Table 11.4.
[b] Includes purchase of land for $60,000 in year 5.
[c] From Table 11.5B.

NPV at 12% = $4,965,730
IRR = 23.89%

Thus, break-even point requires that $S = \$2,794,000 + 0.07 S$, Therefore BEP = $3,004,000. After adjustments for rounding, this is why Paisley Brothers Enterprises is able to make a small profit in its first year (Table 11.15) and raise its IRR from 14% to 24% (Tables 11.12 and 11.17).

SUMMARY

Investing in self-storage facilities presents good risk-return opportunities for today's investor. Demand for such facilities is strong and many localities are underserved, either because of restrictive zoning laws or because developers have not yet recognized the opportunity being presented. Self-storage facilities used to be low-budget investments. Indeed, at one time it was thought that developing land could be used as a self-storage facility while the land awaited more intensive development.

The market today demands facilities that are expensive to construct because of the need for air conditioning, heating, and an array of other amenities. Also, a key to success of such facilities is a convenient location. This translates into more expensive land costs and a building that must conform to community standards. A modern self-storage facility can be as expensive on a square-foot basis as an office building or a high-rise apartment.

This is not to preclude the desirability of investing in this type of real estate. Strong demand can generate revenue streams that results in very favorable cash flow structures. Such opportunities are made even more desirable by the opportunities for financial leverage and the tax offsets such a facility can generate.

The investor, looking at a self-storage facility, should be careful not just to assess the existing competition, but the potential competition as well. Where an opportunity for self-storage facilities exists, it would not be impossible for a number of investors to see this opportunity and enter the market simultaneously. Under these circumstances, the market could be seriously overbuilt and generate a rate structure and vacancy level that would not support these projects. This, of course, is just another manifestation of the "cobweb" cycle of high demand, rising prices, overbuilding, increasing supply, and falling prices that characterizes so many areas of the commercial real estate market.

CHAPTER 12

Restaurant Real Estate

The restaurant industry is huge, accounting for almost 4% of our GNP. There are over 890,000 restaurants operating in the United States with over 12 million employees doing over $800 billion in sales.[1] Future growth is estimated to be between 4% and 7% annually. Americans have not lost their taste for eating out.

Not only is the industry huge, it is dynamic. Old restaurants go out of business and new restaurants spring up. How successful restaurants are depends on a wide variety of factors ranging from broad social issues (the events of 9/11), broad economic issues (the cost of energy), industry-wide issues (Mad Cow Disease), population trends (from the Rust Belt to the South, revitalizing inner cities), as well as the tastes and preferences of individual consumers (high-protein diets, low-carbohydrate diets, low-fat diets, organic foods, ethnic foods). All these factors contribute to a rapidly changing mix for success as a restaurant.

This is great news for commercial real estate investors. The combination of the size of the industry, along with its dynamic character, creates a mosaic of opportunities for commercial real estate investors. Investment in this industry can either be indirect (through holding a lease) or direct (through owning the property and managing the restaurant itself).

There are two basic divisions in the food service industry: (1) fast foods (characterized by both the speed of service and the limited amount of service available) and (2) full-service restaurants. These two sectors in the industry are of roughly equal size. Full-service restaurants may be further broken down into categories based on how expensive they are. These categories are (1) midscale (average check below $20),

---

[1] The National Restaurant Association, www.restaurant.org; U.S. Bureau of the Census, Census of Retail Trade, 1998 and supplements.

(2) casual dining (average check \$20–\$40), and (3) upscale or fine dining (average check above \$40). Each segment of the restaurant industry
has its individual attributes that make for success and failure. However,
a common theme among restaurants of all types is the importance of its
location.

LOCATION AS A FACTOR IN RESTAURANT SUCCESS

It is important that the restaurant's location be appropriate to its sector of
the restaurant industry and to the individual restaurant's particular business strategy. What works for a fast-food restaurant will not necessarily
work for a fine-dining establishment. What works for a Greek restaurant
may not work for a pancake house.

For each type of restaurant, the variables that need to be examined
to determine whether the location is good are basically the same: population, demographics, highway traffic, tourism, seasonal demand, business trade, and competition. Each of these variables may be important
in determining whether a particular location would be good for a particular type of restaurant.

Knowing these variables is critical to developing a good business
plan. A good business plan for a restaurant should target a specific segment of the population and design the restaurant's food, service, and
amenities around that target population segment. The more data that
can be found impacting the ability of the restaurant to work its specific
business plan, the more will be known about the probability of success
or failure of that particular location.

Population

To evaluate a business plan, one needs to get the number of people who
live in the area from where the business will be drawn. In a smaller town,
probably the whole town population is fine. In a big city, the immediate
area relative to the focal point of your business plan will define the relevant population. Census data can be obtained, broken down by small
geographic units called *enumeration districts*, and substantial amounts
of population (and other socioeconomic) data are available by ZIP code.
In our Internet world, a surprising amount of this type of data is available online and free. The Bureau of the Census makes a large amount of
this data available also. Local groups such as the chamber of commerce
or economic development group also can be good sources of data. There
are, of course, no shortages of marketing companies or consultants who
are happy to do this analysis for a fee.

Demographics

Knowing the basic size of the population that can be expected to become a customer base is important; but it is only a first step towards identifying whether the business plan is viable. What is needed is information about the kinds of people live in your market area. This includes such facts as income level breakdowns, ethic groupings, age group breakdowns, and other useful information that relates to who your customer base will be. If you want to open a fine-dining restaurant, you can use demographics to see how many people there are with incomes over a certain amount that will be most likely to be your core customers. Demographic data can be found hand-in-hand with the population data sources discussed above.

Highway Traffic

For many types of restaurants (especially fast food), this is a critically important variable. During the peak dining hours of breakfast, lunch and supper, what could be more convenient than a restaurant located on the way to where you are going. Today's consumers appear to value convenience above virtually every other good or service that they can consume. The daily volume of traffic passing on the streets fronting your restaurant location is also important for generating impulse purchasing during nonpeak hours, and any nearby highway or other main arteries that will bring you your daily customers. Such data is often available from the state or municipal highway or traffic safety department. Many municipalities today publish such information online.

Tourism

The number of annual visitors to your area can have a dramatic impact on restaurant success depending on the business plan of the restaurant. In many vacation areas, this is by far the biggest factor in determining success. Even in what are not normally thought of as tourist destinations, there may be a lot of people, at any given time, just "passing through." And they are going to need to eat. Such data may often be obtained from the local chamber of commerce, visitor's center, tourism board, or other related agencies should have a good estimate of this information. This is especially likely if the market is located in a place that attracts a good number of vacation or convention business.

Seasonal Demand

If the area has a seasonal population fluctuation, the result of skiing opportunities, a summer beach season, a fishing season, and the like that brings in people from out of town, this may often be a factor in determining the success of a business plan. Similarly, there may be seasons when the population leaves the area. Such population movements should also be taken into account. This information is often available at the same places that have tourist information.

Business Trade

The number of businesses operating in your area, and the number of workers who arrive each day, can play a very important role in determining the volume of restaurant business in a given locale. This is particularly important if you are expecting to serve a large lunch crowd, and your restaurant is based in a nonresidential area, where few people are likely to come for dinner, shopping, or other activities that would provide you with business during the nonweekday, nonworking hours. Information of this type should be available from the same sources as population or demographic data.

Competition

The presence of competitors in a particular locale may be bad or may be good. Their presence is bad if such competitors reduce your number of customers. Such competitors are good if they increase your number of customers.

There is strong evidence that "clustering" competitors is good for individual restaurants. A single Italian restaurant, with no other Italian restaurants around it, may have a hard time drawing sufficient customers. Put several Italian restaurants in a cluster and that location becomes a "Little Italy" that attracts crowds of people resulting in more diners per restaurant. This is because clustering creates a destination effect. That is, the area becomes a destination for a product or service in general and is more attractive on that basis alone. Burger King has no fear of locating next to a McDonald's, in fact that is one of their criteria for identifying "good" locations. More fast-food restaurants located in a single place will create a destination effect that increases business for all.

As a general rule, it is the rare situation where the presence of competition reduces the desirability of a particular location. If a restaurant has a well-defined business plan, with a correctly identified target market, and "does the little things right," it should be successful because the demand for food service is so huge. There is plenty of room.

FAILED RESTAURANTS

From the perspective of the commercial real estate investor, there are two approaches to take to the restaurant industry. The first is to own the property and operate the business. The second is to own the property and lease it to the business.

If you are going to own and operate the property, then the importance of having a successful business is obvious. If you are just going to play a passive role and just hold the lease, the success of the business is still just as important in determining your success as an investor. Successful restaurant operators pay their rent on time, have a better attitude about maintaining the property, and are happy to renew their leases (at higher rents) when that time comes. Failing restaurant operators are slow on their payments, are a source of constant complaints (somebody has to take the blame for their situation), do not maintain the property, and do not renew their leases. Even where the lease is tightly drawn and well secured, compliance is always difficult with failing operators. At best, this situation is a constant source of aggravation and concern. (Who likes to write threatening letters?) Holding the lease of a successful restaurant owner is infinitely preferable.

This situation can and should be avoided by a little effort on the part of a nominally passive leaseholder. Some effort needs to be expended to determine the likelihood of success for the potential lessee. Does the potential lessee have a plan? Does this plan make sense? A few easy questions at this point save a wealth of headaches later on.

The mistakes discussed in the following sections are easy to avoid with a little advance planning and research. The best way to establish a highly profitable venture is to find the best fit for the best area and go with that. If your lessee were thinking upscale French, but it is clear the area is begging for a Mexican quick-serve, this needs to be discussed for his or her good and yours. Or if your lessee has his or her heart set on an original concept, then is the property under consideration appropriate to that concept? The trick to answering this type of question is to do the research, which really is not that hard and does not take long, but does pays huge dividends. The high rate of failure in the restaurant business is testimony to the fact that many restaurant operators do not do any research at all.

Causes of Restaurant Failure

Poor Management

This is the number one cause of restaurant failures. Poor management is a broad problem that covers a lot of ground—and usually means that there are many things wrong with the restaurant's operations. These could include excessive staffing, poor inventory control, unchecked employee theft, low enforcement of service standards, and a variety of other problems.

The secret to running a professional, highly successful and profitable restaurant is having a great manager. In fact, taking over a troubled restaurant is very often a good way for a new restaurant owner to inexpensively acquire what turns out to be a very healthy operation, once properly run, from a previous owner anxious to get rid of it because he or she does not know how to run it or fix what is wrong. And not managing a restaurant well is the fastest way to bankruptcy!

The key to addressing management quality is benchmarking. The numbers tell the story. Know your numbers inside and out. Industry standards are widely available for cost of food, cost of service, inventory shrinkage, and every other imaginable dimension of the restaurant business. You cannot prevent food waste, inventory overstocking, poor pricing, incorrect staffing levels, or employee theft (to name a few) if you do not know what the numbers should be. This is especially true if you are not religious about tracking everything and keeping clean, accurate, and up-to-date books.

Be ruthless with cost control—a few extra dollars here and there adds up much faster than one would ever imagine.

Service

Every customer enters a restaurant as a matter of choice. They always have alternatives. If they are not delighted by what they experience, why should they come back? Repeat customers are the lifeblood of any restaurant. Without them, the restaurant dies.

Demand your employees provide A+ service at all times, and A+ quality work. If they do not, they should not be kept.

Remember at all times that the only reason you have a business is because people decide to come and eat at your restaurant—they have other choices, and you want to make sure they always leave happy—even if you have to give a free a meal or apologize for something that was not your fault.

Lack of Financial Resources

Many times a restaurant would have been successful if it just could have lasted a few more months—but bills piled up and the owner miscalculated how long it would be before the new operation broke even. Many restaurants begin with a break-in period, where customers learn about the positive attributes of the restaurant and begin to patronize it. It takes time for word-of-mouth to build and repeat business to develop. Consequently many restaurants will run a negative cash flow during their break-in period. The break-in period may last six months to a year. Many restaurants end up shutting their doors because of they fail to allow for this expense.

Financial Planning

The financial planning of a restaurant is a very critical part of the over-all success of the venture; but few people really have the knowledge and experience to do it right. Some get lucky, but some do not. Why trust in luck? The numbers for a restaurant should be run before it opens its doors so the manager knows what his goals and constraints are. Not only should numbers be run initially, they should be run regularly (at least monthly). If there are problems, running the numbers daily or weekly allow these problems to be specifically identified and solved. There is no business that cannot be run better by knowing what is going on, what is possible, and what is not possible.

Poor Service

People will stop coming to a restaurant much faster if they experience poor service than for any other reason, including high prices and bad food. And by providing great service, an otherwise mediocre restaurant can thrive. Unfortunately for them, many restaurant owners fail to real-ize this basic truth about the industry.

Providing good service sounds obvious, but what does it mean? And how do you get your staff to do it, when they make minimum wage and work long hours day after day? The secret is first to hire the very best people you can find—based on attitude and willingness to follow high standards. Not all experience is equal. Hiring needs to be followed up with training that emphasizes the fundamentals of good service. Often-times, a restaurateur will find it advisable to spend resources to develop a team effort among the employees to stimulate employees to consis-tently provide good service.

To properly motivate your employees, the carrot normally works bet-ter than the stick. The carrot does not have to be money. To merely thank your employees for a job well done or some extra effort they have put forth goes a long way to making them feel appreciated. Everybody wants to be appreciated for what they do. With a good attitude will come better service, with better service more tips. The spiral works both ways.

Having good service, no matter what type of restaurant, will make a huge difference to all aspects of your business, especially the bottom line. People will buy more and visit more often if they like the people who serve them, and they will not come back at all if they do not!

Poor Market Analysis

Restaurants, more than any other business, need to focus on a particular market segment. Trying to be all things to everybody is self-defeating. In the end, you will please nobody. Your location, type of operation, menu, pricing, layout, and many other factors should reflect this focus. Clarity of focus is enhanced by having a formal business plan in which all this is thought out. The restaurants that could have succeeded elsewhere, but failed because it was put in the wrong place or was the wrong concept for the area are legion.

Excessive Costs

Excessive costs are a design issue. It is a matter of scale. Where you have a focus on a particular market niche, all cost factors should scale to that niche. Running the numbers should check that this is so. There have been many cases of restaurants that met or exceeded their projections for sales and number of customers, but still went out of business because they also underestimated their costs. It does not matter if you are doing $2 million in annual sales if your annual costs are $2.5 million. Many first time restaurant owners get caught up in the idea of making their dream a reality and decide to "spare no expense" in bringing their vision to life. Unfortunately, that is a great way to turn the dream into a nightmare.

Without careful planning and a good understanding of what it costs to open and run a restaurant, it is hard to get a restaurant as profitable and successful as it can be, especially in the beginning years.

ILLUSTRATION #1: ROUTE 66 McDONALD'S

Bob and Ray Hudpohl were operators of a gas station on the fringe of a rapidly growing Southwestern town that was being rapidly populated by northern "snowbirds." Their gas station was located at the intersection of two major highways that led into town from nearby metropolitan areas. On the other side of the highway, the county had just constructed a large regional high school.

The gas station was located on 600 acres that they had inherited from their father. The years prior to this recent growth had been a struggle for the family, and they maintained ownership of the land through great sacrifice and hard work. Their recently deceased father had once told them, "Hold on to the land boys, through thick and thin. It will be a constant in your lives." Bob and Ray took this advice to heart. They saw clearly that there were opportunities to develop this land. They were not sure if they should develop the land themselves or lease it to others, but they knew they did not want to sell.

As the town grew towards them, they had numerous offers to sell their land, which were summarily rejected. They had been considering putting up a variety of businesses (motels, restaurants, a strip mall, etc.) that they would operate themselves. After much thought, they rejected this idea on the basis that the thing they knew most about was fixing cars. That is when they were approached by a McDonald's franchisee that already owned several stores in that town (McDonald's is the largest national fast-food restaurant) and wanted to put another store right next to their gas station.

The franchisee proposed leasing three-quarters of an acre from them for building a 2,500 sq. ft. restaurant with plenty of parking and drive-through access. They wanted an absolute prime location for their restaurant. The topography and layout of the intersection gave this particular property a commanding presence. Bob and Ray felt that the use to which this land was put would set the tone for developing the remaining parcel, both in terms of style and rent level. There had been no recent transactions in that area, so there were no "comps" (i.e., comparisons) with which to establish value.

The franchisee planned to spend $3 million on the building, improvements, and equipment. When pressed on the volume of business he expected, the franchisee said that he had run the numbers and, between sales from the considerable highway traffic, high school students, and visitors to the high school, expected to do about $4 million in sales, but, of course, there was no guarantee of this. He offered to take a 20-year triple net lease from Bob and Ray for $600,000 a year, with an option to renew at $600,000, adjusted for whatever the percentage increase in the Consumer Price Index occurred over the next 20 years.

The question for Bob and Ray was whether this was a good deal. Should they demand more or different terms. Analyzing the potential profitability of this restaurant and then considering their own costs, can answer this question. Bob and Ray then asked their accountant how profitable this McDonald's was likely to be.

To do this, the accountant developed NOPAT, income, and cash flow statements for the proposed McDonald's store without any lease expense whatsoever. The accountant took a very conservative approach to constructing these financial statements. To identify McDonald's cost and growth rates, he used the national averages. This was conservative because wages were relatively low in this region, and growth was occurring much faster than in other areas. The results of his analysis are presented in Tables 12.1, 12.2, and 12.3. Table 12.1 shows high levels of positive NOPAT that would support a highly leveraged store. The store's projected sales of $4 million will be highly profitable are presented in Table 12.2.

Part of the reason for this level of profitability is a cost structure that only has 56% variable costs. Each additional dollar of sales will contribute $.44 to the bottom line before taxes. The break-even level of operation for the store is clearly around $1 million. (Assuming TC = $450,000 + 0.56VC, where $TR = TC$, then BEP = $1,023.) It does not

TABLE 12.1 Route 66 McDonald's, Holding Period NOPAT, Pro Forma Net-Operating Profits after Taxes without Land Lease

Year	Revenues[a]	Food Cost[b]	Salary and Wages[c]	Overhead	Depreciation[d]	EBIT	Taxes (40%)	NOPAT EBIT(1 – tx)
1	$4,000,000	$1,440,000	$800,000	$250,000	$151,282	$1,358,718	$543,487	$815,231
2	4,120,000	1,483,200	824,000	257,500	224,615	1,330,685	532,274	798,411
3	4,243,600	1,527,696	848,720	265,225	180,171	1,421,788	568,715	853,073
4	4,370,908	1,573,527	874,182	273,182	150,186	1,499,832	599,933	899,899
5	4,502,035	1,620,733	900,407	281,377	129,319	1,570,200	628,080	942,120
6	4,637,096	1,669,355	927,419	289,819	129,858	1,620,646	648,258	972,388
7	4,776,209	1,719,435	955,242	298,513	96,917	1,706,102	682,441	1,023,661
8	4,919,495	1,771,018	983,899	307,468	90,832	1,766,277	706,511	1,059,766
9	5,067,080	1,824,149	1,013,416	316,693	85,559	1,827,264	730,906	1,096,358
10	5,219,093	1,878,873	1,043,819	326,193	80,989	1,889,219	755,688	1,133,531
11	5,375,666	1,935,240	1,075,133	335,979	77,028	1,952,286	780,914	1,171,372
12	5,536,935	1,993,297	1,107,387	346,058	73,595	2,016,598	806,639	1,209,959
13	5,703,044	2,053,096	1,140,609	356,440	70,620	2,082,279	832,912	1,249,367
14	5,874,135	2,114,689	1,174,827	367,133	68,042	2,149,444	859,778	1,289,667

TABLE 12.1 (Continued)

Year	Revenues[a]	Food Cost[b]	Salary and Wages[c]	Overhead	Depreciation[d]	EBIT	Taxes (40%)	NOPAT EBIT$(1 - tx)$
15	$6,050,359	$2,178,129	$1,210,072	$378,147	$65,807	$2,218,204	$887,281	$1,330,922
16	6,231,870	2,243,473	1,246,374	389,492	145,694	2,206,837	882,735	1,324,102
17	6,418,826	2,310,777	1,283,765	401,177	51,282	2,371,825	948,730	1,423,095
18	6,611,391	2,380,101	1,322,278	413,212	51,282	2,444,518	977,807	1,466,711
19	6,809,732	2,451,504	1,361,946	425,608	51,282	2,519,392	1,007,757	1,511,635
20	7,014,024	2,525,049	1,402,805	438,377	51,282	2,596,512	1,038,605	1,557,907

[a] Same store sales at McDonald's nationally increase at 3% per year.
[b] Food cost at McDonald's nationally average 36%.
[c] Wages and salaries at McDonald's nationally average 20%.
[d] Represents $2 million building depreciated over 39 years using the half-year convention; $750,000 of building improvements depreciated over 15 years using the double-declining balance and half-year convention; and $250,000 of equipment depreciated over five years using the double-declining balance and half-year convention.

TABLE 12.2 Route 66 McDonald's, Pro Forma Income Statement, without Land Lease

Year	Revenues[a]	Food Cost[b]	Salary and Wages[c]	Overhead	Depreciation[d]	Interest[e]	EBT	Taxes (40%)	Net Income
1	$4,000,000	$1,440,000	$800,000	$250,000	$151,282	$250,000	$1,108,718	$443,487	$665,231
2	4,120,000	1,483,200	824,000	257,500	224,615	245,635	1,085,050	434,020	651,030
3	4,243,600	1,527,696	848,720	265,225	180,171	240,834	1,180,954	472,382	708,573
4	4,370,908	1,573,527	874,182	273,182	150,186	235,552	1,264,280	505,712	758,568
5	4,502,035	1,620,733	900,407	281,377	129,319	229,742	1,340,457	536,183	804,274
6	4,637,096	1,669,355	927,419	289,819	129,858	223,352	1,397,294	558,918	838,377
7	4,776,209	1,719,435	955,242	298,513	96,917	216,322	1,489,780	595,912	893,868
8	4,919,495	1,771,018	983,899	307,468	90,832	208,589	1,557,688	623,075	934,613
9	5,067,080	1,824,149	1,013,416	316,693	85,559	200,083	1,627,180	650,872	976,308
10	5,219,093	1,878,873	1,043,819	326,193	80,989	190,727	1,698,492	679,397	1,019,095
11	5,375,666	1,935,240	1,075,133	335,979	77,028	180,435	1,771,851	708,741	1,063,111
12	5,536,935	1,993,297	1,107,387	346,058	73,595	169,113	1,847,485	738,994	1,108,491
13	5,703,044	2,053,096	1,140,609	356,440	70,620	156,660	1,925,619	770,248	1,155,372
14	5,874,135	2,114,689	1,174,827	367,133	68,042	142,961	2,006,484	802,593	1,203,890

TABLE 12.2 (Continued)

Year	Revenues[a]	Food Cost[b]	Salary and Wages[c]	Overhead	Depreciation[d]	Interest[e]	EBT	Taxes (40%)	Net Income
15	$6,050,359	$2,178,129	$1,210,072	$378,147	$65,807	$127,892	$2,090,312	$836,125	$1,254,187
16	6,231,870	2,243,473	1,246,374	389,492	145,694	111,316	2,095,521	838,208	1,257,312
17	6,418,826	2,310,777	1,283,765	401,177	51,282	93,083	2,278,742	911,497	1,367,245
18	6,611,391	2,380,101	1,322,278	413,212	51,282	73,026	2,371,492	948,597	1,422,895
19	6,809,732	2,451,504	1,361,946	425,608	51,282	50,964	2,468,428	987,371	1,481,057
20	7,014,024	2,525,049	1,402,805	438,377	51,282	26,695	2,569,817	1,027,927	1,541,890

[a] Same store sales at McDonald's nationally increase at 3% per year.
[b] Food cost at McDonald's nationally average 36%.
[c] Wages and salaries at McDonald's nationally average 20%.
[d] Represents $2 million building depreciated over 39 years using the half-year convention; $750,000 of building improvements depreciated over 15 years using the double-declining balance and half-year convention; and $250,000 of equipment depreciated over five years using the double-declining balance and half-year convention.
[e] Based on a $2.5 million 20-year mortgage at 10%.

267

TABLE 12.3   Route 66 McDonald's, Pro Forma Cash Flow Statement without Land Lease

Year	Net Income[a]	Depreciation[a]	Equity Payments	Capital Contributions[b]	Net Cash Flows[c]
0				$500,000	–$500,000
1	$665,231	$151,282	$43,649		772,864
2	651,030	224,615	48,014		827,631
3	708,573	180,171	52,815		835,928
4	758,568	150,186	58,097		850,657
5	804,274	129,319	63,907		869,686
6	838,377	129,858	70,297		897,937
7	893,868	96,917	77,327		913,458
8	934,613	90,832	85,060		940,385
9	976,308	85,559	93,566		968,302
10	1,019,095	80,989	102,922		997,162
11	1,063,111	77,028	113,214		1,026,924
12	1,108,491	73,595	124,536		1,057,550
13	1,155,372	70,620	136,989		1,089,002
14	1,203,890	68,042	150,688		1,121,243
15	1,254,187	65,807	165,757		1,154,237
16	1,257,312	145,694	182,333		1,220,673
17	1,367,245	51,282	200,566		1,217,961
18	1,422,895	51,282	220,623		1,253,554
19	1,481,057	51,282	242,685		1,289,654
20	1,541,890	51,282	266,954		1,326,218

[a] See Table 12.2.
[b] Total cost equal $3 million financed by $2.5 million mortgage and $500,000 equity.
[c] Assumed value of property at end of lease equals zero.

NPV at 12% = $5,786,050

IRR = 159.37%

seem that this location contains any risk for the McDonald's franchisee (assuming his sales projections are not totally off).

The cash flows indicated in Table 12.3 suggest that this store will earn the franchisee an NPV of $5,786,050 on an investment of $500,000, a return of 159% over 20 years! (That is without any lease expense whatsoever.) These numbers make it clear that the franchisee can afford a lease higher than the proffered $600,000.

The accountant then experimented with a number of different lease options and finally decides that a lease of $1,260,000 would be fair in implying a correct value for the land and still leaving a return large enough (24%) to encourage the franchisee to do the project. In addition, a lease of $1,260,000, if it were valued at a 20% rate of discount (that is, five times earnings) gives the land a value of $6.3 million. That sets a nice tone indeed for valuing the remainder of Bob and Ray's land.

The impact of a lease of $1,260,000 on the financial returns to the franchisee can be seen in Tables 12.4, 12.5, and 12.6. NOPAT is still sufficiently large to allow for a high degree of financial leverage on the part of the franchisee. However, both NOPAT and net income are negative during the first two years of operation, implying some level of risk for the franchisee. The significance of these negative numbers is diminished by the fact that cash flow is always positive for each year of operation. Even with the substantial lease payments on the income statement in Table 12.5, the cash flow indicated in Table 12.6 is still sufficiently high to permit the franchisee to capture a net present value of $744,175, representing a return of 24% on his investment. (Actually, the likely returns are higher because the costs and sales estimates are on the low side.)

When presented with the demand for a $1,260,000 lease, the franchisee balks and counteroffers saying "That return doesn't take into account the risk of my financial exposure on this store. However, if you will do a build-to-suit deal at this lease rate ($1,260,000), I'll do it because I get a bigger tax break." Bob and Ray ask their accountant to figure that one out.

In constructing this analysis, the first problem the accountant had to solve was to determine the value of the land. The fact that Bob and Ray already owned the land does not impact its value as that should be determined by it's opportunity cost. *Opportunity cost* is the value something has in its next best use. The next best use for this land is leasing it out to the McDonald's franchisee. This would give the land a value of $6.3 million (as discussed above.) The accountant talks to the local bank and finds the Hudpohls can get better terms than the franchisee. The bank will lend them the whole $3 million (securing the loan with the land title) at 9.5% in the form of a conventional 20-year mortgage preceded by a bridge loan at the same rate. The cash flows necessary for Bob and Ray to build the McDonald's are indicated in Table 12.7.

TABLE 12.4 Route 66 McDonald's, Holding Period NOPAT, Pro Forma Net-Operating Profits after Taxes with Land Lease

Year	Revenues[a]	Lease	Food Cost[b]	Salary and Wages[c]	Overhead	Depreciation[d]	EBIT	Taxes (40%)	NOPAT EBIT(1 − tx)
1	$4,000,000	$1,260,000	$1,440,000	$800,000	$250,000	$151,282	$98,718	$39,487	$59,231
2	4,120,000	1,260,000	1,483,200	824,000	257,500	224,615	70,685	28,274	42,411
3	4,243,600	1,260,000	1,527,696	848,720	265,225	180,171	161,788	64,715	97,073
4	4,370,908	1,260,000	1,573,527	874,182	273,182	150,186	239,832	95,933	143,899
5	4,502,035	1,260,000	1,620,733	900,407	281,377	129,319	310,200	124,080	186,120
6	4,637,096	1,260,000	1,669,355	927,419	289,819	129,858	360,646	144,258	216,388
7	4,776,209	1,260,000	1,719,435	955,242	298,513	96,917	446,102	178,441	267,661
8	4,919,495	1,260,000	1,771,018	983,899	307,468	90,832	506,277	202,511	303,766
9	5,067,080	1,260,000	1,824,149	1,013,416	316,693	85,559	567,264	226,906	340,358
10	5,219,093	1,260,000	1,878,873	1,043,819	326,193	80,989	629,219	251,688	377,531
11	5,375,666	1,260,000	1,935,240	1,075,133	335,979	77,028	692,286	276,914	415,372
12	5,536,935	1,260,000	1,993,297	1,107,387	346,058	73,595	756,598	302,639	453,959
13	5,703,044	1,260,000	2,053,096	1,140,609	356,440	70,620	822,279	328,912	493,367
14	5,874,135	1,260,000	2,114,689	1,174,827	367,133	68,042	889,444	355,778	533,667

TABLE 12.4 (Continued)

Year	Revenues[a]	Lease	Food Cost[b]	Salary and Wages[c]	Overhead	Depreciation[d]	EBIT	Taxes (40%)	NOPAT EBIT$(1 - tx)$
15	$6,050,359	$1,260,000	$2,178,129	$1,210,072	$378,147	$65,807	$958,204	$383,281	$574,922
16	6,231,870	1,260,000	2,243,473	1,246,374	389,492	145,694	946,837	378,735	568,102
17	6,418,826	1,260,000	2,310,777	1,283,765	401,177	51,282	1,111,825	444,730	667,095
18	6,611,391	1,260,000	2,380,101	1,322,278	413,212	51,282	1,184,518	473,807	710,711
19	6,809,732	1,260,000	2,451,504	1,361,946	425,608	51,282	1,259,392	503,757	755,635
20	7,014,024	1,260,000	2,525,049	1,402,805	438,377	51,282	1,336,512	534,605	801,907

[a] Same store sales at McDonald's nationally increase at 3% per year.

[b] Food cost at McDonald's nationally average 36%.

[c] Wages and salaries at McDonald's nationally average 20%.

[d] Represents $2 million building depreciated over 39 years using the half-year convention; $750,000 of building improvements depreciated over 15 years using the double-declining balance and half-year convention; and $250,000 of equipment depreciated over five years using the double-declining balance and half-year convention.

271

TABLE 12.5 Route 66 McDonald's, Pro Forma Income Statement with Land Lease

Year	Revenues[a]	Lease	Food Cost[b]	Salary and Wages[c]	Overhead	Depreciation[d]	Interest[e]	EBT	Taxes (40%)	Net Income
1	$4,000,000	$1,260,000	$1,440,000	$800,000	$250,000	$151,282	$250,000	-$151,282	-$60,513	-$90,769
2	4,120,000	1,260,000	1,483,200	824,000	257,500	224,615	245,635	-174,950	-69,980	-104,970
3	4,243,600	1,260,000	1,527,696	848,720	265,225	180,171	240,834	-79,046	-31,618	-47,427
4	4,370,908	1,260,000	1,573,527	874,182	273,182	150,186	235,552	4,280	1,712	2,568
5	4,502,035	1,260,000	1,620,733	900,407	281,377	129,319	229,742	80,457	32,183	48,274
6	4,637,096	1,260,000	1,669,355	927,419	289,819	129,858	223,352	137,294	54,918	82,377
7	4,776,209	1,260,000	1,719,435	955,242	298,513	96,917	216,322	229,780	91,912	137,868
8	4,919,495	1,260,000	1,771,018	983,899	307,468	90,832	208,589	297,688	119,075	178,613
9	5,067,080	1,260,000	1,824,149	1,013,416	316,693	85,559	200,083	367,180	146,872	220,308
10	5,219,093	1,260,000	1,878,873	1,043,819	326,193	80,989	190,727	438,492	175,397	263,095
11	5,375,666	1,260,000	1,935,240	1,075,133	335,979	77,028	180,435	511,851	204,741	307,111
12	5,536,935	1,260,000	1,993,297	1,107,387	346,058	73,595	169,113	587,485	234,994	352,491
13	5,703,044	1,260,000	2,053,096	1,140,609	356,440	70,620	156,660	665,619	266,248	399,372
14	5,874,135	1,260,000	2,114,689	1,174,827	367,133	68,042	142,961	746,484	298,593	447,890

TABLE 12.5 (Continued)

Year	Revenues[a]	Lease	Food Cost[b]	Salary and Wages[c]	Overhead	Depre-ciation[d]	Interest[e]	EBT	Taxes (40%)	Net Income
15	$6,050,359	$1,260,000	$2,178,129	$1,210,072	$378,147	$65,807	$127,892	$830,312	$332,125	$498,187
16	6,231,870	1,260,000	2,243,473	1,246,374	389,492	145,694	111,316	835,521	334,208	501,312
17	6,418,826	1,260,000	2,310,777	1,283,765	401,177	51,282	93,083	1,018,742	407,497	611,245
18	6,611,391	1,260,000	2,380,101	1,322,278	413,212	51,282	73,026	1,111,492	444,597	666,895
19	6,809,732	1,260,000	2,451,504	1,361,946	425,608	51,282	50,964	1,208,428	483,371	725,057
20	7,014,024	1,260,000	2,525,049	1,402,805	438,377	51,282	26,695	1,309,817	523,927	785,890

[a] Same store sales at McDonald's nationally increase at 3% per year.
[b] Food cost at McDonald's nationally average 36%.
[c] Wages and salaries at McDonald's nationally average 20%.
[d] Represents $2 million building depreciated over 39 years using the half-year convention; $750,000 of building improvements depreciated over 15 years using the double-declining balance and half-year convention; and $250,000 of equipment depreciated over five years using the double-declining balance and half-year convention.
[e] Based on a $2.5 million 20-year mortgage at 10%.

TABLE 12.6   Route 66 McDonald's, Pro Forma Cash Flow Statement with Land Lease

Year	Net Income[a]	Depre- ciation[a]	Equity Payments	Capital Contributions[b]	Net Cash Flows[c]
0				$500,000	-$500,000
1	-$90,769	$151,282	$43,649		16,864
2	-104,970	224,615	48,014		71,631
3	-47,427	180,171	52,815		79,928
4	2,568	150,186	58,097		94,657
5	48,274	129,319	63,907		113,686
6	82,377	129,858	70,297		141,937
7	137,868	96,917	77,327		157,458
8	178,613	90,832	85,060		184,385
9	220,308	85,559	93,566		212,302
10	263,095	80,989	102,922		241,162
11	307,111	77,028	113,214		270,924
12	352,491	73,595	124,536		301,550
13	399,372	70,620	136,989		333,002
14	447,890	68,042	150,688		365,243
15	498,187	65,807	165,757		398,237
16	501,312	145,694	182,333		464,673
17	611,245	51,282	200,566		461,961
18	666,895	51,282	220,623		497,554
19	725,057	51,282	242,685		533,654
20	785,890	51,282	266,954		570,218

[a] See Table 12.5.
[b] Total cost equal $3 million financed by $2.5 million mortgage and $500,000 equity.
[c] Assumed value of property at end of lease equals zero.

NPV at 12% = $744,175

IRR = 24.08%

TABLE 12.7   Hudpohls' McDonald's, Initial Cash Flows, Build

Cash Outflows:	
Value of Land[a]	$6,300,000
Construction of store	2,000,000
Building improvements	250,000
Equipment	750,000
Total cash out	9,300,000
Cash Inflows	
Loan from bank[b]	3,000,000
Equity from Hudpohls	5,850,000
Equity from lessee[c]	50,000
Total cash in	8,900,000

[a] Even though the Hudpohls own the land, it must be valued as if it were a cash payment to themselves.
[b] The loan is drawn down over the first year, and interest is paid only on the funds used.
[c] As a lessor, it is a good practice to have the lessee invest some cash as an incentive for it to honor the lease.

To calculate their costs over the 20-year holding period, Bob and Ray need to know what the value of the building will be 20 years hence. This is provided by the fact that if the McDonald's franchisee operated the store with the $1,260,000 lease—which the Hudpohl's were willing to do—it would be earning $785,890 in its 20th year (Table 12.5). That should give the property a value of $10,229,450 (Table 12.8A). It would be reasonable to assume that the McDonald's store would be worth five times earnings on that basis or $3,929,450 plus the $6.3 million value of the underlying real estate. This would generate an after-tax gain on sale of $2,442,277 and result in a cash gain on sale of $9,478,116 (Table 12.8B).

This allows the calculation of the cash flows associated with the Hudpohl's building and leasing this McDonald's store. As can be seen from their perspective in Table 12.9, the present value of their cash outflows would be $6,413,838, requiring a tax adjusted equivalent lease of $1,073,346 to earn 12% on their investment.

Given the $1,260,000 lease in discussion, this certainly will be in an acceptable range for Bob and Ray, but what will be the outcome of this arrangement for the McDonald's franchisee? That is revealed in Tables 12.10, 12.11, and 12.12. We see the effect of being a lessee on the franchise is to increase NOPAT, net income, and cash flow. Table 12.12 shows that the effect of leasing the property and building to the franchisee is to raise the NPV of his investment to $894,862 (up from $744,175 when the franchisee was leasing only the land) and to raise his return to 31% (from 24%)—which is exactly why the franchisee wanted to move to a build-to-suit. It should be noted that this advantage to the franchisee arises from his high tax rate (compared to the Hudpohls) and his higher cost of borrowing.

Another effect of going to a build-to-suit situation is to increase the risk to the franchisee (there is no exception the higher return, higher risk rule). The break-even level of operation for the store was around $1 million when the franchisee was without leasing costs (Table 12.2). Now that the franchisee is leasing the land and the building, his net fixed costs go up to $1,610,000 ($450,000 + $1,260,000). Given that $TR = TC$, and TC now equals $1.61 million + 0.56 VC, then his BEP = $3.66 million. This comes a lot closer to the expected sales level of $4 million. Whether the franchisee thinks this kind of exposure to risk is worth the gain of 7% in return has to do with his confidence in the sales projections and his tastes and preferences for risk.

The effect of the $1.26 million lease on the Hudpohls can be seen in Table 12.13. Their gains from leasing the land and building appear to generate an NPV of $308,662 and a return on their investment of 13%. These gains seem paltry until one understands what really happens here.

TABLE 12.8A   Hudpohls' McDonald's, Tax Consequences of Sale of Property, 20-Year Holding Period

Sale of building[a]		$10,229,450
Fixed plant and improvements	$3,000,000	
Less accumulated depreciation	2,025,641	
Net fixed plant and improvements		974,359
Cost of land		6,300,000
Gain on sale		2,955,091
Capital gains tax (15%)		443,264
After-tax gain on sale		2,511,828

[a] Five times net income plus the capitalized value of the land.

TABLE 12.8B   Hudpohls' McDonald's, Cash Gain from Sale of Property

Sale of property	$10,229,450
Less:	
Tax liability	443,264
Loan balance	320,344
Cash gain from sale	9,465,842

TABLE 12.9 Hudpohls' McDonald's, Build Decision, Building Costs and Cash Flows[a]

Year	After-Tax Mortgage Interest Payments[b]	Mortgage Principle Payments	Total Depreciation[c]	Depreciation Tax Savings[d]	Equity Contribution[e]	Cash (Gain) on Sale[f]	Net Cash Flow[g]
0	$240,000				$5,850,000		$6,090,000
1	240,000	$52,379	$151,282	$30,256			262,122
2	235,810	57,617	224,615	44,923			248,503
3	231,200	63,378	180,171	36,034			258,545
4	226,130	69,716	150,186	30,037			265,809
5	220,553	76,688	129,319	25,864			271,377
6	214,418	84,357	129,858	25,972			272,803
7	207,669	92,792	96,917	19,383			281,078
8	200,246	102,072	90,832	18,166			284,151
9	192,080	112,279	85,559	17,112			287,247
10	183,098	123,507	80,989	16,198			290,407
11	173,217	135,857	77,028	15,406			293,669
12	162,349	149,443	73,595	14,719			297,073
13	150,393	164,387	70,620	14,124			300,657
14	137,242	180,826	68,042	13,608			304,460

TABLE 12.9 (Continued)

Year	After-Tax Mortgage Interest Payments[b]	Mortgage Principle Payments	Total Depreciation[c]	Depreciation Tax Savings[d]	Equity Contribution[e]	Cash (Gain) on Sale[f]	Net Cash Flow[g]
15	$122,776	$198,909	$65,807	$13,161			$308,523
16	106,863	218,800	145,694	29,139			296,524
17	89,359	240,680	51,282	10,256			319,783
18	70,105	264,747	51,282	10,256			324,596
19	48,925	291,222	51,282	10,256			329,891
20	25,628	320,344	51,282	10,256		$9,465,842	−9,130,126

[a] Note that maintenance, insurance, and taxes are not included. Because this is a triple-net lease, they will be the same whether the building is owned or leased and thus do not affect the comparison.

[b] An 10% fixed rate 20-year conventional mortgage with payments of $352,379.

[c] Represents $2 million building depreciated over 39 years using the half-year convention; $750,000 of building improvements depreciated over 15 years using the double-declining balance and half-year convention; and $250,000 of equipment depreciated over five years using the double-declining balance and half-year convention.

[d] The Hudpohls have a marginal tax rate of 20%.

[e] From Table 12.7.

[f] From Table 12.8B.

[g] The sum of equity contributions, after-tax interest payments, principal payments, less depreciation tax savings, less gain on sale of building.

Present value of cash flows = $6,413,838
Discount rate = 0.12

Equivalent annual annuity = $858,677

Tax-adjusted EAA = $1,073,346
(This is the nominal lease payment, which makes the lessee indifferent between leasing and buying.)

278

TABLE 12.10 Route 66 McDonald's, Holding Period NOPAT, Pro Forma Net-Operating Profits after Taxes, with Land and Building Lease

Year	Revenues[a]	Lease	Food Cost[b]	Salary and Wages[c]	Overhead	EBIT	Taxes (40%)	NOPAT EBIT$(1-tx)$
1	$4,000,000	$1,260,000	$1,440,000	$800,000	$250,000	$98,718	$39,487	$59,231
2	4,120,000	1,260,000	1,483,200	824,000	257,500	70,685	28,274	42,411
3	4,243,600	1,260,000	1,527,696	848,720	265,225	161,788	64,715	97,073
4	4,370,908	1,260,000	1,573,527	874,182	273,182	239,832	95,933	143,899
5	4,502,035	1,260,000	1,620,733	900,407	281,377	310,200	124,080	186,120
6	4,637,096	1,260,000	1,669,355	927,419	289,819	360,646	144,258	216,388
7	4,776,209	1,260,000	1,719,435	955,242	298,513	446,102	178,441	267,661
8	4,919,495	1,260,000	1,771,018	983,899	307,468	506,277	202,511	303,766
9	5,067,080	1,260,000	1,824,149	1,013,416	316,693	567,264	226,906	340,358
10	5,219,093	1,260,000	1,878,873	1,043,819	326,193	629,219	251,688	377,531
11	5,375,666	1,260,000	1,935,240	1,075,133	335,979	692,286	276,914	415,372
12	5,536,935	1,260,000	1,993,297	1,107,387	346,058	756,598	302,639	453,959
13	5,703,044	1,260,000	2,053,096	1,140,609	356,440	822,279	328,912	493,367
14	5,874,135	1,260,000	2,114,689	1,174,827	367,133	889,444	355,778	533,667

TABLE 12.10 (Continued)

Year	Revenues[a]	Lease	Food Cost[b]	Salary and Wages[c]	Overhead	EBIT	Taxes (40%)	NOPAT EBIT$(1 - tx)$
15	$6,050,359	$1,260,000	$2,178,129	$1,210,072	$378,147	$958,204	$383,281	$574,922
16	6,231,870	1,260,000	2,243,473	1,246,374	389,492	946,837	378,735	568,102
17	6,418,826	1,260,000	2,310,777	1,283,765	401,177	1,111,825	444,730	667,095
18	6,611,391	1,260,000	2,380,101	1,322,278	413,212	1,184,518	473,807	710,711
19	6,809,732	1,260,000	2,451,504	1,361,946	425,608	1,259,392	503,757	755,635
20	7,014,024	1,260,000	2,525,049	1,402,805	438,377	1,336,512	534,605	801,907

[a] Same store sales at McDonald's are assumed to increase at 3% per year.
[b] Food cost at McDonald's are assumed to average 36%.
[c] Wages and salaries at McDonald's are assumed to average 20%.

280

TABLE 12.11 Route 66 McDonald's, Pro Forma Income Statement with Land and Building Lease

Year	Revenues[a]	Lease	Food Cost[b]	Salary and Wages[c]	Overhead	EBT	Taxes (40%)	Net Income
1	$4,000,000	$1,260,000	$1,440,000	$800,000	$250,000	-$151,282	-$60,513	-$90,769
2	4,120,000	1,260,000	1,483,200	824,000	257,500	-174,950	-69,980	-104,970
3	4,243,600	1,260,000	1,527,696	848,720	265,225	-79,046	-31,618	-47,427
4	4,370,908	1,260,000	1,573,527	874,182	273,182	4,280	1,712	2,568
5	4,502,035	1,260,000	1,620,733	900,407	281,377	80,457	32,183	48,274
6	4,637,096	1,260,000	1,669,355	927,419	289,819	137,294	54,918	82,377
7	4,776,209	1,260,000	1,719,435	955,242	298,513	229,780	91,912	137,868
8	4,919,495	1,260,000	1,771,018	983,899	307,468	297,688	119,075	178,613
9	5,067,080	1,260,000	1,824,149	1,013,416	316,693	367,180	146,872	220,308
10	5,219,093	1,260,000	1,878,873	1,043,819	326,193	438,492	175,397	263,095
11	5,375,666	1,260,000	1,935,240	1,075,133	335,979	511,851	204,741	307,111
12	5,536,935	1,260,000	1,993,297	1,107,387	346,058	587,485	234,994	352,491
13	5,703,044	1,260,000	2,053,096	1,140,609	356,440	665,619	266,248	399,372
14	5,874,135	1,260,000	2,114,689	1,174,827	367,133	746,484	298,593	447,890
15	6,050,359	1,260,000	2,178,129	1,210,072	378,147	830,312	332,125	498,187
16	6,231,870	1,260,000	2,243,473	1,246,374	389,492	835,521	334,208	501,312
17	6,418,826	1,260,000	2,310,777	1,283,765	401,177	1,018,742	407,497	611,245
18	6,611,391	1,260,000	2,380,101	1,322,278	413,212	1,111,492	444,597	666,895
19	6,809,732	1,260,000	2,451,504	1,361,946	425,608	1,208,428	483,371	725,057
20	7,014,024	1,260,000	2,525,049	1,402,805	438,377	1,309,817	523,927	785,890

[a] Same store sales at McDonald's are assumed to increase at 3% per year.
[b] Food cost at McDonald's are assumed to average 36%.
[c] Wages and salaries at McDonald's are assumed to average 20%.

TABLE 12.12   Route 66 McDonald's, Pro Forma Cash Flow Statement with Land and Building Lease

Year	Net Income[a]	Capital Contributions[b]	Net Cash Flows[c]
0		–$50,000	–$50,000
1	–$90,769		–90,769
2	–104,970		–104,970
3	–47,427		–47,427
4	2,568		2,568
5	48,274		48,274
6	82,377		82,377
7	137,868		137,868
8	178,613		178,613
9	220,308		220,308
10	263,095		263,095
11	307,111		307,111
12	352,491		352,491
13	399,372		399,372
14	447,890		447,890
15	498,187		498,187
16	501,312		501,312
17	611,245		611,245
18	666,895		666,895
19	725,057		725,057
20	785,890	50,000	835,890

Note that McDonald's franchisee has no depreciation since he owns neither the land nor buildings.
[1] See Table 12.11.
[2] See Table 12.7.
[3] Assumed value of property at end of lease equals zero.

They have taken their real gains in the form of validating the valuation of this piece of their property at $6.3 million. When that land is fully valued, their build-to-suit becomes a pure lease play. In that context, their return of 13% is above their cost of capital of 12%, so they should do the lease. Plus, valuing this particular piece of property at $6.3 million has significant implications for the value of the remainder of their 600 acres.

The Hudpohls' father was right!

TABLE 12.13 Hudpohls' McDonald's, Build-and-Lease Decision, Income and Cash Flows[a]

Year	Lease Income	Interest Payments[b]	Total Depreciation[c]	EBT	Taxes (20%)	Net Income	Depreciation	Principal Payments	Equity Contribution[d]	Cash (Gain) on Sale[e]	Net Cash Flow[f]
0		$300,000		-$300,000	-$60,000	-$240,000			$5,850,000		-$6,090,000
1	$1,260,000	300,000	$151,282	808,718	161,744	646,974	$151,282	$52,379			745,878
2	1,260,000	294,762	224,615	740,623	148,125	592,498	224,615	57,617			759,497
3	1,260,000	289,000	180,171	790,829	158,166	632,663	180,171	63,378			749,455
4	1,260,000	282,663	150,186	827,152	165,430	661,721	150,186	69,716			742,191
5	1,260,000	275,691	129,319	854,990	170,998	683,992	129,319	76,688			736,623
6	1,260,000	268,022	129,858	862,120	172,424	689,696	129,858	84,357			735,197
7	1,260,000	259,587	96,917	903,497	180,699	722,797	96,917	92,792			726,922
8	1,260,000	250,307	90,832	918,860	183,772	735,088	90,832	102,072			723,849
9	1,260,000	240,100	85,559	934,341	186,868	747,473	85,559	112,279			720,753
10	1,260,000	228,872	80,989	950,139	190,028	760,111	80,989	123,507			717,593
11	1,260,000	216,522	77,028	966,451	193,290	773,161	77,028	135,857			714,331
12	1,260,000	202,936	73,595	983,469	196,694	786,775	73,595	149,443			710,927
13	1,260,000	187,992	70,620	1,001,388	200,278	801,111	70,620	164,387			707,343
14	1,260,000	171,553	68,042	1,020,406	204,081	816,324	68,042	180,826			703,540

TABLE 12.13 (Continued)

Year	Lease Income	Interest Payments[b]	Total Depreciation[c]	EBT	Taxes (20%)	Net Income	Depreciation	Principal Payments	Equity Contribution[d]	Cash (Gain) on Sale[e]	Net Cash Flow[f]
15	$1,260,000	$153,470	$65,807	$1,040,723	$208,145	$832,578	$65,807	$198,909			$699,477
16	1,260,000	133,579	145,694	980,727	196,145	784,581	145,694	218,800			711,476
17	1,260,000	111,699	51,282	1,097,019	219,404	877,615	51,282	240,680			688,217
18	1,260,000	87,631	51,282	1,121,087	224,217	896,869	51,282	264,747			683,404
19	1,260,000	61,157	51,282	1,147,561	229,512	918,049	51,282	291,222			678,109
20	1,260,000	32,034	51,282	1,176,684	235,337	941,347	51,282	320,344		$9,465,842	10,138,126

[a] Note that maintenance, insurance, and taxes are not included. Because this is a triple-net lease, they will be the same whether the building is owned or leased and thus do not affect the comparison.

[b] An 10% fixed rate 20-year conventional mortgage with payments of $352,379.

[c] Represents $2 million building depreciated over 39 years using the half-year convention; $750,000 of building improvements depreciated over 15 years using the double-declining balance and half-year convention; and $250,000 of equipment depreciated over five years using the double-declining balance and half-year convention.

[d] From Table 12.7.

[e] From Table 12.8B.

[f] The sum of net income, depreciation, less principal payments, less equity contributions, plus cash gain on sale.

NPV at 12% = $308,662

IRR = 10%

284

ILLUSTRATION #2: BAXTER'S INTERSTATE #32

Bill and Jean Munstead were divorced after 30 years of less-than-blissful marriage. Bill was a successful developer in a large Southern metropolitan area. As part of her divorce settlement, Jean received clear title to five acres adjacent to an interstate exchange on the northern side of town. The northern side of down was rapidly developing an urban feel after being primarily upper-middle-class residential. Jean could sell the land outright—she had offers—for $3 million, but after taxes, that would leave her with only $2.4 million. If she invested the money in local utility stocks (her broker's recommendation) she would likely earn 5% on her investment. That was only $120,000, thought Jean. If she paid 40% in taxes that would be $72,000. Not enough to live on, she thought.

Jean wondered if leasing her land could bring her more money. One of the offers to buy her land had come from Baxter Corporation, a holding company for a well-known, midscale restaurant chain that wanted to build a large restaurant catering to the interstate traffic on this site. They were very interested in using this site for their 32nd restaurant. Jean approached Baxter, through her counsel, to ask about that possibility. Baxter responded by offering to lease the land for $100,000 per year for five years with three options to renew for five years with lease rates of $110,000, 120,000, and $130,000. Jean was surprised by the size of the offer and wondered if she should jump at this opportunity. She asked her accountant to take a look at the offer and evaluate it.

The accountant found the restaurant chain that had made the offer had store sales averaging $8 million, and which were growing at a rate of 5% per year. He also found out the cost of food sold at these stores averaged 45% and labor added another 25%. Through a little research, the accountant thought that Baxter would have to spend about $3.5 million to construct the building, $2 million for improvements (because of the way the land was situated, a long access road was needed) and $1 million for equipment and finishes. Thus, the total cost of the building would be $6.5 million. The accountant, when he was checking Baxter's credit status, found that Baxter had a standing line of credit for bridge loans and mortgages with a bank syndicate that basically allowed them to do 90% financing with conventional 20-year mortgages at 12%.

The first thing the accountant wanted to do was to see how profitable this restaurant would be for the chain without any land costs at all. He did this by constructing the pro forma financial statements presented in Tables 12.14, 12.15, and 12.16. Table 12.14 shows store #32 is able to support heavy financing costs with its high levels of NOPAT. Table 12.15 shows that with a 90% mortgage on its property (and that is high

TABLE 12.14 Baxter's Interstate No. 32, Holding Period NOPAT, Pro Forma Net-Operating Profits after Taxes, without Land Cost

Year	Revenues[a]	Food Cost[b]	Salary and Wages[c]	Overhead	Depreciation[d]	EBIT	Taxes (40%)	NOPAT EBIT$(1 - tx)$
1	$8,000,000	$3,600,000	$2,000,000	$1,000,000	$423,077	$976,923	$390,769	$586,154
2	8,400,000	3,780,000	2,100,000	1,030,000	658,632	831,368	332,547	498,821
3	8,820,000	3,969,000	2,205,000	1,060,900	497,447	1,087,653	435,061	652,592
4	9,261,000	4,167,450	2,315,250	1,092,727	391,887	1,293,686	517,474	776,212
5	9,724,050	4,375,823	2,431,013	1,125,509	320,881	1,470,825	588,330	882,495
6	10,210,253	4,594,614	2,552,563	1,159,274	333,839	1,569,963	627,985	941,978
7	10,720,765	4,824,344	2,680,191	1,194,052	211,437	1,810,741	724,296	1,086,444
8	11,256,803	5,065,562	2,814,201	1,229,874	195,211	1,951,956	780,782	1,171,174
9	11,819,644	5,318,840	2,954,911	1,266,770	181,149	2,097,974	839,190	1,258,785
10	12,410,626	5,584,782	3,102,656	1,304,773	168,961	2,249,453	899,781	1,349,672
11	13,031,157	5,864,021	3,257,789	1,343,916	158,399	2,407,032	962,813	1,444,219
12	13,682,715	6,157,222	3,420,679	1,384,234	149,245	2,571,336	1,028,534	1,542,801
13	14,366,851	6,465,083	3,591,713	1,425,761	141,311	2,742,983	1,097,193	1,645,790
14	15,085,193	6,788,337	3,771,298	1,468,534	134,436	2,922,589	1,169,035	1,753,553

TABLE 12.14 (Continued)

Year	Revenues[a]	Food Cost[b]	Salary and Wages[c]	Overhead	Depreciation[d]	EBIT	Taxes (40%)	NOPAT EBIT(1 − tx)
15	$15,839,453	$7,127,754	$3,959,863	$1,512,590	$128,477	$3,110,769	$1,244,308	$1,866,462
16	16,631,425	7,484,141	4,157,856	1,557,967	341,509	3,089,951	1,235,980	1,853,971
17	17,462,997	7,858,349	4,365,749	1,604,706	89,744	3,544,449	1,417,780	2,126,669
18	18,336,147	8,251,266	4,584,037	1,652,848	89,744	3,758,253	1,503,301	2,254,952
19	19,252,954	8,663,829	4,813,238	1,702,433	89,744	3,983,710	1,593,484	2,390,226
20	20,215,602	9,097,021	5,053,900	1,753,506	89,744	4,221,431	1,688,572	2,532,858

[a] Same store sales at Baxter's increase at 5% per year.
[b] Food cost at Baxter's nationally average 45%.
[c] Wages and salaries at Baxter's average 25%.
[d] Represents $3.5 million building depreciated over 39 years using the half-year convention; $2 million of building improvements depreciated over 15 years using the double-declining balance and half-year convention; and $1 million of equipment depreciated over five years using the double-declining balance and half-year convention.

TABLE 12.15 Baxter's Interstate No. 32, Pro Forma Income Statement, without Land Cost

Year	Revenues[a]	Food Cost[b]	Salary and Wages[c]	Overhead	Depreciation[d]	Interest[e]	EBT	Taxes (40%)	Net Income
1	$8,000,000	$3,600,000	$2,000,000	$1,000,000	$423,077	$702,000	$274,923	$109,969	$164,954
2	8,400,000	3,780,000	2,100,000	1,030,000	658,632	692,257	139,110	55,644	83,466
3	8,820,000	3,969,000	2,205,000	1,060,900	497,447	681,345	406,308	162,523	243,785
4	9,261,000	4,167,450	2,315,250	1,092,727	391,887	669,124	624,563	249,825	374,738
5	9,724,050	4,375,823	2,431,013	1,125,509	320,881	655,435	815,390	326,156	489,234
6	10,210,253	4,594,614	2,552,563	1,159,274	333,839	640,105	929,858	371,943	557,915
7	10,720,765	4,824,344	2,680,191	1,194,052	211,437	622,934	1,187,806	475,122	712,684
8	11,256,803	5,065,562	2,814,201	1,229,874	195,211	603,704	1,348,252	539,301	808,951
9	11,819,644	5,318,840	2,954,911	1,266,770	181,149	582,165	1,515,809	606,324	909,485
10	12,410,626	5,584,782	3,102,656	1,304,773	168,961	558,042	1,691,411	676,564	1,014,847
11	13,031,157	5,864,021	3,257,789	1,343,916	158,399	531,024	1,876,007	750,403	1,125,604
12	13,682,715	6,157,222	3,420,679	1,384,234	149,245	500,764	2,070,571	828,229	1,242,343
13	14,366,851	6,465,083	3,591,713	1,425,761	141,311	466,873	2,276,110	910,444	1,365,666
14	15,085,193	6,788,337	3,771,298	1,468,534	134,436	428,915	2,493,673	997,469	1,496,204

TABLE 12.15 (Continued)

Year	Revenues[a]	Food Cost[b]	Salary and Wages[c]	Overhead	Depreciation[d]	Interest[e]	EBT	Taxes (40%)	Net Income
15	$15,839,453	$7,127,754	$3,959,863	$1,512,590	$128,477	$386,402	$2,724,367	$1,089,747	$1,634,620
16	16,631,425	7,484,141	4,157,856	1,557,967	341,509	338,787	2,751,164	1,100,466	1,650,698
17	17,462,997	7,858,349	4,365,749	1,604,706	89,744	285,459	3,258,990	1,303,596	1,955,394
18	18,336,147	8,251,266	4,584,037	1,652,848	89,744	225,731	3,532,522	1,413,009	2,119,513
19	19,252,954	8,663,829	4,813,238	1,702,433	89,744	158,836	3,824,874	1,529,949	2,294,924
20	20,215,602	9,097,021	5,053,900	1,753,506	89,744	83,913	4,137,518	1,655,007	2,482,511

[a] Same store sales at Baxter's increase at 5% per year.
[b] Food cost at Baxter's nationally average 45%.
[c] Wages and salaries at Baxter's average 25%.
[d] Represents $3.5 million building depreciated over 39 years using the half-year convention; $2 million of building improvements depreciated over 15 years using the double-declining balance and half-year convention; and $1 million of equipment depreciated over five years using the double-declining balance and half-year convention.
[e] Based on a $5.85 million mortgage at 12%.

TABLE 12.16   Baxter's Interstate No. 32, Pro Forma Cash Flow Statement, without Land Cost

Year	Net Income[a]	Depre-ciation[a]	Equity Payments	Capital Contributions[b]	Net Cash Flows[c]
0				$1,014,000	–$1,014,000
1	$164,954	$423,077	$81,191		506,840
2	83,466	658,632	90,934		651,165
3	243,785	497,447	101,846		639,386
4	374,738	391,887	114,067		652,557
5	489,234	320,881	127,755		682,359
6	557,915	333,839	143,086		748,668
7	712,684	211,437	160,256		763,864
8	808,951	195,211	179,487		824,675
9	909,485	181,149	201,026		889,608
10	1,014,847	168,961	225,149		958,659
11	1,125,604	158,399	252,166		1,031,837
12	1,242,343	149,245	282,426		1,109,161
13	1,365,666	141,311	316,318		1,190,660
14	1,496,204	134,436	354,276		1,276,364
15	1,634,620	128,477	396,789		1,366,308
16	1,650,698	341,509	444,404		1,547,804
17	1,955,394	89,744	497,732		1,547,406
18	2,119,513	89,744	557,460		1,651,797
19	2,294,924	89,744	624,355		1,760,313
20	2,482,511	89,744	699,278		1,872,977

[a] See Table 12.15.
[b] Total capital = 10% of $6.5 million mortgage plus 12% on first-year construction loan.
[c] Assumed value of property at end of lease equals zero.

NPV at 12% = $4,784,100

IRR = 60%

leverage for a restaurant that tends to be fairly risky enterprises), the first year's net income will be $164,954 and grow strongly to $2,482,511 by the 20th year. Cash flow (Table 12.16) is also positive throughout this period, generating an NPV for Baxter of $4,784,100 and a return of 60% on its investment. That is, of course, without any land costs whatsoever.

The accountant conducted the lease negotiations for Mrs. Munstead and determined to get as much for her as possible. He thought store #32 could support a land lease of around $800,000. He proposed an $800,000, five-year annual triple-net lease with three renewals to Baxter. He pointed out that this lease gave Baxter good positive NOPAT, which rose to over $2 million at the end of the 20-year period (Table 12.17) and that while net income (Table 12.18) was negative the first four years of operations, it also turned positive and reached over $2 million by the 20th year. Even so, cash flow (Table 12.19) was positive throughout the period and generated an NPV of $1,582,910 for Baxter representing a return on its investment of 24%.

Baxter refused this lease proposal outright, saying the accountant did not understand their business. "While it is true our stores average $8 million in sales, we have many restaurants that do a lot less business than that! Further, we have found, that one cannot accurately predict what a restaurant of our type will do until it opens its doors. Even then, its quite possible, even likely, for competitors to put stores nearby and cut significantly into our business. There is no way we are going to lock an unknown store into such high fixed costs. There is no way we are going to open a restaurant looking at the first four years of negative net income."

On that basis, the accountant went back to his drawing board and suggested a triple-net five-year lease with three renewals for $200,000 per year plus 1.5% of the gross revenue. This arrangement substantially increases NOPAT in the early years of the lease without diminishing it significantly later on (Table 12.20). Net income (Table 12.21) was now negative only in the first two years and continued to exceed $2 million in 20 years.

Furthermore, cash flow (Table 12.22) was much stronger rising from $314,840 to $1,571,036 by the 20th year. This generated an NPV of $3,318,040 for Baxter and a return of 44% on its money. The accountant also offered to do a build-to-suit for restaurant #32, knowing that this would probably be advantageous to Baxter because of their high tax rate (40%).

Baxter responded that they did not want to do a build-to-suit because they were committed to their present lender and did not want to interfere with that relationship. Baxter still did not want to do the lease for $200,000 + 1.5% of the gross because of the projected negative net income in the first two years.

The accountant argued that the land's value should not be impacted by Baxter's decision to use so much financial leverage. If Baxter used a more conservative approach to financing their restaurants, they would not incur those losses in the early years of operation. However, the accountant stated that Mrs. Munstead would be willing to work with Baxter, as long as she had reasonable financial incentives to do so.

TABLE 12.17   Baxter's Interstate # 32, Holding Period NOPAT, Pro Forma Net-Operating Profits after Taxes, with Land Lease

Year	Revenues[a]	Lease	Food Cost[b]	Salary and Wages[c]	Overhead	Depreciation[d]	EBIT	Taxes (40%)	NOPAT EBIT(1 − tx)
1	$8,000,000	$800,000	$3,600,000	$2,000,000	$1,000,000	$423,077	$176,923	$70,769	$106,154
2	8,400,000	800,000	3,780,000	2,100,000	1,030,000	658,632	31,368	12,547	18,821
3	8,820,000	800,000	3,969,000	2,205,000	1,060,900	497,447	287,653	115,061	172,592
4	9,261,000	800,000	4,167,450	2,315,250	1,092,727	391,887	493,686	197,474	296,212
5	9,724,050	800,000	4,375,823	2,431,013	1,125,509	320,881	670,825	268,330	402,495
6	10,210,253	800,000	4,594,614	2,552,563	1,159,274	333,839	769,963	307,985	461,978
7	10,720,765	800,000	4,824,344	2,680,191	1,194,052	211,437	1,010,741	404,296	606,444
8	11,256,803	800,000	5,065,562	2,814,201	1,229,874	195,211	1,151,956	460,782	691,174
9	11,819,644	800,000	5,318,840	2,954,911	1,266,770	181,149	1,297,974	519,190	778,785
10	12,410,626	800,000	5,584,782	3,102,656	1,304,773	168,961	1,449,453	579,781	869,672
11	13,031,157	800,000	5,864,021	3,257,789	1,343,916	158,399	1,607,032	642,813	964,219
12	13,682,715	800,000	6,157,222	3,420,679	1,384,234	149,245	1,771,336	708,534	1,062,801
13	14,366,851	800,000	6,465,083	3,591,713	1,425,761	141,311	1,942,983	777,193	1,165,790
14	15,085,193	800,000	6,788,337	3,771,298	1,468,534	134,436	2,122,589	849,035	1,273,553

TABLE 12.17 (Continued)

Year	Revenues[a]	Lease	Food Cost[b]	Salary and Wages[c]	Overhead	Depreciation[d]	EBIT	Taxes (40%)	NOPAT EBIT$(1 - Tx)$
15	$15,839,453	$800,000	$7,127,754	$3,959,863	$1,512,590	$128,477	$2,310,769	$924,308	$1,386,462
16	16,631,425	800,000	7,484,141	4,157,856	1,557,967	341,509	2,289,951	915,980	1,373,971
17	17,462,997	800,000	7,858,349	4,365,749	1,604,706	89,744	2,744,449	1,097,780	1,646,669
18	18,336,147	800,000	8,251,266	4,584,037	1,652,848	89,744	2,958,253	1,183,301	1,774,952
19	19,252,954	800,000	8,663,829	4,813,238	1,702,433	89,744	3,183,710	1,273,484	1,910,226
20	20,215,602	800,000	9,097,021	5,053,900	1,753,506	89,744	3,421,431	1,368,572	2,052,858

[a] Same store sales at Baxter's increase at 5% per year.

[b] Food cost at Baxter's nationally average 45%.

[c] Wages and salaries at Baxter's average 25%.

[d] Represents $3.5 million building depreciated over 39 years using the half-year convention; $2 million of building improvements depreciated over 15 years using the double-declining balance and half-year convention; and $1 million of equipment depreciated over five years using the double-declining balance and half-year convention.

TABLE 12.18 Baxter's Interstate #32, Pro Forma Income Statement, with Land Lease

Year	Revenues[a]	Lease	Food Cost[b]	Salary and Wages[c]	Overhead	Depreciation[d]	Interest[e]	EBT	Taxes (40%)	Net Income
1	$8,000,000	$800,000	$3,600,000	$2,000,000	$1,000,000	$423,077	$702,000	-$525,077	-$210,031	-$315,046
2	8,400,000	800,000	3,780,000	2,100,000	1,030,000	658,632	692,257	-660,890	-264,356	-396,534
3	8,820,000	800,000	3,969,000	2,205,000	1,060,900	497,447	681,345	-393,692	-157,477	-236,215
4	9,261,000	800,000	4,167,450	2,315,250	1,092,727	391,887	669,124	-175,437	-70,175	-105,262
5	9,724,050	800,000	4,375,823	2,431,013	1,125,509	320,881	655,435	15,390	6,156	9,234
6	10,210,253	800,000	4,594,614	2,552,563	1,159,274	333,839	640,105	129,858	51,943	77,915
7	10,720,765	800,000	4,824,344	2,680,191	1,194,052	211,437	622,934	387,806	155,122	232,684
8	11,256,803	800,000	5,065,562	2,814,201	1,229,874	195,211	603,704	548,252	219,301	328,951
9	11,819,644	800,000	5,318,840	2,954,911	1,266,770	181,149	582,165	715,809	286,324	429,485
10	12,410,626	800,000	5,584,782	3,102,656	1,304,773	168,961	558,042	891,411	356,564	534,847
11	13,031,157	800,000	5,864,021	3,257,789	1,343,916	158,399	531,024	1,076,007	430,403	645,604
12	13,682,715	800,000	6,157,222	3,420,679	1,384,234	149,245	500,764	1,270,571	508,229	762,343
13	14,366,851	800,000	6,465,083	3,591,713	1,425,761	141,311	466,873	1,476,110	590,444	885,666
14	15,085,193	800,000	6,788,337	3,771,298	1,468,534	134,436	428,915	1,693,673	677,469	1,016,204

TABLE 12.18 (Continued)

Year	Revenues[a]	Lease	Food Cost[b]	Salary and Wages[c]	Overhead	Depreciation[d]	Interest[e]	EBT	Taxes (40%)	Net Income
15	$15,839,453	$800,000	$7,127,754	$3,959,863	$1,512,590	$128,477	$386,402	$1,924,367	$769,747	$1,154,620
16	16,631,425	800,000	7,484,141	4,157,856	1,557,967	341,509	338,787	1,951,164	780,466	1,170,698
17	17,462,997	800,000	7,858,349	4,365,749	1,604,706	89,744	285,459	2,458,990	983,596	1,475,394
18	18,336,147	800,000	8,251,266	4,584,037	1,652,848	89,744	225,731	2,732,522	1,093,009	1,639,513
19	19,252,954	800,000	8,663,829	4,813,238	1,702,433	89,744	158,836	3,024,874	1,209,949	1,814,924
20	20,215,602	800,000	9,097,021	5,053,900	1,753,506	89,744	83,913	3,337,518	1,335,007	2,002,511

[1] Same store sales at Baxter's increase at 5% per year.
[2] Food cost at Baxter's nationally average 45%.
[3] Wages and salaries at Baxter's average 25%.
[4] Represents $3.5 million building depreciated over 39 years using the half-year convention; $2 million of building improvements depreciated over 15 years using the double-declining balance and half-year convention; and $1 million of equipment depreciated over five years using the double-declining balance and half-year convention.
[5] Based on a $5.85 million mortgage at 12%.

295

TABLE 12.19   Baxter's Interstate #32, Pro Forma Cash Flow Statement, with Land Lease

Year	Net Income[a]	Depre-ciation[a]	Equity Payments	Capital Contributions[b]	Net Cash Flows[c]
0				$1,014,000	−$1,014,000
1	−$315,046	$423,077	$81,191		26,840
2	−396,534	658,632	90,934		171,165
3	−236,215	497,447	101,846		159,386
4	−105,262	391,887	114,067		172,557
5	9,234	320,881	127,755		202,359
6	77,915	333,839	143,086		268,668
7	232,684	211,437	160,256		283,864
8	328,951	195,211	179,487		344,675
9	429,485	181,149	201,026		409,608
10	534,847	168,961	225,149		478,659
11	645,604	158,399	252,166		551,837
12	762,343	149,245	282,426		629,161
13	885,666	141,311	316,318		710,660
14	1,016,204	134,436	354,276		796,364
15	1,154,620	128,477	396,789		886,308
16	1,170,698	341,509	444,404		1,067,804
17	1,475,394	89,744	497,732		1,067,406
18	1,639,513	89,744	557,460		1,171,797
19	1,814,924	89,744	624,355		1,280,313
20	2,002,511	89,744	699,278		1,392,977

[a] See Table 12.18.
[b] Total capital = 10% of $6.5 million mortgage plus 12% on first year construction loan.
[c] Assumed value of property at end of lease equals zero.

NPV at 12% = $1,582,910

IRR = 24%

TABLE 12.20 Baxters Interstate # 32, Holding Period NOPAT, Pro Forma Net-Operating Profits after Taxes, with Land Lease

Year	Revenues[a]	Lease	Food Cost[b]	Salary and Wages[c]	Overhead	Depreciation[d]	EBIT	Taxes (40%)	NOPAT EBIT(1 − tx)
1	$8,000,000	$320,000	$3,600,000	$2,000,000	$1,000,000	$423,077	$656,923	$262,769	$394,154
2	8,400,000	326,000	3,780,000	2,100,000	1,030,000	658,632	505,368	202,147	303,221
3	8,820,000	332,300	3,969,000	2,205,000	1,060,900	497,447	755,353	302,141	453,212
4	9,261,000	338,915	4,167,450	2,315,250	1,092,727	391,887	954,771	381,908	572,863
5	9,724,050	345,861	4,375,823	2,431,013	1,125,509	320,881	1,124,964	449,986	674,979
6	10,210,253	353,154	4,594,614	2,552,563	1,159,274	333,839	1,216,809	486,724	730,086
7	10,720,765	360,811	4,824,344	2,680,191	1,194,052	211,437	1,449,929	579,972	869,957
8	11,256,803	368,852	5,065,562	2,814,201	1,229,874	195,211	1,583,104	633,242	949,862
9	11,819,644	377,295	5,318,840	2,954,911	1,266,770	181,149	1,720,680	688,272	1,032,408
10	12,410,626	386,159	5,584,782	3,102,656	1,304,773	168,961	1,863,294	745,318	1,117,976
11	13,031,157	395,467	5,864,021	3,257,789	1,343,916	158,399	2,011,564	804,626	1,206,939
12	13,682,715	405,241	6,157,222	3,420,679	1,384,234	149,245	2,166,095	866,438	1,299,657
13	14,366,851	415,503	6,465,083	3,591,713	1,425,761	141,311	2,327,480	930,992	1,396,488
14	15,085,193	426,278	6,788,337	3,771,298	1,468,534	134,436	2,496,311	998,524	1,497,786

TABLE 12.20 (Continued)

Year	Revenues[a]	Lease	Food Cost[b]	Salary and Wages[c]	Overhead	Depreciation[d]	EBIT	Taxes (40%)	NOPAT EBIT$(1 - tx)$
15	$15,839,453	$437,592	$7,127,754	$3,959,863	$1,512,590	$128,477	$2,673,178	$1,069,271	$1,603,907
16	16,631,425	449,471	7,484,141	4,157,856	1,557,967	341,509	2,640,480	1,056,192	1,584,288
17	17,462,997	461,945	7,858,349	4,365,749	1,604,706	89,744	3,082,504	1,233,002	1,849,502
18	18,336,147	475,042	8,251,266	4,584,037	1,652,848	89,744	3,283,211	1,313,284	1,969,926
19	19,252,954	488,794	8,663,829	4,813,238	1,702,433	89,744	3,494,915	1,397,966	2,096,949
20	20,215,602	503,234	9,097,021	5,053,900	1,753,506	89,744	3,718,197	1,487,279	2,230,918

[a] Same store sales at Baxter's increase at 5% per year.
[b] Food cost at Baxter's nationally average 45%.
[c] Wages and salaries at Baxter's average 25%.
[d] Represents $3.5 million building depreciated over 39 years using the half-year convention; $2 million of building improvements depreciated over 15 years using the double-declining balance and half-year convention; $1 million of equipment depreciated over five years using the double-declining balance and half-year convention.

TABLE 12.21 Baxter's Interstate #32, Pro Forma Income Statement, with Land Lease

Year	Revenues[a]	Lease	Food Cost[b]	Salary and Wages[c]	Overhead	Depre- ciation[d]	Interest[e]	EBT	Taxes (40%)	Net Income
1	$8,000,000	$320,000	$3,600,000	$2,000,000	$1,000,000	$423,077	$702,000	−$45,077	−$18,031	−$27,046
2	8,400,000	326,000	3,780,000	2,100,000	1,030,000	658,632	692,257	−186,890	−74,756	−112,134
3	8,820,000	332,300	3,969,000	2,205,000	1,060,900	497,447	681,345	74,008	29,603	44,405
4	9,261,000	338,915	4,167,450	2,315,250	1,092,727	391,887	669,124	285,648	114,259	171,389
5	9,724,050	345,861	4,375,823	2,431,013	1,125,509	320,881	655,435	469,529	187,812	281,717
6	10,210,253	353,154	4,594,614	2,552,563	1,159,274	333,839	640,105	576,704	230,682	346,023
7	10,720,765	360,811	4,824,344	2,680,191	1,194,052	211,437	622,934	826,995	330,798	496,197
8	11,256,803	368,852	5,065,562	2,814,201	1,229,874	195,211	603,704	979,400	391,760	587,640
9	11,819,644	377,295	5,318,840	2,954,911	1,266,770	181,149	582,165	1,138,514	455,406	683,109
10	12,410,626	386,159	5,584,782	3,102,656	1,304,773	168,961	558,042	1,305,252	522,101	783,151
11	13,031,157	395,467	5,864,021	3,257,789	1,343,916	158,399	531,024	1,480,540	592,216	888,324
12	13,682,715	405,241	6,157,222	3,420,679	1,384,234	149,245	500,764	1,665,331	666,132	999,198
13	14,366,851	415,503	6,465,083	3,591,713	1,425,761	141,311	466,873	1,860,607	744,243	1,116,364
14	15,085,193	426,278	6,788,337	3,771,298	1,468,534	134,436	428,915	2,067,396	826,958	1,240,437

TABLE 12.21 (Continued)

Year	Revenues[a]	Lease	Food Cost[b]	Salary and Wages[c]	Overhead	Depreciation[d]	Interest[e]	EBT	Taxes (40%)	Net Income
15	$15,839,453	$437,592	$7,127,754	$3,959,863	$1,512,590	$128,477	$386,402	$2,286,776	$914,710	$1,372,065
16	16,631,425	449,471	7,484,141	4,157,856	1,557,967	341,509	338,787	2,301,692	920,677	1,381,015
17	17,462,997	461,945	7,858,349	4,365,749	1,604,706	89,744	285,459	2,797,045	1,118,818	1,678,227
18	18,336,147	475,042	8,251,266	4,584,037	1,652,848	89,744	225,731	3,057,479	1,222,992	1,834,488
19	19,252,954	488,794	8,663,829	4,813,238	1,702,433	89,744	158,836	3,336,079	1,334,432	2,001,648
20	20,215,602	503,234	9,097,021	5,053,900	1,753,506	89,744	83,913	3,634,283	1,453,713	2,180,570

[a] Same store sales at Baxter's increase at 5% per year.
[b] Food cost at Baxter's nationally average 45%.
[c] Wages and salaries at Baxter's average 2.5%.
[d] Represents $3.5 million building depreciated over 39 years using the half-year convention; $2 million of building improvements depreciated over 15 years using the double-declining balance and half-year convention; and $1 million of equipment depreciated over five years using the double-declining balance and half-year convention.
[e] Based on a $5.85 million mortgage at 12%.

EXHIBIT 14.22   Baxter's Interstate #32, Pro Forma Cash Flow Statement, with Land Lease

Year	Net Income[a]	Depre-ciation[a]	Equity Payments	Capital Contributions[b]	Net Cash Flows[v]
0				$1,014,000	–$1,014,000
1	–$27,046	$423,077	$81,191		314,840
2	–112,134	658,632	90,934		455,565
3	44,405	497,447	101,846		440,006
4	171,389	391,887	114,067		449,208
5	281,717	320,881	127,755		474,843
6	346,023	333,839	143,086		536,775
7	496,197	211,437	160,256		547,377
8	587,640	195,211	179,487		603,364
9	683,109	181,149	201,026		663,232
10	783,151	168,961	225,149		726,964
11	888,324	158,399	252,166		794,556
12	999,198	149,245	282,426		866,017
13	1,116,364	141,311	316,318		941,358
14	1,240,437	134,436	354,276		1,020,597
15	1,372,065	128,477	396,789		1,103,753
16	1,381,015	341,509	444,404		1,278,121
17	1,678,227	89,744	497,732		1,270,239
18	1,834,488	89,744	557,460		1,366,771
19	2,001,648	89,744	624,355		1,467,036
20	2,180,570	89,744	699,278		1,571,036

[a] See Table 12.21.
[b] Total capital = 10% of $6.5 million mortgage plus 12% on first-year construction loan.
[c] Assumed value of property at end of lease equals zero.

NPV at 12% = $3,318,040

IRR = 44%

The accountant then proposed a lease for a flat $125,000 per year for the first two years. After that as long as total revenues were lower than $8 million, the lease would remain at $125,000. If revenues were higher than $8 million after the first two years, then the lease would be $100,000 plus 2% of gross revenues. While this did not do a whole lot to reduce the financial exposure of Baxter (the consequence of the high overhead incorporated in their business plan and their high degree of financial leverage), the landlord was making as much a concession to Baxter's concerns as could reasonably be expected.

The proposed lease of a minimum of $125,000 and, after two years, $100,000 and 2% of the gross if total revenue exceeded $8 million are examined in Tables 12.23, 12.24, and 12.25. The effect of this lease proposal is to increase NOPAT, particularly in the early years of operation. The increase in NOPAT is strong enough to eliminate the previous pro forma losses anticipated at #32 (Table 12.24). Table 12.24 shows consistently strong cash flows and a 20-year NPV of $3,621,911 for Baxter resulting in a 50% annual return on their initial investment. This, of course, happens only if they hit their expected sales level. But as the accountant said, "Hey! Some risks are worth taking."

Baxter decided to accept this offer and the accountant said he would take it to Mrs. Munstead.

The accountant then explained to Jean that the worst thing that could happen to her would be a lease income of $125,000 for the next 20 years and then she would still own the property. Furthermore, that there was a good chance that the restaurant would hit its sales projections and then lease income would rise to $504,312 in 20 years and she would still own the property. However, he cautioned her, this is not an investment in utilities. They are much more predictable than restaurants. There is an outside chance Baxter's could default on its lease (although it does not seem likely) or not renew it after the first five years. Higher return is always associated with higher risk. Then the accountant opinioned that, "All in all, this looks like a pretty good deal."

As a result, Jean Munstead accepted the proffered lease.

ILLUSTRATION #3: BARRY'S BASTILLE

Barry Potts had been an entrepreneur for years. He was an owner of a bar, three fast-food ventures, two casual dining restaurants, and a tire store. Some were moderately successful, some were not. Barry now had a vision for two acres on the outskirts of his rapidly growing metropolis. The two acres contained an old Victorian-style farmhouse located on a busy road that led to a subdivision that used to be the farm. The farmhouse can best be described by noting that the local Jaycees used it as a "haunted house" every Halloween. An elderly widow owned the farmhouse and wanted to move to a rest home. She was considering an offer to buy the land for $190,000.

Barry saw the house differently. He wanted to remodel the house and put an upscale French restaurant in it. The area surrounding this

TABLE 12.23 Baxter's Interstate #32, Holding Period NOPAT, Pro Forma Net-Operating Profits after Taxes, with Land Lease

Year	Revenues[a]	Lease	Food Cost[b]	Salary and Wages[c]	Overhead	Depreciation[d]	EBIT	Taxes (40%)	NOPAT EBIT$(1 - tx)$
1	$8,000,000	$125,000	$3,600,000	$2,000,000	$1,000,000	$423,077	$851,923	$340,769	$511,154
2	8,400,000	125,000	3,780,000	2,100,000	1,030,000	658,632	706,368	282,547	423,821
3	8,820,000	276,400	3,969,000	2,205,000	1,060,900	497,447	811,253	324,501	486,752
4	9,261,000	285,220	4,167,450	2,315,250	1,092,727	391,887	1,008,466	403,386	605,080
5	9,724,050	294,481	4,375,823	2,431,013	1,125,509	320,881	1,176,344	470,538	705,806
6	10,210,253	304,205	4,594,614	2,552,563	1,159,274	333,839	1,265,758	506,303	759,455
7	10,720,765	314,415	4,824,344	2,680,191	1,194,052	211,437	1,496,325	598,530	897,795
8	11,256,803	325,136	5,065,562	2,814,201	1,229,874	195,211	1,626,820	650,728	976,092
9	11,819,644	336,393	5,318,840	2,954,911	1,266,770	181,149	1,761,581	704,633	1,056,949
10	12,410,626	348,213	5,584,782	3,102,656	1,304,773	168,961	1,901,241	760,496	1,140,744
11	13,031,157	360,623	5,864,021	3,257,789	1,343,916	158,399	2,046,409	818,563	1,227,845
12	13,682,715	373,654	6,157,222	3,420,679	1,384,234	149,245	2,197,681	879,073	1,318,609
13	14,366,851	387,337	6,465,083	3,591,713	1,425,761	141,311	2,355,646	942,258	1,413,388
14	15,085,193	401,704	6,788,337	3,771,298	1,468,534	134,436	2,520,885	1,008,354	1,512,531

TABLE 12.23 (Continued)

Year	Revenues[a]	Lease	Food Cost[b]	Salary and Wages[c]	Overhead	Depreciation[d]	EBIT	Taxes (40%)	NOPAT EBIT$(1 - tx)$
15	$15,839,453	$416,789	$7,127,754	$3,959,863	$1,512,590	$128,477	$2,693,980	$1,077,592	$1,616,388
16	16,631,425	432,629	7,484,141	4,157,856	1,557,967	341,509	2,657,323	1,062,929	1,594,394
17	17,462,997	449,260	7,858,349	4,365,749	1,604,706	89,744	3,095,189	1,238,076	1,857,113
18	18,336,147	466,723	8,251,266	4,584,037	1,652,848	89,744	3,291,530	1,316,612	1,974,918
19	19,252,954	485,059	8,663,829	4,813,238	1,702,433	89,744	3,498,650	1,399,460	2,099,190
20	20,215,602	504,312	9,097,021	5,053,900	1,753,506	89,744	3,717,119	1,486,848	2,230,271

[a] Same store sales at Baxter's increase at 5% per year.
[b] Food cost at Baxter's nationally average 45%.
[c] Wages and salaries at Baxter's average 25%.
[d] Represents $3.5 million building depreciated over 39 years using the half-year convention; $2 million of building improvements depreciated over 15 years using the double-declining balance and half-year convention; and $1 million of equipment depreciated over five years using the double-declining balance and half-year convention.

304

TABLE 12.24 Baxter's Interstate #32, Pro Forma Income Statement, with Land Lease

Year	Revenues[a]	Lease	Food Cost[b]	Salary and Wages[c]	Overhead	Depreciation[d]	Interest[e]	EBT	Taxes (40%)	Net Income
1	$8,000,000	$125,000	$3,600,000	$2,000,000	$1,000,000	$423,077	$702,000	$149,923	$59,969	$89,954
2	8,400,000	125,000	3,780,000	2,100,000	1,030,000	658,632	692,257	14,110	5,644	8,466
3	8,820,000	276,400	3,969,000	2,205,000	1,060,900	497,447	681,345	129,908	51,963	77,945
4	9,261,000	285,220	4,167,450	2,315,250	1,092,727	391,887	669,124	339,343	135,737	203,606
5	9,724,050	294,481	4,375,823	2,431,013	1,125,509	320,881	655,435	520,909	208,363	312,545
6	10,210,253	304,205	4,594,614	2,552,563	1,159,274	333,839	640,105	625,653	250,261	375,392
7	10,720,765	314,415	4,824,344	2,680,191	1,194,052	211,437	622,934	873,391	349,356	524,034
8	11,256,803	325,136	5,065,562	2,814,201	1,229,874	195,211	603,704	1,023,116	409,247	613,870
9	11,819,644	336,393	5,318,840	2,954,911	1,266,770	181,149	582,165	1,179,416	471,766	707,650
10	12,410,626	348,213	5,584,782	3,102,656	1,304,773	168,961	558,042	1,343,199	537,279	805,919
11	13,031,157	360,623	5,864,021	3,257,789	1,343,916	158,399	531,024	1,515,384	606,154	909,231
12	13,682,715	373,654	6,157,222	3,420,679	1,384,234	149,245	500,764	1,696,917	678,767	1,018,150
13	14,366,851	387,337	6,465,083	3,591,713	1,425,761	141,311	466,873	1,888,773	755,509	1,133,264
14	15,085,193	401,704	6,788,337	3,771,298	1,468,534	134,436	428,915	2,091,970	836,788	1,255,182

TABLE 12.24 (Continued)

Year	Revenues[a]	Lease	Food Cost[b]	Salary and Wages[c]	Overhead	Depreciation[d]	Interest[e]	EBT	Taxes (40%)	Net Income
15	$15,839,453	$416,789	$7,127,754	$3,959,863	$1,512,590	$128,477	$386,402	$2,307,578	$923,031	$1,384,547
16	16,631,425	432,629	7,484,141	4,157,856	1,557,967	341,509	338,787	2,318,535	927,414	1,391,121
17	17,462,997	449,260	7,858,349	4,365,749	1,604,706	89,744	285,459	2,809,730	1,123,892	1,685,838
18	18,336,147	466,723	8,251,266	4,584,037	1,652,848	89,744	225,731	3,065,799	1,226,319	1,839,479
19	19,252,954	485,059	8,663,829	4,813,238	1,702,433	89,744	158,836	3,339,815	1,335,926	2,003,889
20	20,215,602	504,312	9,097,021	5,053,900	1,753,506	89,744	83,913	3,633,205	1,453,282	2,179,923

[a] Same store sales at Baxter's increase at 5% per year.
[b] Food cost at Baxter's nationally average 45%.
[c] Wages and salaries at Baxter's average 25%.
[d] Represents $3.5 million building depreciated over 39 years using the half-year convention; $2 million of building improvements depreciated over 15 years using the double-declining balance and half-year convention; and $1 million of equipment depreciated over five years using the double-declining balance and half-year convention.
[e] Based on a $5.85 million mortgage at 12%.

TABLE 12.25   Baxter's Interstate #32, Pro Forma Cash Flow Statement, with
Land Lease

Year	Net Income[a]	Depre- ciation[a]	Equity Payments	Capital Contributions[b]	Net Cash Flows[c]
0				$1,014,000	–$1,014,000
1	$89,954	$423,077	$81,191		431,840
2	8,466	658,632	90,934		576,165
3	77,945	497,447	101,846		473,546
4	203,606	391,887	114,067		481,425
5	312,545	320,881	127,755		505,671
6	375,392	333,839	143,086		566,145
7	524,034	211,437	160,256		575,215
8	613,870	195,211	179,487		629,594
9	707,650	181,149	201,026		687,773
10	805,919	168,961	225,149		749,732
11	909,231	158,399	252,166		815,463
12	1,018,150	149,245	282,426		884,969
13	1,133,264	141,311	316,318		958,257
14	1,255,182	134,436	354,276		1,035,342
15	1,384,547	128,477	396,789		1,116,235
16	1,391,121	341,509	444,404		1,288,227
17	1,685,838	89,744	497,732		1,277,850
18	1,839,479	89,744	557,460		1,371,763
19	2,003,889	89,744	624,355		1,469,277
20	2,179,923	89,744	699,278		1,570,389

[a] See Table 12.24.
[b] Total capital = 10% of $6.5 million mortgage plus 12% on first-year construction loan.
[c] Assumed value of property at end of lease equals zero.

NPV at 12% = $3,621,911

IRR = 50%

location was affluent, and developing rapidly (primarily with "McMansions" on three or four acres). There were two other French restaurants within two miles of this location, and they seemed to be doing well. Barry reasoned that there was certainly room for another French restaurant in this area. Barry was in love with this idea and the kind of person who would not take no for an answer. Barry wanted to call the restaurant the "Bastille" because it sounded romantic.

Barry secured a triple-net, five-year lease on the property for $25,000 per year by charming the elderly widow with his plans for the farmhouse. He explained to her that she would have more income this way and still own the land. She told him the income from her lease was all she would have to supplement her Social Security and meager savings.

Then Barry went to his banker and negotiated a loan for $350,000 to remodel the house and equip the restaurant that was estimated to cost about $500,000. The loan was a 10-year personal 14% note amortized by monthly principal and interest payments and secured by Barry's personal residence and some stock his wife had just inherited from her side of the family. Barry had $250,000 of his own money and was going to put $150,000 into the business.

Barry thought he would substitute his experience in the industry for doing some hard research on the area's population and demographics. His vision was for a restaurant that offered exceptional food in the finest and most elegant surroundings. This translated into cost overruns during the remodeling process of $100,000 that consumed all Barry's cash reserves. The high-quality food Barry was going to serve was expected to run about 50% of sales (a very high ratio for a restaurant). Barry also wanted the business fully staffed with expert cooks and top rate waiters, waitresses, and a maitre d'hôtel. That was expected to drive his labor costs up to 30% (also a high rate for a restaurant).

As the time neared for opening the restaurant, Barry was out of money, but he prevailed on his vendors, many of whom were personal friends and past business acquaintances, to extend him the credit that he needed for supplies.

The Bastille opened auspiciously enough. Business was brisk, quite crowded on weekends, but very little lunch crowd and weekday evening sales were weak. As can be seen from Table 12.26, sales totaled $212,000 the first quarter generating a positive NOPAT of $4,720. However, this meant net income was somewhat negative at –$6,303 as can be seen from Table 12.27. Still Barry was given comfort by the fact that cash flow was positive (Table 12.28) and that he was able to pay his vendors in a timely manner. (This was important, because he had no cash reserves).

The second quarter was tough. Business fell off by one-third to $145,000. This reflected a spell of unusually inclement weather and the fact that the other two French restaurants in their market began to fight back by promoting "specials" in the local newspaper. The cash loss of more than $10,000 meant Barry began to be a little "slow" in his payments to the vendors.

TABLE 12.26 Bastille, Holding Period NOPAT, Net-Operating Profits after Taxes

Quarters	Revenues[a]	Food Cost[b]	Salary and Wages[c]	Lease and Overhead	Depreciation[d]	EBIT	Taxes (20%)	NOPAT EBIT$(1 - tx)$
Year 1, first quarter	$212,000	$106,000	$63,600	$6,500	$30,000	$5,900	$1,180	$4,720
Year 1, second quarter	145,000	72,500	43,500	6,500	30,000	-7,500	-$1,500	-6,000
Year 1, third quarter	199,000	99,500	59,700	6,500	30,000	3,300	-$680	3,980
Year 1, fourth quarter	84,000	42,000	25,200	6,500	30,000	-19,700	$0	-19,700
Year 2, first quarter	80,000	40,000	24,000	6,500	48,000	-38,500	$0	-38,500
Year 2, second quarter	72,000	36,000	21,600	6,500	48,000	-40,100	$0	-40,100

[a] The reasons for the revenue pattern are described in the text.
[b] The high food costs of 50% reflected a strategic decision to go "upscale."
[c] The high labor costs also reflected the strategic decision to go "upscale."
[d] Restaurant improvements were depreciated over 15 years using the double-declining balance option.

TABLE 12.27 Bastille, Income Statement

Quarters	Revenues[a]	Food Cost[b]	Salary and Wages[c]	Lease and Overhead	Depreciation[d]	Interest[e]	EBT	Taxes (40%)	Net Income
Year 1, first quarter	$212,000	$106,000	$63,600	$6,500	$30,000	$12,203	-$6,303	$0	-$6,303
Year 1, second quarter	145,000	72,500	43,500	6,500	30,000	12,057	-19,557	0	-19,557
Year 1, third quarter	199,000	99,500	59,700	6,500	30,000	11,907	-8,607	0	-8,607
Year 1, fourth quarter	84,000	42,000	25,200	6,500	30,000	11,751	-31,451	0	-31,451
Year 2, first quarter	80,000	40,000	24,000	6,500	48,000	11,590	-50,090	0	-50,090
Year 2, second quarter	72,000	36,000	21,600	6,500	48,000	11,423	-51,523	0	-51,523

[a] The reasons for the revenue pattern are described in the text.
[b] The high food costs of 50% reflected a strategic decision to go "upscale."
[c] The high labor costs also reflected the strategic decision to go "upscale."
[d] Restaurant improvements were depreciated over 15 years using the double-declining balance option.
[e] Reflecting monthly interest payments on a $350,000 loan for 10 years at 14%.

TABLE 12.28   Bastille, Cash Flow Statement

Year	Net Income[a]	Depreciation[a]	Equity Payments	Capital Contributions[b]	Net Cash Flows[c]
0				$600,000	−$600,000
1	−$6,303	$30,000	$8,169		15,528
2	−19,557	30,000	20,760		−10,317
3	−8,607	30,000	33,796		−12,403
4	−31,451	30,000	47,294		−48,746
5	−50,090	48,000	61,270		−63,360
6	−51,523	48,000	75,741		−79,264

[a] See Table 12.27.
[b] Total capital = 10% of $6.5 million mortgage plus 12% on first-year construction loan.
[c] Assumed value of property at end of lease equals zero.

NPV at 15% = ($764,058)

Barry was no slouch and fought back with a number of "specials" and local promotions of his own. So, in his third quarter, sales climbed back to almost $200,000. However, this boost in sales was not able to bring cash flow back to a positive level. (Due to his high food and labor costs, Barry had very little operating leverage. That is, a dollar increase in sales only has him $0.20 to defray his fixed costs.) Barry fell further behind in paying his vendors, but was still managing to pay the elderly widow who held the lease on time.

The fourth quarter brought disaster. A Greek restaurant opened a quarter mile south of him and a new Italian restaurant opened up a half mile north of him. Sales nose-dived to $84,000 and cash flow was −$48,746. This was money Barry did not have and could not get. He was unable to pay the elderly widow, who began to send him the most heart rendering, pleading letters. Barry would have paid her if he could, but he did not have the money. His vendors and former friends began seriously dunning Barry for payment.

Disaster continued in the first quarter of his second year. Sales fell slightly, but they were already at too low a level. Operating the restaurant began to take on a crisis mode. Barry was forced to find new suppliers when his former vendors refused to deliver to him any more. By the second quarter of the second year lawsuits began arriving and Barry was forced to declare bankruptcy for both his business and personally. Two weeks after closing, the Bastille burned to the ground from a fire of "suspicious" origin.

The elderly widow who had given Barry the five-year lease for $25,000 had received exactly $14,000 from Barry over those 18 months. Plus liens of $16,000 were attached to the land for a failure to pay property taxes. The land was caught up in a squabble between the creditors in bankruptcy for 24 months. During this period the elderly widow died. The net value of the land that passed to the estate after legal fees, court costs, and taxes was $63,000.

Barry and his wife lost all their money and had their house repossessed. Barry suffered a nervous breakdown and had to be hospitalized. After his recovery, Barry went to work as the manager of a local Pizza Hut. Barry's wife lost her inheritance and divorced him.

CHAPTER 13

Shopping Centers

Shopping centers cover a broad range of investment opportunities. Shopping centers may be invested in directly or indirectly through a partnership, general partnership, master limited partnership, limited liability corporation (LLC), Subchapter S corporation, or REIT. Rarely are large shopping centers held in the form of a regular corporation because of the problem of double taxation. Most shopping centers are owned indirectly because of the need to raise substantial capital and the advantage of spreading the risk.

Often overlooked for their inherent profitability, shopping centers frequently provide a great opportunity for the small- or medium-sized real estate investor. Shopping centers have desirable real estate investment characteristics. The largest portion of the value of the shopping center is depreciable, generating a substantial tax shield. Shopping centers generate their return through a continuous, relatively predictable cash flow, rather than requiring a one-time windfall in the distant future. Shopping centers usually can be acquired in a manner that provides for substantial leverage. Furthermore, the wide array of available types of shopping centers allows the investor to pick and choose the exact combination of risk and return that they prefer.

SHOPPING CENTER THREATS AND OPPORTUNITIES

The basic idea behind the shopping center is that its whole must be more than the sum of its parts. In other words, by virtue of their being grouped together, a number of retailers will do better than if they each located in different areas. Such benefits are technically known as *positive externalities*. These positive externalities can arise from a number of sources.

313

Examples of positive externalities would be the increased convenience for consumers arising from physical proximity, shared common amenities (e.g., a parking lot, security services), or from a more effective or efficient marketing effort. Retailers grouped in a shopping center are able to capture marketing economies of scale (e.g., an advertising campaign or flyer for the shopping center, rather than for individual stores). An important source of positive externalities would be a set of retailers offering complimentary goods and services, such as a shoe store next to a clothing store, a convenience store next to a retail video store, and so on. Relative to the market being served, it is important to reach a sufficiently critical mass to become a destination for shopping excursions. All of these attributes create value by virtue of physical proximity that would not be possible were the stores not grouped together. A shopping center creates value for its tenants and provides an investor with a reward based upon the value created.

Unfortunately, negative externalities can also be created by a shopping center. There was a well-sited strip center of 40 stores serving a market with great demographic and economic attributes. It was doing quite well until the market served by its roller rink tenant changed. This situation came about because of a change in the public transportation system that permitted inner-city adolescents to inundate the roller rink. Crowd control became an issue, vandalism and theft increased, and shoppers felt intimidated. Existing retailers saw sales and profits drop and many left. The shopping center went into a steep decline as a result.

While many small shopping centers can create positive externalities simple by bringing together tenants of roughly equal market appeal, an effective strategy is to allow one larger tenant to be the major draw with the other tenants feeding off that store's presence. Such a store is popularly called an "anchor." (Very large shopping centers may have multiple anchors.) Supermarkets are the classic anchors in small and medium-sized strip shopping centers. However, large discount stores—particularly Wal-Mart—drug chains, department stores, or the larger movie complexes have all served effectively as anchors.

Shopping centers are defined in terms of the market served. This market can be a few square blocks for a community shopping center or cover the whole metropolitan area for a large regional shopping mall. Location, access, and traffic patterns define a mall's success relative to the market served. Securing aerial photographs that allow the shopping center to be identified within the context of its physical infrastructure can begin the analysis of a shopping center's potential. Such photographs are readily available from local or state government agencies. Traffic counts on key nearby thoroughfares can also be obtained from such agencies. Economic and demographic data by ZIP codes and census tracts are readily available, making it possible to pinpoint the characteristics of the market to be served.

The bane of shopping centers is overdevelopment. No matter how cleverly constructed and marketed, a particular shopping center serving a particular market is vulnerable to the arrival of new market entrants. A pie can only be sliced so many times. An excessive number of shopping centers in a particular market will reduce tenant revenue and consequently, the value of the shopping center itself.

Less immediate threats to shopping center success are changes in the market's demographic and economic characteristics. Urban and suburban population patterns are inherently dynamic. Thus, change is natural. These can occur as the result of the passage of time, evolving ethnic and racial patterns, waves of immigration, and shifts in the public transportation system, and changes in employment opportunities. Generally, such changes do not spell doom for the shopping center. Where performance falls off because of such changes, it just means the shopping center is serving the wrong market. Success requires a re-deployment of assets and a change in the tenant mix. Change is to be expected and, being expected, can be planned for.

Successful shopping centers have successful tenants. No matter how strong the lease, a tenant who is not able to earn a profit will find a way to break the lease—or be broken by the lease. Either way, the shopping center itself loses. If an error was not made in locating the shopping center and, in the unlikely instance that demographic and economic changes have not predestined failure, the difference between success and failure for the shopping center will be the quality of the shopping center management.

LEASING CHARACTERISTICS

Although exceptions may be found, the typical shopping center will own all the physical property and lease it to the various tenants. The shopping center will spell out the terms and conditions with its tenants in a lease. These terms and conditions will be comprehensive and spell out details like signage requirements, hours of operation, product lines offered, and the like. The attempt will be to create a consistent image and positive externalities that will benefit each lessee in turn.

A critical element of the lease will be the level of rent. Ultimately, the determination of rent is a matter of supply and demand, not of cost alone. A developer may calculate that a 100,000 sq. ft. facility will cost $8 million. Furthermore, the facility will need to bring in about $15 per sq. ft. in net rent, or $1.5 million annually, to make the project economically viable. If competitive market rates are $12 per sq. ft., the shopping center is just not going to be built. Or if already built, the shopping center will not cover its cost and will go bankrupt. It should be noted that if area rentals are $12 per sq. ft., but there exists a reason that lessees would be willing to pay a premium for this shopping center, it might still be viable. The key is in whether or not the advantages of the shopping center, relative to alternative locations, are perceived by the potential retailers as worth the difference.

Negotiations over the terms of the lease may be contentious. The landlord often takes an optimistic outlook of the retailer's prospects and the retailer takes a more conservative view. Because there is uncertainty necessarily inherent in the outcome, a solution to this problem is provided by making the lease partially contingent on the performance of the retailer. Thus it is quite common to have a lease that requires a minimum level of rent, but may range upward as a fixed percent of the retailer's gross sales. Such percentages frequently range between 2% and 8% depending on the relative bargaining power of the landlord and the tenant.

In this context it should be noted that the bargaining advantage of an anchor with an established track record of success is large. Such an anchor is usually an experienced negotiator (or represented by experienced negotiators). The anchor will be aware of the size and type of the positive externalities it will bring to the shopping center and their value. The anchor will argue that it should be compensated for this value.

Depending on market conditions, a variety of lease arrangements are possible:

- **Gross Lease.** The landlord pays all expenses except remodeling costs and nonstructural maintenance costs in the tenant area. Thus the landlord pays taxes, insurance, utilities, and so on. The tenant pays a fixed rent for the life of the lease. Obviously, this is a relatively undesirable state of affairs for the landlord because it is a situation in which costs may well rise and revenues will not.
- **Net Lease.** Similar to the gross lease, except that the tenant pays a pro rata share of property taxes—still an undesirable lease from the point of view of the landlord.
- **Double-Net Lease.** Like a net lease, except that the tenant must now pay a proportionate share of the insurance costs.
- **Triple-Net Lease.** Like a double-net lease, except the tenant must now pay a proportionate share of building maintenance expenses (including common-area expenses). This is a more desirable type of lease from the landlord's perspective because the expected cash flow will not be eroded by rising costs.
- **Triple-Net Lease with Percentage.** Similar to a triple-net lease, except that, after some minimum level, the rent will include a percentage of the tenant's gross sales.

■ **Triple-Net Lease with Ups.** Similar to a triple-net lease, except that the underlying rent is indexed to some official measure of inflation. This is obviously a very desirable type of lease from the landlord's perspective.

TYPES OF SHOPPING CENTERS

Strip Shopping Centers

A *strip shopping center* is three to 10 small independent stores clustered on a heavily traveled road. The businesses are generally dependent on the volume of traffic and their exposure to this traffic. Convenience stores, fast-food restaurants, liquor stores, video stores, specialty produce, meats, or seafood, gas stations, dry cleaners, and so on typically dominate this environment.

Neighborhood Shopping Centers

A *neighborhood shopping center* is three to 10 small independent stores serving a localized market. Such a shopping center is not necessarily located on a high-volume thoroughfare, although ease of access to the market served is critical. Convenience stores, fast food, small restaurants, liquor stores, video stores, drug stores, hardware store, toy store, and the like typify this environment. Neighborhood shopping centers frequently may be in close proximity to apartment complexes, office buildings, hospitals, large employers, or in a densely populated urban area.

Community Shopping Centers

A *community shopping center* is five to 25 small stores with a major anchor that is a proven traffic builder. Such a shopping center is typically located at the junction of heavily traveled roads. Stores have sufficient breadth and diversity to generate strong positive externalities. The community shopping center has a mix of tenants that give it a strong destination appeal.

Inner-City Shopping Centers

An *inner-city shopping center* is three to 10 small independent businesses located on the first floor of a large building. This shopping center serves both a neighborhood and transitional clientele. The shopping center may either be leased from the building's owners or purchased as a condominium from the building's owners.

Regional or Super-Regional Shopping Centers

A *regional or super-regional shopping center* is a significant concentration of retailers combined to draw shoppers from great distances. Such a shopping center contains 25 to 250 independent stores and may contain several anchors; and it is frequently located beside one or more interstate routes. The 1990s saw an overbuilt market for this type of shopping center. The resultant hypercompetitive environment resulted in the newer, even larger shopping centers doing severe damage to older shopping centers. The competition between these large centers reached such an extent as to draw some business away from community and neighborhood shopping centers in the same metropolitan area, resulting in a more difficult situation for those retailers.

A properly located shopping with the right tenant mix affords investors excellent risk and return combinations—as long as the retail market served is not oversaturated with competitors. These opportunities are particularly attractive if the investor has the expertise to manage the shopping center itself. However, this management expertise is not absolutely necessary. In any given metropolitan area, the investor will be able to find a number of firms who specialize in managing shopping centers. It is sufficient that investors in shopping centers are entrepreneurs who are act as catalysts to bring economic resources together to create something where there was nothing before.

The following illustrations are examples of this type of entrepreneurial activity.

ILLUSTRATION #1: BIG SKY SHOPPING CENTER WITH CONVENTIONAL FINANCING

This is an example of developing a strip shopping center with conventional fixed financing.

Acquisition Phase

The Development Process

An individual investor sees the potential for developing a strip shopping center on the fringe of an existing suburban development. A potential six-acre site is identified along an existing heavily traveled four-lane highway. The highway is not heavily developed in this area at present because most of the traffic is transient. The investor sees potential as suburban growth continues, and the state completes a planned major highway that will intersect with the existing highway where the six-acre site fronts. The investor forms a general partnership with four friends to develop the site. Each partner contributes $20,000 to commission a feasibility study. The location under consideration proves highly promising. (Note: This $20,000 will be considered a sunk cost and, therefore, does not influence subsequent financial calculations.)

The partners envision a 100,000 sq. ft. anchored strip shopping center with 15 stores. It is expected that such a shopping center would take 18 months to complete at a cost of $8,000,000 ($6,000,000 to construct the building, $1,500,000 for land improvements, and $500,000 for staff and operating expenses). Negotiations are begun with local contractors and the planning and permitting process is initiated.

Negotiations are undertaken with a popular aggressive local supermarket chain to secure a 10-year, triple-net lease for 25,000 sq. ft. for $12.50 per sq. ft. (This rent is below market, but the investors feel it necessary to have a strong anchor in the shopping center.) Further negotiation are undertaken to secure eight other tenants (mostly national franchises), with 3-year, triple-net leases, each averaging 5,000 sq. ft. at an average of $16 per square foot. The decision is made to proceed without any commitments on the remaining 35,000 sq. ft.

The local bank is approached for a $6 million, 15-year mortgage on the shopping center. The bank feels the mortgage will be well secured by the $2 million equity that the partnership is putting into the project, the partners' willingness to sign personally for the loan—they each have substantial net worth—and a presently committed annual cash flow of $952,500. The bank offers 8% and 5 points for a 15-year loan with monthly flat principle and interest payments. The resultant payment and equity schedule is presented in Table 13.1. This is important because interest payments are tax deductible, equity payments are not. In addition, the loan requires "5 points," which means an additional cash outflow to the partnership of $300,000 when they get the loan. However, IRS rules require that these interest points be amortized on a straight-line basis over the life of the loan.

The partnership hires staff to implement a formal accounting system to control costs, keep work on schedule, resolve contractor disputes, and begin developing a marketing plan. With the project on schedule after 12 months the seven final tenants are found for the remaining 35,000 sq. ft. with 2-year triple-net leases averaging $14.50 per square foot. The project is successfully completed within budget and on schedule. Prior to the opening of the shopping center, the developer secures the services of a professional shopping center management company, whose fee will be 8% of the shopping center's gross revenues.

Even though the leases used by the partnership do not contain an escalation clause, it would be expected that there would be some turn-

TABLE 13.1 Big Sky Shopping Center, Schedule of Interest and Principal Payments, Conventional $6 Million Loan

Year	Annual Fixed Payment	Loan Interest Component	Equity Contribution	Amortized Points	Total Interest Payments
1	$700,977	$480,000	$220,977	$20,000	$500,000
2	700,977	462,322	459,633	20,000	482,322
3	700,977	443,229	717,381	20,000	463,229
4	700,977	422,610	995,748	20,000	442,610
5	700,977	400,340	1,296,385	20,000	420,340
6	700,977	376,289	1,621,074	20,000	396,289
7	700,977	350,314	1,971,737	20,000	370,314
8	700,977	322,261	2,350,453	20,000	342,261
9	700,977	291,964	2,759,466	20,000	311,964
10	700,977	259,243	3,201,201	20,000	279,243
11	700,977	223,904	3,678,274	20,000	243,904
12	700,977	185,738	4,193,514	20,000	205,738
13	700,977	144,519	4,749,972	20,000	164,519
14	700,977	100,002	5,350,947	20,000	120,002
15	700,977	51,924	6,000,000	20,000	71,924

over among tenants giving the partnership the opportunity to raise rents. The use of short leases for all but the center anchor will give the partnership further opportunity to raise rents. It is expected that after the first full year of operation, rents will rise by an average of 5% per year. Due to the partnership's use of triple-net leases and a professional management company, there are no direct operating expenses to the partnership other than those incurred in the 18-month startup period. The partnership will make the interest and principal payments and take the tax shield generated by depreciation on the shopping center.

Holding Stage

As a result of the efforts put into the planning stage and the assemblage of an effective administrative staff, the shopping center comes on line as planned. A large housing development is undertaken adjacent to the shopping center during construction. The state completes the highway and interchange on schedule. With the completion of the shopping center, the partnership feels it does not have the expertise to manage the facility, so it hires professional management for 8% of gross rentals.

Under the guidance of the professional managers, the shopping center retailers prosper as sales steadily increase.

The operating income (NOPAT) resulting from these circumstances are depicted in Figure 13.2. After losing money in the first two years, Big Sky shows increasing positive income throughout the remainder of the 15-year mortgage culminating with almost $1.5 million in NOPAT in year 15.

Net income (Table 13.3) is more modest (as a result of interest and depreciation charges), reaching $1,261,173 in the 15th year.

The use of net income reflects the definition of income in the IRS Tax Code and is a widely used convention. NOPAT, in contrast, tells the investor about the basic operating characteristics of the investment, abstracting from the conventions of net income that are structured to determine tax liability. Neither net income nor NOPAT is as relevant to an investor's perspective of evaluating an investment as the eventual cash flows expected to be derived from that investment. A better measure of investment performance would, therefore, be the total cash flows associated with the shopping center. To calculate these cash flows, the terminal value of the Big Sky Shopping Center must be calculated.

Disposal Phase

The assumption is the partners' wish to have a 15-year holding period. The holding period may be longer or shorter depending on the partners' preference. Whatever the desired holding period, the methodology for determining the returns to the partners remains unaffected.

As the area has now grown up and there are competitive shopping centers in operation, a list of comparables ("comps") can be obtained. It is found that comparable shopping centers sell for 8 to 12 times net income. The partnership finds a large REIT that wishes to expand its holding in this area and sells the shopping center for 11 times earnings or $9 million.

The cash gained on this sale is analyzed in Table 13.4.

The total cash flows associated with the Big Sky Shopping Center for a 15-year holding period are presented in Table 13.5.

It should be noted from Table 13.5 that the partners expected capital contribution of $2 million was actually exceeded by $426,000. While not a large sum in the context of this project, a requirement of unexpected capital contributions can jeopardize the project, however, potentially profitable. It is not uncommon in projects of this type, no matter how carefully and conservatively the budget is drawn up, unexpected events will require additional capital. Wise investors will tend to keep some capital in reserve under these circumstances.

TABLE 13.2 Big Sky Shopping Center, Strip Shopping Center with Conventional Fixed Financing, Net-Operating Profit after Taxes

Year	Rental Income[a]	Depreciation Buildings[b]	Depreciation Improvements[c]	Management Fees[d]	Operating Expense	EBIT	NOPAT EBIT(1 − tx)
1	$0	$0	$0	$0	$250,000	−$250,000	−$150,000
2	935,000	95,250	75,000	74,800	250,000	439,950	359,220
3	1,870,000	190,500	142,500	149,600		1,387,400	1,022,940
4	1,926,100	190,500	128,250	154,088		1,453,262	1,062,457
5	1,983,883	190,500	115,500	158,711		1,519,172	1,102,003
6	2,043,399	190,500	103,950	163,472		1,585,478	1,141,787
7	2,104,701	190,500	93,450	168,376		1,652,375	1,181,925
8	2,167,843	190,500	88,500	173,427		1,715,415	1,219,749
9	2,232,878	190,500	88,500	178,630		1,775,248	1,255,649
10	2,299,864	190,500	88,650	183,989		1,836,725	1,292,535
11	2,368,860	190,500	88,500	189,509		1,900,351	1,330,711
12	2,439,926	190,500	88,650	195,194		1,965,582	1,369,849
13	2,513,124	190,500	88,500	201,050		2,033,074	1,410,344
14	2,588,517	190,500	88,650	207,081		2,102,286	1,451,872
15	2,666,173	190,500	88,500	213,294		2,173,879	1,494,827

[a] Rental income in year 2 is only for half the year because the shopping center took six months to build. Annual rental income includes $337,500 (supermarket), $990,000 (the first 12 national tenants), and $542,500 (the last seven tenants) for a first-year total of $1,870,000. After year 3, with tenant replacement and lease renewals, rents are expected to rise 3% per year.

[b] Commercial buildings have a recovery period of 39 years and are straight-line depreciated.

[c] Land improvements (streets, blacktop, sidewalk, drainage ditches, etc.) have a recovery period of 15 years and are depreciated 150% double-declining balance using the half-year convention.

[d] Management fees are 8% of gross rentals.

TABLE 13.3 Big Sky Shopping Center, Strip Shopping Center with Conventional Fixed Financing, Statement of Income

Year	Rental Income[a]	Interest Expense[b]	Depreciation Buildings[c]	Depreciation Improvements[d]	Management Fees[e]	Operating Expense	Earnings Before Taxes	Taxes (0.40)	Net Income
1						$250,000	-$250,000	-$100,000	-$150,000
2	$935,000	$500,000	$95,250	$75,000	$74,800	250,000	-60,050	-24,020	-36,030
3	1,870,000	463,229	190,500	142,500	149,600		924,171	369,668	554,502
4	1,926,100	442,610	190,500	128,250	154,088		1,010,652	404,261	606,391
5	1,983,883	420,340	190,500	115,500	158,711		1,098,832	439,533	659,299
6	2,043,399	396,289	190,500	103,950	163,472		1,189,188	475,675	713,513
7	2,104,701	370,314	190,500	93,450	168,376		1,282,061	512,824	769,237
8	2,167,843	342,261	190,500	88,500	173,427		1,373,154	549,262	823,892
9	2,232,878	311,964	190,500	88,500	178,630		1,463,284	585,314	877,970
10	2,299,864	279,243	190,500	88,650	183,989		1,557,482	622,993	934,489
11	2,368,860	243,904	190,500	88,500	189,509		1,656,447	662,579	993,868
12	2,439,926	205,738	190,500	88,650	195,194		1,759,844	703,937	1,055,906
13	2,513,124	164,519	190,500	88,500	201,050		1,868,555	747,422	1,121,133
14	2,588,517	120,002	190,500	88,650	207,081		1,982,284	792,913	1,189,370
15	2,666,173	71,924	190,500	88,500	213,294		2,101,955	840,782	1,261,173

[a] Rental income in year 2 is only for half the year because the shopping center took six months to build. Annual rental income includes $337,500 (supermarket), $990,000 (the first 12 national tenants), and $542,500 (the last seven tenants) for a first-year total of $1,870,000. After year 3, with tenant replacement and lease renewals, rents are expected to rise 3% per year.

[b] Includes interest at 8% on a 15-year mortgage of $6,000,000 with an annual fixed interest and principle payment of $700,977.27.

[c] Commercial buildings have a recovery period of 39 years and are straight-line depreciated.

[d] Land improvements (streets, blacktop, sidewalk, drainage ditches, etc.) have a recovery period of 15 years and are depreciated 150% double-declining balance using the half-year convention.

[e] Management fees are 8% of gross rentals.

TABLE 13.4   Gains from Disposal of Big Sky Shopping Center with Conventional
Financing

Sale of building		$12,611,729
Fixed plant and improvements	$7,500,000	
less accumulated depreciation	$3,938,850	
Net fixed plant and improvements		3,561,150
Earnings before tax		9,050,579
Capital gains tax (20%)		1,810,116
Earnings after tax		7,240,463
Loan amount	6,000,000	
Principal paid to date	5,350,947	
Loan balance to be repaid		649,053
Cash realized from sale		6,591,410

The result of this investment for the investors, in terms of cash flows, is an NPV of $2,706,858 and an IRR of 28%. This level of return would appear adequate to compensate the partners for their investment in the Big Sky Shopping Center

Break-Even Analysis

Determining the approximate risk to the partners may be approached through a break-even analysis. The partner's fixed costs would include the annual $700,977 loan payment. Depreciation can be ignored because it is not a cash outlay. Variable costs would only include the 8% management fee. The 40% tax rate is not a variable cost because it is not a function of revenues, but of earnings.

Where

$$\text{Total costs } (TC) = \text{Fixed costs } (FC) + \text{Variable costs } (VC)$$

Thus,

$$TC = \$700,977 + 0.08 \text{ (revenues)}$$

As the break-even point (BEP) is where total costs are equal to total revenues:

$$BEP = \text{Revenues} - TC = 0: \text{BEP} = \$700,799/0.92 = \$761,738$$

TABLE 13.5 Big Sky Shopping Center, Strip Shopping Center with Conventional Fixed Financing, Statement of Total Cash Flows

Year	Net Income	Total Depreciation	Partnership Capital Contributions[a]	Equity Payments	Financing Charge	Cash Gains From Sale[b]	Net Cash Flow[a]
1	-$150,000		$1,750,000	$220,977			-$2,120,977
2	-36,030	$170,250	750,000	238,655	$300,000		-1,154,435
3	554,502	333,000		257,748			629,754
4	606,391	318,750		278,368			646,774
5	659,299	306,000		300,637			664,662
6	713,513	294,450		324,688			683,275
7	769,237	283,950		350,663			702,524
8	823,892	279,000		378,716			724,176
9	877,970	279,000		409,014			747,957
10	934,489	279,150		441,735			771,905
11	993,868	279,000		477,073			795,795
12	1,055,906	279,150		515,239			819,817
13	1,121,133	279,000		556,458			843,675
14	1,189,370	279,150		600,975			867,545
15	1,261,173	279,000		649,053		$6,591,410	7,482,530

[a] Capital contributions of $2,000,000 in the first year and $1,000,000 in the second year less $250,000 operating expense in each year.
[b] Derived from Table 13.5.

NPV of cash flows at 12% = $2,074,176

IRR = 20%

Thus, in terms of EBT, the Big Sky Shopping Center breaks even in its third year of operation by a margin of over 20% and has a safety margin of over 200% by its 15th year of operation.

This analysis suggests a relatively low risk for the investors. Thus, even though the prospective IRR from the Big Sky Shopping Center is only 28%, the investment may well be attractive to the partners at that level of risk.

ILLUSTRATION #2: BIG SKY SHOPPING CENTER, BUILD-TO-SUIT WITH LEASE

This is an example of developing a strip shopping center build-to-suit with lease.

Acquisition Phase

Build-to-suits arise when a landowner does not wish to relinquish ownership of the land, but is willing to convert the property to meet the unique requirements of a tenant. The owner of the land will then lease the developed property to the tenant. The owner of the property is responsible for financing the improvement of the property. It is typical for the owner of the property to arrange the lease in such a manner that the rental payments cover the cost of the loan, which finances development plus a certain percentage. As the property owner retains ownership of the facilities, the property owner creating a significant tax shield may depreciate such facilities. If it is a triple-net lease, the benefit to the property owner of building-to-suit is a net cash flow consisting of the after-tax rents less interest expense and depreciation plus depreciation plus the capitalized value of the property at the end of the lease.

The risk to the property owner is the loss of liquidity consequent on the unique attributes of the improvements and the assumption of debt to finance those improvements. The risk to the owner of the property is mitigated by his retention of the ownership of the property and the level of financial security provided by the tenants net worth.

Leases for build-to-suits generally take the form of capital leases that (1) do not provide for maintenance, (2) are not cancelable, and (3) are fully amortized (the lessor receives a rental payment equal to the full price of the leased equipment plus a return on invested capital). Such leases effectively shift the tax shield from the lessee (who would normally have bought and depreciated the property) to the lessor (who normally would have just sold the property and not received any tax shield benefits). This creates the possibility of a win-win situation for both the lessor and lessee.

Because there are considerable tax advantages to such an arrangement, the IRS attempts to ensure that such leases are not merely a sham to dodge taxes. They do this by requiring adherence to a set of tax guidelines for leases. The basic requirements of a tax-oriented lease (so that the lessee can deduct the lease payments as expenses) are: (1) The lease term must not exceed 80% of the useful life of the property; (2) at the termination of the lease, the value of the property must be at least 20% of the value of the property at the start of the lease; (3) the lessee cannot have the right to purchase the equipment at a predetermined price at the termination of the lease; (4) the lessee may not make any investment in the property (or provide any financial guarantees for the financing of the property); and (5) the leased property may not be of such "limited use" that it can only be used by the lessee.

The assumptions embedded in this example are that the partnership obtains a 15-year, triple-net lease on the property for an annual rent of $1,200,000 with no option for renewal or purchase. This approach will satisfy the IRS tax-oriented lease requirement as the property has a 39-year life.

The lessor retains the responsibility for financing the $7.5 million property improvements. To identify the advantages and disadvantages of leasing most accurately, the lessor will be assumed to obtain financing on the same basis of the partnership in shopping center financed conventionally in the first illustration (Tables 13.1–13.5). As with conventional financing, the leasehold will be an anchored strip with 15 stores. It is expected that such a shopping center would take 18 months to complete at a cost of $8,000,000 ($6,000,000 to construct the building, $1,500,000 for land improvements, and $500,000 for staff and operating expenses (the lessee will be responsible for these expenses).

The lessor approaches the local bank on the shopping center. The bank feels the $6 million, 15-year mortgage will be well secured by the $1.5 million equity the lessor is putting into the project, a mortgage on the underlying land, and the lessor's willingness to sign personally for the loan. The bank offers 8% and 5 points for a 15-year loan with monthly flat principle and interest payments.

The partnership (the lessee) is not responsible for financing any improvements and contributes no capital except for the $500,000 in administrative and legal fees.

Holding Phase

The results of a leasehold on the Big Sky Shopping Center are presented in Figure 13.6. Everything is held the same as in the conventional financing example presented in the first illustration except the form of financing

TABLE 13.6 Big Sky Shopping Center, Leasehold Financing, Net-Operating Profit after Taxes

Year	Rental Income[a]	Lease Payments	Management Fees[b]	Operating Expense	EBIT	NOPAT EBIT $(1-tx)$
1				$250,000	-$250,000	-$150,000
2	$935,000	$600,000	$74,800	250,000	10,200	6,120
3	1,870,000	1,200,000	149,600		520,400	312,240
4	1,926,100	1,200,000	154,088		572,012	343,207
5	1,983,883	1,200,000	158,711		625,172	375,103
6	2,043,399	1,200,000	163,472		679,928	407,957
7	2,104,701	1,200,000	168,376		736,325	441,795
8	2,167,843	1,200,000	173,427		794,415	476,649
9	2,232,878	1,200,000	178,630		854,248	512,549
10	2,299,864	1,200,000	183,989		915,875	549,525
11	2,368,860	1,200,000	189,509		979,351	587,611
12	2,439,926	1,200,000	195,194		1,044,732	626,839
13	2,513,124	1,200,000	201,050		1,112,074	667,244
14	2,588,517	1,200,000	207,081		1,181,436	708,862
15	2,666,173	1,200,000	213,294		1,252,879	751,727

[a] Rental income in year 2 is only for half the year since the shopping center took six months to build. Annual rental income includes $337,500 (supermarket), $990,000 (the first 12 national tenants), and $542,500 (the last seven tenants) for a first-year total of $1,870,000.
[b] Management fees are 8% of gross rentals.

is now a lease rather than a loan. A characteristic of most leases is the low amount of equity required by the partnership. Such a situation is possible if the lessor feels adequately secured by the net worth of the lessee.

A comparison of NOPAT in Tables 13.2 and 13.6 reveals significantly lower NOPAT for leasehold financing. By the 15th year of the project NOPAT has fallen 50% from $1.5 million using conventional financing to $7.5 million using a leasehold. This dramatic decrease results from the fact that lease payments ($1.2 million) are significantly larger than the charges from interest and depreciation under conventional financing.

Net income (Table 13.7), using a leasehold, is the same as NOPAT. Net income, in comparison to the conventionally financed shopping center, is also dramatically lower, but not as large a difference as with NOPAT because the tax liability is less.

TABLE 13.7 Big Sky Shopping Center, Leasehold Financing, Statement of Income

Year	Rental Income[a]	Lease Payments	Management Fees[b]	Operating Expense	Earnings before Taxes	Taxes (0.40)	Net Income
1				$250,000	-$250,000	-$100,000	-$150,000
2	$935,000	$600,000	$74,800	250,000	10,200	4,080	6,120
3	1,870,000	1,200,000	149,600		520,400	208,160	312,240
4	1,926,100	1,200,000	154,088		572,012	228,805	343,207
5	1,983,883	1,200,000	158,711		625,172	250,069	375,103
6	2,043,399	1,200,000	163,472		679,928	271,971	407,957
7	2,104,701	1,200,000	168,376		736,325	294,530	441,795
8	2,167,843	1,200,000	173,427		794,415	317,766	476,649
9	2,232,878	1,200,000	178,630		854,248	341,699	512,549
10	2,299,864	1,200,000	183,989		915,875	366,350	549,525
11	2,368,860	1,200,000	189,509		979,351	391,740	587,611
12	2,439,926	1,200,000	195,194		1,044,732	417,893	626,839
13	2,513,124	1,200,000	201,050		1,112,074	444,829	667,244
14	2,588,517	1,200,000	207,081		1,181,436	472,574	708,862
15	2,666,173	1,200,000	213,294		1,252,879	501,152	751,727

[a] Rental income in year 2 is only for half the year since the shopping center took six months to build. Annual rental income includes $337,500 (supermarket), $990,000 (the first 12 national tenants), and $542,500 (the last seven tenants) for a first-year total of $1,870,000.
[b] Management fees are 8% of gross rentals.

NPV of net income (cash flows) at 12% = $2,670,084

IRR = 110%

Disposal Phase

The effect of this on the performance of the investment is salutary. While net income (Table 13.8) is lower, this is offset but the significantly reduced capital requirements for the lessee.

As a result, the present value of the net income, which is also the cash flow in this case, increases to $2.250 million and the internal rate of return rises to 110% (Table 13.8.) Further, this increase comes about without relying on the harvesting of the shopping center's terminal value (as in Tables 13.4 and 13.5), resulting in a reduced level of risk from this source of uncertainty. Clearly, this outcome represents an improvement from the investor's perspective.

The Lessor's Perspective

As the feasibility of the build-to-suit lease is dependent on the viability of the project from the lessor's point of view, the underlying viability of the lease needs to be examined.

Leasing is one of those areas where the whole is more than the sum of the parts. This occurs when the advantages of the tax shield are greater to the lessor than the lessee. That can occur when there is a disparity in the marginal tax rate between the lessor and the lessee (the lessor having the higher rate since they will get the benefits of the tax shield). A differential in the benefits of the tax shield may also be due to differences in the absolute amount of income to be taxed between the lessor and lessee.

An analysis of NOPAT, from the lessor's perspective, is presented in Table 13.9. NOPAT is seen as positive in the second year and then plateaus at about $831,600 for the remaining 13 years of the project's holding period. Net income (Table 13.10) is also negative for the first two years of the projects, but rises steadily throughout the life of the project to $509,445 in year 15.

TABLE 13.8   Big Sky Shopping Center, Leasehold Financing Cash Flow

Year	Net Income	Cash Flow	Year	Net Income	Cash Flow
1	-$150,000	-$150,000	9	512,549	512,549
2	6,120	6,120	10	549,525	549,525
3	312,240	312,240	11	587,611	587,611
4	343,207	343,207	12	626,839	626,839
5	375,103	375,103	13	667,244	667,244
6	407,957	407,957	14	708,862	708,862
7	441,795	441,795	15	751,727	751,727
8	476,649	476,649			

NPV at 12% = $2,250,075
IRR = 110%

TABLE 13.9 Big Sky Shopping Center, Lessor, Net-Operating Profit after Taxes

Year	Lease Income	Depreciation Buildings[a]	Depreciation Improvements[b]	EBIT	NOPAT EBIT$(1 - tx)$ + Depreciation
1					
2	$600,000	$103,200	$75,000	$421,800	$431,280
3	1,200,000	190,500	142,500	867,000	853,200
4	1,200,000	190,500	128,250	881,250	847,500
5	1,200,000	190,500	115,500	894,000	842,400
6	1,200,000	190,500	103,950	905,550	837,780
7	1,200,000	190,500	93,450	916,050	833,580
8	1,200,000	190,500	88,500	921,000	831,600
9	1,200,000	190,500	88,500	921,000	831,600
10	1,200,000	190,500	88,650	920,850	831,660
11	1,200,000	190,500	88,500	921,000	831,600
12	1,200,000	190,500	88,650	920,850	831,660
13	1,200,000	190,500	88,500	921,000	831,600
14	1,200,000	190,500	88,650	920,850	831,660
15	1,200,000	190,500	88,500	921,000	831,600

[a] Commercial buildings have a recovery period of 39 years and are straight-line depreciated.
[b] Land improvements (streets, blacktop, sidewalk, drainage ditches, etc.) have a recovery period of 15 years and are depreciated 150% double-declining balance using the half-year convention.

The assumed sale of the project under the same conditions as with conventional financing yield the cash flows indicated in Table 13.11. The NPV of the project is seen to be almost $3.5 million and to generate an IRR of 28%.

From the investor's perspective, this outcome is probably not a bad combination of risk and return. Moreover, the risk to the lessor is not just a function of the success of the shopping center itself. The partnership has pledged its assets with the signing of the lease and this constitutes additional security to the lessor.

Disposal Phase

At the end of 15 years, the relationship between the partnership and the property owner is severed. The property owner is thus free to negotiate a new lease with the partnership or any suitable tenant or to convert the property to another use. The partnership has gained a spectacular

TABLE 13.10 Big Sky Shopping Center, Lessor, Statement of Income

Year	Lease Income	Interest Expense[a]	Depreciation Buildings[b]	Depreciation Improvements[c]	Earnings before Taxes	Taxes (0.40)	Net Income
1	$600,000	$500,000	$103,200	$75,000	-$500,000	-$200,000	-$300,000
2	1,200,000	482,322	190,500	142,500	-60,522	-24,209	-36,313
3	1,200,000	463,229	190,500	128,250	403,771	161,508	242,262
4	1,200,000	442,610	190,500	115,500	438,640	175,456	263,184
5	1,200,000	420,340	190,500	115,500	473,660	189,464	284,196
6	1,200,000	396,289	190,500	103,950	509,261	203,704	305,557
7	1,200,000	370,314	190,500	93,450	545,736	218,294	327,442
8	1,200,000	342,261	190,500	88,500	578,739	231,496	347,243
9	1,200,000	311,964	190,500	88,500	609,036	243,614	365,422
10	1,200,000	279,243	190,500	88,650	641,607	256,643	384,964
11	1,200,000	243,904	190,500	88,500	677,096	270,838	406,258
12	1,200,000	205,738	190,500	88,650	715,112	286,045	429,067
13	1,200,000	164,519	190,500	88,500	756,481	302,592	453,889
14	1,200,000	120,002	190,500	88,650	800,848	320,339	480,509
15	1,200,000	71,924	190,500	88,500	849,076	339,630	509,445

[a] Interest expenses is assumed the same as under conventional financing for consistency in the analysis. Frequently, the lessor would have a better financial standing than the lessor and get better financial terms as a result. Interest is calculated at 8% on a 15-year mortgage of $6 million with flat interest and principal payments of $700,977.27.

[b] Commercial buildings have a recovery period of 39 years and are straight-line depreciated.

[c] Land improvements (streets, blacktop, sidewalk, drainage ditches, etc.) have a recovery period of 15 years and are depreciated 150% double-declining balance using the half-year convention.

TABLE 13.11 Big Sky Shopping Center, Lessor, Statement of Total Cash Flows

Year	Net Income	Total Depreciation	Lessor Capital Contributions[a]	Equity Payments	Financing Charge	Cash Gains from Sale[b]	Net Cash Flow
1	-$300,000		$1,500,000	$220,977	$300,000		-$2,020,977
2	-36,313	$496,800	1,000,000	238,655			-1,078,169
3	242,262	1,009,500		257,748			994,014
4	263,184	1,009,500		278,368			994,317
5	284,196	1,009,500		300,637			993,059
6	305,557	1,009,500		324,688			990,368
7	327,442	1,009,500		350,663			986,278
8	347,243	1,009,500		378,716			978,027
9	365,422	1,009,500		409,014			965,908
10	384,964	1,009,500		441,735			952,730
11	406,258	1,009,500		477,073			938,684
12	429,067	1,009,500		515,239			923,328
13	453,889	1,009,500		556,458			906,930
14	480,509	1,009,500		600,975			889,034
15	509,445	1,009,500		649,053		$6,597,770	7,467,662

[a] Capital contributions include the opportunity cost of $1 million land.
[b] Derived with the same assumption used in Table 13.4.

NPV of cash flows at 12% = $3,497,851

IRR = 28%

333

return on its investment over the years. It would seem that, in this example, the build-to-suit lease offers more return for less initial investment. However, it should be noted that this risk to the partnership is not necessarily less in an absolute sense. The partners had to secure the lease with their personal assets, putting them at risk for that liability.

Break-Even Analysis

The approximate risk to the partners (lessees) from leasehold financing under these circumstances may be approached through a break-even analysis. The partners' fixed costs would include the annual $1.2 million lease payment. Variable costs would again include the 8% management fee. Taxes are not a variable cost, so this analysis is undertaken in terms of EBT.

Where

Total costs (TC) = Fixed costs (FC) + Variable costs (VC)

Thus,

$$TC = \$1,200,000 + 0.08 \text{ (revenues)}$$

As the break-even point (BEP) is where total costs are equal to total revenues:

$$BEP = \text{Revenues} - TC = 0: BEP = \$1,200,000/0.92 = \$1,304,348$$

Thus, the Big Sky Shopping Center breaks even in its first full year of operation by a margin of one third in its first full year of operation and over 100% by its 15th year of operation.

As signatories to the lease, the partners are responsible for that $1.2 million lease payment regardless of the success, or lack of it, of the center. However, the break-even analysis suggests the risks to the lessee are not all that great and the return is spectacular—an internal rate of return of 110% using leasehold financing compared to 20% using conventional financing. All that is necessary to make such a spectacular return is to find a lessor willing to make such a lease!

ILLUSTRATION #3: NEW HOPE SHOPPING CENTER

This is an example of developing an inner-city neighborhood shopping center.

As an SBA-Funded Leasehold

As urban areas cycle through a process of growth, maturation, decline, and renewal, opportunities arise to take advantage of the changing composition of urban neighborhoods. The urban core in many American cities has gone through a long period of decline and decay beginning in the 1960s and extending through the 1990s. Outside of a central business district, characterized more by empty storefronts than bustling shoppers, the urban core became fully blighted. One can see block after block of lots where the homes had been demolished or were in decrepit condition. Abandoned properties became the sad rule. With the decline in population, retail activity was considerably diminished. Middle-class families huddled in the few remaining urban enclaves while those that could fled to the suburbs. A major attraction of the flight to the suburbs was the widely accessible shopping centers suburban life offered.

As a result of aggressive reinvestment in the urban infrastructure and attention to the supply of housing by the Federal Department of Housing and Urban Development and various state and local economic development agencies, the tide appears to have turned. Young professionals, rejecting a daily 30-mile commute to the suburbs, are "gentrifying" the city's urban core. Homes are being renovated and refurbished. Small businesses are being planted. The new city residents are demanding better trash pickup, less crime, parks, and an improved set of urban amenities. As the city responds to these demands, more people are attracted to the area, further increasing the momentum for change. Markets for products and services are being created where none existed before. This process may not be smooth, but the trend is clear. This situation creates opportunities for successful inner-city shopping centers.

Acquisition Phase

Three local store owners in an urban neighborhood see a large apartment building being renovated. They understand that the owners are thinking about converting the ground floor of the apartment to a neighborhood shopping center. They see opportunities for synergy with a small supermarket, a deli, a few boutique restaurants, a fitness center, a day-care center, a bookstore, and a coffee shop. They are aware that local residents do not have easy access to those types of retail establishments at present. Ten years ago the local store owners believed the neighborhood was too thinly populated to support that type of shopping. They believe that now conditions have changed and are likely to improve even further in the future.

The three store owners form a Subchapter S corporation (Hot City Properties, Inc.) and, with the help of the local Small Business Administration (SBA) office, develop a business plan for the neighborhood shopping center. Hot City approaches the apartment owners who appear risk-adverse and are unwilling to enter into a long-term relationship with the store owners. The apartment owners want $15 per square foot for the 50,000 sq. ft. of available space. Hot City feels this is too rich— the store owners are currently renting at $5 or $6 per square foot. The apartment owners argue that in other rejuvenated areas in the city, retail space is currently going for $12 to $15 per square foot. Hot City argues that converting the first floor of the apartment to retail space will constitute an amenity that will prove attractive to the tenants and thus enhance the value of the remaining apartments in the building.

A compromise is reached. The apartment owners offer a five-year lease with a five-year option. The initial lease will be at $7 per square foot in a triple net lease where the store owners pick up the estimated $400,000 of renovation costs. The rent in the (optional) second five years is to rise to $16 per square foot. The store owners put up $50,000 of their own money and arrange for a $350,000 SBA loan that requires fixed annual payments to amortize the loan over five years. The Hot City owners qualify as minorities eligible to receive a below-market interest rate of 3.125% resulting in an annual payment of $76,697.

The lease is signed, the loan taken and renovation is begun immediately. Hot City begins a campaign to find tenants and opens an office for a small staff to market the shopping center and monitor the renovation. In six months, the renovations are complete and Hot City retains its staff to manage the New Hope Shopping Center. Expenses for the office and staff for the first year are $90,000, but that drops to $60,000 in the following year as the initial development and marketing is completed. The Hot City office is moved into the shopping center area and given a 2,000 sq. ft. space.

Hot City initially encounters stiff price resistance from its target retailers. While there are many retailers who would like to establish themselves at this location, they are generally unwilling to pay more than $9 per square foot because the location is, as yet, unproven. Hot City eventually negotiates single-net leases averaging $8.50 per square foot plus 5% of gross revenues with its tenants for the remaining 48,000 sq. ft. of retail space, with the tenants being responsible for maintenance costs. The idea here is that the tenants exchange a lower rent for their willingness to share their success with the lessor. Hot City estimates that its insurance costs will run $35,000 per year and taxes $115,000.

Holding Phase

The New Hope Shopping Center gets off to a relatively slow start. The shopping center mix is not right and some good tenants become discouraged with slow sales and leave. Through strong local promotion efforts and constant experimentation to find the right mixes of tenants, sales volume begins to grow steadily at New Hope. Tenant sales in the first six-month are an anemic $30 per square foot for total sales revenue of $720,000 for the six-month period. At this level of sales, the tenants will fail, causing the New Hope Center—and Hot City—to fail as well. At this level of revenue, the firm faces a cash flow crisis that threatens its viability.

However revenues in the second year pick up to $80 per square foot for total tenant sales of $3,840,000 as neighborhood residents become increasingly acclimated to the shopping center. The Hot City staff double their efforts in promoting the shopping center. Promotions revolving around, or hosting, community organizations prove particularly successful. Sales subsequently increase for the tenants significantly throughout the five-year period as the New Hope Shopping Center establishes itself in its local market. This results in rental income for Hot City as shown in Table 13.12.

The implications of these sales are significant for NOPAT, net income, and cash flow. As seen above, shopping centers with their high fixed costs have high-operating leverage and success is, therefore, driven by sales. With only a half year's operation in its first year and with its struggles to find its market niche, New Hope experiences a large negative NOPAT (Table 13.13) in its first year and then a positive NOPAT increases with only painful slowness in the successive four years.

NOPAT will prove highly sensitive to the success (or lack of it) of New Hope's retailers. The responsibility of Hot City is to make New Hope work. Hot City must create a retail mix that will draw residents from the surrounding community in sufficient volume to make its retailers profitable.

As can be seen from Table 13.14, the net impact of including interest expense and taxes is to slightly lower net income relative to NOPAT.

TABLE 13.12   New Hope Shopping Center, Projected 5-Year Rents

	Projected Tenant		Fixed	5% of	Total
Year	Sales[a] per square foot	Total Sales	Rent[b]	Gross	Rent
1	30	$720,000	$204,000	$36,000	$240,000
2	80	3,840,000	408,000	192,000	600,000
3	120	5,760,000	408,000	288,000	696,000
4	150	7,200,000	408,000	360,000	768,000
5	175	8,400,000	408,000	420,000	828,000

[1] Sales in Year 1 represent six months of retail activity.
[2] $8.50 per square foot.

TABLE 13.13   New Hope Shopping Center, Inner-City Leasehold Shopping Center with SBA Funding, Net-Operating Profits after Taxes

	Rents[a]	Lease Payments[b]	Insurance[c]	Operating Expenses[d]	Depreciation[e]	Property Taxes	EBIT	NOPAT EBIT$(1 - tx)$[f]
1	$240,000	$350,000	$35,000	$90,000	$80,000	$115,000	-$430,000	-$322,500
2	600,000	350,000	36,050	60,000	80,000	118,450	-44,500	-33,375
3	696,000	350,000	37,132	61,800	80,000	122,004	45,065	33,799
4	768,000	350,000	38,245	63,654	80,000	125,664	110,437	82,828
5	828,000	350,000	39,393	65,564	80,000	129,434	163,610	122,708

[a] From Table 13.12.
[b] At $7.00 per square foot.
[c] Insurance costs are expected to increase 3% per year.
[d] Operating costs are expected to increase 3% per year.
[e] While the depreciation of building improvements would normally be over a 39-year period, within a qualifying lease, the improvements may be depreciated over the period of the lease.
[f] The assumed tax rate is 25%.

TABLE 13.14 New Hope Shopping Center, Inner-City Leasehold Shopping Center with SBA Funding, Net Income

	Rents[a]	Lease Payments[b]	Insurance[c]	Operating Expenses[d]	Depreciation[e]	Property Taxes	Interest[f]	EBT	Net Income[g]
1	$240,000	$350,000	$35,000	$90,000	$80,000	$115,000	$10,938	-$440,938	-$330,703
2	600,000	350,000	36,050	60,000	80,000	118,450	8,883	-53,383	-40,037
3	696,000	350,000	37,132	61,800	80,000	122,004	6,763	38,302	28,726
4	768,000	350,000	38,245	63,654	80,000	125,664	4,578	105,859	79,394
5	828,000	350,000	39,393	65,564	80,000	129,434	2,324	161,286	120,964

[a] From Table 13.12.
[b] At $7.00 per square foot.
[c] Insurance costs are expected to increase 3% per year.
[d] Operating costs are expected to increase 3% per year.
[e] While the depreciation of building improvements would normally be over a 39 year period, within a qualifying lease, the improvements may be depreciated over the period of the lease.
[f] Reflecting an annual payment of $76,697.
[g] The assumed tax rate is 25%.

Disposal Stage

The results of five years of operations from the investor's perspective may be seen to generate a positive NPV (Table 13.15). However, the NPV of $32,167 and the modest return on their investment of 20% would not seem to justify the risk exposure of the Hot City partners for their New Hope Shopping Center. Aside from the risk of a less successful tenant experience, it should be noted that cash flows ran –$116,463. Unless the partners were prepared to come up with this sum from their own pockets, in addition to the $50,000 equity they already put in, they would have defaulted on both their lease to the apartment owner and their SBA loan. Either default could have resulted in a bankruptcy action that would have resulted in considerable losses for the Hot City partners.

Break-Even Analysis

As the result of the leases at New Hope being partially structured as a percent of its tenants sales, success at the New Hope Shopping Center is largely defined in terms of its tenants sales. Therefore, a break-even analysis being constructed, which relates profits at New Hope to its tenant's sales per square foot.

Revenues at New Hope are equal to the fixed rent ($408,000) + 5% of 48,000 (dales per square foot) or

$$TR = 408,000 + (0.05)\ 48,000\ (\text{sales per square foot})$$

TABLE 13.15   New Hope Shopping Center, Inner-City Leasehold Shopping Center with SBA Funding, Statement of Total Cash Flows

Year	Net Income[a]	Principal Payments[b]	Depre- ciation	Equity Contribution	SBA Loan	Total Cash Flow
1	–$330,703	$65,760	$80,000	$50,000	$250,000	–$116,463
2	–40,037	67,814	80,000			–27,851
3	28,726	69,934	80,000			38,793
4	79,394	72,119	80,000			87,275
5	120,964	74,373	80,000			126,592

[a] From Table 13.13.
[b] Reflecting an annual payment of $76,697.

NPV at 12% = $32,167

IRR = 20%

Total costs at New Hope are all fixed costs. For year 5, these fixed costs total (from Table 15.13) $666,714 or

$$TC = \$666,714$$

So,

$$BEP = TR - TC; \text{ or } \$408,000 + (0.05)48,000 \text{ (sales per sq. ft.)} - \$666,714$$

Thus

$$BEP \text{ (sales per sq. ft.)} = (\$666,714 - \$408,000)/(0.05)48,000 = \$107.80$$

This is a relatively high level of BEP sales for New Hope's tenants. In two of the five years, sales were 40% below this level. Had New Hope continued to struggle with its tenant mix, had a competitive shopping center opened nearby, had the rate of population growth in the community slowed (or reversed), New Hope would not be able to survive.

Part of the problem with New Hope is that a period of five years is hardly sufficient to capture its efforts in successfully building a community shopping center. As the Hot City partnership has only leased New Hope, there is no income stream to be capitalized at the end of the lease. It should be noted in the conventionally financed Big Sky in the first illustration (Table 13.5) a significant component of its NPV and IRR resulted from the sale of the facility whose value was determined by the capitalized value of its net income. At the termination of its lease, New Hope has no income stream to capitalize.

However, the initial lease did contain an option for an additional five years at $16 per square foot. Taking this option and continuing to operate New Hope for another five years gives Hot City more of an opportunity to capitalize on the success of its shopping center. That is, if New Hope Shopping Center continues to be successful. As in the first five years, everything really depends on the success of New Hope's retailers.

Table 13.16 contains the assumptions about the continued success of New Hope's retailers. In the absence of new competition, and with the continued growth and revitalization of the neighborhood, the retail tenants at New Hope are expected to see 15% sales growth throughout the second five-year period. Indeed, New Hope's retailers are so prosperous that they accept a rise in their fixed rent to $10 per square foot and an increase in their percentage of sales to 6%. This combination of changes significantly enhances revenues at New Hope.

TABLE 13.16   New Hope Shopping Center, Projected 10-Year Rents

Year	Projected Tenant Sales[a] per square foot	Total Sales	Fixed Rent[b]	Percent of Gross[c]	Total Rent
1	30	$720,000	$204,000	$36,000	$240,000
2	80	3,840,000	408,000	192,000	600,000
3	120	5,760,000	408,000	288,000	696,000
4	150	7,200,000	408,000	360,000	768,000
5	175	8,400,000	408,000	420,000	828,000
6	201	9,660,000	480,000	579,600	1,059,600
7	231	11,109,000	480,000	666,540	1,146,540
8	266	12,775,350	480,000	766,521	1,246,521
9	306	14,691,653	480,000	881,499	1,361,499
10	352	16,895,400	480,000	1,013,724	1,493,724

[a] Sales in Year 1 represent six months of retail activity.
[b] $8.50 per sq. ft. for the first five years, and then $10 per square foot.
[c] 5% of sales for the first five years, and then 6% of sales.

The immediate impact of the new lease is to significantly reduce NOPAT at New Hope. NOPAT falls from $123,000 to $14,000 as the increased lease expense more than outweighs the gains in revenues and reductions in expenses (interest and depreciation). However, as indicated in Table 13.17, the continued success of its retailers (embedded in Table 13.16) soon has NOPAT larger than ever at New Hope. This outcome reflects the sensitivity of New Hope to the success of its retailers discussed in the break-even analysis above.

A similar pattern of change is evident in net income (Table 13.18). The immediate effect of the changes is to reduce net income significantly and then to see it increase rapidly as the effect of high-operating leverage takes hold.

The significance of the true impact of the extension of the lease from the perspective of the Hot City partnership is revealed Table 13.19, detailing the cash flows over the entire decade. The result of extending the lease an additional five years is to increase the partner's NPV by a factor of 10 and to more that double the investors' rate of return to 41%. Now the return to the investors approaches the risk they have born in investing in this type of shopping center. It should be noted, however, that their success is driven by the continued success of their retail tenants. Operating leverage under these circumstances has worked in favor of Hot City.

TABLE 13.17 New Hope Shopping Center, Inner-City Leasehold Shopping Center with SBA Funding, Net-Operating Profits after Taxes

	Rents[a]	Lease Payments[b]	Insurance[c]	Operating Expenses[d]	Depreciation[e]	Property Taxes	EBIT	NOPAT EBIT$(1 - tx)$[f]
1	$240,000	$350,000	$35,000	$90,000	$80,000	$115,000	-$430,000	-$322,500
2	600,000	350,000	36,050	60,000	80,000	118,450	-44,500	-33,375
3	696,000	350,000	37,132	61,800	80,000	122,004	45,065	33,799
4	768,000	350,000	38,245	63,654	80,000	125,664	110,437	82,828
5	828,000	350,000	39,393	65,564	80,000	129,434	163,610	122,708
6	1,059,600	800,000	40,575	67,531	0	133,317	18,178	13,634
7	1,146,540	800,000	41,792	69,556	0	137,316	97,876	73,407
8	1,246,521	800,000	43,046	71,643	0	141,435	190,397	142,798
9	1,361,499	800,000	44,337	73,792	0	145,679	297,691	223,268
10	1,493,724	800,000	45,667	76,006	0	150,049	422,002	316,501

[a] From Table 13.16.
[b] At $7.00 per square foot, rising to $16 per square foot.
[c] Insurance costs are expected to increase 3% per year.
[d] Operating costs are expected to increase 3% per year.
[e] While the depreciation of building improvements would normally be over a 39-year period, within a qualifying lease, the improvements may be depreciated over the period of the lease.
[f] The assumed tax rate is 25%.

TABLE 13.18 New Hope Shopping Center, Inner-City Leasehold Shopping Center with SBA Funding, Net Income

	Rents[a]	Lease Payments[b]	Insurance[c]	Operating Expenses[d]	Depreciation[e]	Property Taxes	Interest[f]	EBT	Net Income[g]
1	$240,000	$350,000	$35,000	$90,000	$80,000	$115,000	$10,938	-$440,938	-$330,703
2	600,000	350,000	36,050	60,000	80,000	118,450	8,883	-53,383	-40,037
3	696,000	350,000	37,132	61,800	80,000	122,004	6,763	38,302	28,726
4	768,000	350,000	38,245	63,654	80,000	125,664	4,578	105,859	79,394
5	828,000	350,000	39,393	65,564	80,000	129,434	2,324	161,286	120,964
6	1,059,600	800,000	40,575	67,531	0	133,317	0	18,178	13,634
7	1,146,540	800,000	41,792	69,556	0	137,316	0	97,876	73,407
8	1,246,521	800,000	43,046	71,643	0	141,435	0	190,397	142,798
9	1,361,499	800,000	44,337	73,792	0	145,679	0	297,691	223,268
10	1,493,724	800,000	45,667	76,006	0	150,049	0	422,002	316,501

[a] From Table 13.16.
[b] At $7.00 per sq. ft., then at $16 per sq. ft.
[c] Insurance costs are expected to increase 3% per year.
[d] Operating costs are expected to increase 3% per year.
[e] While the depreciation of building improvements would normally be over a 39 year period, within a qualifying lease, the improvements may be depreciated over the period of the lease.
[f] Reflecting an annual payment of $76,697.
[g] The assumed tax rate is 25%.

344

TABLE 13.19 New Hope Shopping Center, Inner-City Leasehold Shopping Center with SBA Funding, Statement of Total Cash Flows

Year	Net Income[a]	Principal Payments[b]	Depre-ciation	Equity Contri-bution	SBA Loan	Total Cash Flow
1	-$330,703	$65,760	$80,000	$50,000	$250,000	-$116,463
2	-40,037	67,814	80,000			-27,851
3	28,726	69,934	80,000			38,793
4	79,394	72,119	80,000			87,275
5	120,964	74,373	80,000			126,592
6	13,634	0	0			13,634
7	73,407	0	0			73,407
8	142,798	0	0			142,798
9	223,268	0	0			223,268
10	316,501	0	0			316,501

[a] From Table 13.13
[b] Reflecting an annual payment of $76,697.

NPV at 12% = $345,996

IRR = 41%

This is not necessarily the case. Operating leverage can work both ways. Had a new competitor eaten into New Hope's market and slowed the growth of its retail establishments, those new lease payments may have become quite difficult to make. When structuring leases to participate in the sales of its retailers a shopping center faces a certain cost structure and an uncertain revenue structure. The ultimate outcome may be satisfactory, but only at the cost of exposure to significant risk.

SUMMARY

Shopping centers provide investors with a wide range of good risk return outcomes. The opportunities for leverage through direct financing or leasing combined with the tax advantages associated with interest and depreciation write-offs create significant incentives for profitable investment.

An important caveat is that successful investing requires a high degree of business judgment and management skill. As in all real estate investment, location is a critical factor. Over and above this, investors must be able to create a situation in which their retailers flourish. If its retailers are not successful, the shopping center will not be successful. While professional management can be hired, the responsibility for the ultimate success of the project lies with the investor.

The rewards for successfully undertaking a shopping center investment are significant. Not only is there a high probability that a well-conceived project will stand on its own in terms of its profitability, but this investment will also provide significant diversification to an investor's portfolio that cannot be obtained from more traditional investments.

CHAPTER 14

Athletic Clubs, Physical Fitness Centers, and Family Entertainment Centers

America is an increasingly affluent society whose demand for formal opportunities to exercise continues to expand. The Census Bureau has reported a steady growth rate in athletic clubs, physical fitness centers, and family entertainment centers over the past decade.[1] This means that by 2003 there were approximately 11,800 such facilities in existence grossing $6.3 billion in sales. Given the Census population estimate of 283 million for 2003, this means that each facility was supported by a population of 23,729. Even given that the use of such athletic facilities may not be desired by everyone, and that many people live in areas to sparsely populated to make such a facility economically viable, these numbers suggest a tremendous latent demand for such exercise or entertainment facilities.[2] This demand creates opportunities for successful real estate investment.

Unfortunately, the gross population, or the gross population broken down by demographics, does not translate directly into a demand for athletic facilities. Differing segments of the population will have different ideas about what constitutes a desirable athletic facility. What serves for

---

[1] Bureau of the Census, Census of Economic Activity, 1997, 2002.

[2] This analysis refers to a wide variety of facilities ranging from single-purpose indoor basketball, soccer, and ice-skating rinks, through bowling alleys, water parks, racquet ball courts, weight-training rooms, and indoor and outdoor pools to multiple-purpose family entertainment centers, which include many different single-purpose facilities together with locker rooms, child-care centers, snackbars, restaurants, or bar facilities. For purposes of convenience, these will all be called *athletic facilities*.

one segment of the population will not necessarily serve for another. The industry is littered with athletic facilities that did not make it because they aimed to please everyone (and therefore pleased no one) or aimed at the wrong market.

The specificity of athletic facility demand has implications for the optimal investment in a facility. The athletic facility must be properly sized. The conventional approach is to project a given-size athletic facility and build it for the least cost or to estimate demand, revenue, and profit and allow the capitalized amount of profit to determine the investment in the facility. Such approaches reflect simplistic thinking. Because the demand for the facility is not generic, but specific to groups with special socioeconomic attributes and lifestyles, there is an interaction between the market niche to be served and the investment to be undertaken.

The relationship between the investment made in the facility and the market to be served can be defined very precisely. This is normally done in a formal feasibility study that has three components: (1) a market feasibility study that identifies the viable market niches in a given market area; (2) an economic feasibility study that analyzes all cost associated with the construction of an athletic facility relevant to a given market niche target; and (3) a financial feasibility study that identifies all revenues and costs in a series of pro forma financial statements that allow an investor to judge the risk and return parameters of the facility.

FOCUS ON NICHE MARKETING

Isolating the demand for a specific athletic facility is not easy. The general population is not homogeneous. What is needed is a focus on serving the needs of particular population subsegments. The individual characteristics of those subsegments determine its demand for specific types of athletic facilities. This situation is widely recognized and often approached by looking at a market's demographics (income, age, ethnicity, marital status, and education) to determine the relevant population subsegment.

Unfortunately, this approach constitutes a relatively poor way to estimate the demand for an athletic facility. The attributes mentioned above are not specific enough to yield the necessary information to specify the demand for an athletic facility. Markets for specific types and locations of athletic facilities are niche specific. Such market niches are differentiated by socioeconomic characteristics and lifestyles. Socioeconomic characteristics refer to an individual's social and economic standing in the community.

Life-style attributes incorporate how a person lives with particular reference to their values and behavior as consumers.

Socioeconomic characteristics and life-style attributes transcend demographics. Demographics describe the quantitative features of a population that are almost always presented as averages or ranges. Demographics will not tell you the difference between two married males with $75,000 incomes if one is a plumber and the other a librarian. Such individuals may differ significantly in their tastes, likes, and dislikes, and values. In ascertaining the demand for specific types of athletic facilities, such differences are critical. The plumber may like to hunt every fall. The librarian abhors firearms. They may well have different political affiliations, watch different television shows, and dress differently. An athletic facility that may appeal to one, might not appeal to the other.

There is no such thing as a successful athletic facility designed for "everyone." It is impossible to be something special to everyone, because everyone is a set of individuals with different socioeconomic characteristics and lifestyles. Individuals that would be attracted to a country club setting would not feel comfortable visiting a blue-collar bar. Some individuals prefer to play golf, others to watch hockey, and still others have an aversion to all athletics and prefer the opera or symphony. Should the athletic facility offer fruit drinks or soda, coffee or cappuccino, health foods or fries, gourmet food or fast food? The very thing that attracts some individuals to a particular athletic facility will turn others away.

A successful athletic facility must not only attract customers initially, it must keep them. The competition for individual's leisure time and discretionary spending is intense. Competitors are everywhere. For an athletic facility to attract and hold customers, it must give them exactly what they want. These customers need to be delighted with their facility or they will be drawn off by the myriad others ways to spend time and dollars. To create the high level of guest satisfaction necessary to create loyal customers and repeat business, the athletic facility must delight them. If it does not delight them, the customers will stay home or go somewhere else.

Successful athletic centers target particular socioeconomic and life-style groups. The issue for athletic centers is not as much price as it is value. Value arises from what people perceive they are getting from a good or service relative to price. Wal-Mart and Nordstroms flourish in the same community be meeting the needs of different sets of individuals. It is the same with athletic facilities.

Athletic facilities occupy different market niches based on their appeal to:

■ *Family structure.* Singles versus families. Adolescents, young single adults or the elderly. Families with no children, families with young children, families with adolescents, elderly families.

■ *Desired form of socialization.* Passive entertainment versus active experiences. Thrills and rides or interactive games. Competition versus cooperation. Self-development and self-enrichment versus social interaction.

■ *Leisure time availability.* Moms who work outside the home and moms who do not. Fathers with leisure time before normal working hours, after normal working hours, or purely discretionary leisure time.

■ *Occupational affinity.* Managers and professionals versus hourly workers.

■ *Educational values.* This differs from formal education completed (the normal demographic education attribute) and has more to do with personal or educational aspirations. Individuals may want for themselves, or parents for their children, enriching opportunities for personal growth. Or that value may not want to be important to them. Some parents prefer their children read rather than watch TV. Some individuals read Harlequin novels, some read historical novels.

SIZING THE ATHLETIC FACILITY

Sizing the athletic facility requires correctly proportioning the location, physical attributes, and services provided by the facility to the target market niche. The key to success in sizing the athletic facility is focusing on the needs of this target market as it is defined by its socioeconomic characteristics and life-style attributes. Success in developing an athletic facility does not involve minimizing cost. There is certainly nothing wrong with efficiency, but efficiency to what end? Success involves effectively proportioning costs to the needs of that target market. If the outcome of that sizing is a facility that is not economically viable, then it is back to the drawing boards to go through the same process for another market niche or the same market niche in another locality. The most common mistake investors make in developing an athletic facility is to start thinking about cost as an absolute rather than cost as relative to the market niche to be served. Thinking about cost as an absolute goes hand-in-hand with thinking about the demand for an athletic facility in general.

Competition for leisure time and leisure dollars is fierce. Therefore, an athletic facility must satisfy (even more than satisfy) the expectations of the target group. If such expectations are not met and exceeded on a continuing basis, then demand melts like frost in the morning sun. Meeting and exceeding such expectations can be accomplished by focusing on the ambiance desired by the target market niche. *Ambiance* is a term referring to an atmosphere created where that atmosphere is more than the sum of its parts. All the specific elements that contribute to the ambiance must be there, but more than that, those elements must combine and interact in a way that that interaction itself contributes to the whole. Mothers looking for activities for their preschoolers do not just need a clean and safe play area with appropriate toys that will entertain their children. They need other children there who belong to that mother's socioeconomic group and will play with their children. While the children play, the mothers get to talk and share their similar lifestyle experiences. Children and mothers both come away refreshed and pleased with the experience. An experience they will feel is valuable and want to repeat. An experience that is more than just the physical attributes of the building and playroom they visited.

Elements of the desired ambiance include:

- *The attractiveness of the surroundings.* Beauty is certainly in the eye of the beholder. Design and color create an overall impression that provides a context for the desired ambiance.
- *The sensory attributes of the environment.* Sights, sounds, smells, and the physical sensations experienced in the environment play an important role in determining the ambiance of the experience.
- *Interactions with staff and other personnel.* Is the staff sensitive to the needs of the individuals in this market niche? Do they meet their expectations with respect to friendliness, helpfulness, pleasantness, and courtesy?
- *The convenience of the experience.* Travel distances, parking ease, access and identification procedures, facilities layout, and adequacy of lockers, showers and restrooms all contribute to the ambiance of the experience.
- *Interactions with other customers.* If a man wishes to play basketball, he needs to be part of a team. There needs to be sufficient players of an appropriate level to form a team and to form other teams to play against. Developing comradeship with the other players is just as important to individuals as are the physical characteristics of the basketball court. A women seeking an aerobics class will have a much more pleasing experience if there are others in the class who approximate her physical abilities and with whom she can interact socially.
- *The financial and time sacrifices necessary to participate in the use of the athletic facility.* No one expects something for nothing. However,

when the value received for a given expenditure is more than what was expected, that contributes to the desired ambiance of the situation.

■ *The propriety and variety of the activities available within the athletic facility.* It is important that those activities provided suite the needs of the target market. Mothers with young children do not need video game rooms, adolescents do. Young singles need bowling alleys and basketball and volleyball courts, not a nursery. Competitive executives need a running track and handball and racquetball courts, not an aerobics room.

Ambiance does not come without a price tag. The notion that any expense that caters to the needs of the target market niche is as harmful as the notion that costs and available capital should dictate the size and composition of the athletic facility. What is needed is a "value-engineering" approach to this issue. The concept of *value engineering* means to develop the particular set of amenities desired by the target market group at the least possible cost. There is nothing wrong with this concept. The problem lies in properly implementing the concept.

Value engineering as practiced by many developers of athletic facilities involves creating a facility design and plan (either generic or niche targeted) and then as the construction process moves to completion trying to economize by moving to less expensive construction materials, finishes, or equipment. In so doing, they begin to compromise the ambiance envisioned for the target market. This approach often winds up saving some dollars on the cost side, but costs much more in revenue foregone because the target market is not now delighted with the facility. Value engineering is okay, even desirable, but needs to be implemented in the design stage to ensure congruence with the plan to serve the needs and expectations of the target market.

There is no such thing as a good cost per square foot (e.g., $80) in an athletic facility. There is no such thing as an optimal size (e.g., 40,000 sq. ft.) for an athletic facility. Optimal cost and size are always relative to the needs and expectations of the market niche being targeted. The reality of the general demand for athletic facilities today is that many economically viable market niches in this area are either not served at all or are under served. This creates an opportunity for the astute investor. The question then becomes how will the investor know which target niche in a given market will offer the best combination of risk and return and what sort of investment will meet the needs of the niche require.

That answer is best provided through a properly conducted feasibility study.

ATHLETIC FACILITY FEASIBILITY STUDIES

Feasibility studies address the question, "Can this facility be successfully developed?" And answers the question by an explanation of how this can be accomplished, if it is able to be accomplished at all. Feasibility studies generally run between $20,000 and $50,000 and are necessary in developing athletic facilities because targeting a particular niche and value engineering the facility towards that niche is of such critical importance in this industry.

The purpose of the feasibility study is to optimize a specific facility in a given market at a given location. A good feasibility study delivers more than a marketing plan. A good feasibility study synthesizes the demographic and socioeconomic attributes of a particular area with a product concept. The feasibility study then takes this vision for the facility and then considers competitive constraints, site constraints, and from this, projects attendance. These projections suggest the appropriate design and size of the facility. Correlating attendance with the size and attributes of a facility allow estimates of both costs and revenues to be made to determine the potential for profits.

Many athletic facilities are destined to fail. They fail because the facility is not offering the right product mix in its market; they fail because they are "generic" in nature and have not targeted a specific market niche; they fail because they are not sized correctly; and they fail because their facilities and services are not priced right. All of these causes of failure can be traced back to the absence of a feasibility study or a poorly constructed one. All to often would-be developers and investors put their fate in a generic formula for success or go on the basis of intuition.

There may have been times back in the early 1980s when the market for all types of athletic facilities was so underserved that practically any type of athletic facilities or services was successful. Those days are long gone. Today competition is keen for the consumer's discretionary dollar. Consumers have many more options for how to spend their leisure time and money. Consumers of these facilities want to be delighted today. If they are not, they will not come or will go elsewhere.

A good feasibility study allows you to do just that. Good feasibility studies have the following functional components.

A Defined Market Area

Market areas do not necessarily come in circles, squares or rectangles. They are not defined by city or county boundaries. They are not defined by ZIP codes. Contiguous socioeconomic lifestyle groups and traffic routes define most market areas. Hence they are rather uneven, often looking like amoebas. Other factors influencing the size and shape of the market to be served include: the size of the project, which affects market draw, anticipated length-of-stay, and per capita spending; competition and its location; the specific location of the project being considered; the project's exposure to traffic, and cultural perceptions of the location.

Demographic Attributes

As to the feasibility of an athletic center, its not population, age, median income, and the like per se that determines success, it is how they relate to market demand, attendance, financial feasibility, and product design. Even worse is ignoring demographics altogether. Woes betide the investor who looks at an area and says, "There are no athletic outlets here. Families have nothing to do"—and concludes from that there is an opportunity present.

Socioeconomic Lifestyles

While demographics provide pictures of the population in aggregate, they generally do not go deep enough to determine the probability of success for a given type of facility. Socioeconomic attributes and lifestyles bear directly on the demand for athletic facilities. Lifestyles contain more information about what your potential customers are like, their values, their behaviors, and their tastes and preferences.

Knowing how your consumers are likely to behave allows a project to be designed to appeal to their specific wants. The life-style choice an individual makes is reflected in product choice because the values of one reflect their own identity, a concept that retailers call life-style marketing.

Competition

Competition takes many forms. An athletic facility, providing indoor basketball courts, soccer and hockey fields, and video games, is not competition for young mothers who want an aerobics workout and their kids watched while they do it. (And do not forget the double mocha latte afterwards!) What needs to be assessed is relevant competition, and that means athletic facilities that are serving the same age and life-style population you would like to target. Conversely, the lack of direct competition does not mean a project is feasible. The target market must be of sufficient size to support the project. For example, just because a small town does not have a swimming pool or ice skating rink does not mean one is feasible.

One of the interesting attributes of the market for athletic facilities is that demand is variable rather than fixed. The demand for such facilities is not independent of their existence. A successful athletic facility is likely to increase the demand for more athletic facilities of this type or even another type. The better a center matches the values, tastes and preferences of its target market, the more frequently people will visit and spend money.

Product Formula

Given the market area, its demographic and life-style attributes, and the competitive situation, there comes the need to determine what specific type of athletic facility will best meet the market's need. The product formula is more comprehensive than just figuring out an appropriate mix of products and services, but rather every aspect of the facility that will be relevant to the consumer's needs, wants, and expectations. It is not just about racquetball courts, weight rooms, and stairmasters. It is about the size and cleanliness of the locker rooms, the presence or absence of a food service, the presence or absence of child care, the presence or absence of programs on health and nutrition, the presence or absence of music, the general ambiance of the facilities. In short, everything that impinges on the quality of the experience.

Attendance Projections

Valid attendance projections are rooted in the behaviors of the intended target market(s). Attendance projections do not look at the entire population and then project some overall rate of attendance; rather, they should look at the specific age, and lifestyle groups that are targeted. Attendance projections drive revenue expectations. Revenue expectations relative to costs determine the success or failure of the facility.

Operating Capacity

Having the right-size center is critical to success. It should match the expected attendance by offering neither too little nor too much capacity. Too much capacity means costs will be unnecessarily high. Too little will hurt the ambiance of the experience and generate a reputation for being overcrowded.

In summary, a properly drawn feasibility study focuses on a specific target market defined by age and lifestyle. This focus allows for the development of realistic revenue projections, which is then compared to the cost of constructing and operating the facility in a manner that will satisfy the wants, needs, and preferences of the targeted population group. A serious feasibility study is good insurance against undesirable surprises after a commitment is made to develop an athletic facility.

ILLUSTRATION #1: THE MADISON ATHLETIC CLUB

Benny Benito had played 10 years for the major league baseball team that was based in his metropolitan area and was a well thought of sports-personality-now-turned-businessman. Benny lived modestly and had sought professional help in managing his money and, as a result, he had a net worth of about $30 million. Benny had dabbled in local businesses and currently owned two motels and a popular local restaurant. Benny was an actively sought after emcee for local sports banquets and, at 40, still thought of himself of as physically fit. Benny had recently moved to an estate at the northern fringe of the metropolitan area, a previously rural area supporting numerous dairy farms, that was rapidly developing as a bedroom community.

Benny knew quite a few people who lived in the area and a frequent topic of conversation was how rapidly the area was growing and how poorly it was served by a retail and service infrastructure. Benny played in a pickup game of basketball at the local elementary school on Wednesday nights, but had to drive a long distance into town to play racquetball. His wife frequently commented that there was no place in their town that offered aerobics classes. Two of Benny's kids played indoor soccer. So, three nights a week, he took them to the soccer arena that was a 45-minute drive away.

Acquisition Phase

Benny thought his area was ready for a first-class athletic facility. He persuaded two of his friends to each chip-in $20,000 to find a location and do a feasibility study. His thinking was to build a very large, state-of-the-art athletic facility that would have an indoor soccer field, an Olympic-sized swimming pool, three indoor basketball courts, a large weight room, aerobics rooms, and a health bar.

The three partners then found a site that they thought would be a great location for such a facility. The site was a full acre just off an exit on the major interstate that fed into the nearby metropolitan area. The price of the land was $700,000 and the partners secured a six-month option on the land for $25,000.

Benny and his partners next found a consulting company that specialized in assessing and developing family entertainment centers of various types.

After numerous conversations with Benny and his partners, the consultant thoroughly examined the area's present and future population growth, the demographic characteristics of that population, the socio-economic life-styles of that population, and area traffic patterns. The consultant then held a number of focus group interviews with local individuals. As a result of this research, the consultant concluded that the area's population would not support the partner's vision. Not enough population growth had occurred to support the type of facility they envisioned, nor was the interest in athletics as strong as they had personally felt.

However the consultant did feel that the population would be dense enough in several years to support a larger facility. The consultant explained that the largest type of demand for athletic activities in the area came from affluent young women with pre-school children. Such demand would primarily occur during the day. The second largest demand for athletic activities came from affluent married professionals who wanted to "workout" at the end of their day. This demand would primarily be in the evening. The consultant thought these two socioeconomic segments could be served conveniently from a facility that provided an indoor basketball court surrounded by a running track. The basketball court would be used for that purpose at night, but for aerobics during the morning and early afternoon. Because the population being served was education-oriented and upwardly mobile, the consultant though it might be possible to squeeze in educationally oriented activities (ballet, dance, karate, etc.) for preteens after school on the basketball court. The consultant also suggested a fairly large area for free weights and exercise machines, and a good-size child care center. The consultant felt that a small "cappuccino bar" would prove a convenience for the customers and be profitable for the facility as well.

The consultant thought the location that the partners had selected suited the facility under consideration. The consultant thought that a "warehouse" type appearance should be avoided. That these upscale customers would expect high-quality finishes throughout the facility. This meant the facility would be more expensive than the average athletic club, but that the customers in this market niche would be willing to pay for something that delighted them.

This reflected the principle that maximizing profit is not a matter of minimizing cost in developing athletic facilities. Rather maximizing profit involves fitting the right facility to the needs and desires of those who are going to use that facility. This is the concept of the *investment optimum*.

The customer thought that a facility could be created along the lines discussed above in a building of about 45,000 sq. ft. The consultant further estimated that the actual costs of construction would run $120 per square foot and another $20 per square foot in soft costs. Equipment for the facility (basketball backboards, weights, exercise machines, locker room equipment, counters, ID system, and furniture) would cost an additional $1 million. Further a club this size would require a dedicated staff of 15 full-time employees with an annual salary of $450,000. Utilities, insurance, general maintenance, would run about $200,000 per year.

The consultant recommended pricing the facilities at $150 per month per individual and $200 per month for families. One-month trial memberships would be made available to all individuals. The consultant felt that there should be a set of services made available to the patrons without charge. These would include child care, aerobics classes, nutrition classes, weight counseling, and towel service. The consultant thought that a facility this size could comfortably accommodate 300 people at one time and as many as 400 for a short period of time. The consultant felt that aggressive marketing would generate about 700 memberships the first year and about 1,400 by the end of the second year (family memberships would be 600 and 1,200 respectively.) On a net basis, the consultant expected membership to grow at 5% per year as a result of a continued increase in the local population and the popularity of the club. The consultant further noted that membership turnover of about 20% was to be expected and that this was figured into the membership estimates. These conservative estimates mean that the club would reach a capacity level consistent with the desired ambience of the facility in five to seven years. In 10 years the facility would reach absolute capacity and be ready for a major renovation and expansion.

On this basis, the partners thought they would go ahead with the project. They decided to name the facility the Madison Athletic Club (the "MAC," after the county in which the club would be located).

As a result of this strategic approach to the MAC, the consultants estimated that the club would be able to sell 800 family memberships and 200 individual memberships in its first year of operation. These would be priced at $250 and $150 per month respectively. It was recognized that this was a high price; but the consultants felt that the premium facilities being offered would be able to command such a price. Memberships were projected to double the second year and to increase at 10% annually thereafter. With the addition of revenues developed from the cappuccino bar, special services, and merchandise, revenue would grow to $6,096,805 at the end of the third year and, thereafter, grow at 10% per year (Table 14.1).

The cost the MAC would include $700,000 for the initial land purchase, construction costs of (45,000 sq. ft. at $140 per sq. ft.) $6,300,000, plus $1 million for necessary equipment. In addition, the partners had contributed an initial $62,000 for the option on the land and the feasibility study. The necessary legal and accounting services are included in the $20 per square foot soft costs. This brought the first year total cost of the MAC to $8,390,000 (Table 14.2.)

TABLE 14.1   Madison Athletic Club, Three-Year Revenue Structure

Demand Category	Revenue[a]		
	Year 1	Year 2	Year 3
Family memberships[b]	$720,000	$2,160,000	$3,168,000
Individual memberships[c]	90,000	360,000	594,000
Coffee bar revenue[d]	6,000	6,600	7,260
Special services[e]	12,000	13,200	14,520
Merchandise	2,500	2,750	3,025
Total revenue	830,500	2,542,550	3,786,805

[a] Year 1 projections call for 800 initial family memberships projected to double to 1,600 family memberships in the second year and Year 1 individual memberships to be 200, doubling to 400 in the second year. Membership in both categories is expected to increase at 5% annually thereafter. Memberships are expected to ramp up evenly during the first two years.
[b] Membership fees are $250 per month.
[c] Membership fees are $150 per month.
[d] The coffee bar is leased out to an operator for $500 per month.
[e] Rent charged to the operators of ballet and karate classes offered at the facility.

TABLE 14.2   Madison Athletic Club, Acquisition Period Cash Flows

Item	Year 1
Interest-only loan expense[a]	$315,000
Construction expenses	6,300,000
Land acquisition costs[b]	725,000
Equipment expense	1,000,000
Feasibility study	50,000
Total costs	8,390,000
Bridge loan (credit)	−5,000,000
Total cash out	3,390,000

[a] The construction period is one year and the $6.3 million loan is drawn down evenly over this period. Construction costs include both hard and soft costs.
[b] Includes cost of option on land.

The partners decided they would each put up $1,130,000 and borrow the remaining $5 million from a local bank. The local bank was willing to provide an interest-only construction bridge loan of $5 million at 10% and roll this over into a $5 million, 20-year mortgage on the property at 9% upon the completion of construction. This would result in an annual principal and interest payment of $547,732.

Holding Stage

As a result of their careful assessment of the market and their measured approach in constructing the MAC, Benny Benito and his partners experience substantial success. Table 14.3 indicates that, after a small after-tax loss in the first year (primarily a reflection of spreading the acquisition of the MAC's first-year 700 memberships evenly over the entire first year), NOPAT accelerates steadily to over $2 million by year 10.

This pattern is continued in net income. Table 14.4 indicates a fairly substantial first-year, after-tax loss of $300,162. Again this reflects the acquisition of the MAC's first-year 700 memberships evenly over the entire first year, that is, 58 new members a month. Net income then can be seen to rise steadily to just under $2 million (($1,898,000). The strength of the increase in net income suggests a profitable operation.

Disposal Stage

While the partners may well decide to hold on to the property, or even expand it as initially envisioned, the end of 10 years of projected operations is a convenient point to sum up the performance of the project. Athletic clubs are not inherently liquid. Their success is often a function of the quality of management. In this case the club may have benefited from its association with the personality of Benny Benito. However, the MAC is still a commercial property whose value is determined by the capitalized value of its income stream. Athletic facilities of this type are often sold for five to eight times net income. Approaching the value of the MAC conservatively at five times earnings gives MAC a market value of $9,489,744.

The sale of MAC for $9,489,744 after a 10-year holding period may be seen (Tables 17.5A and 17.5B) to generate a cash gain of $5,280,800.

The cash flows associated with the MAC under the given assumptions are presented in Table 14.6. The partner's investment of $3,390,000 is seen to return an NPV of $6,379,928 and an IRR of 35%. Not bad, considering they now have a nice place to work out and Benny no longer has to drive his kids 45 minutes to soccer practice.

TABLE 14.3 Madison Athletic Club, Net-Operating Profits after Taxes

Year	Revenues	Wages and Salaries[a]	Overhead[b]	Building Depreciation[c]	Infrastructure Depreciation[d]	Equipment Depreciation[e]	EBIT	Taxes (40%)	NOPAT EBIT$(1 - tx)$
1	$830,500	$450,000	$200,000	$64,103	$66,667	$100,000	-$50,269	-$20,108	-$30,162
2	2,542,550	495,000	226,000	128,205	124,444	320,000	1,248,900	499,560	749,340
3	3,786,805	544,500	255,380	128,205	107,852	192,000	2,558,868	1,023,547	1,535,321
4	3,976,145	598,950	288,579	128,205	93,472	115,200	2,751,739	1,100,696	1,651,043
5	4,174,953	658,845	326,095	128,205	81,009	69,120	2,911,679	1,164,672	1,747,007
6	4,383,700	724,730	368,487	128,205	70,208	103,680	2,988,391	1,195,356	1,793,035
7	4,602,885	797,202	416,390	128,205	60,847	0	3,200,241	1,280,096	1,920,144
8	4,833,029	876,923	470,521	128,205	52,734	0	3,304,647	1,321,859	1,982,788
9	5,074,681	964,615	531,689	128,205	45,703	0	3,404,469	1,361,788	2,042,682
10	5,328,415	1,061,076	600,808	128,205	39,609	0	3,498,716	1,399,486	2,099,230

[a] Assumes an initial staff of 15 full-time employees. These costs are expected to increase 10% annually as a result of wage increases and additional part time help.

[b] Includes utilities, insurance, and general maintenance increasing at 13% per year.

[c] Of the total construction costs of $6,300,000, $5 million is depreciable over 39 years (with the half year convention), $1 million will be depreciable over 15 years, and $300,000 will be expensed.

[d] $1 million for building infrastructure, double-declining balance over 15 years with half-year convention.

[e] $1 million for equipment, double-declining balance over five years with half-year convention.

TABLE 14.4 Madison Athletic Club, Income Statement

Year	Revenues	Wages and Salaries[a]	Overhead[a]	Total Depreciation[a]	Interest	Earnings before Taxes	Taxes 40%	Net Income
1	$830,500	$450,000	$200,000	$230,769	$450,000	-$500,269	-$200,108	-$300,162
2	2,542,550	495,000	226,000	572,650	441,204	807,696	323,079	484,618
3	3,786,805	544,500	255,380	428,057	431,617	2,127,251	850,901	1,276,351
4	3,976,145	598,950	288,579	336,877	421,166	2,330,573	932,229	1,398,344
5	4,174,953	658,845	326,095	278,334	409,775	2,501,904	1,000,762	1,501,142
6	4,383,700	724,730	368,487	302,093	397,359	2,591,032	1,036,413	1,554,619
7	4,602,885	797,202	416,390	189,052	383,825	2,816,415	1,126,566	1,689,849
8	4,833,029	876,923	470,521	180,939	369,074	2,935,573	1,174,229	1,761,344
9	5,074,681	964,615	531,689	173,908	352,994	3,051,475	1,220,590	1,830,885
10	5,328,415	1,061,076	600,808	167,814	335,468	3,163,248	1,265,299	1,897,949

[a] From Table 14.3.

362

TABLE 14.5A   Madison Athletic Club, Tax Consequences of Sale of Property

Sale of building		$9,489,744
Fixed plant and improvements[a]	$7,000,000	
Less accumulated		
depreciation	2,860,491	
Net fixed plant and improvements		4,139,509
Cost of land		$725,000
Profit		$4,625,235
Capital gains tax (15%)		693,785
After-tax gain on sale		3,931,450

[a] Includes $5 million for buildings, $1 million for improvements, and $1 million for equipment.

TABLE 14.5B   Madison Athletic Club, Cash Gain from Sale of Property

Sale of property	$9,489,744
Less:	
Tax liability	693,785
Loan balance	3,515,159
Cash gain from sale	$5,280,800

TABLE 14.6   Madison Athletic Club, Cash Flow Statement

Year	Net Income	Depre- ciation	Capital Contributions	Gain on Sale of Land	Net Cash Flows
0			-$3,390,000		-$3,390,000
1	-$300,162	$230,769			-69,392
2	484,618	572,650			1,057,267
3	1,276,351	428,057			1,704,408
4	1,398,344	336,877			1,735,221
5	1,501,142	278,334			1,779,476
6	1,554,619	302,093			1,856,712
7	1,689,849	189,052			1,878,901
8	1,761,344	180,939			1,942,283
9	1,830,885	173,908			2,004,793
10	1,897,949	167,814		$5,280,800	7,346,563

NPV at 12% = $6,379,928
IRR = 35%

Break-Even Analysis

Revenues at the MAC are a function of membership (either directly through membership charges or indirectly through the sale of ancillary goods and services) and the price charged for membership. The break-even analysis for the MAC may be constructed on the basis of the number of members assuming price is fixed as a result of being embedded in the array of services and amenities being offered.

At MAC, each member, on the average, is worth an annual revenue of $2,300 (Table 14.1).

Therefore,

$$\text{Total revenue} = M \times \$2,300$$

where M is the number of members.

Total cost at MAC is divided into fixed costs and variable costs. Fixed costs would include the largest component of wages and salaries, interest, overhead, and depreciation. At MAC these total approximately $1,300,000 (Table 14.4). Variable costs consist of marginal part-time help and a small portion of overhead. These may be estimated at 10% (Table 14.4).

Therefore,

$$
\begin{aligned}
\text{Total cost} &= \text{Fixed cost} + \text{Variable cost} \\
&= \$1,300,000 + 0.10 \,(\text{Total revenue})
\end{aligned}
$$

The break-even point for the MAC is therefore,

$$M \times (2,300) = 1,300,000 + 0.1(M \times 2,300)$$

thus,

$$0.9M \times 2,070 = 1,300,000, \text{ or } 0.9M = 1,300,000/2,070$$

thus,

$$0.9M = 628$$

or

$$BEP = 698 \text{ members}$$

As a result of their careful market analysis, the MAC reached this membership level its first year and surpassed that in subsequent years, becoming a great success for its investors.

ILLUSTRATION #2: KIM'S FAMILY ENTERTAINMENT CENTER

Kim Shin, a second generation Korean, had taken over his father's Oriental Food Take-Out located on the boundary between an industrial area and a blue-collar residential neighborhood. Oriental Food Take-Out was popular and successful. Kim had gone to the local school and had many friends in that community. The business itself consisted of a ramshackle 3,000 sq. ft. store located on 10 acres of woodland and marsh that had been used as an informal dump by the community for many years. There were also some dirt bike trails that were used by youths in the community. Kim had noted that the area held a large population of teenagers who hung around a lot and often got into trouble because they had "nothing to do." Kim thought a lot of them hung out in the woods behind his store and was worried about the potential liability of this situation.

Kim thought he might turn this situation to his advantage if he formally developed his woods as a "Family Entertainment Center." He thought he could install a go-cart driving course on three acres. Kim also felt a batting cage would be very popular with local residents. Most of the local population were rabid baseball fans of the area's National League team. He also thought five of these acres could be used as a "Paintball Arena." On these acres friends or groups could arrange to have paintball "wars." Kim could charge admission and rent or sell supplies used for this purpose. Kim thought these three facilities would prove very appealing to the local population and create a critical mass that would attract the youth of the area. Kim also thought he would locate a soda shop and video arcade in the center of these facilities because he knew that the only thing teenagers liked to do more than play videos was to eat.

To create this Family Entertainment Center, Kim needed to spend $30,000 on a zoning variance (successfully because he had broad community support). Kim found the cost of constructing the go-cart track would be $20,000 and the necessary equipment another $20,000. The batting cage and equipment would require $35,000, and all the Paintball Arena needed was a fence. Although Kim would need to carry an inventory of $10,000 in supplies to sell and rent out. The "Soda Shack" was constructed for $25,000 and was stocked entirely by soda and snack vending machines. Kim found a vendor who would supply and stock the machines and give him 35% of the revenues. The Soda Shack had a large area for video machines. Kim found a vendor who agreed to supply and service 20 video machines, five pinball machines and three "claw" machines and split the revenues 50-50 with him.

Acquisition Period

Kim's Family Entertainment Center thus would require $140,000 in startup costs. Kim was willing to put up $25,000 cash for this and take a second mortgage on his store for the remaining $115,000. The second mortgage would be for fixed interest and principal payments for 10 years at 12%. The would result in an annual payment of $20,353.

Kim expected that the business would be highly seasonal because of the region's harsh winters. Kim began construction of the facilities in January and was ready to open in June by the end of the school year.

Holding Period

Kim found the demand for the Paintball Arena to be quite price sensitive. Consequently he charged $1 an hour for entry before 5:00 P.M. and $2 an hour after 5:00 P.M. and on weekends. On weekdays he sold an "All-Day Pass" for $5 and on weekends for $10. During his prime season, Kim averaged $80 per weekday, $250 on Saturday, and $150 on Sunday. Selling the supplies was not particularly profitable because there was a Wal-Mart nearby that stocked paintball supplies.

The demand for go-carts during the day proved to be nil, but quite strong in the evening. Kim charged $5 for a 20-minute ride on a go-cart. Most weekdays, the go-carts would generate about $100 in revenue, $500 on Saturdays, and $300 on Sundays.

The batting cage also proved popular in the evenings and on weekends. By depositing $1 in one of five pitching machines, the patron would get 10 balls to hit. This took approximately 10 minutes. The batting cages generated revenue of about $600 per week.

The Soda Shack did about $2,000 a week in the summer, netting Kim $525 a week and the video games were good for about $3,000 a week, netting Kim $1,500 a week.

Kim found that 80% of his business came in June, July, and August, with 10% in May and another 10% in October. The effective season for his Family Entertainment Center (FET) was 14 weeks.

These activities can thus be expected to generate gross revenues of $67,550 (Table 14.7) over the 14-week season.

As can be seen from Table 14.8, Kim's capital requirements can be met with $25,000 of his own cash and his second mortgage loan of $115,000.

NOPAT (Table 14.9) is positive throughout the 10-year holding period, but is seen to decline steadily as labor costs are expected to rise while demand conditions prohibit a rise in revenues. It should be noted that Kim's largest labor expense is for a uniformed security guard.

TABLE 14.7 Kim's FEC, Revenue Structure

Demand Category	Revenue
Paintball revenues	$12,600
Go-cart revenues	18,200
Batting cage revenues	8,400
Snack shop revenues	7,350
Arcade game revenues	21,000
Total revenue	67,550

TABLE 14.8 Kim's FEC, Acquisition Cash Flows

Item	Year 1
Snack Shack building	$25,000
Improvements	50,000
Equipment	27,000
Inventory	8,000
Zoning appeal	30,000
Total costs	140,000
Bank loan (credit)	–115,000
Total cash out	25,000

A similar pattern can be observed in net income. In Table 14.10, net income is seen as positive throughout, but declining.

Disposal Stage

A FEC is not inherently liquid, but it does have a cash flow that may be capitalized to determine its value. In this case it is likely the restaurant and the take-out would be sold as one unit and the entire revenue stream capitalized at five times earnings. This procedure gives the FEC a market value of $32,947 and yields Kim a net cash gain of $15,722 (Tables 14.11A and 14.11B). Note that the opportunity cost of the 10 acres adjacent to Oriental Food Take-Out was assumed to be zero. However, for tax purposes, the land had an initial cost at purchase, and with a sale, it is necessary to recognize that cost.

The net effect for the FEC can be seen in Table 14.12. Cash flow is positive throughout each of the 10 years in the holding period. Kim Shin can be seen to generate an NPV of $68,242 from his $25,000 investment. An excellent return of 72% on his equity.

TABLE 14.9 Kim's FEC, Net-Operating Profits after Taxes

Year	Revenues	Labor[a]	Overhead[b]	Building Depreciation[c]	Improvements Depreciation[d]	Equipment Depreciation[e]	EBIT	Taxes (40%)	NOPAT EBIT$(1 - tx)$
1	$67,550	$13,100	$16,000	$321	$3,333	$5,400	$29,396	$11,758	$17,638
2	67,550	14,410	16,480	641	6,222	8,640	21,157	8,463	12,694
3	67,550	15,851	16,974	641	5,393	5,184	23,507	9,403	14,104
4	67,550	17,436	17,484	641	4,674	3,110	24,205	9,682	14,523
5	67,550	19,180	18,008	641	4,050	1,866	23,804	9,522	14,283
6	67,550	21,098	18,548	641	3,510	2,799	20,953	8,381	12,572
7	67,550	23,207	19,105	641	3,042	0	21,554	8,622	12,933
8	67,550	25,528	19,678	641	2,637	0	19,066	7,626	11,440
9	67,550	28,081	20,268	641	2,285	0	16,275	6,510	9,765
10	67,550	30,889	20,876	641	1,980	0	13,163	5,265	7,898

[a] Based on two full-time employees, one security guard, and one-part time employee for 14 weeks to increase 10% annually as a result of wage increases and additional part-time help.
[b] Includes utilities, insurance, and general maintenance increasing at 13% per year.
[c] $25,000 for the Snack Shack depreciable over 39 years with the half-year convention.
[d] $50,000 of improvements, double-declining balance over 15 years with half-year convention.
[e] $27,000 for equipment, double-declining balance over five years with half-year convention. Note that inventory is not depreciable.

TABLE 14.10 Kim's FEC, Income Statement

Year	Revenues	Salaries[a]	Overhead[a]	Total Depreciation[a]	Interest	Earnings before Taxes	Taxes 40%	Net Income
1	$67,550	$13,100	$16,000	$9,054	$13,800	$15,596	$6,238	$9,358
2	67,550	14,410	16,480	15,503	13,014	8,143	3,257	4,886
3	67,550	15,851	16,974	11,218	12,133	11,374	4,550	6,824
4	67,550	17,436	17,484	8,425	11,146	13,059	5,224	7,835
5	67,550	19,180	18,008	6,558	10,042	13,763	5,505	8,258
6	67,550	21,098	18,548	6,951	8,804	12,149	4,860	7,289
7	67,550	23,207	19,105	3,683	7,418	14,136	5,654	8,482
8	67,550	25,528	19,678	3,278	5,866	13,200	5,280	7,920
9	67,550	28,081	20,268	2,926	4,128	12,147	4,859	7,288
10	67,550	30,889	20,876	2,621	2,181	10,982	4,393	6,589

[a] From Table 14.9.

TABLE 14.11A Kim's FEC, Tax Consequences of Sale of Property

Sale of FEC		$32,947
Fixed plant and improvements[a]	$102,000	
Less accumulated depreciation	70,217	
Net fixed plant and improvements		31,783
Cost of land		20,000
Profit		–18,836
Capital gains tax (15%)		–2,825
After-tax gain on sale		–16,011

[a] Includes $25,000 for buildings, $50,000 for improvements, and $27,000 for equipment.

TABLE 14.11B Kim's FEC, Cash Gain from Sale of Property

Sale of property	$32,947
Less:	
Tax liability	–2,825
Loan balance	0
Cash gain from sale	35,772
Gain from FEC[a]	$15,772

[a] Excludes cost of land.

TABLE 14.12 Kim's FEC, Cash Flow Statement

Year	Net Income	Depreciation	Capital Contributions	Gain on Sale of Land	Net Cash Flows
0			–$25,000		–$25,000
1	$9,358	$9,054			18,412
2	4,886	15,503			20,389
3	6,824	11,218			18,042
4	7,835	8,425			16,260
5	8,258	6,558			14,815
6	7,289	6,951			14,240
7	8,482	3,683			12,165
8	7,920	3,278			11,198
9	7,288	2,926			10,214
10	6,589	2,621		$0	9,211

NPV at 12% = $63,164
IRR = 72%

Break-Even Analysis

Revenues at the Kim's FEC are a function of attendance—either directly through admission charges or indirectly through the sale of ancillary goods and services—and the revenue generated by each attendee. The break-even analysis for Kim's FEC may be constructed on the basis of the total revenue generated by the FEC.

Therefore,

Total revenue = (Attendees) × (Revenue generated per attendee)

Total cost at Kim's FEC is divided into fixed costs and variable costs. Fixed costs would include the largest component of wages and salaries, interest, overhead, and depreciation. At Kim's FEC these total approximately $50,000 (Table 17.10). Variable costs consist of marginal part-time help and a small portion of overhead. These may be estimated at 6% (Table 17.10).

Therefore,

Total cost = Fixed cost + Variable cost = $50,000 + 0.06(Total revenue)

The break-even point for the MAC is, therefore,

$$TR = \$50,000 + 0.06(TR), \text{ thus } 0.94TR = \$50,000$$

thus,

$$BEP = \$53,191$$

As a result of good fortune and a close knowledge of the local market, Kim Shin's FEC was profitable in its first year and continued that success in subsequent years.

ILLUSTRATION #3: DANCE FOR LIFE

Debbie VanFleet had been a star ballerina for 12 years with the famous Metropolitan Ballet Company until a leg injury had prematurely ended her career. Debbie was a life-long resident of her city and loved urban living. She had long thought that most urban neighborhoods in the area were underserved with the amenities that made life worthwhile. Debbie also loved children, though she had none of her own. She had also thought that when she could no longer dance, she would teach the ballet that she loved so much. It had also been Debbie's experience that many women she met had danced when they were younger and would appreciate the opportunity to return to study this discipline. It seemed to Debbie that this was consistent with modern demands for fitness and a healthy life-style.

At 33, Debbie had only been able to save about $100,000 from her career. She did have a well-to-do brother who cared for her very much. Debbie found a 10,000 sq. ft. deserted loft in an old garment factory at the edge of a trendy neighborhood. Debbie was able to arrange a triple five-year lease for $18 per square foot with a 5% per year escalation clause. Unfortunately, extensive renovation would be called for until the facility could function adequately as a dance studio. In talking with contractors, Debbie found that the necessary renovations would cost $200,000. Debbie recognized that the space she was leasing was more than she needed for her dance studio, so she decided that part of the loft could be devoted to exercise. Consequently, she fitted out a large room with an array of exercise equipment (Nautilus machines, Jogging tracks, stairmasters) that cost an additional $100,000.

Debbie had not done extensive market research on the number of young children who would be willing to take ballet lessons in her immediate vicinity. However, her location had good access through mass transit (although parking was "iffy" and expensive when it could be found), and Debbie felt that with an urban population in the millions, surely there would be an excess of students who would want to study dance with her.

Debbie secured a five-year, interest-only balloon note from her brother for $400,000 at 6% interest. Within six months the renovations had been completed and Debbie threw open the door of "Dance for Life." The conventional approach to ballet and dance lessons was to charge by the quarter. The average cost per quarter per student in her metropolitan area was $250. Debbie thought she would charge $300 owing to the excellence and rigor of her dance pedagogy. Aggressively canvassing her vast network of friends and acquaintances, she was able to begin her dance studio with two beginner classes (12 and 9 students), one intermediate class (11 students), and one advanced class (6 students). While no great shakes with the numbers, even Debbie could see that this would not do. Thirty-eight students at $300 was only $11,400 for the quarter. Rent alone for the quarter was $45,000!

Debbie turned to a friend in marketing who helped her devise an extensive sales campaign for ballet, jazz, tap, and modern dance for both the young and old. She aggressively recruited individuals for membership in her exercise facility. By her Herculean efforts, Debbie was able to moderately increase the number of classes she was offering by the end of the fist year. The first year was still a financial disaster, however.

The marketing campaign began to bear some fruit. By the second year Dance for Life was offering 10 children's classes averaging 11 students per quarter in classes of various types of dance. In addition, Debbie had sold 50 memberships in her exercise facility for $100 per month. This increase reflected an incredible expense of time and effort by Debbie and her closest friends. It turned out that the trendy neighborhood they were located next to was populated largely by yuppies or Dinks (dual income, no kids). So there was little local demand for children's ballet. For potential customers located in other areas of the city, it turned out that parking was an issue. As a result of congestion and crime, mass transit was not seen as a good way to get around. While there was some demand for an exercise facility, many potential members were looking for more than just a roomful of equipment. They wanted a running track, swimming pool, hot tub, and sauna.

By force of personality, an incredible commitment of time and energy, and the excellence of the dance experience offered, Debbie was able to bring revenues up to levels where a small profit could be shown. After five years of frustration and endless toil, Debbie was exhausted. At the end of the lease, she sold the studio to a friend for three times earnings and took a catastrophic loss.

The five-year revenue structure of Dance for Life is depicted in Table 14.13. While revenue shows continuous improvement throughout the period, revenue in the first three years will not be sufficient to cover direct costs. Continued growth of studio revenues is problematic, as so much depended on the exceptional efforts of Debbie personally.

TABLE 14.13 Dance for Life, Revenue Structure

Demand Category	Year 1	Year 2	Year 3	Year 4	Year 5
Childrens' dance[a]	$101,500	$132,000	$198,000	$237,600	$264,000
Adult dance[b]	38,000	60,000	84,000	108,000	132,000
Activity membership[c]	30,000	72,000	78,000	93,600	120,000
Costume and performance fees[d]	8,500	12,000	12,600	13,230	13,892
Total revenue	178,000	276,000	372,600	452,430	529,892

[a] After a disastrous first year, childrens' dance averaged 10 classes per quarter the second year and then climbed to 15, 18, and finally 20 classes per quarter.
[b] After the first difficult year, adult classes averaged 5 per quarter in the second year and slowly inched up to 11 per quarter during the fifth year.
[c] After the first year, activity membership grew to 60 in the second year and edged up to 100 by the fifth year.
[d] These fees are associated with dance recitals given semiannually at the studio.

TABLE 14.14   Dance for Life, Acquisition Period Cash Flows

Item	Year 1
Lease expense	$180,000
Improvements	200,000
Equipment	100,000
Loan from brother	400,000
Total cash out	80,000

Table 14.14 shows that the cash necessary to begin the Dance for Life ballet studio was provided by a loan from Debbie's brother and the bulk of her life savings.

Dance for Life begins with a whopping –$200,000 NOPAT (Table 14.15) that remains negative for the following two years and then moves into positive territory in the fourth and fifth years.

This pattern is mirrored in the income statement for Dance for Life (Table 14.16). Substantial losses are reported the first two years, followed by modest, but increasing, profitability.

Tired and exhausted by the rigors of trying to make Dance for Life successful, Debbie sells out to a friend for three times earnings ($167,808). However, the losses in the early years of Dance for Life precipitated cash flow problems that required another $150,000 from her brother. As can be seen from Table 14.17A and 14.17B the net effect of the sale is to cause Debbie to lose cash of more than $400,000. This will no doubt be a loss that Debbie's brother has to sustain. Had this loan been from a bank, the loan would undoubtedly have been foreclosed, driving Debbie into personal bankruptcy.

The financial saga of Dance for Life is fully told in the cash flow statement (Table 14.18). As a result of misjudging its market, Dance for Life experiences disastrous losses in its early years and, even though it becomes profitable in its later years, the level of profitability is not sufficient to warrant the continuation of the business. For all of her effort, Debbie has lost the equivalent of $454,000 that represents a loss of 468% on her initial investment of $80,000.

Break-Even Analysis

Break-even analysis at Dance for Life suggests the dependence of success on getting adequate numbers of dancers. This should have been done in connection with a market feasibility study before beginning Dance for Life to avoid the subsequent financial disappointment.

TABLE 14.15 Dance for Life, Net-Operating Profits after Taxes

Year	Revenues	Labor[a]	Lease	Overhead[b]	Depreciation[c]	EBIT	Taxes (40%)	NOPAT EBIT(1 − tx)
1	$178,000	$73,000	$180,000	$65,000	$60,000	−$200,000	$0	−$200,000
2	276,000	76,000	189,000	66,950	96,000	−151,950	−60,780	−91,170
3	372,600	79,800	198,450	68,959	57,600	−32,209	−12,883	−19,325
4	452,430	83,790	208,373	71,027	34,560	54,680	21,872	32,808
5	529,892	87,980	218,791	73,158	20,736	129,227	51,691	77,536

[a] Debbie takes an annual salary of $70,000 and employs a part-time receptionist/bookkeeper.
[b] Includes taxes, utilities, maintenance, and insurance.
[c] Building improvements and equipment depreciated over five years, double-declining balance with half year convention.

TABLE 14.16 Dance for Life, Income Statement[a]

Year	Revenues	Labor	Lease	Overhead	Total Depreciation	Interest	Earnings before Taxes	Taxes 40%	Net Income
1	$178,000	$73,000	$180,000	$65,000	$60,000	$36,000	−$236,000		−$236,000
2	276,000	76,000	189,000	66,950	96,000	36,000	−187,950		−187,950
3	372,600	79,800	198,450	68,959	57,600	36,000	−68,209	−$27,283	−40,925
4	452,430	83,790	208,373	71,027	34,560	36,000	18,680	7,472	11,208
5	529,892	87,980	218,791	73,158	20,736	36,000	93,227	37,291	55,936

[a] Data from Table 14.15.

TABLE 14.17A   Dance for Life, Tax Consequences of Sale of Property

Sale of studio		$167,808
Fixed plant and improvements	$300,000	
Less accumulated depreciation	268,896	
Net fixed plant and improvements		31,104
Profit		136,704
Capital gains tax (15%)		20,506
After-tax gain on sale		116,199

TABLE 14.17B   Dance for Life, Cash Gain from Sale of Property

Sale of property	$167,808
Less:	
Tax liability	20,506
Loan balance	550,000
Cash gain from sale	−402,697

TABLE 14.18   Dance for Life, Cash Flow Statement

Year	Net Income	Depreciation	Capital Contributions	Gain on Sale of Land	Net Cash Flows
0			−$80,000		−$80,000
1	−$236,000	$60,000			−176,000
2	−187,950	96,000			−91,950
3	−40,925	57,600			16,675
4	11,208	34,560			45,768
5	55,936	20,736		−$402,697	−326,025

NPV at 12% = −$454,485
IRR = −468%

Revenues at Dance for Live are a function of class size, the number of classes, and the number of exercise memberships, as well as the cost of these services. In year 3 there were 300 attendees at Dance for Life generating an average of $1,242 each.

Therefore,

Total revenue = (Attendees) × (Revenue generated per attendee)
= (Attendees) × $1,242

Total cost at Dance for Life is divided into fixed costs and variable costs. Fixed costs would include the largest component of wages and salaries, interest, overhead, and depreciation. At Dance for Life, these totaled approximately $440,000 (Table 14.15). Variable costs consist of marginal part-time help and a small portion of overhead. These may be estimated at 3% (Table 14.15).

Therefore:

Total cost = Fixed cost + Variable cost
= $440,000 + 0.03(Attendees × $1,242)

The break-even point for Dance for Life is, therefore,

(Attendees × $1,242) = $440,000 + 0.03(Attendees × $1,242)

or

0.97(Attendees) × 0.97($1,242) = $440,000

or

BEP(Attendees) = 376

As a result of her lack of market research, Debbie was not positioned to capture 376 students each year. Consequently, it took her three years to get to the point where she was slightly above her break-even level of attendance. As a result, the business failed and Debbie— and her brother—took a substantial loss.

SUMMARY

The macroconditions for developing all types of athletic facilities in the United States are favorable. Increasing affluence, increasing leisure time, and ascendant social values focusing on health and fitness all portend success in this area. In addition, athletic facilities will carry all the advantages generally associated with investing in commercial real estate: tax shelter from depreciation, interest tax savings, operating leverage, financial leverage, and protection from inflation.

A cautionary note should be sounded in this area: There is no such thing as a generic athletic facility. Athletic facilities have to be carefully designed, sized, and value engineered to meet the needs of specific target markets. If this is the situation, then success is highly likely. The underlying economics of athletic facilities are excellent when demand is there.

If a project is undertaken without due consideration of the market to be served, then disaster portends. Athletic facilities have high fixed costs and, without an appropriate level of demand, simply will not be successful. Depending of the degree of lack of demand, the facility can linger on for years, failing to cover the opportunity cost of its invested capital. Or the facility can die a swift death, being unable to cover even its direct operating costs.

CHAPTER 15

Office Buildings

Office buildings provide excellent opportunities for discerning investors to reap excellent returns for the risk involved. Office buildings can be awesome structures with 50 stories and 1 million sq. ft. of rentable space or modest, simple one-story buildings with 4,000, sq. ft. of space. Whatever the size of the office building, the basic elements in the process of successfully investing in this market are the same. Find a location attractive to potential tenants, design a building that conforms to those tenants' needs, secure leases, find construction financing, find permanent financing, construct the building, and then manage the building in accordance with tenants' expectations. This is the simple recipe for success. Of course, the devil is often in the details. It is one thing to have the recipe for success, another to successfully execute it.

The market for office buildings is highly cyclical, but rather predictable. The low point of the cycle would normally constitute an excellent time to either develop an office building or buy one that is already built, but in financial trouble. Even outside this office building cycle, there may exist a need for an office building that has not been met in a particular location. Such a situation may offer the investor excellent prospects as well. As with other real estate investments, the life cycle of an office building from an investor's perspective goes through an acquisition stage, a holding stage, and a disposal stage.

Where an office building does not currently exist, the acquisition phase will involve finding a suitable piece of land, doing a feasibility analysis, and lining up the financing. In these instances the property must be suitable both in terms of a location that will be attractive to tenants and in compliance with local zoning and environmental laws. The feasibility study attempts to reconcile the costs of construction with the potential tenant demand both in terms of the numbers of tenants and prevailing market rental rates. Financing typically involves both a con-

379

struction loan and permanent financing. Lenders often require preliminary leasing commitments from creditworthy tenants.

Success in developing office buildings is driven by the desirability of the location, the skill with which the building is managed and the financial strength of the project owner. Attracting and retaining tenants is the key to financial stability. The competition for attracting and retaining tenants occurs on the basis of the location and utility of the office building. Unlike shopping centers where issues of critical mass and synergy among center tenants is critical, prospective tenants focus on the extent to which a given office building meets their needs in terms of its location, amenities, design, layout, prestige, and cost.

The architect often plays a critical role in the development of an office building. The architect function is to develop a plan that will create a building that looks attractive and is designed to maximize the use of space, thus resulting in the most potential dollar of revenue relative to cost. Architects should generally be involved as early as possible in the acquisition phase.

Local zoning ordinances often play the critical role in determining the suitability of a property for use as an office building. To promote the general welfare, zoning ordinances are generally delegated to local government by the state. Ordinances must generally be consistent with a comprehensive land-use plan and not result in an unconstitutional restriction on the use of the land. Such general goals and constraints generate plenty of gray areas where differing interpretations of the law is possible. Zoning ordinances regulate the use of land with respect to building height, size, shape, density, placement, and the designated purpose of the land. These ordinances usually differentiate between permitted uses (established as a "right") and conditional uses, which allow for a range of special conditions. Where a building type or use was established prior to the zoning regulations, such nonconforming uses are typically "grandfathered" in and may, or may not, be continued indefinitely.

Where a property considered for an intended office building is apparently not consistent with existing zoning laws—a frequent situation—developers may apply for variance to the zoning law. However, variances are often difficult and expensive to secure. A better approach to this problem is to seek a zoning amendment and submit the application as a conforming use in that context.

A variety of other issues must also be considered in the development of an office building:

- **Design.** A community may often have strong feelings about appearance, construction material and site layout. The requisite approvals from a variety of municipal agencies may be sensitive to the issue of community acceptance of the property design.

■ **Use Intensity.** This is often expressed by the ratio of floor space to the area of the site. The FAR (floor-area ratio) is often addressed in zoning standards.

■ **Access and Circulation.** The intended office building must effectively be integrated into existing traffic flows as well as having a safe and efficient traffic flow of its own.

■ **Traffic Generation.** The impact of the proposed office building on existing traffic patterns is often a point of contention with the local community. Traffic features such as convenience, ease of access, and quality of roads, are often the focus of community concerns about the maintenance of those features.

■ **Parking.** Office buildings must have ample parking to satisfy both the desires of their prospective tenants, the concerns of local residents, and the requirements of zoning ordinances.

■ **Sewer and Water Availability.** Local sewer and water facilities may be at or close to capacity requiring costly investments in infrastructure. This issue may be formally addressed by the municipal government through the imposition of "impact" fees, or the developer may have to fund such facilities as are necessary to make the project feasible.

■ **Environmental Considerations.** Environmental considerations increasingly impinge on land development processes. Environmental considerations would include any relevant natural features of the site (wetlands, floodplains, endangered species, etc.) as well as the more general impact variables covered by clean air, clean water, and environmental hazard regulation.

■ **Disability Accommodations.** The Americans with Disabilities Act (ADA) requires that facilities such as office buildings be accessible and usable by persons with disabilities. This means public entrances such as sidewalks, parking, and meeting places must not have barriers to disabled individuals.

After the office building has been constructed the holding period phase begins. At this point, an investor may continue to be active, functioning as the property manager, or he or she may chose to hire an outside property management firm. Functions that must be carried out during this phase include marketing and leasing activities, maintenance, and security responsibilities. In addition, the occasional services of lawyers and accountants are required throughout this phase.

The disposal of an office building by an investor may come early or later in the life cycle of an office building depending on the objectives of the investor. Disposal could involve selling the building or refinancing to take cash out of an appreciated facility. However, holding the office building long term is often undesirable due to the reduction of tax advantages, such as interest and depreciation shields, that decrease over time.

THE OFFICE BUILDING LIFE CYCLE

Unlike the market for crude petroleum or pork bellies, which are both volatile and unpredictable, the market for office buildings is volatile— and predictable. This later characteristic affords investors who understand the office building market to avail themselves of some very nice risk return outcomes. The office building market is predictable because it has its own internal logic resulting from four separate forces: (1) the national (or regional) business cycle; (2) the local office building life cycle; (3) changes in the preferred geographical location of office buildings; and (4) changes in industrial structure and work mode. The interaction of these four forces creates predictable waves of boom and bust in the market for office space. Since World War II additions to office space have occurred in a series of surges punctuated by low additions to office space.

There was a huge surge in office buildings constructed in the period from 1983 through 1989.[1] This surge created an excess supply of office buildings in many areas and drove down rents to the point where numerous office buildings were placed in receivership with ownership reverting to their creditors. This excess capacity had been largely worked through by 2003 and a new surge in office building appears to be underway.

THE INTERACTION OF THE BUSINESS CYCLE EFFECT AND THE OFFICE-BUILDING LIFE CYCLE

During periods of economic recovery and boom, businesses need more space to conduct their growing operations and the general increase in prosperity tempts businesses to utilize more space per worker. To the extent that vacant space exists at the beginning of a recovery, this increasing demand will not drive up rents. Vacancy rates fall as the economic cycle progresses and businesses increasingly demand more office space. The change in the stage of the business cycle will set the office-building life cycle in motion.

As vacant office space becomes more difficult to find, rents begin to rise. The vacant space in Class A buildings is the first to fill up and some

---

[1] Builders Owners and Managers Association (BOMA), *Property Management* (Washington, DC: Real Estate Education Company, 1991).

of this demand is diverted to vacant space in Class B and C buildings. The need for additional office space becomes more urgent and rents begin to rise dramatically as businesses bid up the existing supply of office space. Rents quickly rise to a level where developing new offices becomes highly profitable. Developers then initiate a new round of office building construction. Since there is at least a two-year time lag between when a building is envisioned and when it becomes available for occupancy, before the new buildings can be completed, rents may soar to very high levels. Once the new buildings begin to hit the market, the pressure on rents will begin to abate. As long as businesses are in an expansionary mode, however, rents continue to increase as supply lags behind demand.

This situation continues to the top of the boom, at which time business no longer need additional space. At this point, the office buildings still in the pipeline continue to come onto the market as they are completed. Because there is no additional demand, supply will exceed demand and rents begin to fall. If the increase in the amount of space coming into the market is large and this coincides with a recession where businesses are cutting back, the fall in rents will be dramatic. Under these conditions, there is excess office space on the market that is not being utilized. Rents will stay depressed until businesses begin to recover and the process starts over again.

Thy cyclical pattern in office building is exacerbated by a "herd" effect among the institutions typically supplying capital to the office construction industry. When rents are high, vacancy rates are low and absorption rates high. Investment money then pours into the industry igniting a feeding frenzy of building. Insurance companies, REITS and pension funds join the rush. When vacancy rates rise and absorption rates fall, the exit of a major lender signals the withdrawal of all from the market. It is as if a water spigot was turned off. At the bottom of the cycle, with rents looking weak and recently built office buildings in default, lenders are nowhere to be found.

This pattern, of alternating periods of excess supply and excess demand, constitutes the office-building life cycle. This pattern has shown great stability throughout the 19th and 20th centuries. Economists refer to this phenomenon as a "cobweb" supply-and-demand pattern resulting from the lag in change in supplies to changes in demand. One attractive strategy in reacting to the existence of this cycle is to begin building when the market is awash in excess office space (because, when no one else is building, all material and service inputs will be cheaper). By the time the market consumes the excess supply, your buildings will be coming "on line," ready to benefit from the situation of escalating rents. Conversely, this line of reasoning suggests withdrawing from the market when there is a clear shortage of office space because, by the time your buildings are ready to come to the market, the situation will be one of excess supply and falling rents.

This business cycle effect can be either national or regional. In the 1980s, the national economy was expanding, but the economy in the Midwest "rust belt" declined; meanwhile the economy of the Southwest boomed with the earliest arrival of the baby boom "snowbirds." It is not unusual for the regional economic situation to be contrary to the national trend. Whether the dominant effect on a particular market for office building space is national or local, the overall impact of the business cycle effect will play a significant role in the market for office buildings.

CHANGES IN THE GEOGRAPHICAL LOCATION OF OFFICE BUILDINGS

Throughout most of the 20th century, office buildings tended to be located in the urban core. This reflected synergism rising from the physical proximity of different offices (i.e., banks could locate next to lawyers and insurance companies), the existence of agglomeration economies resulting from location in the same area (i.e., an infrastructure developed to support office workers), ease of access supported at first by public transportation systems and later by an efficient network of highways. Offices were downtown; workers lived in the suburbs. Towards the end of the 20th century, the advantages of synergism and agglomeration became less important due to increased communication and logistical efficiencies and the increased traffic found in most urban areas significantly increased the cost of transportation. Companies frequently found it more efficient to join their workers in the suburbs, either in office parks or scattered about as determine by zoning laws and the availability of land.

For reasons of historical legacy, community commitment, or prestige, the urban core will most likely remain important locations for many office facilities. Nevertheless, despite the continued importance of the urban core for office locations, the bulk of the growth in new office buildings is likely to be in the suburbs. The primary factor in determining the location pattern of office buildings in suburban locations is largely determined by the desire of communities expressed through their regional economic plans and zoning ordinances. Some communities appear to prefer clustering office buildings to more efficiently provide them with the necessary public services. Other communities appear to prefer to disburse office buildings throughout the area to avoid the negative externalities associated (heavy traffic, dense populations) with large office complexes.

Which pattern is most likely to prevail? This depends on the experiences communities continue to have with office building development. There is a learning curve here. Probably it will not be a matter of "one size fits all." Office location will more likely be a hodgepodge affair, resulting from communities responding to the imperative of a particular set of needs at a particular time. This situation creates a wide array of opportunities for investors.

CHANGES IN INDUSTRIAL STRUCTURE AND WORK MODE

The demand for office space is much affected by the industrial shifts in a dynamic, fluid economy. The latest economic data indicated an increase in paid employees in the Finance Insurance and Real Estate Industries of 12.4% between 1992 and 1997. In the same period, service workers increased a smashing 31%. In contrast, manufacturing employment only increased 3.6%. In 1997, there were 33 million workers in the Finance, Insurance and Real Estate and Service industries, 32% of the all paid workers.[2]

This shift away from factory jobs to office jobs has been a major factor in the increasing demand for office space. Furthermore, it appears that the nature of office work requires more space and higher quality space (i.e., wireless offices or, at least, offices wired for more and better communication facilities such as broadband connectivity). Whether this trend continues is a matter of conjecture. The continued aging of the baby boomers population will no doubt spawn an increasing demand for physician's offices, MRI centers, and the like. An offsetting trend has been the tendency of American business firms to outsource some of their office work to overseas companies (e.g., insurance claims to Ireland, computer programming to India).

An additional factor in the demand for office space has been the changing nature of officework itself. With cellphones so inexpensive and high-speed Internet service so widely available, some workers have been largely freed from the need to work in the office. In some companies, the office has increasingly become a place to gather for meetings rather than actually sit down and do the work. To what extent this trend becomes important in determining the need for office space is also uncertain.

---

[2] Bureau of the Census, *Census of Economic Activity* (Washington, DC: Government Printing Office, 1992).

TYPES OF OFFICE BUILDINGS

Trophy Buildings

A single tenant, willing to pay more for a unique shape and floor plans, unusual building design, and an outstanding location, is typically attracted to "trophy buildings." Such buildings are characterized by the best quality of materials and workmanship and enjoy top-quality maintenance and management. Examples of such buildings include the PPG headquarters building in Pittsburgh and the Bank of America headquarters in San Francisco. Such buildings are always considered Class A.

Character Buildings

Character buildings are typically smaller office buildings (less than 10 floors) that are created by an investor or developer to display a sense of personal accomplishment. Such buildings are typically named after that investor or developer and are intended to stand as a monument to his or her accomplishments. Such buildings are normally well constructed, well located, and well maintained, but are not constructed on as lavish a scale, as trophy buildings. Character buildings may be either Class A or Class B.

Class A

Class A buildings generally constitute the best buildings available in a given market. Such buildings are well located, attractive, and well maintained, and considered highly desirable by prospective tenants. They feature excellent elevators, mechanical systems and air control systems. Class A office buildings are frequently occupied by high-quality, prestigious tenants.

Class B

Class B buildings are constructed along utilitarian lines using standard construction techniques to create as much rentable space as possible for a given cost. The design and layout of such buildings would be considered adequate, but is primarily functional in nature. These buildings also feature adequate elevators, mechanical systems, and air-control systems. Maintenance services and building management are average.

Class C

Class C office buildings are typically unrefurbished older buildings or older buildings with limited refurbishment. Their location may be inferior. Building maintenance may be substandard. Mechanical, heating, and air-conditioning systems may have problems. The building tenants are noticeably inferior to those found in higher-class buildings and in less-desirable areas.

FINANCING THE OFFICE BUILDING

The process of developing an office building begins with a financial commitment from the investor/developer. While occasionally office buildings are financed with 100% equity, the norm is to use bridge financing and a permanent mortgage to gain a degree of financial leverage. The financial terms available to the investor/developer in this industry vary with the office-building life cycle. Generally, borrowers must be able to demonstrate their competence, skill and expertise in developing office buildings or similar projects. A further general prerequisite for debt financing would be preleasing agreement from prospective tenants for 50% to 90% of the proposed space.

Prior to the spectacular boom and bust of the 1980s and 1990s financing would typically be developed through a forward funding facility where a pension fund, insurance company, commercial bank, or savings and loan would commit to a developer for a 30-year fixed rate loan. This would be advanced upon satisfactory completion of the construction phase and upon reaching a specified level of leasing. Another bank would fund the construction advancing funds in stages as construction was completed. The bank providing the construction loan often insisted on a take out provision from the provider of permanent funds insuring that long-term funding would actually take place. Volatility, in both the rental market and the monetary market, has resulted in a blurring of these responsibilities. Many construction loans today extend to five years and many permanent loans have five- to 10-year terms to maturity.

In the construction phase when bridge financing in the form of a construction loan or short-term loan is being used, the lender will want an equity contribution of 25% to 35% of the cost of construction. In addition, the lender will demand a net worth requirement of the project owner equal to the size of the construction loan and total assets on the balance sheet four to eight times the loan size. The borrowers would normally be expected to sign personally, as well as corporately, for the loan.

Permanent long-term mortgage loans would normally follow on the completion and successful inauguration of the office facility. Financial institutions that make office building mortgages frequently are interested in taking equity in the project, once it is established. Prospective lenders to this market generally do not go above a 75% loan-to-value ratio, while 60% may be preferred if the office building market is not healthy. Experience at foreclosure has taught many lenders that relaying on the "collateral" value of a building does not necessarily secure their loan. If the bottom falls out of the office building market, which it certainly did in the 1990s, what was previously a valuable building may suddenly become a lot less valuable as its ability to produce income falls.

Consequently, many lenders look to second criteria of project feasibility—the *debt service coverage ratio* (DSCR). This ratio is calculated as loan principle and interest divided by EBDIT (earnings before depreciation, interest, and taxes) and thus yields a measure of the capacity of the project to service its loan. Even at the most heady stages of the office building life cycle, lenders would want to see this rate being at least 120%. In less promising circumstances, lender requirements may range up to 150%. In the darkest part of the office life cycle, lenders may be so disheartened that funds would not be forthcoming under any circumstances.

Office Building Appraisals

Prior to the *1989 Financial Institutions Reform Recovery and Enforcement Act* (FIRREA), a great deal of variability was possible in the appraisal process even when the appraisers were *members of the Appraisal Institute* (MAI). Title IX of FRREA required a more consistent and rigorous approach to the appraisal than had been common. Value appraisal must now be completely supported by a thorough analysis of the relevant supply-and-demand factors. General appraisal methodology requires three valuations for a development project. An "as-is" value where the property is unimproved, the value at stabilization, and the value at completion. Lenders tend to focus on the value at completion— this approach takes the operating income (the difference between first-year income and expenses) and capitalizes it at 100 basis points over the estimated highest discount rate applied throughout the office building life cycle.

This methodology represents a conservative approach to valuation that may create an artificially low estimate of market value. The reality is that appraisers do not determine value; appraisers only generate an opinion of value. Nevertheless, this approach may result in an unnecessary constraint upon the ability of investors in office buildings to use financial leverage.

ILLUSTRATION #1: THE MARCO BUILDING WITH GOOD DEMAND—SMALL OFFICE BUILDING CONVERSION

Acquisition Phase

Along a well-developed suburban highway strip in a large metropolitan area, Mr. Marco, a successful restaurant proprietor, noticed that a property had become available about a mile from his restaurant. The property consisted of an acre with a single-family residence that had been converted 10 years ago into a two story building the bottom floor of which was occupied by a now defunct bicycle shop and the top floor had been converted into three apartments. The building contained about 20,000 sq. ft. (10,000 sq. ft. on each floor) of leasing space. Mr. Marco was familiar with the location and knew the immediate area to be densely populated by middle-class families and that this highway increasingly served as a transportation corridor for new upper-middle income residents locating in nearby undeveloped areas.

The property was on the market for $800,000 and the general consensus by local businessmen was that the property was overpriced. The value of the land was estimated to be $500,000, the value of the improvements $300,000. Most of the properties on this highway were mixed retail, fast food or restaurants. Very few office sites were available in this part of town and they normally went at a premium. Mr. Marco knew the rental market in the overall metropolitan area was coming off a period of significant excess supply, which had created excess office space and depressed rentals. However, he thought this particular area proved an exception to the general state of the market.

Mr. Marco secured a 6-month option on the property with a price of $800,000 for $10,000. During the six-month period, he investigated and resolved some zoning issues affecting the property, secured the services of an architect, and settled on a building design. He found a contractor who would remodel this building according to the new design for $250,000. With a concrete floor plan in hand, he found two medical practices, that were eager to lease the bottom floor for $20 per square foot, and two dentists and a real estate agency that were willing to lease the top floor of the building for $17 per square foot. The leases were all triple-net pass-throughs with an annual 3% escalation clause. With committed leases of $370,000 per year, Mr. Marco, now an investor/developer, purchased the land for $200,000 cash and an 8%, $600,000 five-year annual loan payment amortized at 20 years from a local savings and loan (with a resultant annual payment of $61,111). Having obtained ownership of the property, Mr. Marco secured a 9% (with 5 points), $250,000 interest-only, three-year construction loan. The loan was secured with the property and his personal signature. Mr. Marco felt a great deal of pride in his approach to this office building as a financier and developer and consequently planned to name it the "Marco Building."

The result of these expenses, Mr. Marco experiences a net outflow of cash of about $500,000 during the first two years of the project. This may be seen in Table 15.1.

TABLE 15.1 Small Office Building Conversion, Acquisition Period Cash Flows

Item	Year 1	Year 2
Land option price	$10,000	
Architectural services	50,000	
Equity in land	200,000	
Accounting and legal expenses	50,000	$10,000
Mortgage payment (land)	61,111	61,111
Interest	48,000	46,951
Principal	13,111	14,160
Construction loan interest	35,000	22,500
Total cash flows out	406,111	93,611

Holding Period Phase

Upon satisfactory completion of the building, evidence of tenant stability (which is why the construction loan had a term of three years), and a DCR ratio of 1.2, the savings and loan would take out the construction loan and land mortgage with an $850,000, 15-year fully amortized mortgage with an 8.5% rate. As the completed property had a value of $1,050,000 ($800,000 land and improvements plus $250,000 in conversion costs), Mr. Marco contributed net equity of $200,000 plus other expenses. The resultant principal and interest payment would be $102,357 on the improved property.

After obtaining the necessary clearances, permits, and site preparation, the actual construction took 18 months. During this period, Mr. Marco maintained an active dialogue with the contractor to ensure that the construction process yielded the intended result. Because the architect had done his job well, there were no change orders and the building came in on target. Two years after taking of the property option, Mr. Marco was able to get his new tenants installed. Mr. Marco then hired a professional property manager for $500 per month.

As can be seen from Table 15.2, NOPAT was positive throughout the holding period rising from $209,669 to $270,629. Net income performs similarly, rising from $166,319 to $246,858 (Tables 15.3). It should be noted that the project substantially exceeded the required 1.2 DCR ratio throughout its holding period (Table 15.3).

Disposal Stage

Following a holding period of 10 years, Mr. Marco wished to pursue other interests and sells the building for eight times earnings (net income) or $1,975,000. Office buildings in town normally sell for between five to

TABLE 15.2 Small Office Building Conversion, Holding Period NOPAT, Net-Operating Profits after Taxes

Year	Revenues	Property Management Fee[a]	Legal and Accounting Expenses[a]	Depreciation[b]	EBIT	Taxes (40%)	NOPAT EBIT$(1 - tx)$
1	$370,000	$6,000	$7,500	$7,051	$349,449	$139,779	$209,669
2	381,100	6,180	7,725	14,103	353,092	141,237	211,855
3	392,533	6,365	7,957	14,103	364,108	145,643	218,465
4	404,309	6,556	8,195	14,103	375,454	150,182	225,273
5	416,438	6,753	8,441	14,103	387,141	154,856	232,285
6	428,931	6,956	8,695	14,103	399,178	159,671	239,507
7	441,799	7,164	8,955	14,103	411,577	164,631	246,946
8	455,053	7,379	9,224	14,103	424,347	169,739	254,608
9	468,705	7,601	9,501	14,103	437,501	175,000	262,500
10	482,766	7,829	9,786	14,103	451,049	180,419	270,629

[a] Increases reflect a 3% escalation clause.
[b] The depreciable basis would consist of the original building ($300,000) plus improvements ($250,000) over 39 years.

TABLE 15.3 Small Office Building Conversion, Conventional Financing, Income Statement

Year	Revenues[a]	Property Management Fee[a]	Legal and Accounting Expenses[a]	Interest[b]	Depreciation	Earnings before Taxes	Taxes (40%)	Net Income	DCR Ratio[c]
1	$370,000	$6,000	$7,500	$72,250	$7,051	$277,199	$110,879	$166,319	3.41
2	381,100	6,180	7,725	69,691	14,103	283,401	113,360	170,041	3.45
3	392,533	6,365	7,957	66,914	14,103	297,194	118,877	178,316	3.56
4	404,309	6,556	8,195	63,902	14,103	311,553	124,621	186,932	3.67
5	416,438	6,753	8,441	60,633	14,103	326,508	130,603	195,905	3.78
6	428,931	6,956	8,695	57,086	14,103	342,092	136,837	205,255	3.90
7	441,799	7,164	8,955	53,238	14,103	358,338	143,335	215,003	4.02
8	455,053	7,379	9,224	49,063	14,103	375,284	150,114	225,170	4.15
9	468,705	7,601	9,501	44,533	14,103	392,968	157,187	235,781	4.27
10	482,766	7,829	9,786	39,618	14,103	411,431	164,572	246,858	4.41

[a] Increases reflect a 3% escalation clause.
[b] Assumes payments of $102,357 on a 15-year loan of $850,000 at 8.5%.
[c] EBIT/$102,397.

eight times earnings. In the case of the Marco Building the premium price reflected the excellent location and stability of rental history that has characterized this property.

Table 15.4A suggests that the sale price of $1,975,000 generates a tax liability of $158,847 and an after-tax gain of $900,132. Adjusting for pay-downs on the mortgage and equity, the sale of this office building can be seen to produce a cash gain of $1,350,060 (Table 15.4B).

The effect of these cash flows for Mr. Marco, as an investor, is to allow him to realize an NPV of $1,312,092 (Table 15.5). These cash flows also represent an annual return on invested capital of 65%. No doubt this represents a resounding success for Mr. Marco and the Marco Building.

However, this whole analysis presupposes that Mr. Marco has correctly estimated the strength of demand for his office space. As noted above, the market for office rental space in the larger metropolitan area was not good. In this example, the strength of the indicated location proved sufficient to attract tenants despite the presence of less expensive office space nearby. If the doctors and dentists Mr. Marco found as tenants were attracted elsewhere by more favorable lease terms, the investment outcome might be considerably different.

TABLE 15.4A Small Office Building Conversion, Tax Consequences of Sale of Property

Sale of building		$1,975,000
Fixed plant and improvements	$550,000	
Less accumulated depreciation	133,978	
Net fixed plant and improvements		416,022
Cost of land		500,000
Gain on sale		1,058,978
Capital gains tax (15%)		158,847
After-tax gain on sale		900,132

TABLE 15.4B Small Office Building Conversion, Cash Gain from Sale of Property

Sale of property	$1,975,000
Less:	
Tax liability	158,847
Loan balance	466,093
Cash gain from sale	1,350,060

TABLE 15.5 Small Office Building Conversion, Conventional Financing, Cash Flow Statement

Year	Net Income	Depre- ciation	Capital Contri- butions[a]	Initial Cash Flows[b]	Gain on Sale of Land[c]	Net Cash Flows
-2				-$406,111		-$406,111
-1			$200,000	-93,611		-293,611
1	$166,319	$7,051				173,371
2	170,041	14,103				184,144
3	178,316	14,103				192,419
4	186,932	14,103				201,035
5	195,905	14,103				210,008
6	205,255	14,103				219,358
7	215,003	14,103				229,106
8	225,170	14,103				239,273
9	235,781	14,103				249,884
10	246,858	14,103			$1,350,060	1,611,021

[a] $1,050,000 costs less $850,000 loan.
[b] From Table 15.1.
[c] From Table 15.4B.

NPV at 12% = $1,312,092
IRR = 65%

ILLUSTRATION #2: THE MARCO BUILDING UNDER CONDITIONS OF EXCESS SUPPLY

Acquisition Phase

Under this scenario, the cost and financing conditions remain unaltered from the first illustration; but Mr. Marco encounters greater difficulty attracting and retaining tenants due to a large supply of office space on the market. As a result, Mr. Marco is able to attract doctors to the ground floor of his building for a two-year lease that does not pass through maintenance costs or taxes (but does pass through insurance costs) for $12 per square foot with no escalation clause. In addition, Mr. Marco is required to remodel the bottom floor to suit the doctors' needs for $10,000. Mr. Marco is not able to secure any dentists for his top floor, but does attract a real estate office for $10 per square foot and an accountant for $8 per square foot who split the available space. Both of these leases are month-to-month and do not pass through maintenance or property taxes. The doctors prove to be steady tenants over the next several years, but the top floor experiences serious turnover, which results in an average 30% vacancy rate. In the 10th year of the building's life, Mr. Marco again chooses to sell it. Because the Marco Building has experienced a spotty occupancy rate and there is a continued overhang of excess office space in the overall market, Mr. Marco is able to sell the building for only five times earnings.

Holding Period Phase

The first result of these adverse market conditions is to reduce annual revenues to $173,000 over the 10-year holding period (Table 15.6). Moreover, the impact of an abundance of competitive office space prohibits raising rents during this decade. This occurs despite a continuous effort on the part of Mr. Marco to secure better tenants throughout the 10-year holding period. During this period, he is in continuous negotiations with his bank that considers their loan to be jeopardized by the failure of the Marco Building to generate a DCR of 1.2.[3] The bank holds off legal action, as Mr. Marco never falls behind the payment on his mortgage obligations. During this period, NOPAT (Table 15.7) falls from $71,669 to $58,935, while net income rises from $28,319 to $66,800 (the difference being smaller interest payments on the outstanding loan balance). This level of income leaves only a razor-thin margin to protect Mr. Marco from absolute disaster (probably a receivership). Even at this, Mr. Marco considers the return inadequate to cover his efforts and the cost of his invested capital.

Disposal Phase

After a decade of sustained effort and low returns, Mr. Marco is ready to leave the industry. After much additional effort, he is finally able to secure a buyer at a fire sale price of five times earnings (Tables 15.8A and 15.8B). This sale produces a nominal loss of $582,023 on the property, but this is mitigated by a tax credit of $87,303. (Mr. Marco has other, more successful investments that produce sufficient profits to use this loss as a tax shelter.)

The net result of this transaction for Mr. Marco is to produce a negative cash flow of $44,791 (Table 15.8B), as a result of his former equity contributions and payments of principal on his mortgage. The success of the Marco Building—or rather the relative lack of success—can be seen in Table 15.9. With the weaker demand structure, Mr. Marco suffers a net loss of $471,710 and a negative return on his investment of 4% (Table 15.9).

---

[3] The DCR ratio measures the debt capacity of the project (EBIT/interest). See Chapter 2 for a more detailed explanation.

TABLE 15.6 Small Office Building Conversion, Holding Period NOPAT, Under Difficult Market Conditions, Net-Operating Profits after Taxes

Year	Revenues[a]	Property Management Fee[b]	Legal and Accounting Expenses[b]	Property Taxes[b]	Maintenance Costs[b]	Depreciation[c]	EBIT	Taxes (40%)	NOPAT EBIT $(1 - tx)$
1	$173,000	$6,000	$7,500	$18,000	$15,000	$7,051	$119,449	$47,779	$71,669
2	173,000	6,180	7,725	18,540	15,450	14,103	111,002	44,401	66,601
3	173,000	6,365	7,957	19,096	15,914	14,103	109,565	43,826	65,739
4	173,000	6,556	8,195	19,669	16,391	14,103	108,085	43,234	64,851
5	173,000	6,753	8,441	20,259	16,883	14,103	106,561	42,624	63,937
6	173,000	6,956	8,695	20,867	17,389	14,103	104,991	41,996	62,994
7	173,000	7,164	8,955	21,493	17,911	14,103	103,374	41,349	62,024
8	173,000	7,379	9,224	22,138	18,448	14,103	101,708	40,683	61,025
9	173,000	7,601	9,501	22,802	19,002	14,103	99,992	39,997	59,995
10	173,000	7,829	9,786	23,486	19,572	14,103	98,225	39,290	58,935

[a] $11 times 10,000 sq. ft. for doctor offices is $110,000. The second floor produces $10 times 5,000 sq. ft. plus $8 times 5,000 sq. ft. less 30%.

[b] Escalates at 3% per year.

[c] The depreciable basis would consist of the original building ($300,000) plus improvements ($250,000) over 39 years.

TABLE 15.7 Small Office Building Conversion, Under Difficult Market Conditions, Income Statement

Year	Revenues[a]	Property Management Fee[a]	Legal and Accounting Expenses[a]	Interest[b]	Property Taxes[a]	Maintenance Costs[a]	Depreciation	Earnings before Taxes	Taxes (40%)	Net Income
1	$173,000	$6,000	$7,500	$72,250	$18,000	$15,000	$7,051	$47,199	$18,879	$28,319
2	178,190	6,180	7,725	69,691	18,540	15,450	14,103	46,501	18,600	27,901
3	183,536	6,365	7,957	66,914	19,096	15,914	14,103	53,187	21,275	31,912
4	189,042	6,556	8,195	63,902	19,669	16,391	14,103	60,225	24,090	36,135
5	194,713	6,753	8,441	60,633	20,259	16,883	14,103	67,641	27,056	40,585
6	200,554	6,956	8,695	57,086	20,867	17,389	14,103	75,459	30,184	45,275
7	206,571	7,164	8,955	53,238	21,493	17,911	14,103	83,706	33,483	50,224
8	212,768	7,379	9,224	49,063	22,138	18,448	14,103	92,413	36,965	55,448
9	219,151	7,601	9,501	44,533	22,802	19,002	14,103	101,610	40,644	60,966
10	225,726	7,829	9,786	39,618	23,486	19,572	14,103	111,333	44,533	66,800

[a] Increases reflect a 3% escalation clause.
[b] Assumes payments of $102,357 on a 15-year loan of $850,000 at 8.5%.

TABLE 15.8 Small Office Building Conversion, Under Difficult Market Conditions, Tax Consequences of Sale of Property

Sale of building		$333,999
Fixed plant and improvements	$550,000	
Less accumulated depreciation	133,978	
Net fixed plant and improvements		416,022
Cost of land		500,000
Gain on sale		−582,023
Capital gains tax (15%)		−87,303
After-tax gain on sale		−494,720

TABLE 15.8B Small Office Building Conversion, Under Difficult Market Conditions, Cash Gain from Sale of Property

Sale of property	$333,999
Less:	
Tax liability	−87,303
Loan balance	466,093
Cash gain from sale	−44,791

TABLE 15.9 Small Office Building Conversion, Under Difficult Market Conditions, Cash Flow Statement

Year	Net Income	Depre- ciation	Capital Contributions[a]	Initial Cash Flows[b]	Gain on Sale of Land[c]	Net Cash Flows
−2				−$406,111		−$406,111
−1			$210,000	−93,611		−303,611
1	$28,319	$7,051				35,371
2	27,901	14,103				42,004
3	31,912	14,103				46,015
4	36,135	14,103				50,238
5	40,585	14,103				54,688
6	45,275	14,103				59,378
7	50,224	14,103				64,327
8	55,448	14,103				69,551
9	60,966	14,103				75,069
10	66,800	14,103			−$44,791	36,112

[a] $1,050,000 costs less $850,000 loan plus $10,000 remodeling fee.
[b] From Table 15.7.
[c] From Table 15.8B.

NPV at 12% = −$471,710
IRR = −4%

Break-Even Analysis

One way to construct a break-even analysis of the Marco Building would be to cast revenues as a function of dollars of rent per square foot. In the two scenarios of the Marco Building presented so far, in the situation with better demand, Mr. Marco was able to negotiate pass-through, triple-net leases. Where demand was less, the leases required Mr. Marco to pick up the tax and maintenance costs. In the latter case, these become a fixed costs, as they must be incurred whether the building is rented out or not. However, who bears these costs really reflects the strength of demand for the property and thus should properly be included as an offset to rent on the revenue side. Thus revenues will be treated below as net of such expenses. That is, such expenses shall be paid by the tenants and are thus embedded in the rent.

Revenues at the Marco Building are equal to the effective average (allowing for vacancies) rent (R) per square foot times 20,000.

$$TR = R \times 20,000$$

Total fixed costs for the Marco Building would include the property management fee ($6,000), legal and accounting fees ($7,500), and a mortgage payment (P&I) of $102,357. There are no variable costs for the Marco Building. As Mr. Marco has also invested net cash into the project of $210,000 ($200,000 equity on the second loan and $10,000 for the land option), the amortized value of that contribution should be included as a cost. Because the planned holding period is for 10 years, the fully amortized value of $210,000 for 10 years at 12% is annual payment of $37,167 and should be included as a fixed cost.

Therefore,

$$TC = \$153,024$$

so,

$$BEP = TR - TC; = R \times 20,000 - \$153,024$$

Thus BEP for R = $153,024/20,000 = $7.65. Note that this is an *effective rent*, which assumes no vacancies or associated expenses (taxes, insurance, and maintenance). To the extent that such vacancies and expenses occur, the rent will need to be proportionately higher.

As an example, in the situation with the Marco Building where the demand was slack, allowance needs to be taken of the 30% vacancy rate of the second floor and the need to cover taxes and maintenance expenses. This means

$$TR = (10,000 + 10,000 \times (1 - 0.3)) \times R = 17,000 \times R$$

And TC will rise by \$33,000 in the first year (Table 16.6), so

$$TC = \$186,024$$

Therefore,

$$BEP = TR - TC; = R \times 17,000 - \$186,024$$

Thus BEP for $R = \$186,024/17,000 = \$11.01$.

Because Mr. Marco in this scenario is unable to charge this effective level of rent, his investment generates the noted loss (Table 15.9).

ILLUSTRATION #3: THE JOHNSON BUILDING

Alfred Johnson owns a small chain of supermarkets (Al's Superfresh). Together, his six stores generate \$1 million of income per year resulting in a tax bill of \$420,000. His stores are so profitable, and his tax liability so large, because the stores are leaseholds. Alfred wonders if he could construct an office building and use its depreciation to shield some of his income. Alfred also manages his enterprises from leased office space that costs him \$150,000 per year (10,000 sq. ft. at \$12 per square foot and \$30,000 for taxes, insurance, and maintenance). He feels Al's Superfresh offices could use a more prestigious location. He also feels his current rent is too high for the quality of space he is leasing. He wonders if there is a better way.

Acquisition Phase

Bill Thompson, a business acquaintance who is a general contractor and has developed numerous office properties in this region in the past, approaches Alfred. Bill suggests using a three-acre parcel that he has just picked up for \$2 million in a desirable part of town and proposes building a 10-story office building on it. Bill has already done some site work and is working with an architect to develop an office building that would have 100,000 sq. ft. of rentable space. The office building itself would cost \$10 million to build and the property would need another \$3 million to put in the necessary access roads, parking, lighting, and landscaping.

Bill proposes that Alfred develop the building himself. Alfred would provide a majority of the financing, and Bill would convey his real estate parcel to Alfred in exchange for \$250,000 for the land per year after the building is constructed, the right to construct the building, and a "call" on 25% of the building for $1 million during the first five years of the building's life. Bill will cosign on Alfred's loan and Alfred will get a "put" on the building that will allow him to sell all or 75% of the building to Bill in five years for the greater of $14 million or 7 times net income. Alfred also receives the right to lease 10,000 sq. ft. of the building for $10 per square foot triple-net for five years, a rate below the anticipated market for space in that building.

Bill's call allows him to gain some ownership equity at a reasonable price if the building proves highly successful. This will allow Bill to share in the success of the project. Al's put limits his downside risk by giving him an "out," that is, the ability to sell the entire project to Bill at a price approximating the building's cost ($14 million).

Bill makes the proposal in this form because he lacks the funds to finance the project himself and would like the work of building the office for his construction company. Alfred is currently liquid and able to finance the building. If successful, Alfred will experience a gain on his investment, a potential tax shield, and a better location for his offices. Furthermore, Alfred's ability to put the project back to Bill in five years provides him with downside protection. Alfred will also get the naming rights to the building and plans to call it the "Johnson Building."

Alfred and Bill engage a commercial real estate broker in the project. With Al's Superfresh headquarters as the lead tenant, they are able to secure commitments for triple-net leases on the remaining 90,000 sq. ft. for $30 per square foot. Alfred and Bill take the project to a local bank that proves willing to advance a bridge loan for $9 million ($4 million the first year and $5 million the second year) on an interest-only basis for 12% with a two-year takeout by a responsible party. Alfred provides the necessary equity and Bill contributes the $2 million property he owns outright. Alfred and Bill then find an insurance company willing to put up long-term financing of $10 million for 25 years at 11% for the finished property. The insurance company has an AA-rating that satisfies the bank's need for a responsible party.

The resulting cash flows require Alfred to contribute equity in the first year of $1.58 million and $4.130 million in the second year. This may be seen in Table 15.10. Bill's construction company begins the building and brings it in on target successfully after two years.

Holding Period Phase

The office building proves an attractive office site for the area's leading companies that are willing to pay premium rates for the prestigious location. The result is that the Johnson Building can sustain a $30 per square foot rent on a triple-net basis with a 3% escalation clause with only a 5%

TABLE 15.10 Johnson Building Partners, Acquisition Period Cash Flows

Item	Year 1	Year 2
Interest Only Loan Expense[a]	$480,000	$1,080,000
Construction Expenses	5,000,000	8,000,000
Accounting and Legal Expenses	100,000	50,000
Bridge Loan (credit)	(4,000,000)	(5,000,000)
Total Cash Out[b]	1,580,000	4,130,000

[a] On the initial bridge loan of $5 million in the first year and $4 million in the second year.
[b] Bill Townsend contributes $2 million worth of real estate in the first year. Alfred Johnson contributes the residual $1.58 million in the first year and $4.13 million in the second year as equity.

vacancy rate to reflect turnover. This produces a NOPAT that rises from $1.161 million to $1.286 million in the fifth year (Table 15.11). A consequence of this is a net income for Al Johnson that rises from $500,923 to $680,046 (Table 15.12). This generates a ROI for Al Johnson of well under 10% and a ROE only slightly above 10%. This does not represent a very strong financial performance given Al's investment and liability. Further confirmation of this may be found in the DCR that is substantially below two at the Johnson Building. A DCR over two was not required in the loan agreement as was the case for the Marco Building.

Disposal Phase

As a consequence of this lackluster performance, Al decides to exercise his put to Bill for $14 million. (Note that Bill does not exercise his call on 25% of the building at year 4. This could reflect either a lack of funds on Bill's part, or Bill's lack of desire to take ownership in a building only marginally profitable). At any rate, as a consequence of the put, Bill buys back the building from Al for $14 million at the end of five years. This (Table 15.13A) generates an after-tax gain for Al of almost $905,449. After paying off the loan, Al has a cash gain on the sale of $4,765,129 (Table 15.13B).

Table 15.14 indicates the net result for Al of financing this project over two years and the resultant cash flows over five years. The first year's cash flow is $1.051 million compared to net income of $500,923, the difference being the net effect of interest charges and the depreciation cash flow. It should be noted that these cash flows include an "opportunity cost" gain on Al's use of the office building at below-market rents. This differential is further modifies by Al's tax rate because any savings would increase income that would be subject to taxation.

TABLE 15.11 Johnson Office Building, Holding Period NOPAT

Year[a]	Revenues[b]	Property Management Fee[b]	Legal and Accounting Expenses[c]	Building Depreciation[d]	Improvements Depreciation[e]	Land Cost[f]	EBIT	Taxes (40%)	NOPAT EBIT (1 − tx)
1	$2,665,000	$25,000	$25,000	$130,128	$300,000	$250,000	$1,934,872	$773,949	$1,160,923
2	2,741,950	25,750	25,750	260,256	540,000	250,000	1,640,194	656,077	984,116
3	2,821,209	26,523	26,523	260,256	432,000	250,000	1,825,907	730,363	1,095,544
4	2,902,845	27,318	27,318	260,256	345,600	250,000	1,992,352	796,941	1,195,411
5	2,986,930	28,138	28,138	260,256	276,480	250,000	2,143,918	857,567	1,286,351

[a] These are the years when the building is completed, after the initial two years of construction.

[b] Al's Superfresh at 10,000 sq. ft. for $10 per square foot and the remaining $90,000 sq.ft. at $30 per square foot with a 3% escalation clause. The 90,000 sq.ft. is adjusted for a 5% vacancy rate reflecting normal turnover.

[c] Assumed to increase 3% per year.

[d] $10,000,000 plus $150 of capitalized legal and accounting fees depreciated over 39 years using the half-year convention.

[e] Land improvements (streets, blacktop, sidewalk, drainage ditches, etc.) have a recovery period of 15 years and are depreciated 150% double-declining balance using the half-year convention. Double-declining balance is a depreciation method in which double the straight-line depreciation amount is taken the first year, and then that same percentage is applied to the undepreciated amount in subsequent years.

[f] Contract rent to Bill Townsend.

403

TABLE 15.12 Johnson Building, Conventional Financing, Income Statement

Year	Revenues[a]	Property Management Fee[a]	Legal and Accounting Expenses[a]	Interest[b]	Total Depreciation[c]	Land Cost[d]	Earnings before Taxes	Taxes (40%)	Net Income
1	$2,665,000	$25,000	$25,000	$1,100,000	$430,128	$250,000	$834,872	$333,949	$500,923
2	2,744,950	25,750	25,750	1,083,663	800,256	250,000	559,530	223,812	335,718
3	2,827,299	26,523	26,523	1,065,530	692,256	250,000	766,467	306,587	459,880
4	2,912,117	27,318	27,318	1,045,402	605,856	250,000	956,223	382,489	573,734
5	2,999,481	28,138	28,138	1,023,059	536,736	250,000	1,133,410	453,364	680,046

[a] Increases reflect a 3% escalation clause.
[b] Annual payments of $1,248,514 on a 25-year loan at 11%.
[c] The sum of building and improvements depreciation from Table 15.11.
[d] Contract rent to Bill Townsend.

TABLE 15.13A Johnson Building Sale by Put, Tax Consequences of Sale of Property

Sale of building		$14,000,000
Fixed plant and improvements	$13,000,000	
Less accumulated depreciation	3,065,234	
Net fixed plant and improvements		9,934,766
Cost of land		3,000,000
Gain on sale		1,065,234
Capital gains tax (15%)		159,785
After-tax gain on sale		905,449

TABLE 15.13B Johnson Building Sale by Put, Cash Gain from Sale of Property to Alfred Johnson

Sale of property	$14,000,000
Less tax liability from sale (Table 15.13A)	159,785
Loan balance	9,075,086
Cash gain from sale	4,765,129

TABLE 15.14 Johnson Building with Sale by Put, Conventional Financing, Cash Flow Statement

Year	Net Income	Depre-ciation	Capital Contri-butions[a]	Gain on Sale of Land[b]	Rent Savings for Al's Superfresh (adjusted for taxes)[c]	Net Cash Flows
-2			$1,580,000			-$1,580,000
-1			4,130,000			-4,130,000
1	$500,923	$430,128			$120,000	1,051,051
2	335,718	800,256			123,600	1,259,574
3	459,880	692,256			127,308	1,279,445
4	573,734	605,856			131,127	1,310,717
5	680,046	536,736		$4,765,129	135,061	6,116,972

[a] From Table 15.10.
[b] From Table 15.13B.
[c] $(10,000 \text{ sq. ft.} \times (\$30 - \$10)) \times (1 - 0.4)$.

NPV at 12% = $1,002,524
IRR = 18%

These cash flows generate an NPV of $1,002,524 for Al and an IRR of 18%. Such returns might be judged modest in nature. Whether or not they are low relative to Al's investment of time, energy, and financial liability is a judgment call. A lot depends on Al's taste and preference for risk. For even though Al had a put on Bill for the cost of the building, Al has no guarantee that Bill will not default. If Bill or his development company goes into bankruptcy, he would be unable to perform his obligation to buy the building. (It is not uncommon for development companies to go into receivership.) This type of risk is called "counterparty risk."

The alternative to exercising the put would be for Al to continue ownership of the building for a longer holding period. Holding the building over a longer period of time would have the advantage of allowing the escalation clause, in its rents, to work the magic of compound interest and take advantage of the operating leverage in the Johnson Building. As a result, as can be seen from Table 15.15, earnings at the end of 10 years would be almost $1.17 million.

Suppose Al holds the building and sells it for $16 million at that point in time. (Such a sale price would be rather improbable because it would require a price earnings ratio of 14, far outside the normal valuation parameters for buildings of this type). However, such an event is not outside the realm of possibility because other factors (e.g., the desire for ownership at this unique location) may play a role. At any rate, if Al is able to sell the property for $16 million, this will generate an after-tax gain of $4,343,541 (Table 15.16A) and a net cash gain of $7,337,037 (Table 15.16B).

Table 15.17 reveals that the resultant cash flows from the 10-year holding period yield an NPV of $3.201 million and an IRR of 22%. This represents a substantial improvement in return. Whether this gain is worth an additional five years of exposure to the vagaries of the real estate market again depends on Al's taste and preference for risk.

Note that if the building sells for only six times earnings (not at all an unrealistic possibility if the local rental market has been deteriorating), Al will encounter an after-tax loss on the sale of $3,312,353 (even with a tax credit of $584,533) as can be seen from Table 15.18A. The result of this loss will be a net cash outflow of $318,856 (Table 15.18B).

The resulting cash flows in Table 15.19 produce an NPV of $1,236,114 and an IRR of 17%. Thus, although the NPV and IRR are lower than when the building is able to be sold for 14 times earnings, it is not a disaster. NPV remains positive and the IRR significantly above the cost of capital. This reflects the relative unimportance of a lump-sum gain 10 years out, compared to the steadily increasing income throughout the 10-year holding period.

TABLE 15.15 Johnson Building, 10-Year Holding Period, Income Statement

Year	Revenues[a]	Property Management Fee[a]	Legal and Accounting Expenses[a]	Interest[b]	Total Depreciation[c]	Land Cost[d]	Earnings before Taxes	Taxes (40%)	Net Income
1	$2,665,000	$25,000	$25,000	$1,100,000	$430,128	$250,000	$834,872	$333,949	$500,923
2	2,744,950	25,750	25,750	1,083,663	800,256	250,000	559,530	223,812	335,718
3	2,827,299	26,523	26,523	1,065,530	692,256	250,000	766,467	306,587	459,880
4	2,912,117	27,318	27,318	1,045,402	605,856	250,000	956,223	382,489	573,734
5	2,999,481	28,138	28,138	1,023,059	536,736	250,000	1,133,410	453,364	680,046
6	3,089,465	28,982	28,982	998,259	481,440	250,000	1,301,802	520,721	781,081
7	3,182,149	29,851	29,851	970,731	437,204	250,000	1,464,512	585,805	878,707
8	3,277,614	30,747	30,747	940,175	401,814	250,000	1,624,131	649,652	974,478
9	3,375,942	31,669	31,669	906,258	373,503	250,000	1,782,843	713,137	1,069,706
10	3,477,221	32,619	32,619	868,610	350,853	250,000	1,942,518	777,007	1,165,511

[a] Increases reflect a 3% escalation clause.
[b] Assumes payments of $102,357 on a 15-year loan of $850,000 at 8.5%.
[c] The sum of building and improvements depreciation from Table 15.11.
[d] Contract rent to Bill Townsend.

TABLE 15.16A   Johnson Building, 10-Year Holding Period, Tax Consequences of Sale of Property

Sale of building		$16,000,000
Fixed plant and improvements	$13,000,000	
Less accumulated depreciation	5,110,048	
Net fixed plant and improvements		7,889,952
Cost of land		3,000,000
Gain on sale		5,110,048
Capital gains tax (15%)		766,507
After-tax gain on sale		4,343,541

TABLE 15.16B   Johnson Building, 10-Year Holding Period, Cash Gain from Sale of Property to Alfred Johnson

Sale of property	$16,000,000
Less tax liability from sale (Table 15.16A)	766,507
Loan balance	7,896,455
Cash gain from sale	$7,337,037

TABLE 15.17   Johnson Building, Ten-Year Holding Period, Cash Flow Statement

Year	Net Income	Depre-ciation	Capital Contri-butions[a]	Gain on Sale of Land[b]	Rent Savings for Al's Superfresh (adjusted for taxes)[c]	Net Cash Flows
-2			$1,580,000			-$1,580,000
-1			4,130,000			-4,130,000
1	$500,923	$430,128			$120,000	1,051,051
2	335,718	800,256			123,600	1,259,574
3	459,880	692,256			127,308	1,279,445
4	573,734	605,856			131,127	1,310,717
5	680,046	536,736			135,061	1,351,843
6	781,081	481,440			139,113	1,401,634
7	878,707	437,204			143,286	1,459,197
8	974,478	401,814			147,585	1,523,877
9	1,069,706	373,503			152,012	1,595,221
10	1,165,511	350,853		$7,337,037	156,573	9,009,975

[a] From Table 15.14.
[b] From Table 15.16B.
[c] (10,000 sq. ft. $\times$ ($30 - $10)) $\times$ (1 - 0.4).

NPV at 12% = $3,201,191
IRR = 22%

TABLE 15.18A Johnson Building, 10-Year Holding Period, Tax Consequences of Sale of Property

Sale of building		$6,993,066
Fixed plant and improvements	$13,000,000	
Less accumulated depreciation	5,110,048	
Net fixed plant and improvements		7,889,952
Cost of land		3,000,000
Gain on sale		–3,896,886
Capital gains tax (15%)		–584,533
After-tax gain on sale		–3,312,353

TABLE 15.18B Johnson Building, 10-Year Holding Period, Cash Gain from Sale of Property to Alfred Johnson

Sale of property	$6,993,066
Less tax liability from sale (Table 15.18A)	–584,533
Loan balance	7,896,455
Cash gain from sale	–318,856

TABLE 15.19 Johnson Building, 10-Year Holding Period, Cash Flow Statement

Year	Net Income	Depreciation	Capital Contributions[a]	Gain on Sale of Land[b]	Rent Savings for Al's Superfresh (adjusted for taxes)[c]	Net Cash Flows
–2			$1,580,000			–$1,580,000
–1			4,130,000			–4,130,000
1	$500,923	$430,128			$120,000	1,051,051
2	335,718	800,256			123,600	1,259,574
3	459,880	692,256			127,308	1,279,445
4	573,734	605,856			131,127	1,310,717
5	680,046	536,736			135,061	1,351,843
6	781,081	481,440			139,113	1,401,634
7	878,707	437,204			143,286	1,459,197
8	974,478	401,814			147,585	1,523,877
9	1,069,706	373,503			152,012	1,595,221
10	1,165,511	350,853		–$318,856	156,573	1,354,081

[a] From Table 15.17.
[b] From Table 15.18B.
[c] (10,000 sq. ft. × ($30 – $10)) × (1 – 0.4).

NPV at 12% = $1,236,114
IRR = 17.37%

The effect of a longer holding period may be seen more clearly in Table 15.20, the income statement for the Johnson Building for 20 years. Net income is seen to rise to $2.343 million by the 20th year. This reflects the continued decline in interest payments, the continued decline in the depreciation of property improvements and the combination of operating leverage and continually increasing rentals.

Assuming the building is sold in its 20th year for six times earnings ($14,059,278), Al will make an after-tax profit of $5,214,133 on the Johnson Building (Table 15.21A). This profit will convert to a cash gain of $11,595,434 on the transaction (Table 15.21B).

The results of the pattern of cash flows over the 20-year period depicted in Table 15.22 yields the owner of the Johnson Building an NPV of $5,377,877 and an IRR of 23%. This is a more satisfactory return, but the increased length of the holding period suggests a loss of liquidity and an increased exposure to the vagaries of the office building market that might not offset this increased return. Again, the investment decision should reflect Al Johnson's tastes and preferences for risk.

Exercising Bill Thompson's Call

The contract between Al Johnson and Bill Thompson featured a call option on the part of Bill Thompson for 25% of the equity in the Johnson Building. In the context of this illustration so far, this option was never exercised because the investment was not sufficiently attractive.

However, it is possible that exercising this option would prove attractive under conditions of a stronger market for office space. If the office space at the Johnson Building were to rent at a premium $45 per square foot after four years—the exercise period for Mr. Thompson—NOPAT would be $2.041 million (Table 15.23) and net income (Table 15.24) would be $1.415 million. Under conditions of strong demand it would be reasonable to value the office building at 10 times earnings resulting in a sale price of $14,145,872 (Table 15.25A). The sale of the property at the price is seen to generate a net gain of $4.541 million. Therefore, it would be profitable for Bill Thompson to exercise his $1 million option and reap an immediate paper profit of $135,000.

Break-Even Analysis

The best way to analyze the Johnson Building from a break-even perspective would be to cast revenues as a function of dollars of rent per square foot. As with most real estate, the majority of the costs of the Johnson Building will be fixed (that is, will not vary with rent). Variations in demand will drive the economic viability of all office buildings. In the illustrations above, taxes, insurance, and maintenance costs were

TABLE 15.20 Johnson Building, 20-Year Holding Period, Income Statement

Year	Revenues[a]	Property Management Fee[a]	Legal and Accounting Expenses[a]	Interest[b]	Total Depreciation[c]	Land Cost[d]	Earnings before Taxes	Taxes (40%)	Net Income
1	$2,665,000	$25,000	$25,000	$1,100,000	$430,128	$250,000	$834,872	$333,949	$500,923
2	2,744,950	25,750	25,750	1,083,663	800,256	250,000	559,530	223,812	335,718
3	2,827,299	26,523	26,523	1,065,530	692,256	250,000	766,467	306,587	459,880
4	2,912,117	27,318	27,318	1,045,402	605,856	250,000	956,223	382,489	573,734
5	2,999,481	28,138	28,138	1,023,059	536,736	250,000	1,133,410	453,364	680,046
6	3,089,465	28,982	28,982	998,259	481,440	250,000	1,301,802	520,721	781,081
7	3,182,149	29,851	29,851	970,731	437,204	250,000	1,464,512	585,805	878,707
8	3,277,614	30,747	30,747	940,175	401,814	250,000	1,624,131	649,652	974,478
9	3,375,942	31,669	31,669	906,258	373,503	250,000	1,782,843	713,137	1,069,706
10	3,477,221	32,619	32,619	868,610	350,853	250,000	1,942,518	777,007	1,165,511
11	3,581,537	33,598	33,598	826,821	332,734	250,000	2,104,787	841,915	1,262,872
12	3,688,983	34,606	34,606	780,434	318,238	250,000	2,271,099	908,440	1,362,659
13	3,799,653	35,644	35,644	728,946	306,642	250,000	2,442,777	977,111	1,465,666
14	3,913,642	36,713	36,713	671,793	297,365	250,000	2,621,058	1,048,423	1,572,635

TABLE 15.20 (Continued)

Year	Revenues[a]	Property Management Fee[a]	Legal and Accounting Expenses[a]	Interest[b]	Total Depreciation[c]	Land Cost[d]	Earnings before Taxes	Taxes (40%)	Net Income
15	$4,031,052	$37,815	$37,815	$608,354	$289,943	$250,000	$2,807,125	$1,122,850	$1,684,275
16	4,151,983	38,949	38,949	537,936	379,003	250,000	2,907,145	1,162,858	1,744,287
17	4,276,543	40,118	40,118	459,773	260,256	250,000	3,226,278	1,290,511	1,935,767
18	4,404,839	41,321	41,321	373,011	260,256	250,000	3,438,929	1,375,572	2,063,357
19	4,536,984	42,561	42,561	276,706	260,256	250,000	3,664,900	1,465,960	2,198,940
20	4,673,094	43,838	43,838	169,807	260,256	250,000	3,905,355	1,562,142	2,343,213

[a] Increases reflect a 3% escalation clause.
[b] Assumes payments of $102,357 on a 15-year loan of $850,000 at 8.5%.
[c] The sum of building and improvements depreciation from Table 15.11.
[d] Contract rent to Bill Townsend.

TABLE 15.21   Johnson Building, 20-Year Holding Period, Tax Consequences of Sale of Property

Sale of building		$14,059,278
Fixed plant and improvements	$13,000,000	
Less accumulated		
depreciation	8,074,996	
Net fixed plant and improvements		4,925,004
Cost of land		3,000,000
Gain on sale		6,134,274
Capital gains tax (15%)		920,141
After-tax gain on sale		5,214,133

TABLE 15.21B   Johnson Building, 20-Year Holding Period, Cash Gain from Sale of Property to Alfred Johnson

Sale of property	$14,059,278
Less tax liability from sale	920,141
Loan balance	1,543,703
Cash gain from sale	$11,595,434

passed through to the tenants by the leases so these costs will not be construed as fixed in the following analysis.

Revenues at the Johnson Building are equal to 95% (allowing for vacancies) of 90,000 sq. ft. times the rent. A fixed component of revenue will be the 10,000 sq. ft. of space allocated to Al's Superfresh at $10 per square foot.

$$TR = (R \times 0.95 \times 90,000) + 100,000$$

Total fixed costs for the Johnson Building would include the property management fee ($25,000), legal and accounting fees ($25,000) and a mortgage payment (P&I) of $1,248,518. There are no variable costs for the Johnson Building. Depreciation does not count as a cost because it does not represent an outflow of cash. Therefore,

$$TC = \$1,298,518$$

so,

$$BEP = TR - TC; = (R \times 0.95 \times 90,000) + 100,000 - \$1,298,518$$

TABLE 15.22 Johnson Building, 20-Year Holding Period, Cash Flow Statement

Year	Net Income	Depreciation	Capital Contributions[a]	Gain on Sale of Land[b]	Rent Savings for Al's Superfresh (adjusted for taxes)[c]	Net Cash Flows
-2			$1,580,000			-$1,580,000
-1			4,130,000			-4,130,000
1	$500,923	$430,128			$120,000	1,051,051
2	335,718	800,256			123,600	1,259,574
3	459,880	692,256			127,308	1,279,445
4	573,734	605,856			131,127	1,310,717
5	680,046	536,736			135,061	1,351,843
6	781,081	481,440			139,113	1,401,634
7	878,707	437,204			143,286	1,459,197
8	974,478	401,814			147,585	1,523,877
9	1,069,706	373,503			152,012	1,595,221
10	1,165,511	350,853			156,573	1,672,937
11	1,262,872	332,734			161,270	1,756,876
12	1,362,659	318,238			166,108	1,847,006
13	1,465,666	306,642			171,091	1,943,399
14	1,572,635	297,365			176,224	2,046,223
15	1,684,275	289,943			181,511	2,155,729
16	1,744,287	379,003			186,956	2,310,246
17	1,935,767	260,256			192,565	2,388,588
18	2,063,357	260,256			198,342	2,521,955
19	2,198,940	260,256			204,292	2,663,488
20	2,343,213	260,256		$11,595,434	210,421	14,409,324

[a] From Table 15.17.
[b] From Table 15.21B.
[c] (10,000 sq. ft. × ($30 − $10)) × (1 − 0.4)

NPV at 12% = $5,377,877
IRR = 23%

414

TABLE 15.23 Johnson Office Building, Excess Demand Conditions, Holding Period NOPAT

Year[a]	Revenues[b]	Property Management Fee[b]	Legal and Accounting Expenses[c]	Building Depreciation[d]	Improvements Depreciation[e]	Land Cost[f]	EBIT	Taxes (40%)	NOPAT EBIT $(1 - tx)$
1	$3,947,500	$25,000	$25,000	$130,128	$300,000	$250,000	$3,217,372	$1,286,949	$1,930,423
2	4,065,925	25,750	25,750	260,256	540,000	250,000	2,964,169	1,185,667	1,778,501
3	4,187,903	26,523	26,523	260,256	432,000	250,000	3,192,601	1,277,041	1,915,561
4	4,313,540	27,318	27,318	260,256	345,600	250,000	3,403,047	1,361,219	2,041,828

[a] These are the years when the building is completed, after the initial two years of construction.
[b] Al's Superfresh at 10,000 sq. ft. for $10 per square foot and the remaining 90,000 sq. ft. at $45 per square foot with a 3% escalation clause. The 90,000 sq. ft. is adjusted for a 5% vacancy rate reflecting normal turnover.
[c] Assumed to increase 3% per year.
[d] $10,000,000 plus $150 of capitalized legal and accounting fees depreciated over 39 years using the half-year convention.
[e] Land improvements (streets, blacktop, sidewalk, drainage ditches, etc.) have a recovery period of 15 years and are depreciated 150% double-declining balance using the half-year convention. Double-declining balance is a depreciation method in which double the straight-line depreciation amount is taken the first year, and then that same percentage is applied to the undepreciated amount in subsequent years.
[f] Contract rent to Bill Townsend.

415

TABLE 15.24 Johnson Building, Excess Demand Conditions, Income Statement

Year	Revenues[a]	Property Management Fee[a]	Legal and Accounting Expenses[a]	Interest[b]	Total Depreciation[c]	Land Cost[d]	Earnings before Taxes	Taxes (40%)	Net Income	DCR Ratio
1	$3,947,500	$25,000	$25,000	$1,100,000	$430,128	$250,000	$2,117,372	$846,949	$1,270,423	2.58
2	4,065,925	25,750	25,750	1,083,663	800,256	250,000	1,880,505	752,202	1,128,303	2.37
3	4,187,903	26,523	26,523	1,065,530	692,256	250,000	2,127,071	850,829	1,276,243	2.56
4	4,313,540	27,318	27,318	1,045,402	605,856	250,000	2,357,645	943,058	1,414,587	2.73

[a] Increases reflect a 3% escalation clause.
[b] Annual payments of $1,248,514 on a 25 year loan at 11%.
[c] The sum of building and improvements depreciation from Table 15.11.
[d] Contract rent to Bill Townsend.

TABLE 15.25A Johnson Building Sale by Put, Excess Demand Conditions, Tax Consequences of Sale of Property

Sale of building		$14,145,872
Fixed plant and improvements	$13,000,000	
Less accumulated depreciation	2,528,497	
Net fixed plant and improvements		10,471,503
Cost of land		3,000,000
Gain on sale		674,369
Capital gains tax (15%)		101,155
After-tax gain on sale		573,214

TABLE 15.25B Johnson Building Sale by Put, Excess Demand Conditions, Cash Gain from Sale of Property

Sale of property	$14,145,872
Less tax liability from sale (Table 15.25A)	101,155
Loan balance	9,503,652
Cash gain from sale	4,541,064

TABLE 15.26 Johnson Building with Sale by Put, Conventional Financing, Cash Flow Statement

Year	Net Income	Depre-ciation	Capital Contri-butions[a]	Gain on Sale of Land[b]	Rent Savings for Al's Superfresh (adjusted for taxes)[c]	Net Cash Flows
-2			$1,580,000			-$1,580,000
-1			4,130,000			-4,130,000
1	$1,270,423	$430,128			$120,000	1,820,551
2	1,128,303	800,256			123,600	2,052,159
3	1,276,243	692,256			127,308	2,095,807
4	1,414,587	605,856			131,127	2,151,571
5	0	0		$4,541,064	135,061	4,676,125

[a] From Table 15.22.
[b] From Table 15.25B.
[c] $(10,000 \text{ sq. ft.} \times (\$30 - \$10)) \times (1 - 0.4)$.

NPV at 12% = $2,291,404
IRR = 26%

Solving for R:

$$0.95\ R = (\$1,298,518 - \$100,000)/90,000;\ R = \$12.65$$

Thus *BEP* for R is $12.65. Note this rent allows for a 5% vacancy rate and assumes taxes, insurance, and maintenance are passed through to the tenants.

As market rents in this example are well above this level, there appears to be little downside risk in this investment. Nevertheless, a better return—one with a satisfactory risk-return outcome—seems to require a longer holding period than Al Johnson might ordinarily prefer.

Johnson Building Conclusion

Al Johnson ventured into developing an office building in search of investment gains, a potential tax shield, and a better location for his offices. The foregoing analysis suggests that if there are potential gains for Al, they are certainly tempered by his exposure to risk. That is not to say that the Johnson Building was a bad investment. In the foregoing iterations of possible outcomes, the desirability of this type of investment can be seen to depend on Al Johnson's taste for risk. Perhaps the most important feature of the investment from this perspective was obtaining of a put to the building developer. If things did not go satisfactorily during the first five years of the project, Al Johnson could probably get out more or less whole.

The potential for a tax shield was seen to be mistaken. The underlying economics of an office building mean that if you are going to run a tax loss owing to depreciation, you will probably experience a net cash outflow as well. This is in contrast to the housing residential market (Chapter 6), where an important feature of the investment activity is the obtainment of a tax shield.

Obtaining a preferred site for the headquarters of Al's Superfresh was seen to generate a relatively small amount of economic value. However, location in this building and cachet—especially the "Johnson Building"—may well have substantial psychic value for Al Johnson.

SUMMARY

Success in developing office buildings is driven by the desirability of the location, the skill with which the building is managed and the financial strength of the project owner. Attracting and retaining tenants is the key to financial stability. Office buildings provide excellent opportunities for discerning investors to reap excellent returns for the risk involved. Whatever the size of the office building, the basic elements in the process of successfully investing in this market are the same. Find a location attractive to potential tenants, design a building that conforms to those tenant's needs, secure leases, find construction financing, find permanent financing, construct the building, and then manage the building in accord with tenant's expectations.

Risk in the market for office building space comes from the market's pronounced cyclical pattern. This predictable cyclical pattern provides opportunities for astute investors. The low point of the cycle would normally constitute an excellent time to either develop an office building or buy one that is already built, but in financial trouble. Paradoxically, many investors enter the office building market at the top of the cycle, when everything seems great. Unfortunately, by the time that building is constructed the cycle may well be on the downswing with tenants hard to find at economically viable rents. As with other real estate investments, the life cycle of an office building from an investor's perspective goes through an acquisition stage, a holding stage, and a disposal stage.

The acquisition phase involves finding a suitable piece of land, doing a feasibility analysis, and lining up the financing. The property must be suitable both in terms of a location that will be attractive to tenants and that will be in compliance with local zoning and environmental laws. The feasibility study attempts to reconcile the costs of construction with the potential tenant demand both in terms of the numbers of tenants and prevailing market rental rates. Financing typically involves both a construction loan and permanent financing. Lenders often require preliminary leasing commitments from creditworthy tenants.

Competition for attracting and retaining tenants is based on location, the utility of the office building relative to tenant needs, and a competitive price. Unlike shopping centers, where issues of critical mass and synergy among center tenants is critical, prospective tenants focus on the extent to which a given office building meets their needs in terms of its location, amenities, design, layout, prestige, and cost. Unfortunately, having the "right" building is only a necessary, but not a sufficient, condition for investor success. As a result of the cobweb effect, proper timing in entering this market is the most important factor in determining the success of a real estate investor.

CHAPTER 16

Industrial Properties

Industrial properties provide great opportunities for good returns with low risk and, when properly structured, they are truly passive investments. Industrial properties are rarely built on speculation (i.e., without a committed lessee). Rather, they generally fall under the category of build-to-suits leases (see Chapter 5).

The opportunity for this type of investment arises when an industrial firm is in a situation where (1) it is already too highly leveraged and has reached its debt capacity on its balance sheet; (2) its marginal cost of debt is prohibitive; (3) it does not have access to capital at any price; or (4) there are significant tax advantages to leasing (usually because it has a very high tax rate) relative to owning.

Such situations are attractive to investors because the returns are generally superior to that obtained from a comparable unsecured industrial debenture bond or even a secured mortgage bond with less risk. This is because the lessor retains title to the property. In the event of default, the investor has an absolute claim on the property and is free to lease it to another party. That is not to say such leases are without counterparty risk. Industrial properties are typically illiquid. Thus, the search for another tenant can be long and expensive or, in a worse care scenario, the investor might end up without any economically viable options.

The general environment for manufacturing activity in the United States is not good. Manufacturing employment has been consistently declining since World War II and recent trade agreements with Mexico, Canada, China, Taiwan, Korea, and other Asian nations have given employers a great opportunity to substitute low-paid foreign workers for higher-paid American workers. In addition, the environmental constraints in these countries may be either lax or nonexistent. These disadvantages to domestic manufacturing are likely to continue. However, this trend is offset to some extent by technology that has reduced the importance of labor as a

421

manufacturing input. This has led to the revitalization of some formerly declining industrial districts and to the location of "clean" manufacturing operations throughout suburbia. The net effect of these trends is that the investment in potential industrial facilities needs to be carefully considered in the context of outsourcing possibilities and changing technology.

Counterparty risk (that of the lessee defaulting) can be dealt with by assessing the credit standing of the potential lessee and evaluating the suitability of the property for other potential lessees. In this dynamic era of rapid technological change and economic dislocation, industrial property may be viewed within a very short time horizon indeed. This presents a significant risk to the lessor. As the form of the build-to-suit lease will almost always be an operating lease (See Chapter 5), the term of the lease will necessarily be for less than the economic life (and most often less than the MACRS' life) of the property. Thus, the investor as the lessor and property owner must look to renewals of the lease, other industrial lessees, or nonindustrial uses of the property to earn a satisfactory return on their investment.

MITIGATING RISK

A firm that desires a build-to-suit because it is already overloaded with debt has some risk of default. The firm may become unable to meet its rent obligations in a timely manner, or might even slide into bankruptcy as the result of some economic adversity. As a general rule this is unlikely. The firm would have to be in dire straights indeed to imperil its production facilities. Many industrial firms struggle under adverse conditions for long periods of time, but generally find a way to keep going and pay the rent.

The lessor can best protect himself from this type of default risk by carefully assessing the five Cs of credit: Character, Capacity, Collateral, Capital, and Condition. The assessment of these attributes allows the lessor to judge the lessee's ability and willingness to pay. It is not necessary that the lessee is "Triple A," but it is necessary for the return embedded in the lease to reflect this risk of default.

A bigger threat to the lessor is nonrenewal of the lease. This can occur because the lessee can get a better deal elsewhere, because the march of technology has lessened the desirability of the property, or the pattern of economic development has caused industrial activity to shift from the area in which the property is located.

This issue can be addressed in the design of the property. Even though it is a "build-to-suit," the lessor can still have input into the design of the building. Convertibility to other types of manufacturing activities or even to other uses can often be inexpensively designed into a particular property, increasing its liquidity should the original lessee not renew.

The pattern of urban development has often taken the form of the creation of industrial facilities adjacent to population centers and then the development of those industrial sites within a densely populated area. As society became more affluent, population would migrate away from the industrial areas. As the population shifts from urban to suburban, industry would eventually migrate out to the suburbs as well, seeking proximity to its labor force. This cycle creates a legacy of industrial buildings that are no longer suited for industrial purposes. Early manufacturing activities in the United States tended to locate along waterways because of transportation and power needs, as well as for water to be used in its manufacturing processes. By and large the need for this type of location has passed with improvements in the industrial infrastructure and environmental regulation. Often today, such locations are being recycled into an array of residential or commercial uses. Factories located on a rural highway that has now grown up to a high-density population area are ripe for similar conversions.

It should be noted that a historical aspect of this problem has been the steady increase in environmental standards. This has created substantial liabilities associated with industrial property and its current owners where there are environmental hazards to be cleaned up. The cost of remediation can be excessive and visited upon those with no connection to the original source of the contamination. The administration of the Toxic Substance and Control Act (1976) and the Comprehensive Environmental and Response Compensation and Liability Act (Superfund Act, 1980 and 1986) have created considerably uncertainty over exactly what environmental contamination is and who should be required to pay for it.

INDUSTRIAL REVENUE BONDS

Industrial revenue bonds (IRBs) are municipal bonds whose proceeds are loaned to private persons or to businesses to finance capital investment projects. *Industrial development revenue bonds* (IDRBs) are municipal bonds whose proceeds are loaned public agencies or nonprofit corporations to private persons or to businesses to finance capital investment projects. The purpose of such funding is usually to attract industrial development to a particular locality. The rational for such funding is that there is little cost to the municipality of using this source of funds to attract development, and there are substantial advantages in terms of jobs created and an expansion of the tax base. For several years the Federal statutory authority for IRBs was constrained by sunset dates, but the exemption for IRBs was made permanent in 1993.

To the investor in industrial real estate, IRBs constitute an advantage in that a significant reduction in the cost of capital is possible. This saving, however, is lessened by a variety of costs associated with issuing the bonds, the necessity of completing the extensive paperwork associated with this activity, and compliance with an array of state or local rules regulating the use of such funds.

Even though they are municipal bonds with interest free of Federal and, possibly, local income taxes, IRBs are not general obligations of the municipality. The municipality is not responsible for debt service, nor is it liable in the case of default. Instead, the person or business for which the bonds are sold is responsible for paying the principal and interest on the bonds. Because IRBs are municipal bonds, they are exempt from federal income tax, so they bear lower interest rates than do other forms of borrowing. This means effectively that the tax status of the municipality is transferred to the borrowing company.

The process of issuing an IRB begins with legal counsel to determine if the project qualifies for IRB financing and whether the interest savings justify the higher initial costs of the borrower's proposed financing. If the project makes sense for IRB financing, the borrower completes an application with the local *industrial development corporation* (IDC). If the project is accepted (sometimes the pool of IRB funds is constrained), the IDC issues an *inducement resolution*, and the bond issuance process begins. The bank performs the credit work, attorneys craft the bond agreement, the state allocates bonding authority from the state pool, and, when all is ready, the IDC issues the bonds. Typically, the underwriter purchases the bonds from the IDC and then sells to the public or institutional buyers. After the bond sale, the proceeds are made available to the borrower.

Projects funded by IRBs can include the cost of building or refurbishing a manufacturing or processing plant. The project must either create new jobs or retain jobs that would have been lost if the project was not done. Specifically, an IDRB can be used to pay for land acquisition, new construction, purchase or renovation of existing facilities, or purchase of new machinery and equipment. The maximum amount that can be borrowed is $10 million. At least 95% of the amount financed must be spent on the qualifying project. Other normal constraints stipulate that no more than 2% of the amount financed may be spent on bond issuance costs and no more than 3% of the amount financed may be used for related noncapital expenses.

ILLUSTRATION #1: AJAX ARMOR MANUFACTURING COMPANY

Ajax manufacturing company makes high-tech body armor that is in wide demand from domestic and international police and security agencies. Only 10 years old, the firm has seen demand rise from virtually nothing to a sales level of $50 million. Next year, Ajax is anticipating $80 million in sales, and it is now at a point where it is producing beyond capacity. The firm employs triple shifts in their only factory and has even been forced to contract out some production. The use of existing facilities on a triple-shift basis has resulted in great inefficiencies and unnecessary expenditures by Ajax. As a result, cost of goods sold has risen from 50% to 64% in three years. The use of other manufactures has raised quality control problems and Ajax's managers are very unhappy. Ajax desperately needs a new manufacturing facility and estimates that the new manufacturing facility will cost $8 million.

The problem with Ajax is that although it was initially well capitalized, its rapid growth has required working capital (for inventory and accounts receivable) that has brought it to an over leveraged situation. Management does not want to sell equity to the public and its bank considers Ajax over extended and will not lend it any more money until they clean up their short-term loans and get more equity in the company. Ajax's financial statements are presented in Tables 16.1 and 16.2.

As can be seen from these financial statements, Ajax is performing well with a ROE of 180%; but it lacks sufficient capital to finance its anticipated rate of growth. Ajax has way too much short-term debt relative to its total debt and it has too much debt altogether with a debt ratio of 71%. Also, with its relatively high tax rate of 46.6%, Ajax is a good candidate for leasing. Clearly Ajax is not in shape to finance an $8 million new manufacturing facility itself.

TABLE 16.1   Ajax Armor Company, Income Statement

Sales	$50,000,000
Cost of goods sold	32,000,000
Gross profit	18,000,000
General administrative	1,500,000
Selling and marketing	2,500,000
Research and development	1,000,000
Interest	1,200,000
Earnings before taxes	11,800,000
Taxes	5,500,000
Net income	6,300,000

TABLE 16.2   Ajax Armor Company, Balance Sheet

Cash	$150,000	Accounts payable	$2,000,000
Accounts receivable	10,000,000	Accrued taxes	500,000
Inventory	8,000,000	Bank notes due	15,000,000
Current assets	18,150,000	Current liabilities	17,500,000
Fixed plant and equipment	7,500,000	Long-term debt	4,000,000
Total assets	25,650,000	Total liabilities	21,500,000
		Owners equity	4,150,000
		Total liabilities and owner's equity	26,650,000

The bottom line is met while Ajax has good profitability and strong cash flow. However, its existing debt structure and excessive financial leverage creates some doubt on the minds of would-be lenders as to its future viability. As it stands, Ajax would be very interested in a new build-to-suit facility and would be willing to pay a premium for it.

Equipleaseco is a leasing company that specializes in industrial leases. It is well capitalized and maintains an AAA-credit rating. It has had discussions with Ajax and understands that the land for the site will cost $1 million, the plant itself will cost $4 million, and the specialized equipment necessary for producing Ajax's armor will cost $3 million. It further understands that Ajax will not commit to a lease longer than five years and wants two five-year extensions of the lease. Ajax also wants a call on the property in the form of the right to buy it at "market price" at the end of each of the lease periods. The lease would be a triple-net lease, with Ajax picking up maintenance, insurance, and tax costs. As a result of Equipleaseco having an interest in a number of property that show losses in net income while being cash flow positive, its tax rate is only 22%.

Equipleaseco can borrow the money for this project. Its bank offers it a $7 million bridge loan at 10%, which rolls over into an 8.5%, 15-year mortgage with $1 million as equity. Under the assumption of a five-year holding period, the lease necessary to fully amortize Equipleaseco's costs would depend on what the property was worth at that time. The property might increase in value or decrease in value depending on the demand for this type of property, its location, or general economic conditions. Such variation might be large because the property is illiquid. Adjustment for this risk will occur when it comes to pricing the lease. For purposes of this analysis, it is assumed the property's value will not change, that is, it will remain at $8 million. Thus, if the property is sold for $8 million at the end of the five-year holding period, it will generate a tax liability of $603,135 for an after-tax gain of $3,417,764 (Table 16.3A). This translates into a cash gain from sale of $1,522,407 (Table 16.3B).

Taking into account all the relevant cash flows from Equipleaseco's perspective, the cost of doing the build-to-suit for Ajax Armor for a five-year lease would be $2,095,972 (Table 16.4). The minimum equivalent five-year annual annuity for the new plant's NPV to Equipleaseco would be $581,443. What this means is that if the annual lease income were $581,443, Equipleaseco would derive zero NPV from the project at 12%. If Equipleaseco were to adjust its NPV to 17% for risk, then lease income of $612,045 would be necessary for Equipleaseco to achieve a NPV of zero. This number then becomes the floor for a five-year lease.

If the first five-year lease is renewed for a second five-year period, it can be seen from Tables 16.5A and 16.5B that the cash gain from the sale of the property increases to $3,547,623. This gain reflects the increased payoff of the underlying mortgage. The assumption is maintained that the property is sold for $8 million at the end of the holding period.

TABLE 16.3A   Ajax Armor, Tax Consequences of Sale of Property, Five-Year Holding Period

Sale of building		$8,000,000
Fixed plant and improvements	$7,000,000	
Less accumulated depreciation	4,020,898	
Net fixed plant and improvements		2,979,102
Cost of land		1,000,000
Gain on sale		4,020,898
Capital gains tax (15%)		603,135
After-tax gain on sale		3,417,764

TABLE 16.3B   Ajax Armor, Cash Gain from Sale of Property

Sale of property	$8,000,000
Less:	
Tax liability	603,135
Loan balance	5,874,458
Cash gain from sale	1,522,407

TABLE 16.4 Equipleasco, Five-Year Holding Period, Cash Flows Out[a]

Year	After-Tax Mortgage Interest Payments[b]	Mortgage Principle Payments[b]	Building Depreciation[c]	Equipment Depreciation[d]	Depreciation Tax (Savings)	Equity Contribution	Cash (Gain) on Sale	Total Cash Flows Out (In)
0	$273,000					$1,000,000		$1,273,000
1	464,100	$247,943	$51,282	$600,000	$143,282			568,761
2	447,661	269,018	102,564	1,360,000	321,764			394,916
3	429,825	291,885	102,564	816,000	202,084			519,626
4	410,473	316,695	102,564	489,600	130,276			596,893
5	389,477	343,614	102,564	293,760	87,191		-$1,522,407	-876,507

[a] Note that maintenance, insurance, and taxes are not included. If the build-to-suit is constructed, it will be under the terms of a triple-net lease.

[b] On an 8.5% fixed rate, 15-year conventional mortgage for $7 million.

[c] Depreciation does not represent a cash expenditure, but depreciation does generate a tax saving which does constitute a cash flow. The building with a basis of $4 million is depreciated over 39 years with the half-year convention.

[d] The equipment is considered to have an economic life of five years due to technological obsolescence. The equipment also has a 5-year MACRS life and will be depreciated at 150% double-declining balance using the half-year convention.

NPV of cash flows at 12% = −$1,359,292
EAA = −$377,081

EAA adjusted for 5%
Risk Factor = −$396,927

However, it can be seen from Table 16.6, that the net effect of extending the lease is to increase the risk adjusted *equivalent annual annuity* (EAA) of the project to $841,781. The reason for this increase lies in the increased time it takes Equipleaseco to recover its initial investment from the sale of the property.

A similar effect can be noted if the holding period is extended to the full 15 years. Tables 16.7A, 16.7B, and 16.8 reveal that the risk adjusted EAA for Equipleaseco has now risen to $1,082,610. Again, this results from the increased length of time it takes Equipleaseco to recover its initial investment.

Conclusion

Ajax Armor is clearly not in a position to finance its own new plant. If it wants a new plant on a build-to-suit from Equipleaseco, then it is going to have to be willing to take an annual lease upwards of $1.3 million. Equipleaseco should be comfortable with this if they feel that the 17% return on their investment satisfactorily compensates them for the risk they are exposed to.

TABLE 16.5A   Ajax Armor, Tax Consequences of Sale of Property, Ten-Year Holding Period

Sale of building		$8,000,000
Fixed plant and improvements	$11,000,000	
Less accumulated depreciation	8,093,079	
Net fixed plant and improvements		2,906,921
Cost of land		1,000,000
Gain on sale		4,093,079
Capital gains tax (15%)		613,962
After-tax gain on sale		3,479,117

TABLE 16.5B   Ajax Armor, Cash Gain from Sale of Property

Sale of property	$8,000,000
Less:	
Tax liability	613,962
Loan balance	3,838,415
Cash gain from sale	3,547,623

TABLE 16.6 Equipleasco, Ten-Year Holding Period, Cash Flows Out[a]

Year	After-Tax Mortgage Interest Payments[b]	Mortgage Principle Payments[b]	Building Depreciation[c]	Equipment Depreciation[d]	Depreciation Tax (Savings)	Equity Contribution	Cash (Gain) on Sale	Total Cash Flows Out (In)
0	$273,000					$1,000,000		$1,273,000
1	464,100	$247,943	$51,282	$600,000	$143,282			568,761
2	447,661	269,018	102,564	1,360,000	321,764			394,916
3	429,825	291,885	102,564	816,000	202,084			519,626
4	410,473	316,695	102,564	489,600	130,276			596,893
5	389,477	343,614	102,564	293,760	87,191			645,900
6	366,695	372,821	102,564	600,000	154,564			584,952
7	341,977	404,511	102,564	1,360,000	321,764			424,724
8	315,158	438,895	102,564	816,000	202,084			551,968
9	286,059	476,201	102,564	489,600	130,276			631,984
10	254,487	516,678	102,564	293,760	87,191		-3,547,623	-2,863,649

[a] Note that maintenance, insurance, and taxes are not included. If the build-to-suit is constructed, it will be under the terms of a triple-net lease.

[b] On an 8.5% fixed rate, 15-year conventional mortgage for $7 million.

[c] Depreciation does not represent a cash expenditure, but depreciation does generate a tax saving that does constitute a cash flow. The building with a basis of $4 million is depreciated over 39 years with the half-year convention.

[d] The equipment is considered to have an economic life of five years due to technological obsolescence. The equipment also has a five-year MACRS life and will be depreciated at 150% double-declining balance using the half-year convention. The assumption is that in five years a new set of equipment will be needed and it will cost as much as the original equipment.

NPV of Cash Flows at12% = $2,882,709
EAA = $799,692

EAA adjusted for 5%
Risk Factor = $841,781

TABLE 16.7A   Ajax Armor, Tax Consequences of Sale of Property, 15-Year Holding Period

Sale of building		$8,000,000
Fixed plant and improvements	$15,000,000	
Less accumulated		
depreciation	12,165,259	
Net fixed plant and improvements		2,834,741
Cost of land		1,000,000
Gain on sale		4,165,259
Capital gains tax (15%)		624,789
After-tax gain on sale		3,540,471

TABLE 16.7B   Ajax Armor, Cash Gain from Sale of Property

Sale of property	$8,000,000	
Less:		
Tax liability	624,789	
Loan balance	0	
Cash gain from sale	7,375,211	

If Ajax's management was correct and its increase in cost of goods sold of 14% results from its running three shifts to capacity, then 14% of $50 million is $7 million. This money after-tax, at the bottom line, is $3.78 million, well above the cost of any lease it will have to pay for the new plant. Ajax Armour's choice is clear.

ILLUSTRATION #2: BATES PUBLISHING CO.

The old eastern seaboard city used to have a thriving port. Its waterfront is lined with old ship repair facilities, canneries, shoe factories, book manufacturers, and textile and rug manufacturers. Where manufacturing once accounted for 50% of the employment in the city, that is now down to 10%. The industrial area is decrepit and continuing to decline. The industrial area is surrounded by ethnic neighborhoods populated by second- and third-generation aging immigrants who historically supplied the labor for the manufacturing industries.

Other parts of the city thrive with burgeoning white-collar industries such as insurance, banking, and an array of financial services. Highly educated, single, young professionals staff these industries.

TABLE 16.8 Equipleasco, 15-Year Holding Period, Cash Flows Out[a]

Year	After-Tax Mortgage Interest Payments[b]	Mortgage Principle Payments[b]	Building Depreciation[c]	Equipment Depreciation[d]	Depreciation Tax (Savings)	Equity Contribution	Cash (Gain) on Sale	Total Cash Flows Out (In)
0	$273,000					$1,000,000		$1,273,000
1	464,100	$247,943	$51,282	$600,000	$143,282			568,761
2	447,661	269,018	102,564	1,360,000	321,764			394,916
3	429,825	291,885	102,564	816,000	202,084			519,626
4	410,473	316,695	102,564	489,600	130,276			596,893
5	389,477	343,614	102,564	293,760	87,191			645,900
6	366,695	372,821	102,564	600,000	154,564			584,952
7	341,977	404,511	102,564	1,360,000	321,764			424,724
8	315,158	438,895	102,564	816,000	202,084			551,968
9	286,059	476,201	102,564	489,600	130,276			631,984
10	254,487	516,678	102,564	293,760	87,191			683,974

432

TABLE 16.8 (Continued)

Year	After-Tax Mortgage Interest Payments[b]	Mortgage Principle Payments[b]	Building Depreciation[c]	Equipment Depreciation[d]	Depreciation Tax (Savings)	Equity Contribution	Cash (Gain) on Sale	Total Cash Flows Out (In)
11	220,231	560,596	102,564	600,000	154,564			626,263
12	183,064	608,246	102,564	1,360,000	321,764			469,546
13	142,737	659,947	102,564	816,000	202,084			600,600
14	98,983	716,043	102,564	489,600	130,276			684,749
15	51,509	776,906	102,564	293,760	87,191		–$7,375,211	(6,633,987)

[a] Note that maintenance, insurance, and taxes are not included. If the build-to-suit is constructed, it will be under the terms of a triple-net lease.

[b] On an 8.5% fixed rate, 15-year conventional mortgage for $7 million.

[c] Depreciation does not represent a cash expenditure, but depreciation does generate a tax saving that does constitute a cash flow. The building with a basis of $4 million is depreciated over 39 years with the half-year convention.

[d] The equipment is considered to have an economic life of five years due to technological obsolescence. The equipment also has a 5-year MACRS life and will be depreciated at 150% double-declining balance using the half-year convention. Again the assumption is made that at the end of 10 years the second set of equipment will have to be replaced with another set whose costs are the same as the first set.

NPV of Cash Flows at 12% = $3,902,566
EAA = $1,082,610

EAA adjusted for 5%
Risk Factor = $1,139,589

433

Many of these individuals reject the thought of living in the distant suburbs (and the resultant long commute) and opt for urban living. A number of neighborhoods in the city have been reclaimed by these yuppies, although not in the old manufacturing waterfront district.

Phil Baker, a successful dentist, and his three partners formed Vision Partners LLC to invest in real estate properties around the city. So far they had purchased and renovated three small office buildings on the periphery of the city's urban core. These acquisitions were successful and were currently generating Vision Partners a 30% return on equity. Vision Partners has a 25% tax rate.

Phil Baker learned of what he thought was a great opportunity and took it to his partners. Bates Publishing Company was a printing and book-publishing company that had been a leading business in the city for 100 years, but had recently fallen on hard times due to increased competition in the industry from Asian imports. Bates Publishing was struggling to stay alive. Tables 16.9 and 16.10 contain its latest financial statements.

These statements show that Bates is losing money and suffering from a liquidity crisis. Its current ratio is 1.3 compared to an industry standard of 2 and its quick ratio is an atrocious 0.3 compared to an industry standard of 1.2. Worse yet, it has a bank note for $3 million due in six months and no way to pay it.

What Bates would like from Vision Partners is to do a sale-leaseback of their plant. They would like Vision Partners to buy the property for $3 million and lease it back for $450,000 per year in a triple-net lease for five years. At the end of the five-year period, they would like to buy the plant back for four times its appraised value. Bates' thinking is that the $3 million cash derived from the sale will enable them to meet their current obliga-

TABLE 16.9   Bates Publishing Co., Income Statement

Sales	$15,000,000
Cost of goods sold	12,000,000
Gross profit	3,000,000
General administrative	1,500,000
Selling and marketing	1,000,000
Interest	750,000
Earnings before taxes	−250,000
Taxes	0
Net income	−250,000

TABLE 16.10   Bates Publishing Co., Balance Sheet

Cash	$25,000	Accounts payable	$1,800,000
Accounts receivable	1,500,000	Bank notes due	3,000,000
Inventory	4,750,000	Current liabilities	4,800,000
Current assets	6,275,000		
		Long-term debt	4,000,000
Fixed plant and equipment	4,000,000		
		Total liabilities	8,800,000
Total assets	10,275,000	Owner's equity	1,475,000
		Total liabilities and owner's equity	10,275,000
	Current ratio =	1.31	
	Quick ratio =	0.32	

tions. Moreover, Bates has some promising printing contracts in the offing that may allow the business to return to profitability. When they do become more solid financially, they would like to buy the building back.

The plant is a dilapidated three-story brick building sitting on three acres of waterfront overlooking the harbor. The property contains a small dump of what the Environmental Protection Agency (EPA) has determined to be biohazardous materials. Best estimates are that remediation will cost $500,000, but could go as high as $1 million. Bates is in discussions with the EPA about cleaning this up, although Bates obviously cannot afford to do so. The property is currently appraised for $750,000.

The neighborhood consists of other industrial building, some of which are still being used, but most are abandoned and in advanced state of decay. Here and there are small clusters of deteriorated townhouses, some occupied, some not. The area is rat infested. The property is zoned for industrial, residential, and commercial use.

Phil Baker finds that Vision Partners can get a conventional 10-year mortgage for $2,500,000 on the building from their bank at 11% if Vision Partners pledges their general credit to the mortgage. (The bank does not feel this property is economically viable.) Given that the property retains its appraised value of $750,000, this would generate an after-tax gain for Vision Partners of $1,195,468 (Tables 16.11A and 16.11B).

An examination of the cash flows (Table 16.12) suggests that the project is acceptable to Vision Partners, as the project has an EAA of $293,126 from Vision Partners perspective. A lease offer of $450,000 suggests the lease would be profitable for Vision Partners if Bates repurchases the building in five years.

TABLE 16.11A   Bates Publishing Co., Tax Consequences of Sale of Property, Five-Year Holding Period

Sale of building[a]		$3,000,000
Fixed plant & improvements	$500,000	
Less accumulated		
depreciation	57,692	
Net fixed plant and improvements		442,308
Cost of land		2,500,000
Gain on sale		57,692
Capital gains tax (15%)		8,654
After-tax gain on sale		49,038

[a] The assumption being the building will still appraise for $750,000 in four years.

TABLE 16.11B   Bates Publishing Co., Cash Gain from Sale of Property

Sale of property	$3,000,000
Less:	
Tax liability	8,654
Loan balance	1,795,878
Cash gain from sale	1,195,468

A cash flow analysis of the $450,000 lease offer (Table 16.13) from Bates indicates Vision Partners will gain a NPV of $102,013 for a 20% return. Phil Baker's partners argue that this is below their LLC's current ROE of 30%, they have serious concerns about being held liable for the contamination cleanup, and they doubt Bates Publishing's ability to return to profitability in which case they will be left holding the bag of a decrepit, useless factory.

Phil Baker argues that the EPA mandated cleanup has been stalled for 10 years at this point, and there is no reason to think the situation will come to a head in the next five years. About being left with the property, Phil says, "That's exactly my point!" Phil thinks the property, as an industrial site is worthless, but could be a prime site for residential condos as the city continues to revitalize itself. Phil anticipates that Bates Publishing will fail. Companies like Bates are always hopeful about tomorrow being a brighter day. He sees this sale-leaseback arrangement as a cheap way to acquire the property. He admits, however, that a lot of this thinking is conjectural.

TABLE 16.12 Vision Partners LLC, Five Year Holding Period, Cash Flows Out[a]

Year	After-Tax Mortgage Interest Payments[b]	Mortgage Principle Payments[b]	Building Depreciation[c]	Depreciation Tax (Savings)	Equity Contribution	Cash (Gain) on Sale	Total Cash Flows Out (In)
1	$206,250	$149,504	$6,410	$1,603	$500,000		$854,151
2	193,916	165,949	12,821	3,205			356,660
3	180,225	184,203	12,821	3,205			361,223
4	165,028	204,466	12,821	3,205			366,289
5	148,160	226,957	12,821	3,205		-$1,195,468	-823,556

[a] Note that maintenance, insurance, and taxes are not included. If the build-to-suit is constructed, it will be under the terms of a triple-net lease.

[b] On an 11% fixed rate, 10-year conventional mortgage for $2.5 million.

[c] Depreciation does not represent a cash expenditure, but depreciation does generate a tax saving which does constitute a cash flow. The building is assumed to have a value of $500,000 and the land $2,250,000. The building will be depreciated over 39 years with a half-year convention.

NPV of cash flows at 14% = $1,056,652
EAA = $293,126

TABLE 16.13 Vision Partners LLC, Cash Flow Analysis

Year	Lease Revenue	Depreciation[a]	Interest[b]	EBT	Taxes	Net Income	Depreciation	Principal Payments	Cash Gain on Sale	Equity Contribution	Cash Flow[c]
1	$450,000	$6,410	$275,000	$168,590	$42,147	$126,442	$6,410	$149,504		$500,000	-$516,651
2	450,000	12,821	258,555	178,625	44,656	133,969	12,821	165,949			-19,160
3	450,000	12,821	240,300	196,879	49,220	147,659	12,821	184,203			-23,723
4	450,000	12,821	220,038	217,142	54,285	162,856	12,821	204,466			-28,789
5	450,000	12,821	197,547	239,633	59,908	179,725	12,821	226,957	$1,195,468		1,161,056

[a] From Table 16.12.
[b] 11% on a conventional 10-year mortgage for $2.5 million.
[c] Consists of net income plus depreciation, less principal payments, plus cash gain on sale less equity contribution.

NPV at 14% = $102,013
IRR = 20%

438

Phil Baker suggests that they push the rent up to $485,000, which will almost double their NPV and increase their return to 25% (Table 16.14). While this is subpar for Vision Partners, Phil proceeds to demonstrate a plan for converting the factory into a condo five years from now. For all practical purposes, Phil sees the investment in this industrial property as a cheap way to acquire and hold what could become very desirable waterfront property. The deal with Bates Publishing is really about acquiring an option on a future condo project. If the city evolves as Phil thinks it will, and if Bates Publishing defaults as Phil thinks it will, then Vision Partners could be looking at a very profitable opportunity indeed.

If—and this is a big if—events evolve fortuitously over the next 10 years as Phil Baker hopes, he estimates that Vision Partners, by doing the sale-leaseback with Bates Publishing, will incur about $100,000 in lost opportunity costs (that is, if they invested in a similar-sized project with a 30% ROE). Phil also feels Vision Partners will incur about $300,000 in carrying costs on a present-value basis (primarily taxes and legal fees after Bates defaults and before the property can be developed as a condo).

If the conversion is undertaken, Phil feels the factory is of sufficient size to convert to 100 upscale condo units. Phil feels that the cost per unit would be roughly $200,000 ($20 million total) and the condos could be sold for $350,000 ($35 million total), yielding roughly a profit of $15 million. Evaluating the project using conventional capital budgeting tools (e.g., NPV) is very difficult because of the great uncertainty associated with the investment. However, the value of this option can be determined through the use of the *Black-Scholes Option Pricing Model* (OPM).

The Black-Scholes Option Pricing Model is a mathematical tool most often applied to valuing stock options. However, this tool has often been applied to real world (nonfinancial) situations where outcomes are not known with certainty and can best be described in terms of probabilities.[1] The idea behind the following equations is to capture how much would be gained weighted by the probability of that particular gain. That result is then expressed in the value of an option "call."

The value of the call (C) is

$$C = SN(d1) - X\, e-rtN(d2)$$

---

[1] Joanne Sammer, "Thinking in Real Options," *Business Finance* (March 2002); Edward Teach, "Will Real Options Take Root," CFO *Magazine* (July 1, 2003); Aswath Damodaran, "Promise and Perils of Real Options," Chapter 11 in *The Dark Side of Valuation* (Englewood Cliffs: Prentice Hall, 2002).

TABLE 16.14   Vision Partners LLC, Cash Flow Analysis

Year	Lease Revenue	Depre- ciation[a]	Interest[b]	EBT	Taxes	Net Income	Depre- ciation	Principal Payments	Cash Gain on Sale	Equity Contri- bution	Cash Flow[c]
1	$485,000	$6,410	$275,000	$203,590	$50,897	$152,692	$6,410	$149,504		$500,000	−$490,401
2	485,000	12,821	258,555	213,625	53,406	160,219	12,821	165,949		0	7,090
3	485,000	12,821	240,300	231,879	57,970	173,909	12,821	184,203		0	2,527
4	485,000	12,821	220,038	252,142	63,035	189,106	12,821	204,466		0	−2,539
5	485,000	12,821	197,547	274,633	68,658	205,975	12,821	226,957	$1,195,468	0	1,187,306

[a] From Table 16.12.
[b] 11% on a conventional 10-year mortgage for $2.5 million.
[c] Consists of net income plus depreciation, less principal payments, plus cash gain on sale less equity contribution.

NPV at 14% = 192,131
IRR = 25%

Where:

$d1$ = $(\ln(S/X) + (r + 0.5s2)t)/((s)(\text{sqrt}t))$
        $d1 - ((s)(\text{sqrt}t))$
S = Current stock price
C = Call option price
X = Strike price of call
r = Short-term risk free-rate of interest
s = Standard deviation of stock (expected volatility)
t = Time remaining (as fraction of a year)
e = 2.718 (natural antilog of 1)
$N(.)$ = Cumulative probability density from Normal Distribution Table for standardized value Z

Vision Partners Condo OPM Evaluation

What Vision Partners needs to ascertain is the value of using the Bates Publishing sale-leaseback arrangement to gain for them the future opportunity to develop this waterfront property. Such an option is often termed a "flexibility" option because it gives a party an opportunity it would not otherwise have. In this case, Vision Partners is getting a unique piece of property on which it can develop its condominium project.

The time of this option could be considered 10 years. (This is the time until the area might be ready for such a project.) The opportunity cost of Vision Partner's money could be its WACC of 14%. (Many financial analysts prefer to use the risk-free rate of interest for this calculation; however, Vision Partners is not in the business of making risk-free investments.) The strike price of the option would be the $15 million expected profit on the condo project, and the analog to the stock price in the OPM would also be the $15 million expected profit. If Vision Partners were in a situation where they had to expend the $20 million to have a chance of creating a $35 million project, then $20 million would be the strike price and $35 million the stock price; however, that is not the situation now. The question at this point to Vision Partners has to do with variance around the $15 million potential profit. The most difficult part of specifying this model would be determining the total variance of the outcome. That is, the city might not develop in the direction of the harbor, the industrial district might not prove a desirable residential area in the mind of the public, the city might go into an economic decline, actual cleanup costs may far exceed the most conservative estimates, and so on. Any number of largely unpredictable events might occur, which would obviate the prospects for the condo project. Given that Vision Partners are expecting a return of 30% return on their projects in general, it would not be unreasonable to say that for this very risky project, that return might have a standard deviation of 40%.

The Black-Scholes application to this project is presented in Table 16.15. This analysis shows the option has the value of $11.86 million to Vision Partners. Because this is way above the cost of the option to Vision Partners ($400,000), they should do the project. It is not certain that they will make this money. The OPM compares the odds of losing with the amount to be lost against the odds of winning with the amount to be won. On this basis, Vision Partners should go ahead with the sale-lease-back to Bates Publishing, not for the gain in that lease per se, but on the basis of the value of the option they gain on the underlying condo project.

Additional consideration needs to be undertaken of the unresolved environmental hazard on the property. However, because the worst that can happen is that this costs Vision Partners an additional $1 million (raising their costs of the option to $1.4 million), it is still a good deal for Vision Partners and it should proceed with the sale-leaseback arrangement with Bates Publishing.

ILLUSTRATION #3: HANDHELD APPLIANCES CORP.— CONVENTIONAL ROUTE

Jacksonville Ventures LLC (JV) is a partnership created to invest in a variety of commercial and industrial real estate ventures throughout the Mississippi River Basin. The partnership currently has $30 million of loans outstanding and a successful track record spanning a decade. JV has a target ROE of 25%, which it has slightly exceeded in each of the past five years. JV is currently paying a corporate tax of 25%.

JV is approached by Handheld Appliances Corporation to do a build-to-suit manufacturing facility for them. Handheld specializes in producing a wide array of molded and injected plastic appliances. Handheld has been in business for 12 years, during which time it has grown steadily to sales of $5 million and has been consistently profitable. Handheld is using all of its productive capacity. Handheld has been successful despite a marginal amount of capitalization. Its steady growth has created working capital demands that have stretched it to the limit. Handheld simply could not afford to build a new manufacturing facility for them.

Handheld is in a position where it has been offered a subcontracting opportunity from a major computer manufacturer. This opportunity would guarantee Handheld sales of $10 million for five years. Handheld thinks that this business would be very profitable. Given the rate of technological innovation in the industry, Handheld assumes this product would become obsolete after five years, but that the demand for plastic appliances of this type will remain strong whatever changes technology brings.

TABLE 16.15   Vision Partner's OPM for Condo, Black-Scholes Version

Call Formula: $C = SN(d1) - X\, e{-}rtN(d2)$
Inputs ($000,000)

Strike price	15
Time	10
Current price	15
Volatility	0.4
Risk-free % rate	0.14

where:

$d1$	=	$(\ln(S/X) + (r + 0.5s2)t)/((s)(sqrtt))$
$d2$	=	$d1 - ((s)(sqrtt))$
S	=	Current stock price
C	=	Call option price
X	=	Strike price of call
r	=	Short-term risk free rate of interest
s	=	Standard deviation of stock (expected volatility)
t	=	Time remaining (as fraction of a year)
e	=	2.718 (natural antilog of 1)
$N(.)$	=	Cumulative probability density (from Normal Distribution Table for standardized value Z

Finding $d1$

ln (S/X)	0	
$(r + 0.5s2)t$	2.2	
s*sqrt$t$	1.264911064	
$d1 =$	1.739252713	
$d2 =$	0.474341649	*Note:*
$N(d1) =$	0.95900488	If the d value > 0, then subtract the Z value of d from 1.
$N(d2) =$	0.682371844	If $d < 0$, then do not subtract the Z value of d from 1.
$e - rt =$	0.246632762	

Thus, solving for C:	Price of Call:
$C = SN(d1) - X\, e{-}rtN(d2)$	11.86064441

The call value to Vision Partners = $11,860,640

The proposed manufacturing facility would be located in a new, thriving industrial park being created on the outskirts of Jackson Mississippi. The Magnolia Industrial Park already features the factories of several "light" manufacturers that were attracted by the excellent transportation infrastructure available, the large pool of qualified labor, and the local Mississippi Industrial Development Corporation that has been very aggressive in promoting the area.

JV understands that the proposed facility will be 60,000 sq. ft., which can be constructed for $100 per square foot for $6 million and require another $2 million for access roads, parking facilities, and landscaping. The cost of the site itself will be $750,000. This funding will be for the building alone, with Handheld supplying all required equipment and machinery. The single-story design of the building would render it appropriate for use as any light manufacturing facility.

JV would ordinarily prefer not to do business with Handheld Appliance, preferring to work with more established, creditworthy firms. However, JV feels that Handheld should be good for at least five years based on the strength of their contract with the computer manufacturer and they like the location and setup of the Magnolia Industrial Park. It feels strongly that this is an excellent location and property in the park will appreciate in value. It expects the value of property in this park to appreciate at 8% over the next five years.

JV found that it could secure both a bridge loan and a mortgage loan for $7 million on the property. The bridge loan would be interest only for 10.5% and would roll over into a conventional 15-year fixed rate mortgage at 10%. This results in a mortgage payment of $920,316. After allowing for appreciation of the property at 8%, which generates a potential cash gain from the sale of the property in five years of $6,017,237 (Tables 16.16A and 16.16B), JV finds that it needs a lease for at least $669,920 to make its 14% cost of capital (Table 16.17). Note, in this income statement, the effect of substantial tax shield generated for JV because net income is negative. Given the uncertainties surrounding the financial situation of Handheld Appliances, it decides it could not possibly do a lease for less tan $750,000.

Handheld Appliances decides that it cannot do a $750,000 lease for the property. Its contract with the computer manufacturer has only a narrow profit margin built in. Handheld Appliances suggests to JV that it can get a better deal if it raises its funding through the Mississippi IDC.

TABLE 16.16A   Jacksonville Ventures LLC, Tax Consequences of Sale of Property, Five-Year Holding Period

Sale of property[a]		$12,856,621
Fixed plant and improvements	$8,000,000	
Less accumulated depreciation	1,639,194	
Net fixed plant and improvements		6,360,806
Cost of land		750,000
Gain on sale		5,745,815
Capital gains tax (15%)		861,872
After-tax gain on sale		4,883,943

[a] $8.75 million at 8% annually for five years.

TABLE 16.16B   Vision Partners LLC, Cash Gain from Sale of Property

Sale of property	$12,856,621
Less:	
Tax liability	861,872
Loan balance	5,977,511
Cash gain from sale	6,017,237

ILLUSTRATION #4: HANDHELD APPLIANCES CORP.— WITH IRB

JV approaches the Mississippi IDC and asks for an evaluation of the project. The IDC is enthusiastic about using RBs to finance the project. After consulting with the IDC, its lawyers and an investment bank, JV finds it can finance a $7 million mortgage for this project for 3.75%, with legal fees, flotation costs, and the like costing another 1.5% to bring its net cost of borrowing through the IRBs to 5.25%.

The lower interest rate effectively means a lower loan balance in five years and thus translates into a larger cash gain on sale ($6,371,941). This may be seen from Tables 16.18A and 16.18B.

As can be seen from Table 16.19, the effect of the lower interest rates is to substantially lower the costs of the project to Jacksonville Ventures. The project now only requires an annual lease of $496,239 to allow JV to make its 14% cost of capital. Note again the importance of the tax shield generated by the project's negative net income for JV. Again, the JV partners are concerned about Handheld's financial viability, so it wants to build in itself a "safety net" and offer Handheld Appliances the lease at $550,000.

TABLE 16.17 Jacksonville Ventures LLC, Five-Year Holding Period, Cash Flows Out[a]

Year	After-Tax Mortgage Interest Payments[b]	Mortgage Principle Payments[b]	Building Depreciation[c]	Improvements Depreciation[d]	Depreciation Tax (Savings)	Equity Contribution[e]	Cash (Gain) on Sale	Total Cash Flows Out (In)
0	$275,625					$1,750,000		$2,025,625
1	525,000	$220,316	$76,923	$133,333	$52,564			2,442,752
2	508,476	242,348	153,846	248,889	100,684			650,141
3	490,300	266,583	153,846	215,704	92,387			664,496
4	470,306	293,241	153,846	186,943	85,197			678,350
5	448,313	322,565	153,846	162,017	78,966		–$6,017,237	–5,325,324

[a] Note that maintenance, insurance, and taxes are not included. If the build-to-suit is constructed, it will be under the terms of a triple-net lease.

[b] On an 10% fixed rate, 15-year conventional mortgage for $7 million.

[c] Depreciation does not represent a cash expenditure, but depreciation does generate a tax saving that does constitute a cash flow. The building is assumed to have a value of $500,000 and the land $2,250,000. The building will be depreciated over 39 years with a half-year convention.

[d] Land improvements (streets, blacktop, sidewalk, drainage ditches, etc.) have a recovery period of 15 years and are depreciated 150% declining balance using the half-year convention.

[e] Land is $750,000, building is $6 million, and improvements $2 million; less the loan of $7 million, this equals equity of $1.75 million.

NPV of cash flows at 14% = $2,414,912
EAA = $669,920

446

TABLE 16.18A   Jacksonville Ventures LLC, Tax Consequences of Sale of Property, Five-Year Holding Period

Sale of property[a]		$12,856,621
Fixed plant and improvements	$8,000,000	
Less accumulated depreciation	1,639,194	
Net fixed plant and improvements		6,360,806
Cost of land		750,000
Gain on sale		5,745,815
Capital gains tax (15%)		861,872
After-tax gain on sale		4,883,943

[a] $8.75 million at 8% annually for five years.

TABLE 6.18B   Vision Partners LLC, Cash Gain from Sale of Property

Sale of property		$12,856,621
Less:		
Tax liability	861,872	
Loan balance	5,622,807	
Cash gain from sale	6,371,941	

Handheld accepts. The region gets increased employment and tax revenues. Jacksonville Ventures gets a handsome return on its investment of 0.27% (Table 16.20), slightly above its target ROE.

SUMMARY

Industrial real estate is seen to offer a potentially good risk and return combination for the commercial real estate investor. Where the industrial firm is unable or unwilling to finance its own properties, their alternative is to have an investor supply that capital in the form of a build-to-suit leasing arrangement. There is little doubt that this arrangement favors the industrial firm, especially where it is subject to a high tax rate.

Risks exist for the real estate investor in this situation, but it can be controlled for with foresight. The first risk to be encountered by the investor is that of nonrenewal of the lease. Because the taxing circumstances will normally dictate the use of an operating lease, the lease cannot be fully amortized over the life of the lease. The investor can address this issue by designing the building so that it has use in a wide number of applications and that it is located in an area that would be attractive to other industrial firms.

TABLE 16.19 Jacksonville Ventures LLC, Five Year Holding Period, Cash Flows Out[a]

Year	After-Tax Mortgage Interest Payments[b]	Mortgage Principle Payments[b]	Building Depreciation[c]	Improvements Depreciation[d]	Depreciation Tax (Savings)	Equity Contribution[e]	Cash (Gain) on Sale	Total Cash Flows Out (In)
0	$275,625					$1,750,000		$2,025,625
1	275,625	$318,340	$76,923	133,333	$52,564			2,291,401
2	263,090	335,053	153,846	248,889	100,684			497,459
3	249,898	352,643	153,846	215,704	92,387			510,153
4	236,012	371,157	153,846	186,943	85,197			521,972
5	221,398	390,643	153,846	162,017	78,966		-6,371,941	-5,838,867

[a] Note that maintenance, insurance, and taxes are not included. If the build-to-suit is constructed, it will be under the terms of a triple-net lease.

[b] The bridge loan remains conventionally financed at 10.5%, but the 15-year bond costs 5.25%. The IRB will be self-liquidating in the same form as a conventional fixed rate mortgage.

[c] Depreciation does not represent a cash expenditure, but depreciation does generate a tax saving that does constitute a cash flow. The building is assumed to have a value of $500,000 and the land $2,250,000. The building will be depreciated over 39 years with a half-year convention.

[d] Land improvements (streets, blacktop, sidewalk, drainage ditches, etc.) have a recovery period of 15 years and are depreciated 150% declining balance using the half-year convention.

[e] Land is $750,000, building is $6 million, and improvements $2 million; less the loan of $7 million, this equals equity of $1.75 million.

NPV of cash flows at 14% = $1,788,832
EAA = $496,239

448

TABLE 16.20 Jacksonville Ventures LLC, Cash Flow Analysis

Year	Lease Revenue	Depre-ciation[a]	Interest[b]	EBT	Taxes	Net Income	Depre-ciation	Principal Payments	Cash Gain on Sale	Equity Contri-bution	Cash Flow[c]
0										$1,750,000	-$1,887,813
1	$550,000	$210,256	$183,750	-$183,750	-$45,938	-$137,813	$210,256	$220,316			-30,877
2	550,000	402,735	367,500	-27,756	-6,939	-20,817	402,735	242,348			7,745
3	550,000	369,550	350,787	-203,522	-50,881	-152,642	369,550	266,583			-11,593
4	550,000	340,789	333,197	-152,747	-38,187	-114,560	340,789	293,241			-31,556
5	550,000	315,864	314,683	-105,472	-26,368	-79,104	315,864	322,565	$6,371,941		6,319,444
			295,197	-61,061	-15,265	-45,796					

[a] From Table 16.19.
[b] 5.25% on a 15-year IRB for $7 million.
[c] Consists of net income plus depreciation, less principal payments, plus cash gain on sale less equity contribution.

NPV at 14% = $1,181,293
IRR = 27%

A second risk could be default by the lessee. This risk can be addressed by assessing the financial solvency of the lessee prior to committing funds. In the event of default, the risk to the lessor is minimized by the fact that he retains title to the property and the industrial firm's creditors cannot attach the property.

An interesting dimension to this type of investing is the availability of IRB financing for industrial properties. As in the case of Handheld above, the possibility of lower interest rates can make an otherwise unattractive venture attractive.

Overall, a built-to-suit lease, with a stable, financially solvent industrial firm that will renew through successive leases, can provide the investor with a handsome low-risk return.

CHAPTER 17

Parking Lots

Parking lots are cash generating machines. Parking lots can be low-cost, low-technology facilities that are simple to operate. Parking lots can also be high-cost, high-technology facilities requiring a sizable staff and sophisticated management controls. The hallmark characteristic of parking lots is their high ratio of fixed to variable expenses. This means that the key to successfully developing (or purchasing) a parking lot is revenue estimation.

The potential revenue of a given parking lot is driven by location and constrained by competition. Location is always of great importance in determining the value of property, never more so than in the case of parking lots. In any suburban or urban area, there is always plenty of free parking—but it is just not in the right place. The demand for parking lots is very location specific. You are either next to the convention center or three miles away. One of these locations will not substitute for the other.

Parking lots generate heavy externalities (benefits that do not accrue to the parking lot itself). Urban hotels, stadiums, shopping mall, hospitals, and large office complexes cannot exist without parking facilities. As a result, parking lots are frequently integrated into the development of such population-intense facilities. Often times, the integrated parking facility will be an important revenue generator in its own right. Municipal governments may see the need to provide parking facilities as part of an infrastructure to support its commercial, industrial, and residential population. We are a nation on wheels. To live in our culture is to be on the go. The large bulk of the population finds the automobile a necessity and as they go from here to there, they need to park that automobile.

FINANCIAL FEASIBILITY STUDY

Success in developing or investing in a parking lot requires a thorough financial analysis. This analysis is performed in the context of a financial feasibility study. The two interrelated components to a financial feasibility study are *cost estimation* and *revenue estimation*. A smaller facility will have less cost and generate less potential revenue. A larger facility will have greater cost, but generate more potential revenue. The trick is to find that facility configuration that has the best risk and return characteristics from an investor's perspective.

Determining the viability of a particular parking facility is best done in two stages: (1) a rough preliminary analysis, and (2) a more formal detailed analysis. Both approaches have the same elements, but differ in terms of the thoroughness and detail of the data collected and analyzed. These elements consist of a revenue estimate and a cost and design estimate.

Revenue Estimation

The fist step in analyzing a potential parking facility should be an estimation of the current demand for and supply of parking at the proposed site. This can be accomplished by observing the success of existing nearby parking facilities (if any). Are they often full, over full, or relatively empty? Inquiries may also be made of the municipal traffic office as to their opinion of the need for additional parking facilities. If the parking demand appears to reflect a need for access to a particular destination (or set of destinations) inquires to those destinations may provide useful insights. This information can be formatted into a schedule detailing the number of spaces needed by day and by time of day. These estimates may be further refined into the type of parking demand desired. This is important because this approach not only yields a sense of the absolute level of demand, but of the sensitivity of that demand to price.

Revenue structures for parking facilities may be complex. Simple or complex, they revolve around a concept known as the *maximum daily rate*. The MDR is the most a single patron will be charged over a 24-hour period. All other parking rates work off the MDR.

General categories of demand include short-term/transient parkers, early-bird parkers, special-event parkers, Saturday and Sunday parkers, holiday parkers, and contract parkers. These categories of demand differ by their elasticity of demand (sensitivity to price) and the effective market area they draw from. The effective market area might be 100 yards for a short-term parker or 1,000 yards for a contract parker. The exact parameters of the effective market area will depend on the topographical characteristics of the area and the nature of the parker's destinations.

Short-Term/Transient Parkers

These parkers may need parking for a fraction of an hour or several hours. On an individual basis, their demand for parking may be only occasional or sporadic. As a group (owing to the "Law of Large Numbers"), their demand may by quite predictable and regular. Generally these parkers pay by the hour and the revenue schedule is set up to "front load" the cost to the patrons. That is, the first fraction of an hour, or the first few hours, is priced much higher than successive hours. Since short-term and transient parkers by definition only have a limited need for the consumption of a parking space, this pricing structure will have a favorable impact on the revenues of the parking facility. Where the demand for this type of parking is predictable, this is the most profitable type of service the parking facility can provide.

Demand from this source tends to have the smallest physical drawing area. The patron demand for parking is a direct and immediate function of the patron's destination. Therefore, this demand will be limited to arising from destinations in the immediate vicinity of the parking facility.

Where demand permits, the goal of the revenue structure is normally to capture 25% of the MDR in the first hour and 50% of the MDR in the first three hours. It may thus be possible to get three or four patrons in a given spot during a 24 period, potentially doubling the MDR revenues for that spot.

Early-Bird Parkers

This category of demand arises from the desire of the parking facility to fully utilize its available capacity. Early-bird parkers are price sensitive shoppers who are able to exercise discretion in determining where they park. If there are competitors nearby in the effective market area, then these parkers must be attracted by offering price discounts. Early-bird parkers have more elastic demand curves than short-term/transient parkers. This market is served by specifying a specific time slot for their parking (e.g., in by 8:00 A.M. out by 5:00 P.M.) and offering these parkers a 40% to 60% discount off the MDR.

Special-Event Parkers

Examples of special-event parking might include a sporting event, a parade, a circus, a concert, and the like. Such time-and-destination-specific parking tends to be highly inelastic. If the parking facility and the site of the event are in close physical proximity, this often means a flat fee can be charged equivalent to the MDR for the event because parking is event dependent rather than time dependent. Where the parking facility is located on the outer edge of the effective market area, price concessions may be warranted to attract parkers.

Saturday and Sunday

In most urban settings, parking demand is weakest on the weekend. Offices and business are closed and the need for short-term and transient parking declines. If the effective marketing area of the parking facility includes attractive retail destinations, price concessions may stimulate the use of the facility. If the local retail destinations are large, they might even be interested in subsidizing parking fees to encourage their business. Downtown retail shopping districts are often at a severe disadvantage to suburban shopping malls on the weekends. Many parking facilities use low flat rates to entice weekend parkers.

Holidays

The demand for holiday parking shares many of the same attributes as the demand for parking on weekends. Offices and business are closed and the need for short-term and transient parking declines. An exception to this may occur over the Christmas holiday season where the demand for retail shopping is so great that parking demand will approach or exceed normal weekday demand. Under these circumstances, the normal rate schedule would apply.

Monthly-Contract Users

The demand for this market segment arises from potential patrons with employment in the effective marketing area. Depending on the degree of competition, such demand tends to be inelastic. Because the cost is large and planned to the parker, price shopping will occur if at all possible. This situation results in a wide dispersion of rates whose ultimate determination will depend on the particular circumstances of a specific facility. Monthly-contract parking rates vary between 10 and 20 times the maximum daily rate. At 21.7 times the MDR, the entire work year of 260 parking days is covered. Providing amenities such as desirable locations within the parking facility, special entrances, special exits, and expedited ticketing often mitigates the expense to monthly contract users.

Cost-and-Design Estimate

The basic dimensional unit of a parking facility is the "parking bay module," which consists of a driving lane and two rows of parking. The amount of space parking facilities allot to a module is a function of the average size of cars. Automobiles were larger in the 1970s, decreased in size in the 1980s and 1990s and, with the increasing popularity of SUVs and LTUVs, have been increasing again. Current parking lots are being built around 300 sq. ft. per module. This translates to a parking space width of about 8 ft., 8 in. It should be noted that the Americans with Disabilities Act require a certain proportion (2% for larger facilities) of parking spaces be for handicapped patrons. These spaces basically require a module twice as large as the standard-size parking module.

Parking facilities fall into two general categories: surface parking or structured parking (when a multistoried parking facility is constructed by going below grade, building up, or both). Surface parking lots are used when plenty of land is available for parking or when the land would otherwise sit idle while its ultimate "highest and best" use is determined. Structured parking lots create parking space when none existed before.

The cost of surface parking lots varies considerably with local zoning requirements and surface conditions. The cost of paving, lighting, drainage, striping, security facilities, landscaping, revenue control, and signage will generally run between $5 to $15 per square foot. This cost is exclusive of land cost.

Successfully designed surface parking lots maximize the number of parking spaces. The basic tradeoff in designing a surface lot is between 90° parking, which requires more modular width (for comfortable ingress and egress) and angled parking, which decreases the size of the parking module but also increases the number of square feet required per parking space.

Structured parking facilities may be divided into those that are self-park and those with attendant parking. Attendant parking tends to permit a more efficient utilization of space, but is associated with higher operating costs. Successful design for structured parking facilities involves finding the right design tradeoffs that maximize the facilities cash flow. It is not just a matter of finding the design that minimizes cost per parking space. The revenue each space produces must be taken into consideration also. What is desired is a design that brings about equality between the marginal revenue generated by a parking space and the marginal cost of building it.

The most common design layout for structured parking facilities is the continuous ramp, where isles and angled parking spaces are both sloped (usually no more than 6%). Convenience for the parker may be defined as continuous driving without having to pass more than 500 spaces before locating a parking space. The design should also favor an expeditious means of exit. This is often accomplished by using a single- or double helix shaped ramp. Zoning requirements require that the design should provide safe and efficient pedestrian circulation and stair fire exits. In multistoried facilities patrons—and the Americans with Disabilities Act—generally require elevators. The typical ratio is four elevators per 1,000 spaces.

The most efficient construction methods available today generally result in a cost per parking space of between $7,500 and $10,000. This translates into a cost per square foot for the gross parking area of between $20 and $25. However, it is possible to spend a lot more. The cost of below grade construction tends to increase exponentially with each level down. The same is only a little less true for building up. These costs are all exclusive of land costs.

The following illustrations are examples of parking lot developments.

ILLUSTRATION #1: SMALL SURFACE PARKING LOT, LEASEHOLD

Acquisition Phase

An investor becomes aware of a site where a small meat packing plant has been torn down to be developed into a large luxury hotel. The site is adjacent to the dense urban core of a large metropolitan area, where downtown parking is a perennial problem. The site is about the size of a football field, about 45,000 sq. ft. It is located about 1,500 ft. from the heart of the downtown area. As a result of the nature of planning, zoning, and other legal constraints, it will be five years before the work can begin on the hotel. The investor feels the site would make an excellent parking lot.

The city-planning agency estimates that, on a normal weekday, there are over 400,000 potential parkers competing for about 100,000 parking spots. Many parkers are forced to park in the outlying suburbs and take public transportation downtown. Existing parking facilities frequently block their entrances with "Parking Full" signs. The downtown area is gridlocked about 20 times a year with a variety of special events when the demand for parking becomes much greater.

A parking consultant is engaged who creates an efficient design for the lot and estimates construction costs at $6 per sq. ft. ($270,000). The resulting design will generate 285 parking slots (141 parking modules). The cost is low because the site is already partially blacktopped, existing lighting around the periphery of the lot is sufficient, and no landscaping will be required. The existing owners of the property are willing to give the investor a five-year lease on the property for $350,000 per year plus 30% of the gross receipts.

The parking consultant also does a revenue analysis. It appears that the parking facility will quickly be filled to capacity at an MDR of $20. (This is the MDR at other facilities in the effective market area.) It is felt that the following demand structure is likely.

Short-Term/Transient Parkers

Weekday demand for short-term transient parking is expected to be strong. The proposed short-term rate structure will be $5 the first hour and $2 for each hour following until the MDR is hit. With this parking structure, it is expected that the facility will be able to accommodate an average of 100 short-term parkers a weekday, at an average rate of $7 each.

Early-Bird Parkers

No early bird discounts will be offered due to the current excess demand for parking in the effective market area.

Special-Events Parkers

It is estimated that 60 special events will take place downtown on weekday evenings over the course of the year. At each of these events, the lot should be able to attract 175 patrons at a flat fee of $10.

Saturday and Sunday Parkers

It is estimated that 12 special events will occur on weekends in the downtown area. For these events the facility should be able to attract 175 patrons for a flat $10 fee. On nonspecial event weekends, the lot expects to attract an average of 50 cars for a flat $4 fee.

Holiday Parkers

As the downtown retail shopping area is moribund, it is not expected that holidays with significantly impact demand at this facility.

Contract Parkers

It is felt that there will be a very strong demand for contract parking at this location, because most other garages in the downtown area have waiting list for contract parkers. Two hundred contract parking spaces are offered at a monthly fee of 15 times the MDR ($300). In order to clear out these cars for evening events, the contract parkers only have parking rights till 6:00 P.M., at which time they are subject to the short-term transient rates.

Holding Phase

The results of the revenue estimation procedure described above can be seen in Table 17.1.

The property for the parking lot is leased and the investor self-finances the needed $270,000 in improvements. As a result, there are no interest expenses and, therefore, NOPAT and net income are the same ($120,720 per year). This can be seen in Tables 17.2 and 17.3.

It should be noted that the investor bears the full risk of carrying the lease. However, with most of the lease's costs being raised from a percentage of revenue, the risk to the investor from this source is minimal.

Break-Even Analysis

Determining the approximate risk to the partners may be approached through a break-even analysis. The investor's fixed costs would include the annual $350,00 lease payment, as well as overhead and labor expenses. Depreciation can be ignored because it is not a cash outlay. Variable costs would only include the portion of lease expense based on gross revenues (30%). The 40% tax rate is not a variable cost because it is not a function of revenues, but of earnings.

Where

$$\text{Total costs } (TC) = \text{Fixed costs } (FC) + \text{Variable costs } (VC)$$

thus,

$$TC = \$420,000 + 0.3(\text{Sales})$$

Because the break-even point (BEP) is where total costs are equal to total revenues:

$$BEP = \text{Revenues} - TC = 0: BEP = \$420,000/0.7 = \$600,000$$

TABLE 17.1 Small Surface Parking Lot, Leasehold, Revenue Structure

Demand Category	Annual Revenue
Short-term/transient[a]	$182,000
Early bird	0
Special events	105,000
Saturday/Sunday	29,000
Holiday	0
Contract	720,000
Total revenue	1,036,000

[a] This assumes a 260-weekday parking year.

TABLE 17.2 Small Surface Parking Lot, Leasehold, Net-Operating Profit after Taxes

| | | Lease Expenses | | | Direct | Overhead | | NOPAT |
Year	Revenue	Base	30%	Depreciation	Labor[a]	Expenses[b]	EBIT	EBIT(1 − tx)
1	$1,036,000	$350,000	$310,800	$54,000	$70,000	$50,000	$201,200	$120,720
2	1,036,000	350,000	310,800	54,000	70,000	50,000	201,200	120,720
3	1,036,000	350,000	310,800	54,000	70,000	50,000	201,200	120,720
4	1,036,000	350,000	310,800	54,000	70,000	50,000	201,200	120,720
5	1,036,000	350,000	310,800	54,000	70,000	50,000	201,200	120,720

[a] Assumes one full-time employee and part-time employees for 16 additional hours per day, seven days per week.
[b] Utilities, accounting, banking, and legal fees.

TABLE 17.3 Small Surface Parking Lot, Leasehold, Income Statement

| | | Lease Expenses | | | Direct | Overhead | Earnings | Taxes | Net |
Year	Revenue	Base	30%	Depreciation	Labor[a]	Expenses[b]	before Taxes	(40%)	Income
1	$1,036,000	$350,000	$310,800	$54,000	$70,000	$50,000	$201,200	$80,480	$120,720
2	1,036,000	350,000	310,800	54,000	70,000	50,000	201,200	80,480	120,720
3	1,036,000	350,000	310,800	54,000	70,000	50,000	201,200	80,480	120,720
4	1,036,000	350,000	310,800	54,000	70,000	50,000	201,200	80,480	120,720
5	1,036,000	350,000	310,800	54,000	70,000	50,000	201,200	80,480	120,720

[a] Assumes one full-time employee and part-time employees for 16 additional hours per day, seven days per week.
[b] Utilities, accounting, banking, and legal fees.

TABLE 17.4   Small Surface Parking Lot, Leasehold, Cash Flow Statement

Year	Net Income	Depreciation	Capital Required	Total Cash Flow
0			$270,000	–$270,000
1	$120,720	$54,000		174,720
2	120,720	54,000		174,720
3	120,720	54,000		174,720
4	120,720	54,000		174,720
5	120,720	54,000		174,720

NPV at 12% = $359,826
IRR = 58%

Thus, in terms of EBT, the leased parking lot's break-even at about one-third of its projected revenues. This analysis suggests a relatively low risk for the investors. In combination with the anticipated expected IRR of 58%, this investment seems wonderfully attractive. Of course, such a favorable outcome results from a combination of strong demand and favorable lease terms particular to this specific property.

This parking lot yields cash flows per year of$174,720 over the five-year holding period (Table 17.4). Having invested $270,000 the investor gains a NPV of almost $360,000 and an IRR of 58%. Parking lots can offer good risk return combinations.

Disposal Stage

With the termination of the lease, the investor no longer has any connection with the parking facility. In this example, the returns to the investor have been large and the risk small. In this location, a property the size of a football field parking at a maximum 285 cars, has shown itself to be capable of generating revenues of over $1 million a year. Parking lots are truly cash-generating machines.

SMALL SURFACE LOT, CONVENTIONAL FINANCING

Holding Phase

An interesting question to be asked about the small surface parking lot in the first illustration is what amount of conventional financing could it carry? That is, because it would be sited in an obviously attractive area (for a parking lot), it will generate gross revenues of $1,036,000 per year (Table 17.1). Labor and overhead expenses (Table 17.2) will run about $120,000 per year. If the cost of improvements for the property remains at $270,000, they would have to be depreciated over a 33-year period, resulting in an annual charge of approximately $6,923. That depreciation would, of course, generate a small tax shield. Exclusive of this tax saving, the investor would have a cash flow of about $909,000 to work with. Given that cash flow, how much property the investor could purchase would depend on the degree of financial leverage possible, the form of the loan (conventional fixed rate, five-year conventional with a balloon, five-year, interest-only with a balloon, etc.), and the interest rate.

This question is first investigated by assuming the property will be purchased for $10,000,000 with the investor taking out a loan for $8,150,000. The loan will be for 20 years with a 9% interest rate and annual payments of $892,804. The investor will make a capital contribution of $1,850,000 to provide equity for the project.

At this price for the property, the parking lot is financially viable. This may be seen by the generated NOPAT of close to $550,000 in Table 17.5. As a result of supporting the interest required by this loan, the net income illustrated in Table 17.6 is considerably reduced from this level of NOPAT. However, net income rises steadily from $105,341 to $215,198 throughout the period as a result of falling interest expenditures. Note depreciation is so small because this parking lot just used the surface ground and there were very few improvements needed so there is little to depreciate. The value of the land cannot be depreciated.

Disposal Phase

The assumption is that the property appreciates at 3% a year throughout the holding period. This yields the after-tax gain on sale of $2,752,635 indicated in Table 17.7A and a cash gain of $6,877,705 (Table 17.7B).

The resulting cash flows may now be calculated and are presented in Table 17.8. These cash flows are seen to represent a modest NPV of $941,864.15 with an IRR of 17%. The effect of going to conventional financing versus leasehold dramatically lowers the return to investors in this instance. It could be argued that this difference reflects the existence of very favorable lease terms skewing the results towards a leasehold. The real import of this distinction however is the importance of the land value in the outcome of a conventional financing versus a leasehold.

For example, if the land under consideration could be purchased for $6 million a much different outcome may be found to occur. Where the land is bought for $6,000,000 and financed with a $5,000,000 loan under the same terms as above, a large difference in the capital gain may be observed. As can be seen from Tables 17.9A and 17.9B, the resulting after-tax capital gain on the land is $6,093,789 and the actual cash gain is now a robust $8,366,366.

TABLE 17.5 Small Surface Parking Lot, Conventional Financing, Net-Operating Profits after Taxes

Year	Revenues	Direct Labor[a]	Overhead Expenses[b]	Depreciation	EBIT	Taxes (40%)	NOPAT EBIT(1 − tx)
1	$1,036,000	$70,000	$50,000	$6,923	$916,000	$366,400	$549,600
2	1,036,000	70,000	50,000	6,923	916,000	366,400	549,600
3	1,036,000	70,000	50,000	6,923	916,000	366,400	549,600
4	1,036,000	70,000	50,000	6,923	916,000	366,400	549,600
5	1,036,000	70,000	50,000	6,923	916,000	366,400	549,600
6	1,036,000	72,100	51,500	6,923	912,400	364,960	547,440
7	1,036,000	72,100	51,500	6,923	912,400	364,960	547,440
8	1,036,000	72,100	51,500	6,923	912,400	364,960	547,440
9	1,036,000	72,100	51,500	6,923	912,400	364,960	547,440
10	1,036,000	72,100	51,500	6,923	912,400	364,960	547,440

[a] Assumes one full-time employee and part-time employees for 16 additional hours per day, seven days per week, with a 3% increase after five years.
[b] Utilities, accounting, banking, and legal fees with a 3% increase after five years.

TABLE 17.6 Small Surface Parking Lot, Conventional Financing, Income Statement

Year	Revenues	Direct Labor[a]	Overhead Expenses[b]	Interest[c]	Depreciation	Earnings before Taxes	Taxes (40%)	Net Income
1	$1,036,000	$70,000	$50,000	$733,500	$6,923	$175,577	$70,231	$105,346
2	1,036,000	70,000	50,000	719,163	6,923	189,914	75,966	113,949
3	1,036,000	70,000	50,000	703,535	6,923	205,542	82,217	123,325
4	1,036,000	70,000	50,000	686,501	6,923	222,576	89,030	133,546
5	1,036,000	70,000	50,000	667,933	6,923	241,143	96,457	144,686
6	1,036,000	72,100	51,500	647,695	6,923	257,782	103,113	154,669
7	1,036,000	72,100	51,500	625,635	6,923	279,842	111,937	167,905
8	1,036,000	72,100	51,500	601,590	6,923	303,887	121,555	182,332
9	1,036,000	72,100	51,500	575,381	6,923	330,096	132,038	198,058
10	1,036,000	72,100	51,500	546,813	6,923	358,664	143,466	215,198

[a] Assumes one full-time employee and part-time employees for 16 additional hours per day, seven days per week, with a 3% increase after five years.
[b] Utilities, accounting, banking, and legal fees with a 3% increase after five years.
[c] Assumes conventional financing for 20 years at 9% with fixed payments of $892,803.77.

TABLE 17.7A　Small Surface Parking Lot, Tax Consequences of Sale of Property

Sale of property		$13,439,164
Fixed plant and improvements	$270,000	
Less accumulated depreciation	69,231	
Net fixed plant and improvements		200,769
Cost of land		$10,000,000
		3,238,395
Capital gains tax (15%)		485,759
After-tax gain on sale		2,752,635

TABLE 17.7B　Small Surface Parking Lot, Cash Gain from Sale of Property

Sale of property	$13,439,164
Less:	
Tax liability	485,759
Loan balance	6,075,700
Cash gain from sale	6,877,705

TABLE 17.8　Small Surface Parking Lot, Conventional Financing, Cash Flow Statement

Year	Net Income	Depreciation	Capital Contributions[a]	Gain on Sale of Land[b]	Net Cash Flows
0	.		-$2,120,000		-$2,120,000
1	$105,346	$6,923			112,269
2	113,949	6,923			120,872
3	123,325	6,923			130,248
4	133,546	6,923			140,469
5	144,686	6,923			151,609
6	154,669	6,923			161,592
7	167,905	6,923			174,828
8	182,332	6,923			189,255
9	198,058	6,923			204,981
10	215,198	6,923		$6,877,705	7,099,826

[a] $270,000 plus $1,850,000.
[b] Consequent on the fixed payments of $910,600 to amortize the loan. See Table 17.7B.

NPV at 12% = $941,864.15
IRR = 17%

TABLE 17.9A   Small Surface Parking Lot, Tax Gain (Loss) on Sale of Land

Sale of property		$13,439,164
Fixed plant and improvements	$270,000	
Less accumulated		
depreciation	0	
Net fixed plant and improvements		270,000
Original cost		6,000,000
Gain on sale of land		7,169,164
Capital gains tax (15%)		1,075,375
After-tax gain on sale		6,093,789

TABLE 17.9B   Small Surface Parking Lot, Cash Gain (Loss) on Sale of Land

Original cost	$6,000,000	
Less mortgage balance	3,727,423	
Recaptured principal		$2,272,577
Cash gain on sale of land		8,366,366

This gain will be augmented by the greater cash flows consequent on reduced financing charges. This may be seen in Table 17.10. NPV is seen to increase by a factor of three to $2,974,840 and the IRR rises to 27%. This improved performance results not from anything having to do with the parking lot per se, but with the value of the underlying property itself. Under these circumstances the parking-lot use becomes a vehicle to hold the property for speculative purposes.

Break-Even Analysis

The risk associated with a conventionally financed parking lot—both with the $6 million and $10 million purchase price—may be approached through a break-even analysis. In a conventionally financed parking lot all costs are fixed! It may be argued that labor costs are variable at least to some extent. While this may be true, as a practical matter the amount of possible variation would be so small as to be inconsequential.

Fixed expenses other than the loan payment would be $126,293, so with a $5 million loan, the BEP would be $684,985 and with a $8.125 million loan the BEP would be $1,036,893. These break-even points are substantially higher than that found in a leasehold situation ($600,000 in the above example). The projected revenues of $1,036,000 (Table 17.1) suggest that if the parking lot were to succeed as a parking lot, the investor would need to be at the $6 million purchase price. The $10 mil-

TABLE 17.10 Small Surface Parking Lot, Conventional Financing, Cash Flow Statement

Year	Net Income	Depre- ciation	Capital Contributions[a]	Gain on Sale of Land[b]	Net Cash Flows
0			$1,270,000		-$1,270,000
1	$105,346	$6,923			112,269
2	113,949	6,923			120,872
3	123,325	6,923			130,248
4	133,546	6,923			140,469
5	144,686	6,923			151,609
6	154,669	6,923			161,592
7	167,905	6,923			174,828
8	182,332	6,923			189,255
9	198,058	6,923			204,981
10	215,198	6,923		$8,366,366	8,588,487

[a] $270,000 plus $1,000,000.
[b] Consequent on the fixed payments of $547,732.38 to amortize the loan. See Table 17.9B.

NPV = $2,974,840
IRR = 27%

lion purchase price puts the investor slightly underwater. Given the validity of Murphy's Law—if anything can go wrong, it will—the higher price would rule out the investment as a pure parking lot. However, if the investor expected strong price appreciation of the underlying property, and has sufficiently deep pockets to absorb a negative cash flow, then the use of the property as a parking lot becomes secondary to supporting land speculation. The use of the land as a parking lot, then, has the function of lowering the carrying costs of the land.

ILLUSTRATION #2: FOUR-STORY ABOVE-GROUND PARKING LOT, CONVENTIONAL FINANCING

Acquisition Phase

As a simple ground-level facility, this 45,000 sq. ft. property was designed to accommodate a maximum of 285 cars. With the most efficient possible, long-span, single-helix design and the necessary columns, elevators, stairwells, and pedestrian walkways, the proposed parking structure would reduce the capacity at each level to 225 cars for a total

TABLE 17.11   Four-Story Parking Lot, Conventional Financing, Revenue Structure[a]

Demand Category	Annual Revenue
Short-term/transient	$618,800
Early bird	0
Special events	357,000
Saturday/Sunday	98,600
Holiday	0
Contract	2,448,000
Total revenue	3,522,400

[a] Compared to the revenue schedule in Table 17.1, the reduction in spaces per level reduces per-level revenue about 15%, based on a 260-weekday parking year and the same demand configuration.

capacity of 900 parking spots. Construction costs are estimated to be $10,000 per parking spot or $9 million in total.

The property itself is to be purchased for $6 million, bringing total capital need to $15 million. The investor forms an LLC, known as "Big City Properties," with three business associates. Big City Properties finances this capital need by putting up $3 million of their own money and obtaining a $12 million conventional 20-year loan at 9% with flat annual principle and interest payments of $1,314,558.

This illustration considers the same basic revenue structure as developed in the above examples. That is, a parking lot in the effective demand area of a downtown urban core that is characterized by excess demand. The presumption here is that this excess demand is sufficient to fill the four stories because it has filled the parking lot when it was just on ground level. Consequently, the revenue structure remains unchanged, except for the reduction in parking spaces per level from 285 to 225. This means total revenue will be projected at $3,522,400 (Table 17.11).

Holding Phase

The projected NOPAT is considerable and reflects the underlying viability of the project consequent on the strong revenue projections made. Thus, this project will consistently generate NOPAT of over $1.9 million for a four-story parking lot that is conventionally financed (Table 17.12).

The income statement for the four-story parking lot (Table 17.13) presents a positive income flow ranging from $1.2 million to $1.3 million. This increase in net income for the parking lot reflects the fact that the increase in construction costs and loss of parking capacity are more than offset by the revenue from the additional parking spaces at the margin.

TABLE 17.12 Four-Story Parking Lot, Conventional Financing, Net-Operating Profits after Taxes

Year	Revenues	Direct Labor[a]	Overhead Expenses[b]	Depreciation	EBIT	Taxes (40%)	NOPAT EBIT$(1-tx)$
1	$3,522,400	$140,000	$90,000	$230,769	$3,292,400	$1,316,960	$1,975,440
2	3,522,400	140,000	90,000	230,769	3,292,400	1,316,960	1,975,440
3	3,522,400	140,000	90,000	230,769	3,292,400	1,316,960	1,975,440
4	3,522,400	140,000	90,000	230,769	3,292,400	1,316,960	1,975,440
5	3,522,400	140,000	90,000	230,769	3,292,400	1,316,960	1,975,440
6	3,522,400	144,200	92,700	230,769	3,285,500	1,314,200	1,971,300
7	3,522,400	144,200	92,700	230,769	3,285,500	1,314,200	1,971,300
8	3,522,400	144,200	92,700	230,769	3,285,500	1,314,200	1,971,300
9	3,522,400	144,200	92,700	230,769	3,285,500	1,314,200	1,971,300
10	3,522,400	144,200	92,700	230,769	3,285,500	1,314,200	1,971,300

[a] Assumes two full-time employees and part-time employees for 32 additional hours per day, seven days per week, with a 3% increase after five years.
[b] Utilities, accounting, banking, and legal fees with a 3% increase after five years.

TABLE 17.13 Four-Story Parking Lot, Conventional Financing, Income Statement

Year	Revenues	Direct Labor[a]	Overhead Expenses[b]	Interest[c]	Depreciation[d]	Earnings before Taxes	Taxes (40%)	Net Income
1	$3,522,400	$140,000	$90,000	$1,080,000	$230,769	$1,981,631	$792,652	$1,188,978
2	3,522,400	140,000	90,000	1,058,890	230,769	2,002,741	801,096	1,201,645
3	3,522,400	140,000	90,000	1,035,880	230,769	2,025,751	810,300	1,215,451
4	3,522,400	140,000	90,000	1,010,799	230,769	2,050,832	820,333	1,230,499
5	3,522,400	140,000	90,000	983,460	230,769	2,078,170	831,268	1,246,902
6	3,522,400	144,200	92,700	953,662	230,769	2,101,069	840,428	1,260,641
7	3,522,400	144,200	92,700	921,181	230,769	2,133,550	853,420	1,280,130
8	3,522,400	144,200	92,700	885,777	230,769	2,168,954	867,581	1,301,372
9	3,522,400	144,200	92,700	847,187	230,769	2,207,544	883,018	1,324,526
10	3,522,400	144,200	92,700	805,123	230,769	2,249,607	899,843	1,349,764

[a] Assumes two full-time employees and part-time employees for 32 additional hours per day, seven days per week, with a 3% increase after five years.
[b] Utilities, accounting, banking, and legal fees with a 3% increase after five years.
[c] Based on a 20-year, 9% loan with annual fixed payments of $1,314,558.
[d] $9 million building depreciated over 39 years.

Disposal Phase

The construction of the $9 million building probably prohibits conversion of the property to another use. Therefore, it becomes necessary to value the property at the end of the holding period. The value of the parking lot will be determined by its ability to earn income. In its 10th year of operation, the parking lot shows net income of $1,349,764. Market data reveal parking lots normally sell between six and 12 times earnings. As this parking lot has shown great stability of revenue and—because it has not raised its rates in 10 years—growth potential, it sells for 11 times earnings or $15 million. This sale produces an after tax gain of $1,961,538 and a cash gain of $8,015,723 (indicated in Table 17.14A and 17.14B).

The net impact of the sale of the parking lot would produce the cash flows indicated in Table 17.15. The investors receive an NPV for their investment of $7,914,515 and a generous return on their equity of 50%, having had positive cash flow from the beginning of the project. This parking lot certainly proved a handsome risk-return opportunity for its investors.

Break-Even Analysis

The risk associated with this four-story, conventionally financed parking lot may be approached through a break-even analysis. As above, con-

TABLE 17.14A   Four-Story Parking Lot, Tax Gain (Loss) on Sale of Land

Sale of property		$15,000,000
Fixed assets	$9,000,000	
Less accumulated depreciation	2,307,692	
Net fixed assets		6,692,308
Cost of land		6,000,000
Gain on sale of land		2,307,692
Capital gains tax (15%)		346,154
After-tax gain on sale		1,961,538

TABLE 17.14B   Four-Story Parking Lot, Cash Gain (Loss) on Sale of Land

Original cost	$15,000,000	
Less mortgage balance	8,945,816	
Recaptured principal		$6,054,184
Cash gain on sale of property		8,015,723

TABLE 17.15 Small Surface Parking Lot, Conventional Financing, Cash Flow Statement

Year	Net Income	Depreciation	Capital Contributions[a]	Gain on Sale of Land[b]	Net Cash Flows
0			$3,000,000		-$3,000,000
1	$1,188,978	$230,769			1,419,748
2	1,201,645	230,769			1,432,414
3	1,215,451	230,769			1,446,220
4	1,230,499	230,769			1,461,268
5	1,246,902	230,769			1,477,671
6	1,260,641	230,769			1,491,411
7	1,280,130	230,769			1,510,899
8	1,301,372	230,769			1,532,141
9	1,324,526	230,769			1,555,296
10	1,349,764	230,769		$8,015,723	9,596,256

[a] $3 million equity plus $12 million loan to capitalize the parking lot.
[b] Consequent on the fixed payments of $1,314,558 to amortize the loan. See Table 17.14B.

NPV at 12% = $7,914,515
IRR = 50%

ventionally financed parking lots only have fixed costs! Fixed expenses other than the loan payment would be $270,000; so, with the $12 million loan, the break-even point would be $1,570,764. That is, less than half of projected revenues. Under the conditions specified above, this is a very good risk return combination for Big City Properties.

ILLUSTRATION #3: EIGHT-STORY PARKING LOT, FOUR ABOVE GRADE, FOUR BELOW GRADE, CONVENTIONAL FINANCING

The above potential success with the four-story, above-grade parking lot raises the interesting question of just what size parking lot would be optimal at this site. Assuming the parking lot is limited to four stories up by zoning regulations, an estimate could be developed for going down an additional four stories.

Acquisition Phase

The assumption will also be of perfectly elastic demand for parking spots at this location. This means that the revenue structure will not change as the supply of parking lots increases. Perhaps this is a version of "Build it, and they will come." While formatted for a simple ground-level facility, this 45,000 sq. ft. property was designed to accommodate a maximum of 285 cars. With the most efficient possible long-span, single-helix design and the necessary columns, elevators, stairwells, and pedestrian walkways, the capacity is reduced at each level to 225 cars for a total capacity of 900 parking spots in the upper four floors and 215 spots in the lower four floors. As a result of the difficulties associated with below-grade construction, construction costs are estimated to be $20,000 per parking spot or $35,200,000.

Given the continuation of the demand pattern noted above, the annual revenue estimate for this eight-story facility will be $6,692,560 as shown in Table 17.16.

In this situation, the investors intend to finance this parking lot with $7,200,000 of their own equity and a loan of $34 million to cover the cost of the building and the land ($6 million). They expect to get a 20-year loan with annual fixed P&I payments at an interest rate of 9%.

Holding Phase

This situation yields a NOPAT (Table 17.17) of around $3.7 million a year over the 10-year period. An ample NOPAT capable of withstanding the financial consequences of the partnership's proposed capital structure.

TABLE 17.16   Eight-Level Parking Lot, Conventional Financing, Revenue Structure[a]

Demand Category	
Short-term/transient	$1,175,720
Early bird	0
Special events	678,300
Saturday/Sunday	187,340
Holiday	0
Contract	4,651,200
Total revenue	6,692,560

[a] Compared to the revenue schedule in Table 17.11, the reduction in spaces in the lower four levels reduces revenue to 90% of the upper four levels, given the same parking year and demand configuration.

TABLE 17.17 Eight-Level Parking Lot, Conventional Financing, Net-Operating Profits after Taxes

Year	Revenues	Direct Labor[a]	Overhead Expenses[b]	Depreciation	EBIT	Taxes (40%)	NOPAT EBIT$(1 - tx)$
1	$6,692,560	$250,000	$180,000	$902,564	$6,262,560	$2,505,024	$3,757,536
2	6,692,560	250,000	180,000	902,564	6,262,560	2,505,024	3,757,536
3	6,692,560	250,000	180,000	902,564	6,262,560	2,505,024	3,757,536
4	6,692,560	250,000	180,000	902,564	6,262,560	2,505,024	3,757,536
5	6,692,560	250,000	180,000	902,564	6,262,560	2,505,024	3,757,536
6	6,692,560	257,500	185,400	902,564	6,249,660	2,499,864	3,749,796
7	6,692,560	257,500	185,400	902,564	6,249,660	2,499,864	3,749,796
8	6,692,560	257,500	185,400	902,564	6,249,660	2,499,864	3,749,796
9	6,692,560	257,500	185,400	902,564	6,249,660	2,499,864	3,749,796
10	6,692,560	257,500	185,400	902,564	6,249,660	2,499,864	3,749,796

[a] Assumes four full-time employees and part-time employees for 40 additional hours per day, seven days per week, with a 3% increase after five years.
[b] Utilities, accounting, banking, and legal fees with a 3% increase after five years.

Despite the reduced parking capacity of the below-grade floors and the doubling of per-parking lot construction costs, net income (Table 17.18) exceeds that generated by the four-story upper level parking lot configuration by $191,000 in the first year to $490,000 in the 10th year (Table 17.12). This is impressive testimony to the ability of parking lots to generate substantial revenue relative to their costs in situations of strong demand.

Disposal Phase

The construction of the $35.2 million building prohibits conversion of the property to another use. Therefore, it becomes necessary to value the property at the end of the 10-year holding period. The value of the parking lot will be determined by its ability to earn income. In its 10th year of operation, the parking lot shows net income of $1,839,548.

Market data reveal parking lots normally sell between six and 12 times earnings. As this parking lot has shown great stability of revenue and—because it has not raised its rates in 10 years—growth potential, it sells for a little over 11 times earnings or $21 million. As the original cost of the land and buildings was $41.2 million, this produces a loss for the partnership. As can be seen from Tables 17.19A and 17.19B, even with a capital gains offset, the paper loss totals almost $9.5 million, although there is an actual cash gain of $6.4 million.

The net impact of the sale of the parking lot would thus produce the cash flows indicated in Table 17.20. The investors receive an NPV for their investment of $11,315,383 and a return on their equity of 33%, having had positive cash flow from the beginning of the project. Note that both the NPV and the IRR are below that produced by the four-story, above-grade parking lot alone. While the eight-level parking lot is profitable in its own right (and certainly has good risk return parameters), this decline in performance suggests that the marginal profitability of parking lot places has ceased to be positive. This undoubtedly reflects the high cost of construction and the reduction in parking capacity. It would seem that, given a choice between the four-story, above-grade parking lot and the eight-level parking lot, the wise investor would choose the former.

Break-Even Analysis

The risk associated with this eight-level, conventionally financed parking lot may be approached through a break-even analysis. As in the previous illustrations, conventionally financed parking lots only have fixed costs. Fixed expenses other than the loan payment would be $430,000, so with the $34 million loan, the break-even point would be $4,228,325. That is about one-third less than projected revenues. Under conditions of strong demand, that would appear to suggest an adequate margin of safety.

TABLE 17.18 Eight-Level Parking Lot, Conventional Financing, Income Statement

Year	Revenues	Direct Labor[a]	Overhead Expenses[b]	Interest[c]	Depreciation[d]	Earnings before Taxes	Taxes (40%)	Net Income	Gain over Four Story Construction
1	$6,692,560	$250,000	$180,000	$3,060,000	$902,564	$2,299,996	$919,998	$1,379,998	$191,019
2	6,692,560	250,000	180,000	3,000,188	902,564	2,359,808	943,923	1,415,885	214,240
3	6,692,560	250,000	180,000	2,934,992	902,564	2,425,003	970,001	1,455,002	239,551
4	6,692,560	250,000	180,000	2,863,930	902,564	2,496,066	998,427	1,497,640	267,141
5	6,692,560	250,000	180,000	2,786,471	902,564	2,573,525	1,029,410	1,544,115	297,213
6	6,692,560	257,500	185,400	2,702,041	902,564	2,645,055	1,058,022	1,587,033	326,391
7	6,692,560	257,500	185,400	2,610,013	902,564	2,737,083	1,094,833	1,642,250	362,120
8	6,692,560	257,500	185,400	2,509,702	902,564	2,837,394	1,134,958	1,702,437	401,064
9	6,692,560	257,500	185,400	2,400,363	902,564	2,946,733	1,178,693	1,768,040	443,514
10	6,692,560	257,500	185,400	2,281,183	902,564	3,065,913	1,226,365	1,839,548	489,783

[a] Assumes four full-time employees and part-time employees for 40 additional hours per day, seven days per week, with a 3% increase after five years.
[b] Utilities, accounting, banking, and legal fees with a 3% increase after five years.
[c] Based on a 20-year, 9% loan with annual fixed payments of $3,724,580.
[d] $35,200,000 building depreciated over 39 years.

TABLE 17.19A Eight-Level Parking Lot, Tax Gain (Loss) on Sale of Land

Property sold		$21,000,000
Fixed assets	35,200,000	
Less accumulated depreciation	9,025,641	
Net fixed assets		26,174,359
Cost of land		6,000,000
Gain (loss) on sale of land		–11,174,359
Capital gains tax (15%)		–1,676,154
After-tax gain (loss) on sale		–9,498,205

TABLE 17.19B Eight-Level Parking Lot, Cash Gain (Loss) on Sale of Land

Original cost	$41,200,000
Less mortgage balance	25,346,478
Recaptured principal	15,853,522
Cash gain on sale of land	6,355,317

TABLE 17.20 Eight-Level Parking Lot, Conventional Financing, Cash Flow Statement

Year	Net Income	Depre- ciation	Capital Contri- butions[a]	Gain on Sale of Land	Net Cash Flows
0			$7,200,000		–$7,200,000
1	$214,240	$2,359,808			2,574,048
2	239,551	2,425,003			2,664,555
3	267,141	2,496,066			2,763,207
4	297,213	2,573,525			2,870,738
5	326,391	2,645,055			2,971,446
6	362,120	2,737,083			3,099,203
7	401,064	2,837,394			3,238,459
8	443,514	2,946,733			3,390,247
9	489,783	3,065,913			3,555,696
10	1,839,548	902,564		$6,355,317	9,097,429

[a] $7.2 million equity plus $34 million loan to capitalize the parking lot for a total cost of $41,200,000.

NPV at 12% = $11,315,383
IRR = 39%

SUMMARY

Where demand conditions support them, parking lots provide excellent opportunities for investors. With strong demand, parking lots are cash generating machines that require relatively little upkeep. Parking lots generally have high fixed costs unless the property is leased for a percentage of the gross. In either case, the parking lot is likely to have a high degree of operating leverage. In the presence of strong demand, this situation makes for profitable outcomes

As a result of their relatively low construction costs and strong cash flow, parking lots may serve as a temporary use for land held for speculative purposes. Investing from this perspective is a far cry from investing in a parking lot as a parking lot. Where the parking lot is used as a vehicle for land speculation, risk and return are likely to be quite high owing to the uncertain nature of future land values. In contrast, investing in a parking lot as a parking lot generally may be expected to have a good return with relatively low risk. The key factor in mitigating that risk is accurately assessing the demand for parking in a particular location.

CHAPTER 18

Hotels and Motels as Commercial Real Estate Investments

Hotels and motels provide wonderful opportunities for passive investors looking for excellent risk-return opportunities—or for active investors short on cash but long on a desire to work hard to build sweat equity in a business. Overall, the "hospitality" business (which offers lodging and food) has tended to the strong secular growth characterizing an affluent society one might expect. Americans will travel on just about any excuse, including trips to resorts, the ocean, national and local parks, visiting relatives, class reunions, weddings and funerals, or just to sight-see. However, the industry is prone to shocks affecting the confidence of travelers or the cost of travel. 9/11 had a significant impact on travel throughout the nation, as well as New York City itself. In the spring of 2003, sniper killings in the Washington, D.C. and northern Virginia area, resulted in a dramatic fall in lodging occupancy in that region. The problems with the cost and availability of gasoline since the 1970s also had a significant impact on the demand for away-from-home lodging.

Despite some unevenness in demand, opportunities for successful hotels and motels are likely to increase in the future. Travel and guest lodging are luxury goods in an ever more affluent society. Our increasingly mobile lifestyle assures a constant increase in the demand for lodging services.

The industry is characterized by a large number of segments providing more or less good substitutes for each other in a given lodging market. Hotels may be huge skyscrapers, costing hundreds of millions of dollars, capable of hosting thousands of guests located in the center of the city next to a convention center or sports arena. At the other end of the spectrum, lies the 10-unit, "ma and pa" guest cottage on the side of a stream in a rural area adjacent to a state forest. It is important to note that there are at least a dozen market segments between these two extremes, which cater to a wide variety of tastes, preferences and expectations.

The economic success of a hotel or motel is driven by "room revenue." That is, how much revenue can be expected to be derived from a room in a given year. Room revenue will be a function of how often it is occupied (the *average occupancy rate* or AOR) and the daily price of the room (the *average daily rate* (ADR) times 365). Hotels and motels properties frequently include restaurant, meeting, and convention facilities. The reason for this has to do with the potential synergy between these businesses and the lodging business. Obviously, providing facilities for a wedding reception increases the likelihood of the lodging function being used by the wedding guests. Tired travelers need food as well as rest. Traveling salespeople and businesspeople frequently like to relax at a bar while away from home. Nevertheless, the underlying economics of those businesses per se are quite different from that of the lodging service and generally require quite a different set of management skills. As a result, most hotel and motel owners lease those facilities to others rather than trying to manage such different businesses themselves.

Room revenue is such an important criteria of economic success that motels are frequently valued as a multiple of room revenue. Hotels and motels are most frequently priced at between two and four times room revenue. Variances in this multiple may arise because of (1) the existence of nonroom revenue associated with the property; (2) the potential for growth in either or both the AOR and ADR; or (3) the physical condition of the property, which may or may not require significant upgrading and maintenance.

Marketing is extremely important in determining the success or failure of a hotel or motel. The industry is highly competitive. The traveler normally has a choice among many alternatives. Location, street appeal, amenities, and price usually determine which destination is selected. However, this selection process can be markedly affected by advertisement or other marketing activities. This is why so much (65%) of the industry is dominated by branded franchises (chains). Hotels and motels not so branded are called "independents." A branded hotel or motel has a well-defined image that gives the traveler a degree of assurance as to what he or she will find. For years, the slogan at Holiday Inn was "No surprises!" Hotels and motels are able to upgrade (or downgrade) themselves as a result of these factors. Most hotels are in a continual state of flux with properties upgrading or downgrading to another market segment.

Hotel and motel franchises charge a flat franchise fee (either one time or annually) and then a percentage of revenues as a royalty. The franchiser generally offers advice and suggestions as to location, operations and local marketing practices, in addition to providing a brand associated image. The decision as to whether or not to operate as a franchisee or an independent depends to a considerable extent on local conditions, the strength of demand in the local lodging market, the degree of competition in the local lodging market, the characteristics of that market (e.g., located next to an interstate or in a remote area away from major highways), the condition of the facility, and/or the experience and expertise of the hotel/motel owner. The general calculus as to whether or not to be an independent (or to select among different franchises) is to determine if room revenue without a franchise is larger than room revenue less franchise expenses with a franchise. The reason that a franchised hotel/motel may have larger room revenue after franchise expenses is largely because the brand image of the franchise provides a higher AOR and/or allows a higher ADR.

One of the interesting attributes of hotels and motels is that their value as a hotel/motel may be less than if the property was converted to another use. It is not uncommon for hotels and motels in resort areas, where facilities are limited, to profitably convert to condos or even timeshares. Hotels and motels may also be converted to apartments, retirement homes, offices, or retail shops. Thinking "out of the box" may prove quite rewarding to the astute investor.

FRANCHISE OPPORTUNITIES

The majority of hotels and motels are members of a franchise chain. The reasons for this are basically that the benefits received from this arrangement exceed the cost of the franchise. The benefits include a standardized image, continuous advertising and promotion of that image, access to an online reservation system, a system of "perks and rewards" that encourage repeat customers, help on local marketing and advertising practices, and technical help in managing and siting the hotel or motel. Costs typically involve a fixed charge franchise fee based on the number of rooms in the hotel/motel (typically running from a few hundred dollars to more than $1,000 per room) and a royalty based on a percent of room revenues (usually 4% to 8%).

The franchise advantages of a standardized image, continuous advertising and promotion of that image, access to an online reservation system, and a system of "perks and rewards" that encourage repeat customers generally will translate into higher average occupancy rates and higher average daily rates for the franchisee. The underlying economics of the motel business is that the response of profitability to any increase in ADR or AOR will be more than enough to pay any reasonable franchise fee or royalty. The only question for the potential franchisee is which franchise works best for them.

Entering into a franchise arrangement is not to be taken lightly. Becoming a franchisee involves signing a contract that commits the franchise to serious obligations. The prospective franchisee should be sure to consider the following elements of the contract:

■ *Term.* The number of the contract years in the franchise agreement. This is important because it permits the franchise to get out of the franchising arrangement without additional costs or if the franchisee wishes to continue as a franchisee, the amount of relicensing fees due at that time.

■ *Liquidated damages.* Lump-sum cash penalties the owner pays to the franchise company if the owner terminates the franchise agreement early.

■ *Exit windows.* Specific times during the agreement that allow termination without liquidated damages.

■ *Fees.* (1) Application fees (franchise agreements are generally nontransferable and prospective purchasers must apply for a new agreement); (2) relicense fees; (3) royalty fees; (4) marketing fees; and (5) reservation system fees.

■ *The property improvement plan (PIP).* A listing of improvements required by the franchise to maintain brand quality and consistency. A PIP for the new purchaser of an existing franchise is generally more extensive than improvements required by the franchise for the existing owner. The PIP is often referred to as the "punch list."

Different franchises offer different benefits and have different costs. What is right for a particular location or situation depends on a number of unique factors. Relative to those factors the prospective franchisee should consider:

■ *The definition of market served.* One of the principal benefits of being a franchisee is having a brand name that is well defined and attractive to its potential market. There are an array of market segments to be served, including full-service, limited-service, budget, economy, upper-economy, midmarket, upper-midmarket, extended-stay, and the luxury market. The greater the clarity of the brand focus and the wider its recognition, the more valuable it will prove.

■ *Percent of room sales.* Most franchises have a proprietary reservation system. A measure of the franchise's strength is the percent that are generated by the reservation system.

■ *Brand average daily rate and occupancy levels.* Another measure of franchise strength. Be sure to get both the national and regional statistics.

■ *Technical support.* One of the best ways to learn is by the experience of others. There are many "tricks of the trade" to be learned in this business. Seemingly small factors can make a big difference to success rates. The franchiser should have an active program to disseminate this type of information.

■ *Area of protection.* The franchiser should provide site location support if necessary or, if the location is already established, a market evaluation process. The franchisee should know how close another property in the same franchise system could be placed to the franchisee's property in the future.

While a number of newly constructed hotels/motels are developed initially as franchise properties, it is quite common for an existing facility to rebrand itself with another franchise. Conversion issues that should be considered include:

■ *Which franchises are available.* Given franchises may or may not be appropriate given the property's physical structure, amenities, location, and distance from other properties of the same brands?

■ *Profitability considerations.* Which franchise is best for the market served, which will allow the property to achieve maximum revenue and profitability? Will the required improvements, franchise fees, and restrictions give a sufficient return on the investment? Is the franchise worth the cost?

Given the dynamic nature of the hotel/motel market, potential franchisee's need the ability to adapt to changing market circumstances. This would include:

■ *Contract negotiability.* The contract terms should not be written in stone. Changing circumstances require different responses. The franchisee should have the ability to renegotiate terms and conditions of the franchise agreement on a case-by-case basis. At times there is a phase-in of fees over the first 2 to 3 years, or a negotiated time frame to complete required upgrades.

ILLUSTRATION #1: SUPER 8 MOTEL CONVERSION

Acquisition Phase

The property under consideration is a Super 8 with 25 units and a manager's apartment on 2.5 acres located on the edge of a town with a rapidly expanding university. The motel is a two-story stucco building with exterior corridors. There is a two-bedroom manager's apartment located at the entrance to the motel. Other than phone service, the motel offers no amenities. The Super 8 has been allowed to deteriorate over the years and could currently be described as "shabby." Room revenue is $6,387.50, reflecting an AOR of 50% and an ADR of $35. The property is offered at two times room revenue for a total price of $319,375 ($6,387.50 × 25).

Ron Smith, a recent university graduate, is a very ambitious person who feels that he would like to be his own boss. He is attracted to this motel because he sees it as full of potential that could be realized if he were manager. It is his opinion that the area will grow rapidly and that it is underserved by hotels and motels. He is also interested in this property as an investment in the underlying value of the land. Aside from the desire to own his own business, Ron feels that within 20 years the town will have expanded to the point where this 2.5 acres will become much more valuable than it is at present. Ron would like the opportunity to try out his business skills in upgrading and more effectively marketing the motel. Ron Smith is willing to act as the motel's manager for five years and live in the manager's apartment, but after that he wishes to find a full-time manager.

Ron estimates that refurbishing the rooms will require $2,000 per room for a total of $50,000 and general refurbishment of the building itself another $50,000. Ron would also like to add a prominent lighted sign with a signboard at the front of the motel for a cost of $20,000. Ron also wishes to install a 36-channel cable TV system that will have an up-front cost of $6,000.

Ron feels the Super 8 affiliation should be severed because it is associated with the poor condition of the motel and wishes to become a franchisee of the Days Inn motel chain to develop a new image. He is also impressed by the efficacy of the Days Inn automated reservation system. The franchise fee for Days Inn is $25,000 plus $5,000 for the reservation system, and a royalty fee of 4% of room revenue. Altogether Ron is looking at an up-front cost of $475,375.

Ron has recently inherited $150,000 that he is willing to put into the motel as equity. He would like to hold the motel as a property within his Subchapter S corporation. He is initially turned down by a local bank for a loan for the remainder of the needed funds, but eventually is successful in securing a Small Business Administration 20-year loan for $335,375. Both the corporation and Ron personally sign for the mortgage. The mortgage is fully amortizing and requires a monthly payment of $35,439. Ron purchases the motel and closes it for three months while the renovations are underway. The cash flows associated with acquiring the property are indicated in Table 18.1.

TABLE 18.1 Super 8 Conversion, Initial Cash Flows

Outflows:	
Hotel cost	$319,375.00
Land	100,000
Building	219,375
Room refurbishment	50,000
Building improvements	50,000
Franchise fee	25,000
Reservation system	5,000
Sign	20,000
Cable TV installation	6,000
Total cash outflows	$475,375.00
Inflows:	
SBA loan	335,375
Equity from Ron Smith	150,000
Total cash inflows	485,375

Holding Phase

Ron hires a general maintenance man for $18,000 per year, two part-time hotel clerks each for 20 hours per week at a cost of another $18,000. He hires two domestics to clean the rooms. They are paid a base salary of $12,000 each plus $5 for each room they clean after it has been used. Ron is attempting to use the $5 as an incentive to have the domestics keep the rooms in tip-top shape. Ron takes a $30,000 annual salary for himself as manager.

As a result of the upgrading and refurbishment of the motel and, as a result of Ron's aggressively talking up the motel with various student groups, community groups, and social clubs in town, demand for the motel's units increases. As more people have a pleasant overnight stay at the Days Inn, word-of-mouth brings in still more business. Ron is also able to trace a number of customers to his use of the Days Inn reservation system. Greater demand allows Ron to raise his prices. This increase in demand is expressed in both the higher AOR and higher ADR noted in Table 18.2.

This higher level of demand generates NOPAT which develops from $28,000 to $118,000 over the first five years (Table 18.3). This looks low relative to the interest on the outstanding mortgage and, in fact, creates net income of only $9,000 the first year of operation (although

TABLE 18.2　Revenue Estimates, Super 8 Conversion

Year	AOR[a]	ADR[b]	Room Revenue[c]	Total Revenue[d]
1	52%	$45.00	$6,406	$160,144
2	55%	47.50	9,536	238,391
3	57%	50.00	10,403	260,063
4	59%	55.00	11,844	296,106
5	61%	60.00	13,359	333,975

[a] Average occupancy rate remains constant after five years.
[b] Average daily rate expected to increase an average of 3% per year after five years.
[c] Normally AOR × ADR × 365, but adjusted to allow for the three-month conversion period in the first year.
[d] Room revenue × 25.

this reflects that the motel was closed for renovations the first three months of that year). Table 18.4 details the elements contributing to net income. While the DCR ratio is positive and grows during this period, it starts out pretty low and is only able to gain as a result of Ron's success in raising the AOR and ADR. This motel is profitable, but the difference between a profitable motel and a losing proposition is small. Ron Smith would be in a position of having the pressure on at all times in order to keep the business successful.

If Ron elected to sell the property following a five-year holding period, as a result of the steadily rising AOR and ADR, he should easily be able to get three times room revenue of $333,975 or $1,001,975 (Table 18.5A). This sale would generate an after-tax gain of $594,790 and a cash gain of $602,665 (Table 18.5B).

A successful outcome for Ron Smith in terms of the net effect of the resultant cash flows is revealed in Table 18.6. The ending NPV of $506.485 on his $150,000 investment represents a solid return reflected in the IRR of 64%. This looks like a very nice risk return outcome for Ron Smith. However, this outcome reflects the industriousness and effort of Ron in making the business a success. Were it not for his unstinting activities in making the motel a more desirable lodging destination, the outcome need not have been as successful as it was. Successful motel management requires an unswerving personal commitment to success. A thousand small efforts resulting from a daily commitment to the success of the enterprise makes the difference in whether AOR and ADR rise or fall.

TABLE 18.3 Small Office Building Conversion, Super 8 Conversion, Holding Period NOPAT

Year	Revenues[a]	Franchise Royalty	Labor Costs[b]	Utilities[c]	Building Depreciation[d]	Furnishings Depreciation[e]	Franchise and Sign Depreciation[f]	EBIT	Taxes (30%)	NOPAT EBIT $(1 - tx)$
1	$160,144	$6,406	$76,294	$21,000	$3,454	$10,000	$3,000	$39,991	$11,997.22	$27,994
2	238,391	9,536	103,094	28,840	6,907	16,000	5,600	68,414	20,524	47,890
3	260,063	10,403	104,006	29,705	6,907	9,600	4,853	94,588	28,376	66,212
4	296,106	11,844	104,919	30,596	6,907	5,760	4,206	131,874	39,562	92,312
5	333,975	13,359	105,831	31,514	6,907	3,456	3,645	169,262	50,779	118,483

[a] From Table 18.1. Note the motel only operated for nine months of its first year.

[b] Includes maintenance man at $18,000, two part-time hotel clerks at $18,000, two domestics with a $12,000 base and a $5 per room incentive, as well as a manager's salary for Ron Smith of $30,000.

[c] Water, electric, phone service, and cable TV.

[d] The land was valued at $100,000 and the building ($219,375) was improved by $50,000 for a basis of $269,375 that was straight-line depreciated over 39 years using the half-year convention.

[e] Furniture of $30,000 is depreciated over five years using the 200% DB method and half-year convention.

[f] The sign and the franchise are depreciated over 15 years using the 200% DB method and half-year convention.

487

TABLE 18.4 Super 8 Conversion, Income Statement

Year	Revenues[a]	4% Franchise Royalty	Labor Costs[b]	Utilities[c]	Interest[d]	Total Depreciation[e]	Earnings before Taxes	Taxes (30%)	Net Income	DCR Ratio[c]
1	$160,144	$6,406	$76,294	$19,500	$28,507	$16,454	$12,984	$3,895	$9,089	1.40
2	238,391	9,536	78,583	26,780	27,918	28,507	67,068	20,120	46,947	2.45
3	260,063	10,403	80,940	27,583	27,278	21,360	92,498	27,749	64,749	3.47
4	296,106	11,844	83,368	28,411	26,585	16,873	129,025	38,708	90,318	4.96
5	333,975	13,359	85,869	29,263	25,832	14,008	165,643	49,693	115,950	6.55

[a] From Table 18.1. Note the motel only operated for nine months of its first year.

[b] Includes maintenance man at $18,000, two part-time hotel clerks at $18,000, two domestics with a $12,000 base and a $5 per room incentive, as well as a manager's salary for Ron Smith of $30,000.

[c] Water, electric, phone service, and cable TV.

[d] The land was valued at $100,000 and the building ($219,375) was improved by $50,000 for a basis of $269,375 that was straight-line depreciated over 39 years using the half-year convention.

[e] From Table 18.3.

TABLE 18.5A Super 8 Conversion, Tax Consequences of Sale of Property

Sale of building		$1,001,925
Fixed plant and improvements	$299,375	
Less accumulated depreciation	97,203	
Net fixed plant and improvements		202,172
Cost of land		100,000
Gain on sale		699,753
Capital gains tax (15%)		104,963
After-tax gain on sale		594,790

TABLE 18.5B Super 8 Conversion, Cash Gain from Sale of Property

Sale of property	$1,001,925
Less:	
Tax liability	104,963
Loan balance	294,297
Cash gain from sale	602,665

TABLE 18.6 Super 8 Conversion, Cash Flow Statement

Year	Net Income[a]	Depreciation[a]	Capital Contributions	Opportunity Apartment Cost[b]	Cash Gain on Sale of Land[c]	Net Cash Flows
0			$150,000			−$150,000
1	$9,089	$16,454		$6,300		31,842
2	46,947	28,507		8,400		83,854
3	64,749	21,360		8,400		94,509
4	90,318	16,873		8,400		115,591
5	115,950	14,008		8,400	$602,665	741,024

[a] From Table 18.4.
[b] A comparable apartment would cost $700 per month.
[c] From Table 18.5B.

NPV at 12% = $506,485
IRR = 64%

The impact of the longer 10-year holding period initially planned highlights the fact that success in the hotel and motel business is not dependent on a one-time gain far down the road, but from the cash flow arising steadily out of the operations of the hotel or motel. In the nature of the need to run faster to stay in place, after five years Ron again needs to upgrade the room furniture and does so for $25,000. Ron has also become tired of being manager and is fortunate in having a cousin who sees Ron's success and wants to get into the business. Ron pays his cousin the $30,000 salary he received and, in addition, promises a $5,000 bonus for every year his cousin can keep the AOR and ADR ratios rising.

This matter of finding an acceptable replacement for Ron is no small matter. An inept or uncaring manager will let cleanliness and service slide little by little until the motel begins to lose its repeat trade and word-of-mouth begins to discourage new guests. This will result in a slide in AOR and ADR that can have a disastrous affect on the success of the motel. It is not uncommon for motels with absentee owners to go into a downward spiral of declining AOR, declining ADR, and declining profitability. This happens because the motel owner and/or his manager becomes burned out by the exhausting daily grind that is the hallmark of this business. This situation creates both opportunities for new market entrants as well as posting a dire warning for those already in the business.

In this case the cousin is a successful replacement for Ron and is able to keep both AOR and ADR rising to 65% and $70 respectively at the end of 10 years. For the 25-room motel, this creates total room revenue of $415,188 (Table 18.7).

The rising AOR and ADR contribute to a substantially healthier NOPAT over time, reaching $167,281 in the 10th year.

Net income (Table 18.9) is also seen to grow substantially to $163,590. As EBIT grows, this has a strong impact on the DCR ratio that practically soars out of sight. This represents a continued lower level of risk exposure to the owner of the motel and his creditor.

Under the assumptions that Ron could sell his motel at three times room revenue as was the case at the end of five years, Ron would be able to sell the building for $1,245,563 for an after-tax gain of $843,733 (Table 18.10A). This sale price may be seen to generate a net cash flow of $849,692 (Table 18.10B) at the end of 10 years.

Table 18.11 shows that the net cash flows generated for Ron Smith at the end of 10 years generates a NPV of $744,347 and an IRR of 55%. It should be noted that this is more NPV (as expected) than that earned after five years but a lower rate of IRR. The lower rate of IRR reflects (1) higher labor costs resulting from the performance bonus; (2) the loss of the apartment opportunity cost; and (3) the increased length of the holding period.

TABLE 18.7   Super 8 Conversion, Revenue Estimates

Year	AOR[a]	ADR[b]	Room Revenue[c]	Total Revenue[d]
1	52%	$45.00	$6,406	$160,144
2	55%	47.50	9,536	238,391
3	57%	51.00	10,611	265,264
4	59%	55.00	11,844	296,106
5	61%	60.00	13,359	333,975
6	62%	62.00	14,031	350,765
7	63%	64.00	14,717	367,920
8	64%	66.00	15,418	385,440
9	65%	68.00	16,133	403,325
10	65%	70.00	16,608	415,188

[a] Average occupancy rate remains constant after five years.
[b] Average daily rate expected to increase an average of 3% per year after five years.
[c] Normally AOR × ADR × 365, but adjusted to allow for the three-month conversion period in the first year.
[d] Room revenue × 25.

Break-Even Analysis

The best way to analyze the Days Inn from a break-even perspective would be to consider income as a function of room revenue that in turn is a function of AOR and ADR. Motels, as is typical of all commercial real estate, are characterized by high fixed costs.

$$TR = \text{Number of rooms} \times (AOR \times 365) \times ADR$$

Total fixed costs for the Days Inn Motel would $78,000 for labor (including the cost of a manager), utilities of $28,000, and interest costs of $28,000 for an approximate annual total of $134,000. Note depreciation does not count as a cost because it does not represent a cash outlay. Variable costs are 4% of room revenue (or in this case, total revenue) and $5 per room actually cleaned ($5 × AOR × 365).

Thus,

$$TC = \$134,000 + 4\% \times (TR)$$

So,

$$BEP = TR - TC = TR - \$134,000 - 4\%(TR)$$

TABLE 18.8 Super 8 Conversion, 10-Year Holding Period NOPAT

Year	Revenues[a]	Franchise Royalty	Labor Costs[b]	Utilities[c]	Building Depreciation[d]	Furnishings Depreciation[e]	Franchise and Sign Depreciation[f]	EBIT	Taxes (30%)	NOPAT EBIT $(1-tx)$
1	$160,144	$6,406	$76,294	$21,000	$3,454	$10,000	$3,000	$39,991	$11,997.22	$27,994
2	238,391	9,536	103,094	28,840	6,907	16,000	5,600	68,414	20,524	47,890
3	265,264	10,611	104,006	29,705	6,907	9,600	4,853	99,581	29,874	69,707
4	296,106	11,844	104,919	30,596	6,907	5,760	4,206	131,874	39,562	92,312
5	333,975	13,359	105,831	31,514	6,907	3,456	3,645	169,262	50,779	118,483
6	350,765	14,031	111,288	32,460	6,907	10,184	3,159	172,737	51,821	120,916
7	367,920	14,717	111,744	33,433	6,907	8,000	2,738	190,381	57,114	133,267
8	385,440	15,418	112,200	34,436	6,907	4,800	2,373	209,306	62,792	146,514
9	403,325	16,133	112,656	35,470	6,907	2,880	2,057	227,223	68,167	159,056
10	415,188	16,608	112,656	36,534	6,907	1,728	1,782	238,973	71,692	167,281

[a] From Table 18.7. Note the motel only operated for nine months of its first year.

[b] Includes maintenance man at $18,000, two part-time hotel clerks at $18,000, two domestics with a $12,000 base and a $5 per room incentive, as well as a manager's salary of $30,000 and performance bonus of $5,000.

[c] Water, electric, phone service, and cable TV.

[d] The land was valued at $100,000 and the building ($219,375) was improved by $50,000 for a basis of $269,375 that was straight-line depreciated over 39 years using the half-year convention.

[e] Furniture of $50,000 is depreciated over the first five years using the 200% DB method and half-year convention. Furniture of $25,000 is depreciated over the next five years on the same basis.

[f] The sign and the franchise are depreciated over 15 years using the 200% DB method and half-year convention.

TABLE 18.9 Super 8 Conversion, Income Statement

Year	Revenues[a]	4% Franchise Royalty	Labor Costs[b]	Utilities[c]	Interest[d]	Total Depreciation[e]	Earnings before Taxes	Taxes (30%)	Net Income	DCR Ratio[3]
1	$160,144	$6,406	$76,294	$19,500	$28,507	$16,454	$12,984	$3,895	$9,089	1.40
2	238,391	9,536	78,583	26,780	27,918	28,507	67,068	20,120	46,947	2.45
3	265,264	10,611	80,940	27,583	27,278	21,360	97,491	29,247	68,244	3.65
4	296,106	11,844	83,368	28,411	26,585	16,873	129,025	38,708	90,318	4.96
5	333,975	13,359	85,869	29,263	25,832	14,008	165,643	49,693	115,950	6.55
6	350,765	14,031	88,445	30,141	25,015	20,250	172,882	51,865	121,018	6.91
7	367,920	14,717	91,099	31,045	24,129	17,645	189,285	56,785	132,499	7.89
8	385,440	15,418	93,832	31,977	23,168	14,080	206,966	62,090	144,876	9.03
9	403,325	16,133	96,647	32,936	22,125	11,844	223,641	67,092	156,549	10.27
10	415,188	16,608	99,546	33,924	20,993	10,417	233,699	70,110	163,590	11.38

[a] From Table 18.7. Note the motel only operated for nine months of its first year.

[b] Includes maintenance man at $18,000, two part-time hotel clerks at $18,000, two domestics with a $12,000 base and a $5 per room incentive, as well as a manager's salary for Ron Smith's cousin of $30,000.

[c] Water, electric, phone service, and cable TV.

[d] The land was valued at $100,000 and the building ($219,375) was improved by $50,000 for a basis of $269,375 that was straight-line depreciated over 39 years using the half-year convention.

[e] From Table 18.3.

TABLE 18.10A   Super 8 Conversion, Tax Consequences of Sale of Property

Sale of building		$1,245,563
Fixed plant and improvements	$324,375	
Less accumulated depreciation	171,439	
Net fixed plant and improvements		152,936
Cost of land		100,000
Gain on sale		992,627
Capital gains tax (15%)		148,894
After-tax gain on sale		843,733

TABLE 18.10B   Super 8 Conversion, Cash Gain from Sale of Property

Sale of property	$1,245,563
Less:	
Tax liability	148,894
Loan balance	246,977
Cash gain from sale	849,692

TABLE 18.11   Super 8 Conversion, Cash Flow Statement

Year	Net Income[a]	Depre-ciation[a]	Capital Contri-butions	Opportunity Apartment Cost[b]	Cash Gain on Sale of Land[c]	Net Cash Flows
0			−$150,000			−$150,000
1	$9,089	$16,454		$6,300		31,842
2	46,947	28,507		8,400		83,854
3	68,244	21,360		8,400		98,004
4	90,318	16,873		8,400		115,591
5	115,950	14,008	−25,000	8,400		113,359
6	121,018	20,250				141,268
7	132,499	17,645				150,144
8	144,876	14,080				158,956
9	156,549	11,844				168,392
10	163,590	10,417			$849,692	1,023,699

[a] From Table 18.9.
[b] A comparable apartment would cost $700 per month.
[c] From Table 18.10B.

NPV at 12% = $746,835
IRR = 56%

Solving for *TR*: 0.96*TR* = \$134,000: *BEP TR* = \$140,000 (Abstracting from the costs of the cleaning room bonus (which equal \$1,095 with a 60% ADR).

Any combination of ADR and AOR (given 25 rooms and a 365 day year) that generates about \$140,000 of total revenue is what is needed to make this motel economically viable. However, in this case, what the motel investor really wants to know is ADR and AOR elasticity.

What is important is, how much EBIT (because that is what is used to pay debt) is generated by a 1% increase in AOR or a \$1.00 increase in ADR. These answers can be obtained from the manipulation of Tables 18.3 and 18.8. For example a 1% increase in AOR in the third year of the motels operation generates an increase of EBIT of 4% (an increase of \$3,924, from \$94,588 to \$98,512). That is a pretty high degree of AOR elasticity and is suggestive of the priority that should be given this variable in developing a strategic plan for operating the motel. As a further example, an increase of \$1.00 in the ADR in the third year will result in an increase of EBIT of \$4,993 (from \$94,588 to \$98,512). In percentage term a rise of 2% (from \$50 to \$51) in the ADR gives an increase in EBIT of 5.3% (from \$94,588 to \$98,512). Again, EBIT is found responsive to changes in the ADR roughly comparable to that of the AOR.

These two variables (the ADR and the AOR) determine the basic success of most hotel operations. The good news is that the financial structure of hotel/motel operations results in both of these variables having an elastic impact on EBIT. This means that efforts directed towards raising AOR or ADSR are capable of paying off in a big way for the hotel/motel investor.

ILLUSTRATION #2: THE STARLIGHT MOTEL, TO BE OR NOT TO BE A FRANCHISEE

A comparison of an independent motel and two types of franchises is illustrated below.

Ravi Patel purchased a two-story, 52-unit independent motel known as the "Starlight Motel" with a swimming pool and a 7,500 sq. ft. meeting room for \$1,150,000 with the help of a \$260,000 interest-only loan (at 10%) from his uncle. The motel is located a half mile from a major interstate exchange, but is not visible from either highway or the interchange itself. The motel is located in a small town that does not generate much local business. Most of his business comes from travelers off the interstate who find the numerous motels located immediately around the interchange full. He has operated the motel for three years now and the pattern of costs and revenues is very clear. In fact, Ravi thinks they are set in concrete. Try as he may, the AOR seems stuck at 52% and the ADR at $49. Attempts to improve these ratios have not been successful. Ravi hires some outside labor but basically operates the motel with the help of his wife, two aunts, a brother, two teenage children, and three cousins. These nine relatives constitute his full-time work force. He pays them minimum wage ($8.00/hour), but provides them with free (but crowded) housing.

Tables 18.12–18.16 detail the financial performance of the Starlight Motel. On his investment (the fruit of 20 industrious years in the motel industry) over a 10-year holding period, Ravi expects to earn a paltry NPV of $194,626 and an IRR of 16%. Although the Starlight Motel is keeping the "wolf from the door," Ravi feels that he should be doing better. Many of his friends seem to be making a lot more money with their motels.

To improve his situation, Ravi is considering affiliating with a number of motel chains. He has three specific offers on the table:

1. An Econo Lodge affiliation will cost him no franchise fee—Econo Lodge nominally charges $17,500, but will credit a franchisee back the $17,500 for improved building improvements—and 7.5% of room revenue. In addition, Ravi will have to put up a new sign for $20,000. Ravi feels that this affiliation will boost his AOR to 56% and allow him to raise his ADR to $54.00.
2. A Knights Inn affiliation will cost $25,000, but only charge 4% of room revenue as a royalty. In addition, Ravi will have to put up a new sign for $20,000. Ravi feels that this affiliation will also allow him to boost his AOR to 56% and his ADR to $54.00.

TABLE 18.12   Starlight Motel, Revenue Estimates

Year	AOR	ADR	Room Revenue[a]	Total Revenue
1	52%	$49.00	$9,300	$483,610
2	52%	49.00	9,300	483,610
3	52%	49.00	9,300	483,610
4	52%	49.00	9,300	483,610
5	52%	49.00	9,300	483,610
6	52%	49.00	9,300	483,610
7	52%	49.00	9,300	483,610
8	52%	49.00	9,300	483,610
9	52%	49.00	9,300	483,610
10	52%	49.00	9,300	483,610

[a] 52 rooms.

TABLE 18.13 Starlight Motel, Holding Period NOPAT

Year	Revenues[a]	Outside Labor Costs	Family Labor Costs[b]	Utilities[c]	Total Depreciation[d]	EBIT	Taxes (30%)	NOPAT EBIT$(1 - tx)$
1	$483,610	$45,000	$149,760	$85,000	$72,500	$131,350	$39,405	$91,945
2	483,610	46,350	149,760	87,550	72,000	127,950	38,385	89,565
3	483,610	47,741	149,760	90,177	71,500	124,433	37,330	87,103
4	483,610	49,173	149,760	92,882	71,000	120,796	36,239	84,557
5	483,610	50,648	149,760	95,668	70,500	117,034	35,110	81,924
6	483,610	52,167	149,760	98,538	70,000	113,145	33,943	79,201
7	483,610	53,732	149,760	101,494	69,500	109,124	32,737	76,387
8	483,610	55,344	149,760	104,539	69,000	104,967	31,490	73,477
9	483,610	57,005	149,760	107,675	68,500	100,670	30,201	70,469
10	483,610	58,715	149,760	110,906	68,000	96,230	28,869	67,361

[a] From Table 18.12.

[b] Includes nine relatives at minimum wage.

[c] Water, electric, phone service, and cable TV.

[d] Includes buildings, equipment, and furnishings.

TABLE 18.14   Starlight Motel, Income Statement

Year	Revenues[a]	Total Labor Costs[a]	Utilities[a]	Interest[b]	Total Depreciation[a]	Earnings before Taxes	Taxes (30%)	Net Income
1	$483,610	$194,760	$85,000	$26,000	$72,500	$105,350	$31,605	$73,745
2	483,610	196,110	87,550	26,000	72,000	101,950	30,585	71,365
3	483,610	197,501	90,177	26,000	71,500	98,433	29,530	68,903
4	483,610	198,933	92,882	26,000	71,000	94,796	28,439	66,357
5	483,610	200,408	95,668	26,000	70,500	91,034	27,310	63,724
6	483,610	201,927	98,538	26,000	70,000	87,145	26,143	61,001
7	483,610	203,492	101,494	26,000	69,500	83,124	24,937	58,187
8	483,610	205,104	104,539	26,000	69,000	78,967	23,690	55,277
9	483,610	206,765	107,675	26,000	68,500	74,670	22,401	52,269
10	483,610	208,475	110,906	26,000	68,000	70,230	21,069	49,161

[a] From Table 18.13.
[b] 10% on a $260,000 interest-only note held by Ravi Patel's uncle.

TABLE 18.15A Starlight Motel, Tax Consequences of Sale of Property

Sale of building		$1,450,831
Fixed plant and improvements	$950,000	
Less accumulated depreciation	702,500	
Net fixed plant and improvements		247,500
Cost of land		200,000
Gain on sale		1,003,331
Capital gains tax (15%)		150,500
After-tax gain on sale		852,832

TABLE 18.15B Starlight Motel, Cash Gain from Sale of Property

Sale of property	$1,450,831
Less:	
Tax liability	150,500
Loan balance	260,000
Cash gain from sale	1,040,332

TABLE 18.16 Starlight Motel, Cash Flows

Year	Net Income[a]	Depre- ciation[a]	Capital Contributions	Cash Gain on Sale of Land[b]	Net Cash Flows
0			−$890,000		−$890,000
1	$73,745	$72,500			146,245
2	71,365	72,000			143,365
3	68,903	71,500			140,403
4	66,357	71,000			137,357
5	63,724	70,500	−25,000		109,224
6	61,001	70,000			131,001
7	58,187	69,500			127,687
8	55,277	69,000			124,277
9	52,269	68,500			120,769
10	49,161	68,000		$1,040,332	1,157,492

[a] From Table 18.14.
[b] From Table 18.15B.

NPV at 12% = $194,626
IRR = 16%

3. Ravi can also become a Howard Johnsons Express. This will cost him a $100,000 franchise fee up-front and 4% of room revenues down the road. In addition, Ravi will have to spend $20,000 on a new sign and undertake improvements costing $50,000. Due to the strength of this brand and its excellent system for referring travelers, Ravi expects this affiliation would boost his ADR to 59% and allow him to charge a $56.50 ADR.

The question confronting Ravi is: "Which of these affiliations, if any, would be best for him?"

Econo Lodge Affiliation

Table 18.17 indicates that even the minimal increase of 1% in the AOR and $2 in the ADR translates into an increase in revenue of more than $39,000 at the Starlight Motel. This, in turn, translates into a NOPAT of between $26,000 and $27,000 in Table 18.18 and net income of $23,000 to $25,000 in Table 18.19. Selling the property in the 10th year for three times earnings can be seen (Tables 18.20A and 18.20B) to bring an increased cash flow of $103,692 at the end of the disposal stage. The net effect on cash flows (Table 18.21) is to reward Ravi Patel with an increase in NPV of $161,004 and an IRR of 161 (!) s a result of his decision to switch from being an independent to being an Econo Lodge franchisee. The exceptionally high return (IRR) reflects the virtual absence of a franchise fee and thus less of an initial cash investment on the part of Ravi Patel.

TABLE 18.17   Starlight Motel, Econo Lodge Conversion, Revenue Estimates

Year	AOR	ADR	Room Revenue[a]	Total Revenue[b]
1	53%	$52.00	$10,059	$523,089
2	53%	52.00	10,059	523,089
3	53%	52.00	10,059	523,089
4	53%	52.00	10,059	523,089
5	53%	52.00	10,059	523,089
6	53%	52.00	10,059	523,089
7	53%	52.00	10,059	523,089
8	53%	52.00	10,059	523,089
9	53%	52.00	10,059	523,089
10	53%	52.00	10,059	523,089

[a] 25 rooms of 3% per year after five years. Normally AOR × ADR × 365, but adjusted to allow for the three-month conversion period in the first year.
[b] Room revenue × 25.

TABLE 18.18   Starlight Motel, Econo Lodge Conversion, Holding Period NOPAT

Year	Change in Revenues[a]	Franchise Fee	Change in Depreciation[b]	Change in EBIT[c]	Taxes (30%)	Change in NOPAT EBIT$(1-tx)$
1	$39,478	$2,961	$1,558	$37,921	$11,376	$26,544
2	39,478	2,961	2,908	36,571	10,971	25,599
3	39,478	2,961	2,520	36,958	11,088	25,871
4	39,478	2,961	2,184	37,294	11,188	26,106
5	39,478	2,961	1,893	37,586	11,276	26,310
6	39,478	2,961	1,640	37,838	11,351	26,487
7	39,478	2,961	1,422	38,057	11,417	26,640
8	39,478	2,961	1,232	38,246	11,474	26,772
9	39,478	2,961	1,068	38,411	11,523	26,887
10	39,478	2,961	925	38,553	11,566	26,987

[a] Resulting from an increase in AOR from 52% to 53% and an increase in the ADR from $49 to $52.
[b] From an expenditure on the building of $17,500 and a sign of $20,000. *Note:* No additional labor costs from the added occupancy; Cost absorbed by family workers.
[c] Includes additional utility costs."

TABLE 18.19   Starlight Motel, Econo Lodge Conversion, Income Statement

Year	Change in Revenues[a]	Franchise Fee	Change in Depreciation[b]	Earnings before Taxes	Taxes (30%)	Change in Net Income
1	$39,478	$2,961	$1,558	$34,960	$10,488	$24,472
2	39,478	2,961	2,908	33,610	10,083	23,527
3	39,478	2,961	2,520	33,998	10,199	23,798
4	39,478	2,961	2,184	34,334	10,300	24,033
5	39,478	2,961	1,893	34,625	10,387	24,237
6	39,478	2,961	1,640	34,877	10,463	24,414
7	39,478	2,961	1,422	35,096	10,529	24,567
8	39,478	2,961	1,232	35,285	10,586	24,700
9	39,478	2,961	1,068	35,450	10,635	24,815
10	39,478	2,961	925	35,592	10,678	24,914

[a] Reflecting a 1% increase in the AOR to 53% and a $3 increase in the ADR to $52.
[b] Depreciating building improvements of $17,500 over 39 years and a $20,000 sign over 15 years.

TABLE 18.20A   Starlight Motel, Econo Lodge Conversion, Tax Consequences of Sale of Property

Sale of building		$1,569,266
Fixed plant and improvements[a]	$987,500	
Less accumulated depreciation	719,850	
Net fixed plant and improvements		267,650
Cost of land		200,000
Gain on sale		1,101,616
Capital gains tax (15%)		165,242
After-tax gain on sale		936,374

[a] Includes new sign and $17,500 building improvements.

TABLE 18.20B   Starlight Motel, Econo Lodge Conversion, Cash Gain from Sale of Property

Sale of property		$1,569,266
Less:		
Tax liability	165,242	
Loan balance	260,000	
Cash gain from sale		1,144,024
Change in cash gain from sale[a]		103,692

[a] From Table 18.15B.

TABLE 18.21   Starlight Motel, Econo Lodge Conversion, Cash Flows

Year	Change in Net Income	Depreciation	Capital Contributions	Change in Cash Gain on Sale of Land	Net Cash Flows
0			-$20,000		-$20,000
1	$24,472	$1,558			26,030
2	23,527	2,908			26,435
3	23,798	2,520			26,318
4	24,033	2,184			26,217
5	24,237	1,893			26,130
6	24,414	1,640			26,054
7	24,567	1,422			25,989
8	24,700	1,232			25,932
9	24,815	1,068			25,883
10	24,914	925		$103,692	129,532

NPV at 12% = $161,004
IRR = 131%

Knights Inn Affiliation

A similar patter may be observed for the Knights Inn franchise. Here a slightly larger increase in the AOR (to 54%) and ADR (to $53) reward the franchisee with $59,997 increase in NOPAT (Table 18.22 and 18.23) and corresponding increases in net income from $39,000 to $41,000 (Table 18.24). If the property is sold in the tenth year for three times room revenue, the corresponding gain in cash will be $152,393 (Tables 18.25A and 18.25B). The resultant cash flows in Table 18.26 suggest a significantly higher NPV (of $216,040), but a lower IRR (66%) than that resulting from the Econo Lodge franchise option. The fall in the IRR reflects the fact that the up front cash requirements of the Knights Inn franchise were higher that the cash required for the Econo Lodge. Although the cash flows of the Knights Inn were much larger than those of the Econo Lodge, they were not large enough to offset the increase in capital requirements.

The Howard Johnson Express Affiliation

The Howard Johnson's franchise would definitely be a step up for the Starlight Motel. Its brand image is much stronger than that provided by either Econo Lodge or the Knights Inn. More importantly, the Starlight's location of being close to the interstate, but not observable from it, would benefit greatly from its becoming part of Hojo's well-developed reservation system.

Consequently, the anticipated increases in both AOR and ADR are larger for this franchise than the Econo Lodge and the Knights Inn.

TABLE 18.22   Starlight Motel, Knights Inn Conversion, Revenue Estimates

Year	AOR	ADR	Room Revenue[a]	Total Revenue
1	54%	$53	$10,446	$543,208
2	54%	53	10,446	543,208
3	54%	53	10,446	543,208
4	54%	53	10,446	543,208
5	54%	53	10,446	543,208
6	54%	53	10,446	543,208
7	54%	53	10,446	543,208
8	54%	53	10,446	543,208
9	54%	53	10,446	543,208
10	54%	53	10,446	543,208

[a] 25 Rooms.

TABLE 18.23   Starlight Motel, Knights Inn Conversion, Holding Period NOPAT

Year	Increase in Revenues[a]	Franchise Fee	Change in Depreciation[b]	Change in EBIT[c]	Taxes (30%)	Change in NOPAT EBIT$(1 - tx)$
1	$59,597	$2,384	$1,558	$58,040	$17,412	$40,628
2	59,597	2,384	2,908	56,690	17,007	39,683
3	59,597	2,384	2,520	57,077	17,123	39,954
4	59,597	2,384	2,184	57,413	17,224	40,189
5	59,597	2,384	1,893	57,704	17,311	40,393
6	59,597	2,384	1,640	57,957	17,387	40,570
7	59,597	2,384	1,422	58,175	17,453	40,723
8	59,597	2,384	1,232	58,365	17,510	40,856
9	59,597	2,384	1,068	58,529	17,559	40,971
10	59,597	2,384	925	58,672	17,602	41,070

[a] Resulting from an increase in AOR from 52% to 54% and an increase in the ADR from $49 to $53.
[b] From an expenditure on the building of $17,500 and a sign of $20,000. *Note:* No additional labor costs from the added occupancy, cost absorbed by family workers.
[c] Variable utility costs.

TABLE 18.24   Starlight Motel, Knights Inn Conversion, Income Statement

Year	Change in Revenues[a]	Franchise Fee	Change in Depreciation[b]	Earnings before Taxes	Taxes (30%)	Change in Net Income
1	$59,597	$2,384	$1,558	$55,656	$16,697	$38,959
2	59,597	2,384	2,908	54,306	16,292	38,014
3	59,597	2,384	2,520	54,693	16,408	38,285
4	59,597	2,384	2,184	55,029	16,509	38,521
5	59,597	2,384	1,893	55,321	16,596	38,724
6	59,597	2,384	1,640	55,573	16,672	38,901
7	59,597	2,384	1,422	55,792	16,737	39,054
8	59,597	2,384	1,232	55,981	16,794	39,187
9	59,597	2,384	1,068	56,145	16,844	39,302
10	59,597	2,384	925	56,288	16,886	39,401

[a] From Table 18.23.
[b] From an expenditure on the building of $17,500 and a sign of $20,000.

TABLE 18.25A Starlight Motel, Knights Inn Conversion, Tax Consequences of Sale of Property

Sale of building		$1,629,623
Fixed plant and improvements[a]	$987,500	
Less accumulated		
depreciation	737,200	
Net fixed plant and improvements		250,300
Cost of land		200,000
Gain on sale		1,179,322
Capital gains tax (15%)		176,898
After-tax gain on sale		1,002,424

[a] Includes new sign and $17,500 building improvements.

TABLE 18.25B Starlight Motel, Knights Inn Conversion, Cash Gain from Sale of Property

Sale of property	$1,629,623
Less:	
Tax liability	176,898
Loan balance	260,000
Cash gain from sale	1,192,724
Change in cash gain from sale[a]	152,393

[a] From Table 18.15B.

Table 18.27 shows that this franchise will increase AOR from its current level of 52% (as an independent) to 59% over a 10-year period. Similarly, ADR will rise from its present level of $49 (as an independent) to $56.50 over the 10-year period. The resulting increase in revenues drives NOPAT up from $43,000 to $101,000 (Table 18.28) and net income up from $41,000 to $97,000 (Table 18.29). Again, at the end of the holding period if the motel is sold for three times room revenue, it will generate an additional cash gain for Ravi Patel of $387,059 (Tables 18.30A and 18.30B). The net effect of the affiliation with Howard Johnsons would be to generate an NPV for Ravi of $459,931 and an IRR of 52% on his cash investment of $137,500.

Table 18.32 illustrates a comparison of the costs and benefits of the different franchises. Each in turn offers the opportunity to significantly increase the Starlight's financial performance. Which one Ravi would choose will reflect his personal tastes and preferences for risk. However, it is clear, each of these franchises offer Ravi a nice risk-reward opportunity.

TABLE 18.26 Starlight Motel, Knights Inn Conversion, Cash Flows

Year	Change in Net Income[a]	Depreciation[a]	Capital Contributions[b]	Change in Cash Gain on Sale of Land[c]	Net Cash Flows
0			−$62,500		−$62,500
1	$38,959	$1,558			40,517
2	38,014	2,908			40,922
3	38,285	2,520			40,805
4	38,521	2,184			40,705
5	38,724	1,893			40,617
6	38,901	1,640			40,541
7	39,054	1,422			40,476
8	39,187	1,232			40,419
9	39,302	1,068			40,370
10	39,401	925		$152,393	192,720

[a] From Table 18.24.
[b] Includes $25,000 Franchise Fee, $20,000 sign, and $17,500 building improvements.
[c] From Table 18.25B.

NPV at 12% = $216,040
IRR = 66%

TABLE 18.27 Starlight Motel, Howard Johnson Conversion, Revenue Estimates

Year	AOR	ADR	Room Revenue[a]	Total Revenue
1	54%	$54.00	$10,643	$553,457
2	55%	55.00	11,041	574,145
3	56%	56.00	11,446	595,213
4	57%	56.50	11,755	611,251
5	58%	56.50	11,961	621,975
6	59%	56.50	12,167	632,698
7	59%	56.50	12,167	632,698
8	59%	56.50	12,167	632,698
9	59%	56.50	12,167	632,698
10	59%	56.50	12,167	632,698

[a] 52 rooms.

TABLE 18.28 Starlight Motel, Howard Johnson Conversion, Holding Period NOPAT

Year	Increase in Revenues[a]	Franchise Fee	Change in Depreciation[b]	Change in EBIT[c]	Taxes (30%)	Change in NOPAT EBIT$(1 - tx)$
1	$69,846	$2,794	$8,224	$61,622	$18,487	$43,135
2	90,535	3,621	15,352	75,182	22,555	52,628
3	111,602	4,464	13,305	98,297	29,489	68,808
4	127,641	5,106	11,531	116,109	34,833	81,277
5	138,364	5,535	9,994	128,371	38,511	89,859
6	149,088	5,964	8,661	140,427	42,128	98,299
7	149,088	5,964	7,506	141,582	42,474	99,107
8	149,088	5,964	6,506	142,582	42,775	99,808
9	149,088	5,964	5,638	143,450	43,035	100,415
10	149,088	5,964	4,886	144,202	43,260	100,941

[a] Resulting from an increase in AOR from 52% to 59% and an increase in the ADR from $49 to $56.50.
[b] From an expenditure on the building of $17,500, a sign of $20,000, and a franchise fee of $100,000. *Note:* No additional labor costs from the added occupancy; cost absorbed by family workers.
[c] Includes additional utility costs."

TABLE 18.29 Starlight Motel, Howard Johnson Conversion, Income Statement

Year	Change in Revenues[a]	Franchise Fee	Change in Depreciation[a]	Earnings before Taxes	Taxes (30%)	Change in Net Income
1	$69,846	$2,794	$8,224	$58,828	$17,648	$41,180
2	90,535	3,621	15,352	71,561	21,468	50,093
3	111,602	4,464	13,305	93,833	28,150	65,683
4	127,641	5,106	11,531	111,004	33,301	77,703
5	138,364	5,535	9,994	122,836	36,851	85,985
6	149,088	5,964	8,661	134,463	40,339	94,124
7	149,088	5,964	7,506	135,618	40,685	94,933
8	149,088	5,964	6,506	136,619	40,986	95,633
9	149,088	5,964	5,638	137,486	41,246	96,240
10	149,088	5,964	4,886	138,238	41,471	96,767

[a] From Table 18.28.

TABLE 18.30A Starlight Motel, Howard Johnson Conversion, Tax Consequences of Sale of Property

Sale of property		$1,898,095
Fixed plant and improvements[a]	$1,087,500	
Less accumulated depreciation	794,104	
Net fixed plant and improvements		293,396
Cost of land		200,000
Gain on sale		1,404,699
Capital gains tax (15%)		210,705
After-tax gain on sale		1,193,994

[a] Includes new sign, $17,500 building improvements and $100,000 franchise fee.

TABLE 18.30B Starlight Motel, Knights Inn Conversion, Cash Gain from Sale of Property

Sale of property	$1,898,095
Less:	
Tax liability	210,705
Loan balance	260,000
Cash gain from sale	$1,427,390
Change in cash gain from sale[a]	$387,059

[a] From Table 18.15B.

It is these types of tradeoffs that are responsible for the preponderance of franchising in the hotel and motel industry.

ILLUSTRATION #3: PEACEFUL VALLEY RESORT

Acquisition Phase

Igor Brodsky has been a cabdriver in New York City for the past 18 years, having immigrated from his native Poland when he was 30 years old. He is tired of the hassle and stress of New York City traffic and wishes to go into semi-retirement in the "North Country," which reminds him of the forests in his native country. He has saved up $70,000 from his labor as a cabdriver. He has a wife and two teenaged sons and the combined family income is about $80,000 a year. All family members are eager to leave the rigors of urban life for the bucolic countryside.

TABLE 18.31 Starlight Motel, Howard Johnson Conversion, Cash Flows

Year	Change in Net Income[a]	Change in Depreciation[a]	Capital Contributions[b]	Change in Cash Gain on Sale of Land[c]	Net Cash Flows
0			−$137,500		−$137,500
1	$41,180	$8,224			49,404
2	50,093	15,352			65,445
3	65,683	13,305			78,988
4	77,703	11,531			89,234
5	85,985	9,994			95,979
6	94,124	8,661			102,785
7	94,933	7,506			102,439
8	95,633	6,506			102,139
9	96,240	5,638			101,879
10	96,767	4,886		$387,059	488,712

[a] From Table 18.28.
[b] Includes $100,000 franchise fee, $20,000 sign, and $17,500 building improvements.
[c] From Table 18.30B

NPV at 12% = $459,931
IRR = 52%

TABLE 18.32 Starlight Motel, Howard Johnson Conversion, Franchise Comparison[a]

Franchise	10th Year AOR	10th Year ADR	Capital Required	Increase in NPV	IRR
Econo Lodge	53%	$52.00	$20,000	$161	131%
Knights Inn	54%	53.00	67,500	216,040	44%
Howard Johnson Express	59%	56.50	137,500	459,931	52%

[a] From Table 18.21, 18.26, and 18.31.

Igor finds a "Route 30 Motel and Cottages" about 200 miles from New York City on a minor state highway in a small town bordering the state forest. The town has a population of 500 and serves as a retail center for the scattered local residents and farmers. The nearest urban area is 100 miles away. The motel is located on five picturesque acres bordering a small trout fishing stream that supports a population of native fish. The Route 30 Motel and Cottages consists of a dilapidated 12-unit motel, 10 even more dilapidated cottages, and a restaurant. Rust, decay, and mold are everywhere. The restaurant has been closed and vacant for five years, none of the cottages have been rented the past two years, and the motel has a 20% AOR and a $25 ADR. The property has been owned and managed by an elderly couple who are now too frail to continue in that role and want to get out of the business very badly.

The elderly couple has had the property appraised for $100,000, but Igor finds the property has been on the market for two years and has not generated a single offer to purchase it. Igor makes an offer to the owners for $25,000 cash and $75,000 in 10 years with no interest.

Igor has a vision for the property not as a rest stop for the very few travelers who pass by that way, but as a restful vacation spot for residents of metropolitan New York who would like a peaceful getaway from the hustle and bustle of the city. Igor recognizes that the vacation season in his area is only about 10 weeks long—winters are hard in that part of the country—and that would prohibit the financial success of the motel as a vacation destination. However, Igor recognizes that many of the local residents are rather elderly and are either having trouble keeping up their residences or are living with younger relatives. The nearest "home for the elderly" is over 90 miles away and local residents consider it too expensive. Igor feels that his motel and cottages could provide inexpensive housing for elderly residents that would allow them their independence, but not be too far away from their relatives. Igor develops a strategy for renting out the cottage and motel units as apartments in the off-season and as a vacation destination for the summer. Implementing this strategy will require extensive renovation of the existing buildings. Fortunately, Igor and his sons have carpentry and "fix-up" skills and feel they can do most of the work themselves.

Igor purchases the property at the beginning of the vacation season. It takes one month and $25,000 to convert one of the cottages into a satisfactory home for Igor and his family. Igor obtains an 8%, $100,000 loan on the property with a conventional 30-year, fixed-rate mortgage from a local bank. The next six weeks the Brodskys work feverishly to renovate the remaining nine cottages and the restaurant. The restaurant is remodeled into a "common area" with kitchen facilities that can be used by the anticipated cottage residents. The total cost of these renovations to the Brodskys is $50,000. During this 10-week period, the Brodsky's (frugal) living expenses have been $2,000 per month.

The Brodskys rename their property the "Peaceful Valley Resort" and find renters eager for these unfurnished apartments at $75 per week. During the winter, Mrs. Brodsky takes a job driving the local school bus while father and sons begin to work on remodeling the motel components of the property. By the end of the winter, the motel units are remodeled and furnished to give a "rustic" air at a cost of $3,000 per unit. The remodeling was extensive with Mr. Brodsky and his sons doing all the carpentry, plumbing, and electrical work.

Holding Phase

Mr. Brodsky begins the vacation season by inviting all his old friends from New York City to come to Peaceful Valley Resorts for a special of only $200 per week. Mr. Brodsky then takes out advertisements in a local newspaper back in the area of New York City advertising Peaceful Valley as a restful vacation site at $400 per week. Takers are slow at first, but business grows throughout the season as the virtues of Peaceful Valley are spread by word of mouth. By the end of the second year, the motel is full up, with a waiting list. Furthermore, summer vacationers begin to come back for a holiday (Thanksgiving, Christmas) retreat, or just to enjoy the pristine wilderness in the dead of winter. The increasing popularity of a stay at the Peaceful Valley Resort allows for a slow but steady increase in the ADR. The Brodskys provide their visitors with consistently immaculate rooms and a cheerful atmosphere. The Brodskys together do all the necessary work. The buildings are well maintained and the property acquires a reputation as a desirable vacation spot.

Although the property has been reclaimed and is an esthetic success, it is a financial struggle. The cash flow required to acquire the property and get it developed took substantially all the cash the Brodskys had (Table 18.33). As picturesque as Peaceful Valley may have been, its climate dictated that it would not experience much demand during the majority of the year. Consequently raising revenue was a perennial struggle (Table 18.34). Then, in the first year, cash flow was substantially negative while the property was being reclaimed because much of the property could not be rented out (Table 18.35). Tables 18.35 and 18.36 show NOPAT was not strong enough to turn net income positive until the third year. Any mishap during this period of time would have spelled financial disaster for the Brodskys. Net income never does rise to levels that might be expected of a resort motel. As an economic entity Pleasant Valley suffered because of its climatic difficulties and its relatively small size. Of course the Brodskys enjoyed the psychic income arising from their location.

TABLE 18.33 Peaceful Valley, First Year, Initial Cash Flows

Cash Outflows:	
Property purchase[a]	$25,000
Initial cottage renovation	25,000
Cottage and restaurant renovation	50,000
Brodsky living expenses	24,000
Motel renovations	36,000
Motel supplies and linens	6,000
Utilities	10,000
Mortgage payments[b]	8,071
Advertising	500
Total cash out	184,571
Cash Inflows:	
Bank loan	100,000
Mrs. Brodsky's bus driver wages	8,000
Equity contribution from the Brodskys	70,000
Apartment rentals[c]	26,933
Total cash in	204,933
Ending cash balance	20,361

[a] The property is purchased for $100,000, $25,000 down and a 10-year note at no interest for the balance.
[b] Payments of $733.76 per month for 11 months and a 5% vacancy rate for turnover.
[c] The apartments are rented for 42 weeks at $75 per week.

Disposal Phase

After 10 years of hard work developing the property, Igor Brodsky dies of a massive heart attack. His wife and children decide they have had enough of hard work and the bucolic life and wish to return to the city. The now much-improved property immediately receives an offer of eight times earnings (net income) for their property. They take the offer and return to the city.

The financial consequences of Pleasant Valley are revealed in Tables 18.37 and 18.38. Table 18.37A shows the after-tax profit on the sale of Pleasant Valley being $173,567. This translates (Table 18.37B) into a cash gain of $219,509. Table 18.38 takes that gain along with the cash flows generated throughout the 10-year period and finds that the original investment of their life savings ($70,000) has generated a NPV of $90,305 and an IRR of 23%. As it turns out, Peaceful Valley is not a financial disaster. The 23% return is not to be sneezed at, but whether or not it compensates the investor's for the risks they have taken is another matter. Only the Brodskys can say for sure whether the pleasantries of the environment more than compensated them for the financial risk they took and the years of grinding toil necessary to achieve success.

SUMMARY

The "hospitality" business is dynamic, providing both passive and active investors a wealth of opportunities and risks. The basic economic context of the industry is positive. The industry will continue to grow as society grows and becomes more affluent. Americans love to travel: visits to relatives, short vacations, long vacations, just plain sight-seeing, going to class reunions, weddings, or funerals. The American life-style is on the move and likely to be increasingly so. Consequently, the hotel and motel industry is well developed and often highly competitive. Economy, midlevel, and luxury hotels and motels compete on the basis of location, image, amenities, and price.

TABLE 18.34   Peaceful Valley, Revenue Estimates

Year	AOR[a]	Motel Revenue ADR[b]	Room Revenue	Total Motel Revenue[c]	Cottage Revenue[d]	Total Revenue
1	0%				$26,933	$26,933
2	19%	$375	$3,705	$44,460	33,345	77,805
3	24%	400	4,992	59,904	33,345	93,249
4	28%	425	6,188	74,256	33,345	107,601
5	30%	425	6,630	79,560	33,345	112,905
6	30%	446	6,962	83,538	37,791	121,329
7	30%	469	7,310	87,715	37,791	125,506
8	30%	492	7,675	92,101	37,791	129,892
9	30%	517	8,059	96,706	37,791	134,497
10	30%	542	8,462	101,541	37,791	139,332

[a] Average occupancy rate on a weekly basis.
[b] Average weekly rate.
[c] For 12 rooms.
[d] Based on $75 per week with a 95% occupancy for the first five years, $85 thereafter.

TABLE 18.35 Peaceful Valley, Holding Period NOPAT

Year	Revenues[a]	Labor Costs[b]	Utilities[c]	Building Depreciation[d]	Furnishings Depreciation[e]	EBIT	Taxes (15%)	NOPAT EBIT$(1-tx)$
1	$26,933	$66,560	$10,000	$1,423	$1,200	-$52,251	-$7,837.59	-$44,413
2	77,805	66,560	10,300	2,846	1,920	-3,821	-573	-3,248
3	93,249	66,560	10,609	2,846	1,152	12,082	1,812	10,270
4	107,601	66,560	10,927	2,846	691	26,576	3,986	22,590
5	112,905	66,560	11,255	2,846	415	31,829	4,774	27,055
6	121,329	66,560	11,593	2,846	622	39,708	5,956	33,752
7	125,506	66,560	11,941	2,846	0	44,159	6,624	37,535
8	129,892	66,560	12,299	2,846	0	48,187	7,228	40,959
9	134,497	66,560	12,668	2,846	0	52,423	7,863	44,559
10	139,332	66,560	13,048	2,846	0	56,878	8,532	48,346

[a] From Table 18.34.

[b] The Brodsky family pays itself a minimum wage for 40-hour weeks to ensure Social Security coverage, workman's compensation, and unemployment insurance.

[c] Water, electric, fuel oil, phone service, and cable TV.

[d] The land was originally valued at $50,000 and the buildings valued at $50,000. The buildings were subsequently improved for $61,000, creating a depreciable basis of $111,000, which was then depreciated over 39 years using the half-year convention.

[e] Furnishings of $6,000 are depreciated over five years using the 200% DB method and half-year convention

TABLE 18.36 Peaceful Valley, Income Statement

Year	Revenues[a]	Labor Costs[b]	Utilities[c]	Building Depreciation[d]	Furnishings Depreciation[e]	Interest	EBT	Taxes (15%)	Net Income
1	$26,933	$66,560	$10,000	$1,423	$1,200	$7,308	-$59,559	-$8,933.82	-$50,625
2	77,805	66,560	10,300	2,846	1,920	7,930	-11,751	-1,763	-9,989
3	93,249	66,560	10,609	2,846	1,152	7,857	4,224	634	3,591
4	107,601	66,560	10,927	2,846	691	7,779	18,798	2,820	15,978
5	112,905	66,560	11,255	2,846	415	7,694	24,135	3,620	20,515
6	121,329	66,560	11,593	2,846	622	7,601	32,107	4,816	27,291
7	125,506	66,560	11,941	2,846	0	7,501	36,658	5,499	31,159
8	129,892	66,560	12,299	2,846	0	7,393	40,794	6,119	34,675
9	134,497	66,560	12,668	2,846	0	7,276	45,147	6,772	38,375
10	139,332	66,560	13,048	2,846	0	7,149	49,729	7,459	42,270

[a] From Table 18.34.

[b] The Brodsky family pays each member a minimum wage for 40-hour weeks to ensure Social Security coverage, workman's compensation, and unemployment insurance.

[c] Water, electric, fuel oil, phone service, and cable TV.

[d] The land was originally valued at $50,000 and the buildings valued at $61,000. The buildings were subsequently improved for $61,000, creating a depreciable basis of $111,000, which was then depreciated over 39 years using the half-year convention.

[e] Furnishings of $6,000 are depreciated over five years using the 200% DB method and half-year convention.

TABLE 18.37A Peaceful Valley, Tax Consequences of Sale of Property

Sale of property		$338,158
Fixed plant and improvements	$117,000	
Less accumulated depreciation	33,038	
Net fixed plant and improvements		83,962
Cost of land		50,000
Gain on sale		204,196
Capital gains tax (15%)		30,629
After-tax gain on sale		173,567

TABLE 18.37B Peaceful Valley, Cash Gain from Sale of Property

Sale of property	$338,158
Less:	
Tax liability	30,629
Loan balance	88,020
Cash gain from sale	219,509

TABLE 18.38 Peaceful Valley, Cash Flow Statement

Year	Net Income[a]	Depreciation[a]	Capital Contributions	Opportunity Apartment Cost[b]	Cash Gain on Sale of Land[c]	Net Cash Flows
0			-$70,000			-$70,000
1	-$50,625	$2,623		$7,200		-40,802
2	-9,989	4,766		7,200		1,978
3	3,591	3,998		7,200		14,789
4	15,978	3,537		7,200		26,715
5	20,515	3,261		7,200		30,976
6	27,291	3,468		7,200		37,959
7	31,159	2,846		7,200		41,205
8	34,675	2,846		7,200		44,721
9	38,375	2,846		7,200		48,421
10	42,270	2,846		7,200	$219,509	271,824

[a] From Table 18.36.
[b] A comparable apartment would cost $600 per month.
[c] From Table 18.37B.

NPV at 12% = $90,305
IRR = 23%

The critical success factor in the lodging industry is "room revenue." That is, the revenue that can be expected to be derived from a room in a given year. As a result, room revenue will be a function of how often it is occupied (the AOR) and the daily price of the room (the ADR times 365). An important additional factor in hotel or motel success is often ancillary businesses such as restaurant, meeting, and convention services. Such businesses may be considered complimentary goods to lodging. Providing facilities for a wedding reception increase the likelihood of the lodging function being used by the wedding guests. Tired travelers need food as well as rest.

Generally, the necessary skills to succeed in these businesses are quite different from that of the lodging service and generally require other management skills. As a result most hotel and motel owners lease those facilities to others rather than trying to manage such different businesses themselves.

Image is extremely important in determining the success or failure of a hotel or motel. Because the industry is highly competitive, travelers normally have a choice among the different hotels and motels that are available. As a result branding is very important in the industry and most hotels and motels brand themselves through affiliation with a franchisor. In many cases, the fees and royalties charged by the franchisor are more than offset by an increase in the AOR or the ADR. The decision to operate as a franchisee or an independent will often hinge on local conditions such as the strength of demand in the local lodging market, the degree of competition in the local lodging market, location factors, the condition of the facility, the experience and expertise of the hotel/motel owner.

Aside from their desirability as hotels or motels, properties being used in this manner occasionally could be worth more if they were converted to a "higher and better" use. Often this opportunity is present because no one has been thinking about the property in an alternative use. Thinking "out of the box" may prove quite rewarding to the astute investor.